The Finleys of Early Sonoma County California

by Carmen J. Finley

HERITAGE BOOKS
2009

HERITAGE BOOKS
AN IMPRINT OF HERITAGE BOOKS, INC.

Books, CDs, and more—Worldwide

For our listing of thousands of titles see our website
at
www.HeritageBooks.com

Published 2009 by
HERITAGE BOOKS, INC.
Publishing Division
100 Railroad Ave. #104
Westminster, Maryland 21157

Copyright © 1997 Carmen J. Finley

Art Direction & Design
Brad Scott, Spyder Graphics

Editor
Doris Dickenson

Scan Photography
Simone Wilson

Copy Photography
Pierre Zogg, Photoworks

All rights reserved. No part of this book may be reproduced or transmitted in any form or by any means, electronic or mechanical, including photocopying, recording or by any information storage and retrieval system without written permission from the author, except for the inclusion of brief quotations in a review.

International Standard Book Numbers
Paperbound: 978-0-7884-0780-2
Clothbound: 978-0-7884-8246-5

This work is dedicated to

Clara Keithly Tarwater, 1875-1973
&
Nettie Head McDonald, 1906-1993

*two earlier researchers of
John and Keziah Finley
whose endeavors
were the inspiration
for my interest
and efforts.*

Clara Keithly Tarwater

Nettie Head McDonald

THE FINLEYS OF EARLY SONOMA COUNTY, CALIFORNIA

FOREWORD & PREFACE

INTRODUCTION
The Coming of Three Finley Families to Sonoma County

CHAPTER 1
John and Keziah (Head) Finley
PAGE 2

CHAPTER 2
William Asa and Sarah (Latimer) Finley
PAGE 16

CHAPTER 3
Harrison and Livonia (Ray) Finley
PAGE 28

CHAPTER 4
Early Virginia Beginnings:
1. John Caldwell 2. Reverend John Thomson
PAGE 35

THE FINLEYS OF EARLY SONOMA COUNTY, CALIFORNIA

CHAPTER 5
Ancestors and Descendants of John Finley (1823-1910)
PAGE 45

CHAPTER 6
Ancestors and Descendants of William Asa Finley (1839-1912)
PAGE 140

CHAPTER 7
Ancestors and Descendants of Harrison Finley (1836-1917)
PAGE 180

NOTES & REFERENCES
PAGE 208

INDEX
PAGE 238

FOREWORD

The millennium is fast approaching and with it's arrival we can look back on one hundred fifty years of statehood and immigration to California. The process is still going on and no doubt will continue into the future.

Members of the Finley family were early settlers on the western frontier of Pennsylvania, Virginia, and North and South Carolina. Always moving west, younger generations settled in Trans-Mississippi Missouri and surrounding states.

There was immigration to California since the 1820s and 1830s; the 1840s ushered in organized overland emigrant parties to Oregon and California. Many of these people were of Scotch descent and described as Scotch-Irish (or Scots-Irish as purists say) because they had come from Northern Ireland in the eighteenth and nineteenth centuries. These people had moved to the frontier upon their arrival in America and had continued their western movement from the eastern seaboard over the mountains to Kentucky, Tennessee, Ohio, Indiana, and on to Missouri.

Much attention has been given to the effects the discovery of gold at Sutter's Mill in Coloma in 1848. This discovery was tantamount to a huge beacon in the sky, visible around the world, drawing multitudes to California. There probably was no county in all of the United States at that time that did not contribute citizens to this venture. Many came and returned home, some with more than they came with, but more commonly with experiences of a lifetime but little or no gold. There were those who could see that they had been pursuing the wrong kind of gold in California, that there were other ways to make one's fortune there. Some stayed. Others returned to their homes in the East, and after a while California began festering in their conscience like some non-malignant fever. This fever was contagious and others were drawn to it, and to the Golden State.

Carmen Finley has researched and woven this story of the Finley experience from the eastern coast line to their arrival in California, and Sonoma County in particular. These hardy and enterprising citizens of Sonoma County have added more than their share to the general welfare of our wonderful Sonoma County, California. The story continues as you read these lines.

Harold A. Lapham,
Past President and Archivist
Sonoma County Historical Society
March 26, 1996

PREFACE

Compilation of this history of the Finleys who came to Sonoma County, California, prior to 1900, really began in 1979 when I first became interested in my own family history. As most family historians do, I looked for other family members who knew more about my ancestors than I did—and found a second cousin Nettie (Head) McDonald. I had never met Nettie, although I had heard my father speak of her. He had been the person who took Nettie to her first day of school, for he had been living and working on the ranch owned by Nettie's father at the time. When I raised the general question to both parents, "Who in the family knows anything about our ancestors?" it was Father who resoundingly told me to go see Nettie. And it was he who took me the next week to meet my second cousin who had lived all her married life within twelve miles of where we lived.

Nettie owned a wonderful trunk full of original documents, mostly deeds, that had been the property of our great-grandfather, John Finley, who had come to Sonoma County in 1852. Among these documents was also a family Bible record that identified his parents as Samuel and Martha (Downing) Finley. They were living in Indiana when John was born. Beyond that our earlier Finley ancestors were still to be discovered.

Being new to this self-hewn art of tracing one's ancestors, I did what many family researchers did. I hired a person to find the parents of Samuel Finley. In fact I ended up hiring two persons to do the job. But it was Rosemary Richardson of Louisburg, North Carolina, who successfully discovered the link between Samuel and his father, David Finley of Garrard County, Kentucky. As the story of this new ancestor unfolded, I began to learn some of the techniques of researching ones family and became a working participant in tracing the next generation back. After several false starts which made me think David may have come from North Carolina, I eventually established a tie to Augusta County, Virginia. Nearby I found a particularly capable researcher in the person of Sharon Hamner, then living in Charlottesville, who worked with me for many years digging out the facts about the numerous Finleys who lived in and around Beverly Manor. From Sharon I learned many of the finer points of how to research my family. She was an excellent teacher as well as researcher and I began to learn my way around such things as deeds, court orders, tax lists, and census records.

About this time I found another researcher who was interested in the same group of Finleys in Virginia as I. This was James D. Finley of Modesto, California. Jim and I maintained a fairly constant interchange on our findings and concerns for the next eleven years, until his death in 1993. As it turned out, Jim's ancestor Thomas, was a brother to my ancestor David. Substantial information on Thomas is included in chapter 5, provided by Jim Finley. For a substantial period of the time that Jim and I maintained our working relationship on the study of Finleys, we were joined by J. Wayne Johnson, M.D., of Andalusia, Georgia. Wayne's Finley ancestors crossed paths with ours, but were not identified as of the same line within the time frame of our correspondence. Never-the-less, Wayne also contributed much to our understanding of Finleys in the broader scene—in Pennsylvania and in the Carolinas as well as Virginia.

In 1983 I retired and moved back to Santa Rosa, my birth place, and was now proudly touting the fact that I was a fourth generation native of Sonoma County. I re-established contacts with Sonoma State University and set up a scholarship program with them to provide funds for students in family history who were interested in in finding Virginia Hershey who was completing her master's degree in history and who also just happened to be an Accredited Genealogist. Virginia was the first recipient of the Finley-McFarling Scholarship. Her paper contributed substantially to the research of the Augusta County Finleys, but more important, she extended my understanding of the finer points in genealogical research.

As my knowledge of the Finleys who lived in Augusta County, Virginia, grew, so did the realization that earlier researchers of this line had confused two separate John Finley families living near each other in early eighteenth century Virginia. Then the hard work began. Sorting out the many Finleys who lived in that area is still not complete, but the identification of two separate John Finley families emerged. One John Finley lived on South River and was an early Commissioner and Elder who helped establish and serve Tinkling Spring Meeting House from about 1737 until 1765. He was the ancestor of two of the early Finley families of Sonoma County. The other John Finley lived on Middle River, just outside the bounds of Beverly Manor. He also had his children baptized at Tinkling Spring during the 1740s before Brown's Meeting House was built nearer his home. This, of course, added to the confusion. The Middle River John Finley was the ancestor of the third early Finley family to settle in Sonoma County. Two key figures in my sorting of these various Finleys were Mary McCampbell Bell of Arlington, Virginia, who first pointed out the possibility the Middle River and the South River Finleys were not directly related—at least in that generation—and Elizabeth Shown Mills of Tuscaloosa, Alabama, who critiqued my manuscript, *The John Finleys of Augusta County, Virginia: Some Hypotheses*, and made many helpful comments. Other substantial contributors to this effort included Katharine G. Bushman of Staunton, Virginia, who searched for Augusta County documents; Barbara Vines Little of Orange,

at that time; and Marie E.B. DeLaney of Farmville, Virginia, who dug into the files of Prince Edward County.

Meanwhile, I was searching for additional information about David Finley, son of John of South River. David struck out for Kentucky while still a young man and raised a family of ten children along the Dix River in what is now Garrard County, Kentucky. An invaluable researcher of Kentucky information was Alma Ray Ison of Harrodsburg, who patiently dug out information from many sources. While digging about in Kentucky, contact was made with Mary Heple of Salinas, California, who is descended from David's half-brother George. David's later years were spent in Orange County, Indiana, and Pearl Wilson of Paoli was my constant source of information in that area. She even trudged through cemeteries to read gravestone markings when published records were in question. Through her, another descendant of David was located, George Altenberger of Fairborn, Ohio, although the exchange of information on his family branch was through his wife, Eileen.

Following David's children took me briefly into Illinois, and then on to Missouri and Texas. Samuel, the direct ancestor of the first Finley to arrive in Sonoma County, moved to Decatur, Illinois, probably shortly after the death of his wife. He remarried, but died at the age of forty-five leaving five minor children. I am grateful for the Abstracts of Macon County, Illinois Probate Court Records, compiled by Jean Parke Hauffe. These were rich in the amount of information about Samuel's probate proceedings and provided information about his children as well. Records filmed by the Mormon Church in Salt Lake City added even more information.

After the death of Samuel, several of his children spent some time in Missouri, so the next research efforts were directed towards

Bates County and vicinity, where the John Finley who migrated to Sonoma County in 1852 was found in the 1850 census. My best source of information came from Marjorie Rector of Sedalia, Missouri. In the process, it was discovered that two of Samuel's brothers, Edmund and Jesse, also lived for a while in Missouri and later moved on to Texas. I located two cousins who were descendants of Jesse, Peggy Harding of Kilgore, Texas, and Jeanne Branom of Commerce, Texas. They added much on their branch of the family, and it is their work that provided the basis for that portion of chapter 5 which deals with Texas. Edmund's eldest child, also a John Fin(d)ley, migrated to California and settled in Tulare County. One of his descendants, Michelle Yahnian of Visalia, has been a continuous and faithful correspondent, supplying much information on her branch of the family, which is also found in chapter 5. Some time later Josephine Williams, a descendant of Samuel's sister Mary (Finley) Maxwell, was found in Lake Hughes, California. Josephine provided information on Mary's family. When I finally got around to reconstructing the generations within my own memory, I enlisted the aid of living cousins—Ed and Horace Wilds, Marie (Wilds) Naish, Lorraine (Wilds) Piazza, and Diane (Piazza) Starkey.

My real research of Finley families living in Sonoma County prior to 1900 started in 1994, although by this time I had many threads, not only of my own ancestors, but also of the others. Christine (Sloat) Faux and I had compared notes years before and she had generously provided access to all her notes and documents on the Mark West Finleys. Now down to serious work, I haunted the Sonoma County Library for several months during the fall and winter of 1994 and am grateful for the assistance provided by Audrey Herman, keeper and archivist of the historical and genealogical collections. Many hours were also spent in the offices of the Sonoma County recorder and the county clerk. Their staffs were generous with their time and assistance. Also on the home front, selected chapters were read by Harry Lapham, archivist and past president of the Sonoma County Historical Society, and by Ruth Burke, local historian of the Bodega area. Important information was also gleaned from Dr. Stephen E. Yale, Director of Archives at the Commission on Archives and History, California-Nevada Conference, United Metho-dist Church in Berkeley; from Herbert Hucks, Jr., archivist, Wofford College, Spartanburg, South Carolina; and from Lawrence Landis, Oregon State University Archives, Corvallis, Oregon.

I would be remiss not to mention the help received from the Family History Library in Salt Lake City and the Family History Centers provided by the Church of Jesus Christ of Latter-Day Saints. The Mormons are dedicated to genealogy and have the most comprehensive set of records in the world. I learned early in my venture into the study of my own family about this exceptional resource and have made several trips to Salt Lake City. Their collection grows daily with the active pursuit of records world-wide. Most of their records are also available at a nominal cost through Family History Centers located in local Mormon churches throughout the United States.

And a very special thank you goes to Doris M. Dickenson, Guerneville, California, not only for her editorial assistance, but for her moral support during the final phases of the compilation of this history.

A NOTE ON THE FALLIBILITY OF HISTORICAL INFORMATION

This story of the Finley families who came to Sonoma County prior to 1900, as with all family histories, has been put together from many sources, including both recollections of living persons and existing records which document various events in the lives our ancestors. Any experienced family historian knows that both the memories of persons on whom we rely and the records that remain are fallible. It is not uncommon to find records which contradict each other. For example, dates on a death certificate may not agree with dates on cemetery records or with ages found on census records. It is up to the family historian either to reconcile these differences or acknowledge such discrepancies where they exist.

Primary sources, those which have been prepared near the time of the event by someone directly involved, are generally the best sources of information.

Secondary sources, those prepared by individuals who abstract or summarize a body of information, vary in their usefulness depending on the accuracy of the person preparing the material. However, secondary sources may provide valuable insights where primary records do not exist. This writer has used primary records as a preferred source, but has also used secondary sources where information would otherwise be missing or unavailable.

A great many original documents have been examined in preparation for this history of the early Finley families of Sonoma County, including journals, letters, deeds, wills, court records, vital records, church records, census records, tax lists, military records, pension applications, and probate and estate records. It is not unusual to find spelling variations in both given and surnames among documents, or even within a single document especially during the eighteenth century. Among these early records are found a number of spelling variations for Finley, such as Finla, Findly, Findley, Finlay, and Finly. Spelling simply was not too important in the early history of our country. Finley became the preferred spelling for those families which settled in Sonoma County, but the Findley spelling was adopted by another closely related line that settled in Tulare County, California. The reader will also note occasional inconsistencies in the spelling of either given or surnames, which reflect the differences found in the original documents.

Of greater concern is the accuracy of the vital data contained herein. Every effort has been made to reconcile differences which occur in the primary records or to acknowledge them where they exist. Careful attention has also been paid to proofing the many dates, but there is always the danger that an error might creep in. The author encourages any reader who has additional relevant information or conflicting information to contact her.

INTRODUCTION: THE COMING OF THREE FINLEY FAMILIES TO SONOMA COUNTY

Between 1852 and 1888 three families by the name of Finley settled in Sonoma County. The first to arrive was John Finley with his wife, Keziah, and their three young sons, Samuel Emanuel, John Jay, and Henry Head, who ranged in age from six years to six months. They spent the winter of 1852 in Santa Rosa and then settled in the Bloomfield area in 1853. The next to arrive was William Asa Finley with his wife, Sarah, and their six-year-old son, Ernest Latimer. They arrived in 1876 and settled in Santa Rosa. Last to arrive, in 1888, was Harrison Finley with his wife, Livonia, and their nine children, Mattie Zoe, Matilda Narcissus, Eliza Belle, Wilson Ebenezer, Mary Frances, Abigail Josephine, Lucy Ray, Livonia Louise, and Alicia V., who ranged in age from three to twenty-four years. They settled in the Mark West area about five miles north of Santa Rosa.

As I was growing up in Santa Rosa in the 1930s and 1940s, I knew of no connection between these various Finleys and assumed we were not related. At a young age I learned to bear the cross of not being related to *The Finleys*. *The Finleys* were those associated with Ernest Latimer Finley, who by this time had established the town's leading newspapers, *The Press Democrat*, a morning paper, and *The Santa Rosa Republican*, an evening paper, both published out of the same plant. By 1937 he had added the establishment of Santa Rosa's first radio station, KSRO, to his growing list of community achievements. Later, in the mid-1940s, while attending the University of California, I spent my summers working at *The Press Democrat* where Ruth Finley, E.L.'s widow, approached me one day asking, "Are you my relative?" I replied that I did not think so, but that turned out not to be strictly true. However, it wasn't until the mid-1980s, after becoming absorbed in my own family history, that I discovered my fourth great-grandfather John Finley, was a third great-grandfather of Ernest L. Finley. However, we were descended from different wives of John Finley. Digging a little deeper I found descendants of the Mark West Finleys living in Santa Rosa. Christine (Sloat) Faux provided me with much information about the Mark West Finleys and another cousin, Annabel Wesson, helped piece together enough information to discover that their progenitor, another John Finley, lived within fifteen miles of my John Finley in Augusta County, Virginia, for the period between the late 1730s and 1765. It would not be surprising to learn that another generation back these two lines also converged, but the early Finley history in Pennsylvania, from whence they came, is totally muddled. The best prediction that can be made at this time is that our ancestors arrived about 1720 from Ireland, and their ancestors before them from Scotland, the Scotch-Irish heritage that provided the "skirmish line of civilization"[1] as the American frontier expanded to the West.

Having discovered the real and potential ties that bound the three early Sonoma County Finley families together,

I set about filling in the information back to our early Virginia ancestors. By 1990 I had published four generations of my branch of the family, from John Finley of Virginia to John Finley of Bodega.[2] In 1995 I added the story of Ernest L. Finley's ancestors.[3] In the meantime, I worked intermittently on trying to fill in the gaps about the Mark West Finleys from their Virginia ancestor, another John Finley, to their arrival in Sonoma County. From that came the idea of compiling all this information into a single volume under the title, *The Finleys of Early Sonoma County, California.*

Chapters 1, 2, and 3 focus on the early Finley immigrants, John Finley of Bodega, William Asa Finley of Santa Rosa, and Harrison Finley of Mark West. Chapter 4 gives some background on our early Virginia beginnings. The next three chapters give the detailed family history of their early Finley ancestors beginning with the earliest proven progenitor in the 1730s. These later chapters are written in the style of the *National Genealogical Society Quarterly,* which does not generally make for interesting reading but is most efficient in documenting the facts about our ancestors and their families. I hope future genera-

tions of Finleys with early ties to Sonoma County, as well as Sonoma County Historians, will find this of interest.

& their story begins...

CHAPTER ONE: JOHN AND KEZIAH (HEAD) FINLEY

In the summer of 1852 John and Keziah Finley, with their three young sons, Samuel Emanuel, John Jay, and Henry Head,[1,2] left their homestead in Bates County, Missouri, and headed north to St. Joseph. That was one of the departure points for wagon trains heading West. There, according to family tradition, they were joined by Keziah's parents in anticipation of their joint trek across the country to Texas, or so Keziah thought at the time of their departure. However, when they reached that point in the trail where the Texas bound travelers were to turn off, a change in plans occurred. As the story goes, Keziah's parents continued to Texas, but John and Keziah headed for California.[3] They came across the Sierras by way of Donner Pass. Perhaps their change in plans had something to do with the fact that John's brother Samuel, his wife, Prudence, and their young daughter had already gone to California and settled in Sonoma County. John and Keziah arrived late in the year of 1852 and, reaching the Santa Rosa Valley, they rested first in the old adobe just east of

CARMEN J. FINLEY COLLECTION

John Finley, 1823-1910

Santa Rosa, (the Carrillo Adobe).

Sonoma County, in 1852, had a population of 2,332 persons, 371 of which were Indians. There were 2.5 males for every female. It was a young population with only twelve percent over the age of forty and twenty-two percent aged ten or under. Eighty-three percent were white, sixteen percent Indian and the remainder were black, mulatto, Spanish, or Mexican. Eighty percent had been born in

America. Of the foreign-born, English, Germans, and the Irish together made up about eight percent of the remaining population. Of those who migrated from outside the state, the largest proportion, forty percent, came from Missouri and they had migrated to Missouri from Virginia, North Carolina, Tennessee, and Kentucky.[4]

On their arrival, John was not yet thirty, Keziah was twenty-four, and their children were ages seven, two, and about six months old. While John was born in Indiana, his heritage was from Kentucky and Virginia; Keziah had been born in Tennessee. So John and Keziah were pretty representative of the "norm" for the population.

After spending the winter in Santa Rosa and looking over the valley, John decided there was too much adobe soil to suit his plans and he looked west for better farm land. In the spring of 1853 he and Keziah continued west and leased farm land in the Bloomfield area.

John's first farming venture was to raise potatoes which had become a very lucrative agricultural pursuit in the

Bodega area where John and Keziah were located. In 1853 the price was almost five and a half cents per pound.[5] According to the 1852 State census, Sonoma County, with less that one percent of the State's population, provided twenty-one percent of the State's potatoes. This helped provide some of the agricultural needs of San Francisco, Sacramento, and the mining counties in the Sierras. Wheat, corn, onions, barley, and oats were also produced, but not nearly in so great quantities as potatoes.[6] So it would appear that John was a pretty "savvy" farmer. After about five years, John and Keziah leased a larger tract on English Hill.[7] However, continued overproduction soon drove the price of potatoes down and John switched to dairy ranching, which was more stable. About 1859 they leased a 600 acre tract on Sugar Loaf Hill in the Bodega settlement and began a dairying operation.[8]

By February 1863 John had saved enough money to buy their first piece of property. Their family had grown to seven children, including four born in California, Nancy Caroline, Elizabeth Finetta, James Preston, and Jefferson Davis. James Preston, born 18 January 1860 was a twin, but his sister, Marenda, did not survive the day of their birth. The two oldest boys, Sam and John, were now in their teens, Henry was eleven and all were able to help do the work required on the new dairy ranch. Even as they made the move, Keziah was four months pregnant with their tenth child, Andrew Jackson.[9] He was the first of four additional children born to John and Keziah. More information on all the children is given in chapter 5.

They bought 486.12 acres extending from the ridge of Irish Hill to a small tributary which became Finley Creek. It was bordered on the south by the center of Salmon Creek on Despard Taylor's line. John purchased this property from Tyler Curtis for $2,430.60, a rate of $5 per acre.[10]

Tyler Curtis had married Manuela Torres Smith, the widow of Capt. Stephen Smith, original owner of the Bodega Rancho which was granted to Smith by the Mexican government in 1843. It was Smith's arrival with the first steam operated sawmill, gristmill, shingle mill, and distillery west of the Rockies that gave a boost to the development of the Bodega area. Smith was a fifty-seven-year-old sea captain from Massachusetts when he arrived in Bodega with his sixteen-year-old bride, Manuela, daughter of a Peruvian aristocrat. Manuela, who became known as the Mistress of Rancho Bodega, was one of the primary moving forces in the establishment of St. Teresa's, the first Catholic Church in the area.[11] The original Rancho was more that 35,000 acres, running from the Russian River to the Estero Americano. A portion of the survey states:

> The greater part of this "Rancho" is rough, hilly and broken. The land for about a half or three fourths of a mile

Keziah (Head) Finley, 1828-1903

back from the coast and along the Estero Americano is of a fine quality and suitable for agricultural pursuits. All the northern portion is very rough and broken, but is thickly covered with fine redwood timber and scattering oak. It is well watered throughout.[12]

And so it was that John and Keziah purchased a little piece of this land along Salmon Creek that was eventually to grow to about 1,000 acres. The nearest post office, established in 1854, was at Smith's Ranch, as the Bodega Rancho was called after California ceased to be part of Mexico. When the Smith influence waned, and as the present town of Bodega grew, the post office was moved into town. However, it was still called Smith's Ranch Post Office until 1901 when Howard McCaughey, then postmaster, had the named changed to Bodega.[13]

John and Keziah built their home and dairy facilities on the north bank of Salmon Creek. They continued to raise potatoes and shipped both dairy and farm produce to market. Nettie McDonald describes their system of shipment:

In those earlier days, the lower part of Salmon Creek was navigable, especially at high tide so they could transport the produce by raft down the creek to where it was hauled by team to Campbell's Wharf at Bodega Bay. From there it was shipped by boat to the San Francisco markets and sold. They received supplies the same way. In later years, the trip was made around the road by team, hauling the produce to Campbell's Wharf and bringing supplies back to the ranch. In 1875 the North Pacific Coast Narrow Gauge Railroad began operation between San Francisco and the Russian River Country with stations all along the way.[14] The one at Bodega Roads, approximately three miles east of Bodega, became the main shipping and receiving point for all the farmers and ranchers around the Bodega country. Farm and dairy produce of all kinds was hauled by team (later by truck) to the station for shipment to San Francisco and supplies were received at the station for the ranches.[15]

That John was not literate is assumed from a deed of sale he made in 1876.[16] John signed with an "X" although Keziah was able to sign her name. However, the Finley children attended school, either the Pacific District School, established in 1859 on Irish Hill,[17] or Potter District School, established in 1866 in Bodega. Samuel, the oldest, may have been an exception since in a later deed, where all the brothers and sisters assigned their interests to Henry Head Finley, he was the only one to sign with an "X."[18] Acquiring an education in those days in the Bodega area was not easy. In the winter the roads were flooded by heavy rains which would wash out the bridges, making it impossible to get to school. Schools had only started to appear in Sonoma County shortly before John and Keziah arrived. Bodega was one of the five townships which had a school by 1850, but it was a private school on Capt. Smith's Rancho, mainly for his children, and lessons were taught in Spanish. By 1855 there were twenty-three schools in the county with a total enrollment of 1,253.[19]

As the children grew up on the family homestead, they helped with the many chores. The boys milked cows and helped with making butter, general farming, and getting the produce to market. They also found jobs in nearby lumber mills, did logging in the woods or worked on other ranches as they grew

Bodega at the turn of the century, reconstructed by Dick Shell from the early accounts of Bodega Corners.

older. The girls, Nancy and Nettie, helped with the housework, sewing, and did lighter outside chores.

They [the girls] learned how to knit and crochet sweaters, socks, mittens, gloves, caps; to piece quilts and comforters; and to make mattresses and pillows from feathers and down plucked from the geese the family raised. They learned how to plant and tend a vegetable garden, the secret of raising turkeys and chickens, and how to make butter and cheese with the cream and milk from the dairy. In the summer they learned how to can fruit, make pickles, relishes, jams, and jellies. Blackberries grew in abundance all around the country and every one went berry-picking. Fresh blackberry

CARMEN J. FINLEY COLLECTION

John and Keziah's homestead on Salmon Creek

shortcake was a special treat, but plenty of the fruit also went into jam, jelly, and canning to store away for winter.[20]

During the 1860s and 1870s the town of Bodega, a few miles southeast of the Finley ranch, included the Potter School; Shiloh Presbyterian Church, to which Keziah belonged; St. Teresa's Catholic Church; three saloons; two general stores, Goodman's & McCaughey's; and a post office. The post office alternated its location between Goodman's and McCaughey's stores.

Social life of the area was pretty much whatever was created among themselves. There were picnics, dances, parties, and socials at the churches, lodges, schools, and homes. There were hay rides, coast parties, fishing trips, and horseback rides. Apparently there was a lot of local talent and together they put on their own programs and entertainment to the enjoyment of everyone. The Finley family loved music. They had an organ which Henry, Nancy, and Nettie all learned how to play and the family would gather around to sing. Jim played the violin and, in addition to playing at home, he would play for local dances. Some of the music they played at home consisted of hymns. Keziah was a very devout person and read the Bible every day. The Shiloh Presbyterian Church was holding services in a partially completed building as early as 27 September 1868. The completed building was dedicated 26 March 1871 and Keziah officially joined 2 April 1871. The family participated in many church activities.

In August of 1871 John's youngest sister, Elizabeth, who had married their first cousin, another John Findley, was suddenly widowed when her husband was shot to death, a deliberate homicide reported in chapter 5. They were living in Tulare County at the time and had six children under the age of sixteen. Shortly thereafter, Elizabeth and all her brood moved to Sonoma County and bought 160 acres adjacent to the Estero Americano Grant,[21] near her brothers John and Sam. Legal guardianship of her six children was transferred to John in February 1873.[22] When Elizabeth remarried a few months later, John bought her property.[23]

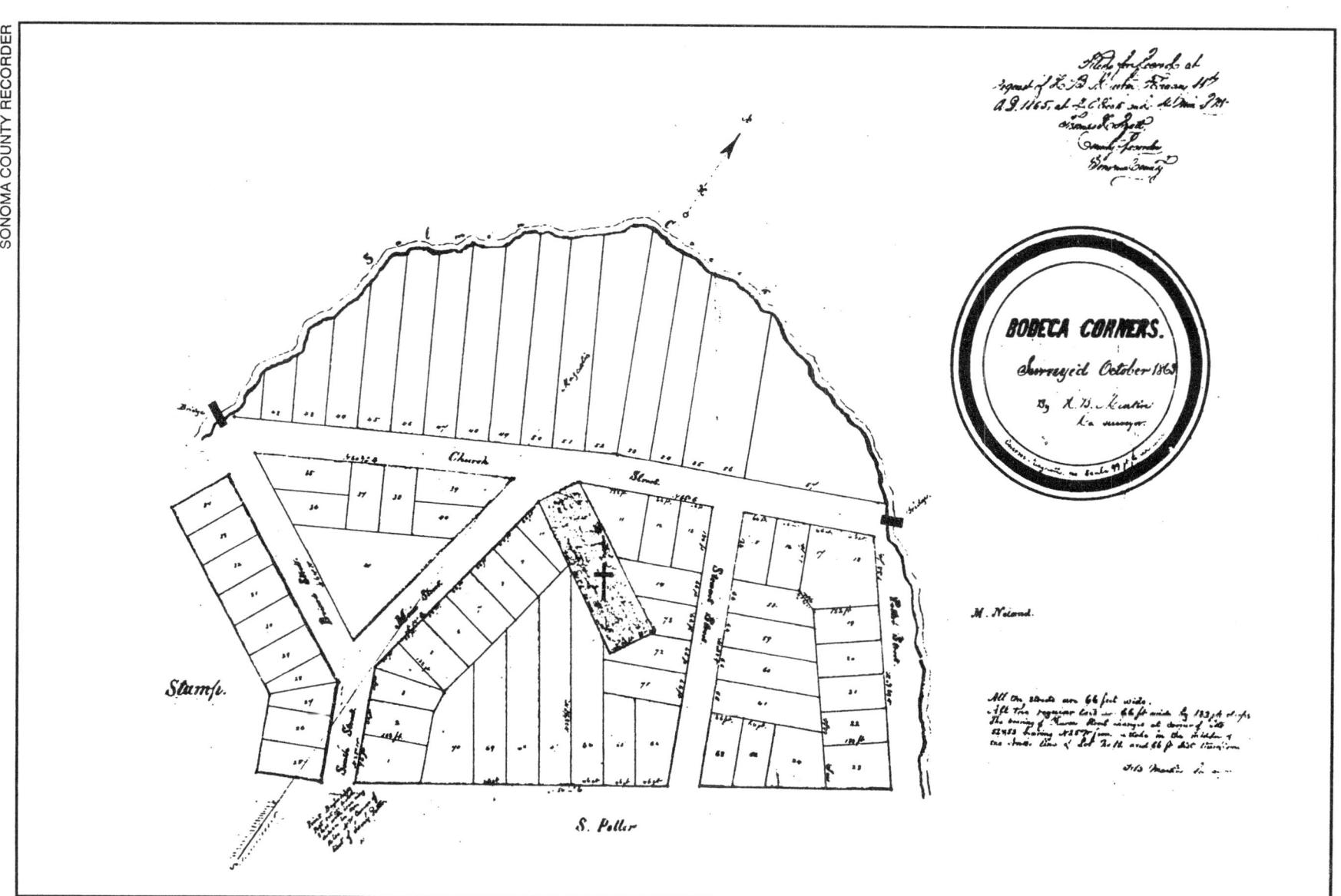

Bodega Corners, 1863

Receipt for State and County Taxes.   No. 2110

$185.89

CAUTION.—Examine the following and have errors (if any) corrected before leaving the office.

STATE OF CALIFORNIA, COUNTY OF SONOMA.
Tax Collector's Office, Santa Rosa, _____ 188_

State Tax, $ .59
County Tax, $ .85
Total Tax, $1.45

Received of _Finley John_
One hundred & eighty four 84/100 DOLLARS,

in full for the State and County Taxes for the Fiscal year 1882, as per Assessment Roll, on the following property, to wit:

483 Acres Bd N By Hitchcock E By Finley
S By Taylor W By Gomer Rco.   5800 Imp 400
408 Acres Bd N By Fay E By McQuade
S By Salmon Creek W By Finley   3600 " 800

Real Estate, - - $ 9400
Improvements, - $ 700
Personal Property $ 2720
Total, - - $ 12820
Less Mortgage, - $
Total, - $

Property Tax, - - $
Five Per Cent., - - $
Advertising, - - - $
Total, - - - $

_____ Tax Collector.
By _____

SANTA ROSA REPUBLICAN PRINT.

John Finley's tax receipt on 891 acres of his property in 1882.

PAGE 8

He continued as official guardian for her children and tended their finances until 1891, when the youngest child came of age. This was only the beginning of a strong patriarchal role which John was to play for the remainder of his life.

In 1875 Nancy and Sam were the first of John and Keziah's children to marry. Nancy married Calvin Keithly who had been teaching at the Potter School in Bodega. They were married under the trees near the house on Fay Creek which was a part of John and Keziah's ranch, property they had bought from George Owens in 1872.[24] But Nancy was destined to return to the Finley ranch less than two years later, after the birth of her daughter, Clara, in December 1875, and the death of her husband, Calvin, in September 1876. Sam had been given half of the 330 acre sheep ridge portion of the ranch, which was situated between Finley and Coleman Valley Creeks. Sam had been working in a sawmill in Gualala, Mendocino County, when he met and married Mary Jane Stanley. They soon returned to the Finley ranch to set up housekeeping.

In July of 1876 another tragedy struck the Finley family when John's brother, Sam, was shot and killed in the streets of Guerneville, a nearby community. Sam had the dubious distinction of being the first homicide to occur in Guerneville. A feature story of this event was carried in a recent issue of the *Journal of the Sonoma County Historical Society*[25] and is told in chapter 5. Sam's oldest daughter, Martha, was married to a James F. Oliver, who, from the records he left, was not a very good businessman. He accumulated a string of mortgages and promissory notes culminating in a foreclosure in 1879 in which John Finley was named as a co-defendant.[26] So once again it was John to the rescue. When last heard from, Oliver gave power of attorney to Henry Finley to sell all his property. That order was executed from Madison County, Montana on 26 March 1880.[27]

Nettie (Elizabeth Finetta) was the next to be married. In 1880 she was wed to Albert Pike Head at her parents home on Salmon Creek. But her health was not good. She suffered from rheumatism and had never really been strong. Nettie had three children between 1881 and 1887, but then died later that year. Albert felt he could not take care of the children by himself, so their children, Clarence Elmore, Lulu Myrtle, and Robertson Calvin Head also came back to the Finley ranch to be reared. This turn of events precipitated new living arrangements and Nancy, together with her bachelor brother Henry, set up housekeeping in a house on the east bank of Coleman Valley Creek. There they cared for Nancy's daughter, Clara, and Nettie's three children. The four children grew up together.

In addition to Sam, only three of John and Keziah's other sons married, Jeff (Jefferson Davis), Jack (Andrew Jackson), and Alvin Wesley. All of Jeff's children were born in or near Bodega. Jack moved around a bit to Arizona, Orange County, California, back to Bodega, then Trinity County but eventually returned to the Finley ranch where he lived out his life. Alvin began his married life in Sonoma County, but also moved around. He and his family lived in the San Francisco Bay area, and in Mendocino, Merced, Monterey, Santa Cruz, and San Mateo Counties. John Jay, Henry Head, James Preston, and William David never married, but lived on or near the Finley homestead during their lives.

Nancy's daughter, Clara, who grew up on the Finley ranch in a home shared with her mother, Nancy, Uncle Henry, and her Head cousins, was the first real family historian. Her articles appear in the early issues of the Journal of the Sonoma County Historical Society. In one, she comments on her Grandmother Keziah:

> Grandma had geese and ducks. It was her ambition to make a feather bed for each of her nine children. This she accomplished. Grandpa admired her for her "spunk."[28]

Keziah, according to family tradition, was half Cherokee Indian. This may well be true. The few photos of her which exist portray a stern looking woman with dark hair and high cheekbones. John, according to information from the Great Register of Sonoma County for 1892, was of fair complexion, with blue eyes and gray hair. Their sons, who appeared in the same Great Register were Alvin, Henry, Jim, John, Jeff, and Samuel. All except Henry had a dark complexion; all had brown eyes; all had either brown or black hair. Joseph Jefferson Finley, a nephew of John's who lived nearby, was fair with gray eyes and brown hair.[29]

In another of her writings, Clara tells how butter was made on the Finley

DAIRY METHODS IN THE 1890s by Mrs. Clara Tarwater
(Excerpt from article published in the *Journal of the Sonoma County Historical Society*, September 1964)

Another room with butter brake and also hardwood shelf for the finished article, and the sheltered porch where the big iron kettle held water over a wood fire for washing the many utensils. Also in this porch stood the box-shaped churn supported on a frame. Here the man who made the butter would stand, and by means of a crank, turn the churn of cream over and over until the butter was separated from the milk.

In those days the cows depended on the pasture for feed. The dairy work began at 3 A.M., when the men, two or three on each dairy, would rise, get their coal-oil lanterns and drive the cows in for milking. Nor should I forget to mention the good dog which helped in this chore. It use to amuse me to notice how the individual cows each remembered their favorite place to stand, and there they would quietly chew their cud until the milking was finished and they were driven towards the pasture until 3 P.M. for the second milking.

The men milked into five-gallon buckets. This was strained into pans previously arranged in up and down rows in racks around three sides of the room. There it was left for two or three days for the cream to rise. For this purpose the room was to be kept at a certain temperature. This was done in cold weather by a wood fire in a stove near the center of the room, thus making an attractive haven of warmth on cold days. But not much time to enjoy this for skimming must be done. Of course there were several separate milkings around the room and the oldest one was always ready to be skimmed. For this purpose there was a special type of stand waiting by the fourth wall. It had a curved opening in each end for a cream can to fit into. The center was a funnel shaped opening into which the milk was poured. It ran into a covered trough down to a tank by the pig-pen. Thus the porkers had "curds and whey" for their meals. These porkers were eventually turned into spare-ribs, sausage, smoked hams or shoulders for the dining table.

If the milk was just right, it was fun to skim. The skimming knife was of wood, curved with a handle. The skimmer would circle the milk with this knife to cut the cream loose from the pan, roll the cream up and slide it off into the large cream can, send the milk down to the pigs and stack the pans. Then the cleaning up. Pans - dozens of them - and three or four buckets must be washed and scalded. Now the milkers were free and off to look after the stock, fences or other farm work - except the man who made the butter. He now emptied the large can of cream - maybe two, of 30 or 40 gallons each, into the churn, and clamp on the lid over a cloth which sealed it. Then turn by crank over and over until the butter separated from the milk. (The better equipped dairies had power machinery outside which connected with the churn. This was operated by a horse going around and around until the churning was completed.)

Then the buttermilk was drawn, a little saved in pans for the cook, excellent for drinking, or for making soft biscuits or hotcakes, the rest down the chute for the pigs. After the milk was drawn off, bucket after bucket of clean cold water was poured into the churn for washing out whatever milk was left, for milk will sour or turn unsavory with age. The product was now carried to the butter brake where the water was worked out of it. This brake was a triangular shaped table slanting towards the apex where the excess water worked off by means of a long pole arranged as a lever, then salt was worked into the butter, the amount being judged by the operator.

Now the final step of shaping the product into rolls, and preparing it for shipment. For this procedure there were three paddles of hardwood, two of which were alike and used to shape a chunk of approximately two pounds for the molds. The third paddle was narrower and sharper for trimming the excess from the mold thereby leaving a two pound roll about six inches long. These rolls were stood on end on the shelf of hardwood to become firm. Then more cleaning up, a hinged cover being let down over the butter.

The next day the rolls were wrapped in clean cloth and stood on end in a box made for that purpose. This "butter cloth" was bought by the bolt and when needed was torn into strips and cut into sections by help of a measuring board. These sections must be just right to fit the roll, leaving a narrow border turned over each end. Now being packed, they were ready to be stamped. This impression gave the initial of the owner circled by a wreath, and when the rolls were all stamped the effect was a small work of art. Finally the butter was covered by a larger cloth, lid closed and the product was ready for shipment to a commission merchant in San Francisco.

Often it was Grandfather who took the butter by horses and "spring wagon" to Bodega Roads, a station on the old narrow gauge railroad by which it was carried to its destination. In a few days the "Returns" came, including payment, with a brief letter of commendation or suggestion for improvements.

This description is typical of the dairies of the 90s. But soon the creameries with inspectors came in and methods changed.

ranch during the time she lived there. Her earliest recollections were of Keziah "churning and shaping butter and then taking it on horseback down to the store in Freestone where it was exchanged for more needed articles." Keziah must have been at least in her fifties at the time. Clara then describes the corral dairy house with its large milk-room. By this time, in the 1890s, John was running two different dairies on the ranch.

Clara, in her story of *The Corners, Smith's Ranch*, also describes what life was like in Bodega in the 1880s and 1890s:

> . . . life there was interesting, with chatter of school experiences around the evening meal; entertainments at end of the terms; monthly church socials; and occasional picnics at the beach.[30] Our Fourth of July celebration was the main event of the year in those days (the 90s). It was an open-air affair in Joy's Woods of Redwood trees where there was a platform for the musicians and orator. This a patriotic program before noon during which all was quiet and respectful, even the children. Then to the picnic lunches and refreshment stand. The afternoon was passed in dancing and visiting.[31]

Apparently the Finleys did their share of entertaining. The following is an excerpt from a letter written by one of the Finley neighbors, Mrs. James McCaughey:

> We held our church social yesterday (Saturday) at Finley's and had a nice time. Watsons came with their spring wagon and took us along. Howard went horseback. It was something like a picnic - they wanted it there in the daytime as the roads are not safe to drive on at night. They had a nice croquet grounds and a large swing erected, also a hammock and all just before you go to Henry's house on the left on the other side of the creek in a lovely place under the trees. They had every accommodation in the way of amusements. They carried the organ out and had nice exercises first. Then had a delicious lunch and after that

The fruit ranch on Frei Road near Graton, Keziah's residence in her later years where she lived to ease her asthma condition. She is shown here with her youngest son, Alvin, his wife, Frances, and their child, Claude, around 1902.

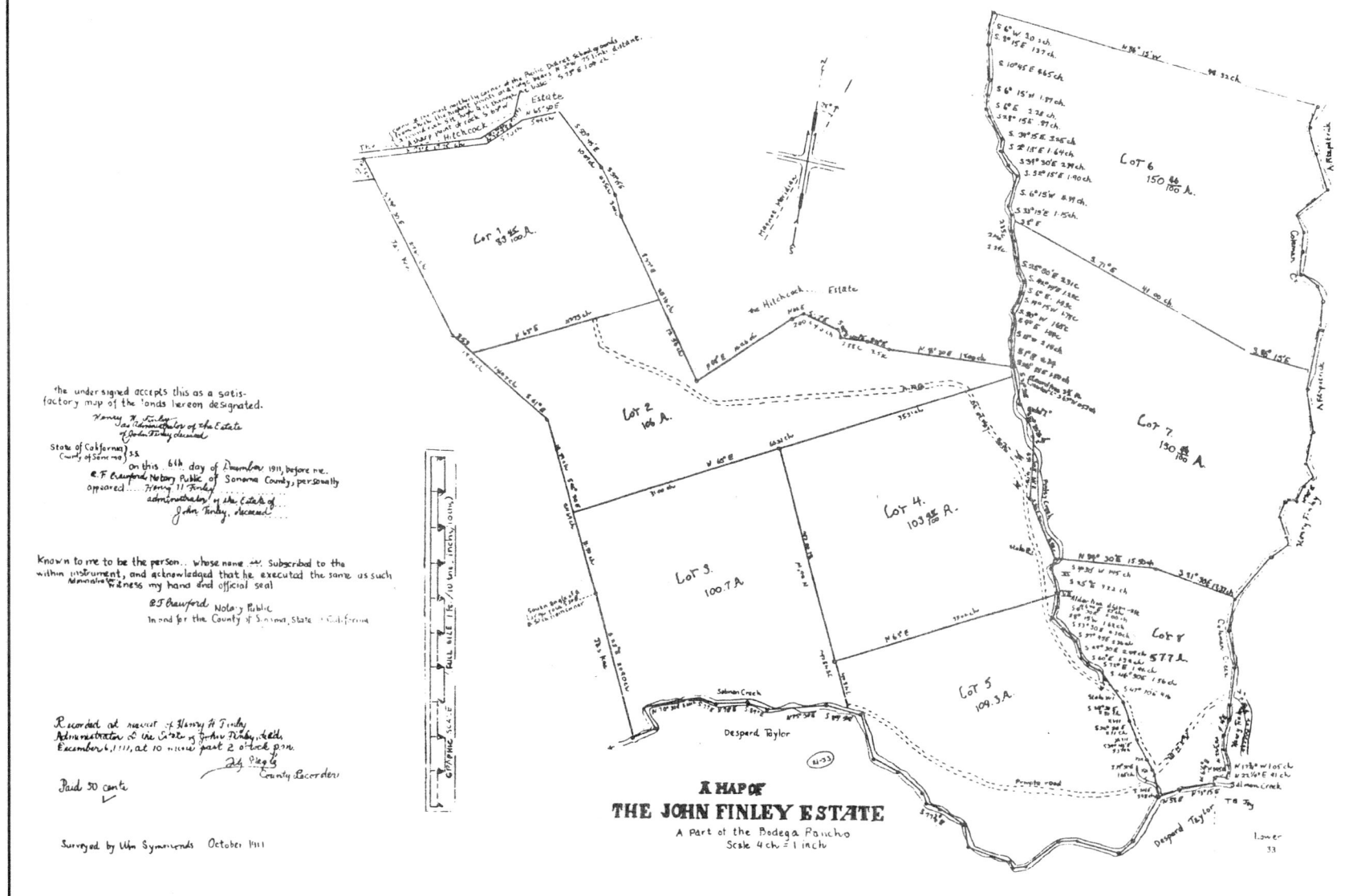

John Finley's land consisted of eight parcels and was divided among his heirs as follows:

HEIR	LOT No.
James P. Finley	1
Samuel E. Finley	2
Clarence Head Lulu McKune Robert C. Head	3
Alvin W. Finley	4
Jefferson D. Finley	5
Samuel E. Finley (this was deeded to him by his father in 1871)	6
Andrew J. Finley	7
John J. Finley	8

had games, races and all kinds of fun.[32]

Clara, in her later years, dug up this little gem, whose source she gives only as *The Press Democrat*:

During Bodega's "golden Age" (1890) there were five saloons, two churches, a school, a blacksmith shop, and a livery stable. Mc-Caughey's store, far from being an anachronism left over from the last century is as much alive today as it was when butter sold for 12 cents a pound and a customer had to use a wagon to take home $5 worth of groceries.[33]

Keziah's health began to fail in the 1880s and she suffered from asthma. She began to stay with her children who lived in drier climates during the times when the weather was bad at home. Son Jack and his wife, Alfaretta, lived in Arizona when they were first married, and she would visit them there. She also visited Southern California where her youngest son, Alvin, attended college in Santa Ana. Because of Keziah's health problems, John bought a forty-eight and one half acre fruit ranch near Graton in 1899.[34] This property was located in Analy Township, about three and a half miles north of Sebastopol and about a mile east of Graton, on what is now Frei Road. Keziah lived there with different members of the family, mainly her son Alvin, and her granddaughter Clara. Her grandson Rob Head, stayed with her a year and went to Oak Grove School when he was in the fourth grade. Alvin married Frances Head in 1901 and they made their home with Keziah until she died in 1903 at the age of seventy-five. Two years later, at the age of eighty-two, John retired from the ranch at Bodega and made his home at the fruit ranch until his death in 1910.

Henry was the executor for his father's estate. The Finley ranch at that time consisted of approximately 1,000 acres, which was divided among his heirs. The property was divided into eight parcels ranging in size from 58 acres to 150 acres. This proved to be good planning since in the final accounting of John Finley's estate is found, "that there is no inheritance tax whatsoever, the appraised value of the property received by each heir being less than the exemption allowed by law."[35] In addition to John's children, the Head grandchildren,

Clarence, Lulu, and Rob, who were reared by Henry and Nancy, received one of the lots. John's cash reserves amounted to $3,507.80 and his personal property included a herd of 118 cows, five horses, four hogs, ten pigs, two shoats, poultry, plus four wagons, his dairy equipment, farm tools and implements, and household furniture. Both John and Keziah are buried at the Spring Hill Cemetary, which, as of this writing, has been abandoned.

For this period of time, 1852 to 1910, this story is probably fairly typical of the successful rural Sonoma County farmer and the workings of an extended patriarchal family. The story of John and Keziah's descendants is told in chapter 5.

CHAPTER TWO: WILLIAM ASA AND SARAH (LATIMER) FINLEY

In a number of ways, the early history of William Asa Finley parallels that of John and Keziah Finley. Before coming to California he was living in Missouri, having moved there from Kentucky. He left Missouri on a wagon train in 1852, just a few months before John and Keziah. They shared a common ancestor. John Finley of Virginia was the second great-grandfather of William Asa and the great-grandfather of John of Sonoma County. But there the parallel stops.

William Asa was younger than John by sixteen years. He migrated with his parents and siblings at the age of twelve, although he reached his thirteenth birthday before they reached California. Their destination was San Jose, Santa Clara County, where he lived to young adulthood. But that is getting ahead of the story.

The family's migration across the country was chronicled by William's younger brother Newton Gleaves, who wrote it in retrospect seventy years later.[1] Their family joined three other families and left from Saline County, Missouri.

Counting the necessary teamsters and cooks, the party totaled forty-four persons, of which twenty-seven were children. The following information, gleaned from Newton's account, is probably fairly typical of pioneer trips of the 1850s.

A party of that size required eight prairie schooners drawn by oxen and two family carriages pulled by mules.

William Asa Finley, 1839-1912

ALTON LOVELL ALDERMAN, M. D. COLLECTION

The accompanying livestock consisted mostly of cows, plus a few oxen, and numbered about three hundred head. There were also about twenty mules and a few choice saddle horses.

According to Newton's account, the food was "bountiful and of best grade and also of great variety," . . . including cornmeal flour, buckwheat flour, ham, bacon, sausages, dried beef, beans, peas, potatoes, rice, coffee, tea, sugar, honey, syrup, milk, butter, as well as dried fruits, apples, walnuts, hickory nuts, and hazel nuts. They had fresh milk twice daily and butter fresh daily, which was made simply by placing milk in the churn in the morning and carrying it aboard a wagon. The wagon and rough roads did the rest! Fortunately, water was abundant and of good quality.

The wagon train went by the Little and Big Blue Rivers to the South Fork of the Platte River, then to the North Platte, the Rocky Mountains and through the Black Hills to Green River. From there it went over the Wasatch Mountains to the plateau below, Fort Hall and Bear River, and on to the Great Salt Lake. Next it crossed over the Humboldt Mountains to the headwaters of the Humboldt River and across the desert to Rag Town (now Reno), across Carson River and the Sierras near Truckee Lake. Finally the travelers reached Hang Town (now Placerville), where the children were allowed to pan for gold using milk pails. With the worst behind them, it was just a few more days into Livermore Valley and San Jose. Newton ends his memoirs with this verse:

Many things more remain untold
Of this trip to the land of Gold
By the way:–sufficient to say
We landed safe in San Jose

Sadly, they did not all land safely in San Jose as the Finley children's mother died the day they arrived. But the family resumed its goal of settlement in their new location and soon there was a new step-mother.

Here William Asa grew to adulthood and attended first, the University of the Pacific in Santa Clara, and then Pacific Methodist College in Vacaville where he obtained his Master of Arts degree in 1864.[2] The graduating class of 1864[3] had a total of three graduates and William Asa gave the valedictory address: *God In Science*.[4] In addition, William was the only one, and the first in the history of the college, who chose to apply for admission into the ranks of the itinerancy of the Methodist Church. That year he was appointed to the Ukiah Circuit in Mendocino County and traveled to perform his duties. In 1865 he was offered and accepted the position of President of Corvallis College in Oregon (later Oregon State University).[5] The school, established in 1856 under Presbyterian leadership, came under the direction of the Methodist Episcopal Church, South, in 1865, and William Asa Finley was appointed their first administrator. He made the trip by stagecoach, arriving in October of that year. Still unmarried when he accepted this position, he returned to California at the end of his first year to claim his bride, Sarah Latimer, who had been a college classmate.[6] They were married 8 August 1866 at their alma mater, Pacific Methodist College. Their return to Corvallis was by ship from San Francisco to Portland, and by river steamer from Portland to Corvallis. His wife, Sarah, at the age of eighty, wrote a series of four articles describing their experience at Corvallis.

Sarah (Latimer) and William Asa Finley wedding picture.

These were published in the Oregon State Monthly in the spring of 1930.

During the school year 1866-67, Corvallis had a faculty of five persons and one hundred sixty-seven students, eighty-six males and eighty-one females. The small size required that William do a lot of teaching himself and his offi-

Home of President William Finley, of Corvallis College (now Oregon State University), and wife, Sarah. The young couple are on the balcony, Sarah holding young Ernest L. Finley, ca.1870.

cial title was "President of the College and Professor of Languages."

The high point of his tenure in Corvallis came in 1868 when the college was chosen over Willamette University as "the agricultural college of Oregon." This carried with it "a land-grant of 1862, under the Morrill Act, which allowed Oregon 90,000 acres of land as a perpetual endowment for a state agricultural college."[7]

It was truly a triumph, but the problems it brought soon proved almost impossible to handle. The grant required major additions to the curriculum in agriculture, science, foreign languages, and military exercises, to mention only a few. This, despite the college being deeply in debt and the state very slow and slight in its support. Teachers often went unpaid and had to support themselves with other work.[8]

Recognition of his work during these years came when, in June 1871, William was given an honorary degree of Doctor of Divinity by Wofford College, Spartanburg, South Carolina.[9] He was the sixth person to be so honored by Wofford.[10] The *History of Southern Methodism* noted William as "being the youngest man to receive this title that has ever been amongst us."[11]

William resigned his position on 4 May 1872, to take effect at the close of the academic year.[12] He gave as his reason that the health of Mrs. Finley, "demanded the continuous sunshine of a southern climate." A later article in the college newspaper written in 1938 pointed out that, "singularly enough, while President Finley, who continued his professional career in California, died 19 July 1912, at the age of about seventy years, Mrs. Finley, whose frailty in 1872 led to his departure from Oregon, lived until November 14, 1937, approaching within four months of ninety years of age."[13]

In September 1872 the church assigned him to a position as head of Gilroy High School, and Sarah was appointed vice-principal.[14] The school was abandoned two years later and he was appointed pastor of the Grace Methodist Episcopal Church, South, in Stockton.[15] However, he watched for an opportunity to return to his alma mater and that soon came. Pacific Methodist College had moved to Santa Rosa in 1871 from Vacaville after the Vacaville facility had been burned to the ground, presumably by Yankee sympathizers. Ten acres of land were donated by Santa Rosa citizens and a "spacious college building" was erected at a cost of $25,000. It was located in the northeastern part of the city on what is now College Avenue, at the site of the present Santa Rosa Junior High School, and could accommodate 300 students.

In 1876 William accepted a professorship at his former alma mater. His appointment came just as A.L. Fitzgerald resigned as president. It was all very timely and William was elected acting president in October and later became president.[16] In addition to being president, he was also professor of mental and moral science, Greek language and literature. The college also offered Latin, mathematics, natural science, music, and commercial and business courses.[17]

So this is how the second Finley family came to live in Sonoma County and settle in Santa Rosa just the year after the arrival of Luther Burbank. In subsequent years both Burbank and the son of William and Sarah, then six-year-old Ernest Latimer Finley, were destined to leave powerful marks on the community.

At the beginning of the 1870s Santa Rosa was a small rural town. According to one contemporary historian:

> The 1870 census marked Santa Rosa as the most insular of all Sonoma County communities. One of five in the Analy township was foreign-born, the average for the county. In Petaluma, Sonoma, and Bodega, one in four was foreign-born. In Santa Rosa township only one of every nine inhabitants was born outside the United States. One in ten, bearing out old contentions, was a Missourian.[18]

Prior to 1870, "The streets were mud. It was an all-day trip to anywhere. The saloons outnumbered the book shops five to one, and it was only the second-largest town in Sonoma County."[19] But all this was about to change. With the coming of the railroad, businesses began to expand. William and Sarah's arrival was shortly after the "railroad cyclone"

Pacific Methodist College
Santa Rosa, California
The Thirty-second semi-annual session
of
Pacific Methodist College
will begin

Tuesday,..........January 2d, 1877

Faculty
REV. W.A. FINLEY, Acting President and Professor of Mental and Moral Science
CHARLES S. SMYTH A.M., Professor of Mathematics.
O.H. ROBERTS, A.M., Professor of the Latin, Oriental and Modern Languages
E.J. GRIFFITH, A.M., Professor of Natural Science.
W.A. FINLEY, A.M., Professor of Greek Language and Literature
WM. .A. WRIGHT, A.M., Principal of Commercial and Business Department
FERDINAND KENJOY, A.B., Tutor in Mathematics
MISS LIZZIE M. YATES, A.B., Tutor of Languages
MISS LILLA WERLEIN, Teacher of Music

The scholastic year is divided into two sessions of twenty weeks each.

Expenses
tuition, per session
Primary Department	$15
Preparatory Department	$20
Preparatory Department-with algebra	$25
Preparatory Department - with Latin or Greek	$25
Collegiate Department-Irregular	$30
Collegiate Department-Regular	$35

Board in good families, including all expenses for fuel, lights, etc., $20 per month.

The College is open to both Ladies and Gentlemen. Parents will confer a great favor upon us by sending their children at the opening of the session.
For further particulars, address
Dr. W.A. Finley, President

ADVERTISEMENT FROM SONOMA DEMOCRAT, 27 JANUARY 1877

COURTESY, THE SONOMA COUNTY LIBRARY

COURTESY, THE SONOMA COUNTY LIBRARY

Santa Rosa Ladies' College, established in 1884 by William Asa Finley, operated until circa 1890.

Pacific Methodist College, Santa Rosa, California, was located on College Avenue between King Street and North Street (now Brookwood Avenue). William Asa Finley was president from 1876 to 1884.

had hit Sonoma County. This, in turn, brought on a real estate boom and the community began to grow. Many of the people who relocated in Santa Rosa were from San Francisco.

Shortly after his appointment, William and Sarah bought their first piece of property on the northwest corner of Cherry and Orchard Street in what was the Farmer & Ames Addition. They bought it at auction in the sale of the Mary Gallagher Estate for $650, the highest bid. The property included three adjacent lots and occupied approximately one-fourth of the block.[20] That corner, 801 Cherry Street, is today occupied by the Gospel Promotion Church.

Sometime before 1880 William and Sarah took in a foster daughter, Julia Cannon,[21] reported to be thirteen years old in the 1880 census, three years older than Ernest.[22] The circumstances surrounding her becoming a member of the household, or for how long she stayed, are unknown. Quite possibly she stayed until her marriage to Eugene Wakefield Brown on 21 May 1888. The service was performed by William.[23] In March of 1882 the family expanded with the addition of a daughter, Willie C.; Ernest was now twelve. This may have contributed to William's next major professional step and a change in housing.

In 1884 William bought eight lots in the McDonald Addition from Horace Clark for $3,000. This property had a 200 foot frontage on McDonald Avenue between 17th and 18th Streets and ran the full length of 17th Street to Monroe Street, a distance of 312 feet.[24] It was occupied by what had been the Santa Rosa Shoe and Boot Factory and William converted it into a school for young women.[25] Also, about that time, he sold his Cherry Street property and purchased a home on King Street in the Benton Addition, a temporary move.[26] The next year, he sold his King Street home and purchased more property on McDonald Avenue and 17th Street adjacent to his college. This finally became his permanent resi-

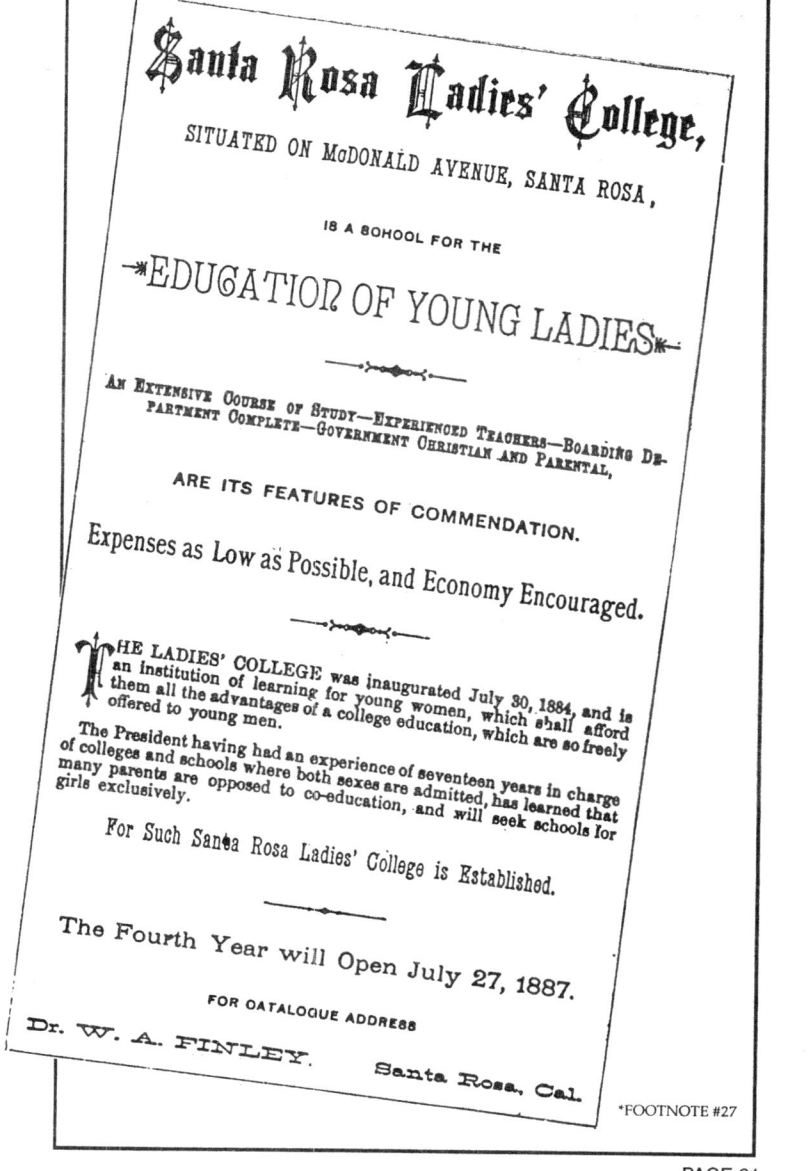

*FOOTNOTE #27

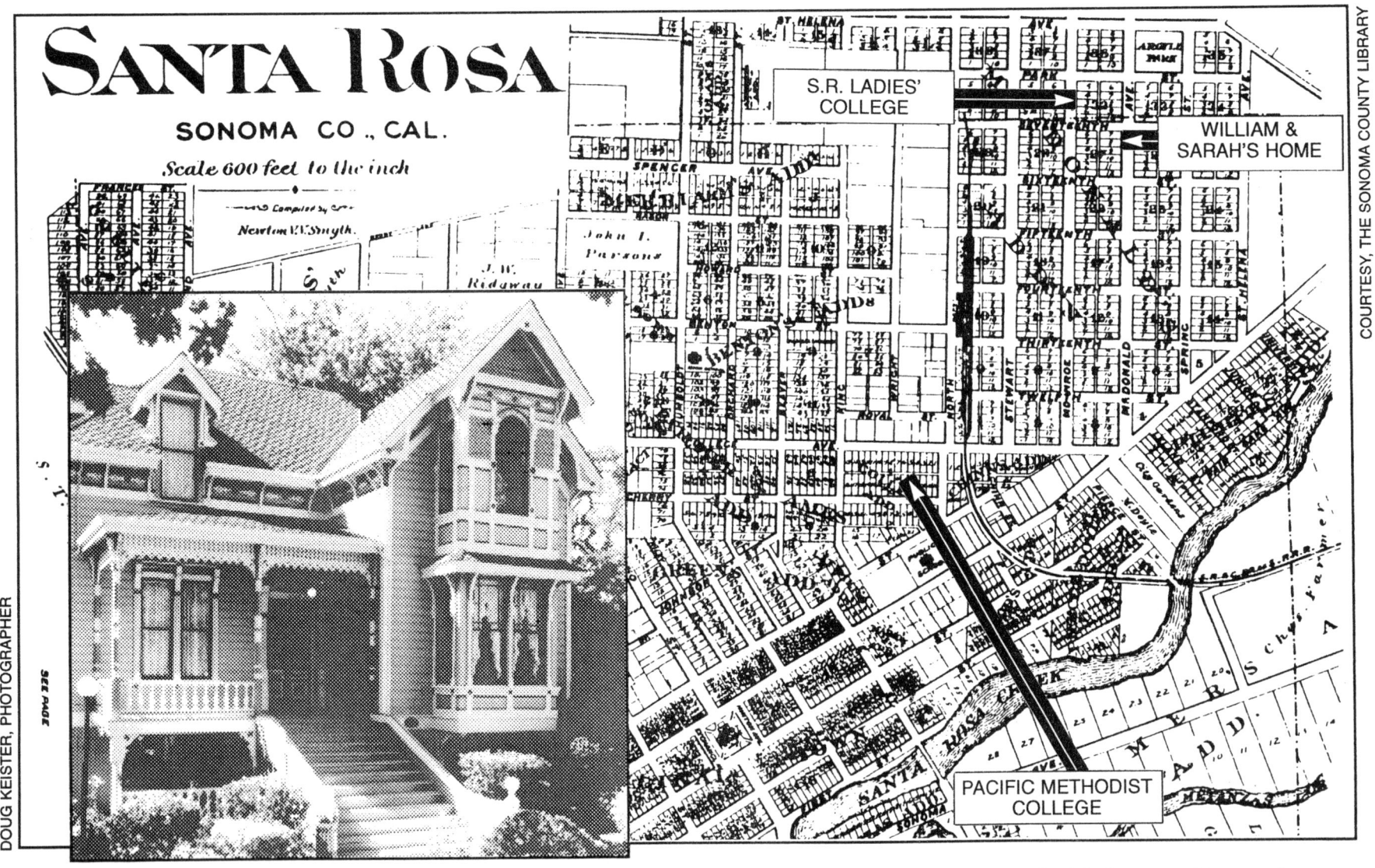

Northeast section of Santa Rosa showing location of Pacific Methodist College, Santa Rosa Ladies' College, and home of William and Sarah Finley. 1127 McDonald Avenue (inset), home of William and Sarah Finley.

dence.[28]

William and Sarah's home at 1127 McDonald Avenue is, today, one of the most attractive and well-kept Victorian homes in the area.[29] The street is named for Mark McDonald, Santa Rosa's leading entrepreneur at the time, who developed the town's water company and the area which was called McDonald's Addition of Homesteads. Construction of homes in this tract began in 1877. McDonald Avenue was designed to be elegant and is, to this day, Santa Rosa's most exclusive street. McDonald built his own summer home,[30] Mableton, an ornate Victorian mansion, at 1015 on the west side of the street about mid-way into his tract of homes and just a block south of William and Sarah's house. When McDonald opened his tract, he also built the Santa Rosa Street Railway to connect his new development with the railroad depot. Many years later Ernest L. Finley wrote about these horse-drawn vehicles:

> People living on McDonald avenue could pay $1.50 a month and ride as much as they pleased. It was quite the common custom for mothers to put their children aboard and let them ride back and forth for an hour or two, without charge. The cost was all included in the monthly "ticket," although there was no actual ticket so far as I ever knew. You just paid your $1.50 and that ended it.[31]

Santa Rosa's growth continued. By the mid-1880s a new county courthouse had been built in the center of Santa Rosa Plaza and a new City Hall constructed nearby. Not far away was Santa Rosa's Chinatown which had developed from early railroad workers and now included China-born residents who worked in hotels, homes, and as farm workers. By 1885 Santa Rosa boasted ten industrial plants, eight hotels, seven churches, five schools, two lodges, two cemeteries, two town parks, a public library, a railroad depot, a skating rink, a hospital, and a theater.[32]

William Finley made a few more land transactions. He did what amounted to a "swap" with his father-in-law, Robert A. Latimer, in 1888. He purchased the two remaining lots on the north side of his college from Latimer, which gave him the entire block on McDonald Avenue running between 17th and 18th Streets.[33] On the same date, he sold to Latimer the property at 1127 McDonald, where he and his family were living.[34] A few months later he purchased two lots in the South Park Addition.[35]

In the early 1880s William's brother Newton Gleaves Finley, moved to Santa Rosa and established himself on a fruit ranch in the Lewis district. He purchased twenty-three and one third acres from Eldad Rogers for $2,400, the property bordering on Santa Rosa Creek.[36] Newton was known to his family as a "pioneer prune grower." He may have been influenced in his decision to relocate by Luther Burbank, who had just established himself as the "plant wizard" by delivering 19,500 prune trees to Warren Dutton on a very tight schedule in 1881.[37] Burbank's most often quoted phrase describing the area, "I firmly believe from what I have seen that this is the chosen spot of all this earth as far as Nature is concerned," was printed for years at the bottom of the first page of *The Press Democrat*, published by William and Sarah's son, Ernest Latimer Finley.

The Great Register of Voters established by California Code in 1866 was the official record of men eligible to vote and gives both occupation and a description of physical characteristics in some years. In it William is variously listed either as a "minister" or "clerical teacher," while Newton is listed either as an "orchardist" or "fruitgrower."[38] William was not a tall man, being just 5'8", with dark complexion, hazel eyes, and black hair. In contrast Newton was 5'11", with fair complexion, gray eyes, and brown hair.[39]

In 1889 William was offered a position as professor of mathematics in the College of Liberal Arts at the University of Southern California in Los Angeles, which he accepted.[40] The announcement, following, was on the front page of *The Sonoma Democrat.*[41]

That year his visits at home during Christmas and Easter were duly noted in the local press.[42]

Apparently, the Santa Rosa Young Ladies' College went out of existence sometime in 1890 or 1891. In the 1890 business directory William was still listed as president, and Sarah was listed as "lady principal" at the Santa Rosa Ladies' College.[43] However, in *1891 The Resources of California* did a sixteen-page feature article on Sonoma County, which included a section on schools. William's school was not mentioned, although the Pacific Methodist College was boldly

---

DR. FINLEY'S CALL

Dr. W. A. Finley, President of the Ladies' College, informs us that having no senior class the present year and since his school is thoroughly organized and in competent hands, he has accepted a call to the University of Southern California, in Los Angeles, for the year beginning Oct. 1, 1889.

The patrons of his College in the meantime may rest assured that their interests will in no wise be neglected.

---

featured with pictures of the campus and other private schools were also mentioned.[44] In September 1891 the local paper carried a notice that, "Dr. W.A. Finley has joined the Los Angeles Conference, and is stationed at Downey."[45] He must have known of this appointment at least as early as June of that year since during a convention of the American Bible Association in Santa Rosa, he "extended an invitation to the Association to hold its next meeting in Los Angeles."[46] In November of that year he gave one of the major addresses at the Sunday School Mass Meeting sponsored by the Los Angeles County Sunday School Association. His address was

titled, *Child Religion.*[47]

The Los Angeles Methodist Conference was a separate administrative unit from the Pacific Coast Conference to which he formerly belonged, and the records for those years are not intact.[48] However, in 1895 he rejoined the Pacific Conference and was assigned to a church position in Madera where he served as pastor for the next four years. While in Madera he was appointed County Superintendent of Schools to fill an unexpired term.[49] He apparently returned to Santa Rosa around the turn of the century and subsequent city directories, and the Great Register, show him alternately retired and/or selling securities and investments. The 1908 business directory, for example, shows William selling securities at 409 Mendocino Avenue and living at 1127 McDonald Avenue.[50]

In 1906 Sarah's father, Rev. Robert Atwell Latimer, then in his nineties, who had been the legal owner of the 1127 McDonald Avenue home in which William and Sarah lived, made a deed of gift of that property to Sarah.[51] A few months later, he and his ailing wife, Martha, Sarah's step-mother, came to live with them. Martha died shortly thereafter, but Robert lived another four years to the age of almost ninety-six.⁵² A year and a half later, 19 July 1912, William Asa Finley died, at the age of seventy-three, while visiting his daughter in San Francisco.⁵³

William did not leave a will, but his son, Ernest, was appointed administrator of his estate. At his death William owned no real property. In 1895 he had sold the entire block on McDonald Avenue between 17th and 18th Streets, where his Ladies' College stood, to Thomas Kyle⁵⁴ and J.H. Brush.⁵⁵ His last parcel he bought in the South Park Addition was sold to Ernest in 1898.⁵⁶ It would appear that William suffered considerable financial losses with the failure of his Ladies' College.

William's total assets consisted entirely of stock he held in five companies, the largest of which was the Bank of Ukiah, and the total value of his estate was $17,235. The claims filed against his estate totalled $17,123, the largest of which was a claim by F.A. Brush, trustee, in the amount of $7,175. Frank A. Brush⁵⁷ was the son of J.H. Brush, who had bought the largest piece of William's McDonald property and together Brush and his son held the controlling interests in the Santa Rosa National Bank. The bank also filed a claim against the estate in the amount of $950.⁵⁸

Sarah Finley, daughter of a minister, also made her mark. She was born 22 March 1848 in Clarksville, Johnson County, Arkansas, the daughter of Robert Atwell and Malinda (Logan) Latimer.⁵⁹ Although her father came to California during the Gold Rush years, she remained on a large cotton plantation near Clarksville and attended school in Little Rock until she was twelve. After coming to California in 1860, she attended Pacific Methodist College in Vacaville, where her father was business agent.⁶⁰ The college offered both a primary and a preparatory program which is most likely what Sarah would have entered when she arrived. However, by the time she reached her sophomore year in 1864, the regular curriculum through which she passed included Latin and Greek grammar, Cicero's orations, algebra, geometry, elocution, physiology, Horace's odes and epodes, and Herodotus. Extras offered by the College for added fees included music (piano, melodeon, guitar), drawing or painting, wax work (fruit or flowers), embroidery, hair work, leather work, and modern languages. We can surmise from Sarah's later years that

Sarah Elizabeth Latimer, before her marriage to William Asa Finley.

she took music.⁶¹

Pacific Methodist College was where Sarah met and married her future husband then returned with him to Corvallis after their marriage. While at Corvallis she served as a music instructor, was active in the Methodist Church, operated a boarding house for women students, and acted as counselor. While it has been more difficult to follow Sarah's career path, we do know that she served as a vice-principal at Gilroy, and as an

English teacher and vice-principal at the Santa Rosa Ladies' College.[62]

While living in Santa Rosa her community activities included a keen interest in the Rose Carnival. In fact in 1894, which marked the first Rose Carnival, she designed the butterfly float, which was a part of the floral parade, and was mentioned as a sponsor.[63]

As noted earlier, at age eighty Sarah wrote a series of articles on her stay in Corvallis for publication in the *Oregon Monthly* in 1930. Even at this age she was articulate and wrote with a flair. Her opening article, *Oregon State College in an Incubator*, began like this:

It has ever been the mission of the church to teach. To found schools and to foster literature with the strong hand of endeavor has always been its most coveted task, and it has never refused to plant where others might reap. Corvallis College, organized in 1865, was one of such institutions; and so it transpired that Oregon State College came to Corvallis College in its swaddling clothes. No, we recall now that it had no clothes; it was "shirtless." It came a naked fact and was generously taken in. And this is how it all came about.[64]

In this same article she says of her husband, "The Rev. W.A. Finley, already a master of arts, later to be a doctor of divinity, was an optimist, courting responsibility . . . hence the president was given a free hand to install the incubator and see what he could do with this embryonic enterprise wished upon the state by the national government."[65]

In a later article she tells of their wedding, originally scheduled at 7 a.m. on the morning of 8 August 1866 at their alma mater. "The fashionable hour for weddings at that remote date was seven o'clock in the morning and Dame Fashion could not be denied. A compromise was a seven o'clock breakfast, after which the wedding party went immediately to the chapel, where the assembled guests were waiting." She then tells of their honeymoon on an angry sea saying, "We heartily concurred in the vehement comments on our chosen mode of travel. Why invade the sea when a stage coach or a covered wagon on terra firma might have been more fittingly chosen?" Finally, they arrived at Portland and continued their trip around Willamette Falls "in a diminutive box car drawn by an amiable donkey along iron rails; our spirits rose. Witicism after witicism was hurled at that poor donkey. We, seeing no engineer, assumed the role." Once around the falls their trip continued by boat up the Willamette. On their arrival, they were met by a college representative and driven to their boarding house in a wagon drawn by a team of two fine horses.[66]

In her final article, Sarah comments, "As we write, once familiar forms come trooping by and my pen is in despair; for I fear that ere now, the editor, responsible for digging out this fossil, regrets his discovery!" She also alludes briefly to a daughter who was "transferred to the 'everlasting gardens where angels walk and seraphs are the wardens.'" And her final comment:

Dr. Finley's capacity for work was limitless. His whole soul was wrapped up in his work for Corvallis College. The cornerstone of Corvallis College was soul with the will to work. Without a soul no work ever yet touched the human heart. No institution can live forever in which has not been kindled somewhere, somehow the fires of an immortal soul.[67]

The History of Sonoma County, edited

by her son, Ernest, records her in this manner:

> Some of the most interesting stories, articles, essays, sketches and comments brightening newspaper pages, club papers and magazines for many years were the contributions of Sarah E. Latimer Finley, who from earliest adult life has ranked as an intellectual leader and uncompromising advocate of women's rights. Her facile pen never faltered in urging support of the need of the moment in social or civic welfare. Mrs. Finley is the daughter of an old and distinguished Southern family. Her stories of life in the South "before the war" are regarded as classics. She made her home in Santa Rosa for more than a half century, dating from 1873; her later years have been spent in Oakland, California.[68]

Being an advocate for women's rights, it was no surprise when *The Press Democrat*, published by her son, was one of the first newspapers in the state to endorse the constitutional amendment which gave women the right to vote. At the first opportunity after the passage of the amendment (1911), Sarah's name was found in the Great Register list of 1912.[69]

Sarah Elizabeth (Latimer) Finley, ca1930

And she was found continuously on the list for Sonoma County through 1924.[70] In the fall of 1921 she leased her home at 1127 McDonald Avenue to Charles B. Schoenfeld for a period of two years and moved in with her son, Ernest, and his family. She also gave Schoenfeld an option to buy the home for $8,000 at the end of the lease.[71] However, he did not exercise the option, and when she finally sold in 1926, it was to Anna St. John Barrett.[72]

Sarah lived for twenty-five years after the death of her husband, spending the last eleven or twelve years in Oakland, where she died 14 November 1937.[73] Her burial service was conducted from the home of her son, Ernest, at 1020 McDonald Avenue.[74]

As recently as February 1993, *The Oregon Stater* carried a front page story featuring William and Sarah in their 125th anniversary issue saying, "and we begin with William L.(sic) Finley, whose work and vision led to Oregon State's land-grant university status."[75] This was shortly after the publication of an issue featuring the Oregon Trail, with William and his picture an integral part of the historic route from Independence, Missouri, to the shores of the Columbia River.[76]

The real legacy William and Sarah left Santa Rosa was developed by their son, Ernest L. Finley and is summarized in chapter 6.

CHAPTER THREE   HARRISON AND LIVONIA (RAY) FINLEY

The third Finley family to arrive in Sonoma County, prior to the turning of the century, was Harrison Finley and his family. He shared a number of characteristics with the two previous Finley families. Like William Asa, he was born in Missouri, his family having moved there from Kentucky. He had lived, for a while, in Bates County, the departure point for John and Keziah. His great-grandfather was another John Finley of Virginia, not the one shared by the first two Sonoma County Finleys, but one who lived in Augusta County within a fifteen mile proximity of the John Finley who was the ancestor of the first two. He was closer in age to William Asa, being just three years older. And like William Asa, his migration to California was not directly to Sonoma County, but rather he went to Calaveras County.

Harrison's migration began on 12 May 1860, later than the other two Finley families, with a group in five ox-team drawn wagons. It took four months, slightly less time than his predecessors. At age twenty-four he was still single,

but it took him less than two years to find a wife in the person of Livonia Josephine Ray. They married 3 April 1862 in Amador County. Both Calaveras and Amador, neighboring counties in the Sierras, were still primarily mining areas of the state. They lived in Amador County until the birth of their first child, whom they named Missouri. She lived just short of three months, and Harrison and Livonia left a few months later to settle in the Tassajara Valley near Danville in Contra Costa County where they leased a 160 acre ranch. Here they farmed and raised stock. Five more children were born to Harrison and Livonia, Mattie Zoe, Matilda Narcissus, Eliza Belle, Wilson Ebenezer, and Mary Frances. In 1875 they purchased their own ranch, containing 1,080 acres, in the foothills north of Pleasanton.[1] There the family increased by another four children, Abigail Josephine, Lucy Ray, Livonia Louise (Lulu), and Alicia V.

What prompted their move to Sonoma County after twenty-five years in Contra Costa County is not known, but in the fall of 1888 they sold their

holdings there and purchased a 225 acre ranch in the Mark West area, about five miles north of Santa Rosa (now Larkfield Estates).[2] In 1911 he added another 69.5 acres.[3] Their land was adjacent to Fountain Grove, which has a unique history of its own. They raised hops, prunes, apples, hay, and turkeys on the ranch.

The Mark West area was a part of the San Miguel Rancho, claimed in 1841 by William Marcus West, an English sailor who had married into a prominent Mexican family. The area was in the midst of rich agricultural country and had established a post office by 1865. However, any hopes of Mark West developing into a real town were preempted by the Fulton Brothers, Thomas and James, when the railroad came through in 1871. The town of Fulton, only a half mile west of Mark West, began with the building of a warehouse capable of storing 1,200 tons of grain. Soon the railroad company built a freight warehouse and a passenger depot. The post office established at Mark West was moved to Fulton, and by 1880 Fulton was des-

PAGE 28

cribed as "a flourishing town on the San Francisco and North Pacific Railroad." By then Fulton had a church, two stores, two blacksmith shops, a boot and shoe store, one hotel, a livery stable, a saloon, and a post office.[4] In 1890, two years after Harrison and his family arrived, the population of Mark West was approximately sixty persons[5]—and his family accounted for ten of them!

A graphic description of what the Finley family of mostly girls was like in 1890 was given many years later by Grant Laughlin, who eventually married Abigail (Abbie) Finley.

Harrison Finley home on Mark West Springs Road, Santa Rosa, California

> I drove up to the front gate and tied the horses. My errand was to get a gobbler for our flock of hen turkeys, and Mrs. Finley, expecting me, had the big bird tethered in the back yard. As I followed her, I saw bashful little girls peeking around the corner of the house, from in back of hedges and fences and from around the smokehouse and barn corners. Gosh, it seemed as if there were a lot of them, and I noted that they were all right pretty. My mother had been very friendly with Mrs. Finley since the Finley family had arrived here from Contra Costa County two years before, but this was the first time I'd seen any of them except Mr. and Mrs. Finley when they came to visit us.[6]

By the time Harrison and Livonia moved into the area, hops had become one of the leading crops in Sonoma County and especially in the area where they had settled.

Fortunes were made in the hop yards during the boom, and Santa Rosa gained a reputation as the hop capital of the nation. The harvest brought migrant workers to the area and provided employment for towns-people. Hop picking took on a folkloric aspect. In 1898 San Francisco newspapers wrote about Huie Hughes, a picker who walked to Santa Rosa

Harrison Finley family. Back row: Belle, Abbie, Mary, Wilson, and Lucy. Next row forward: Matilda, Harrison, Livonia, and Mattie. Seated in front, Lulu, ca.1893

each year for the harvest—from his home in Kentucky. By the turn of the century hop picking was a competitive sport with much speculation about who the next champion would be.[7]

In 1898 Harrison and Livonia's seventeen year old daughter, Lulu, to the surprise of all, took the championship by picking 400 pounds of hops in the twelve hour period between 6 a.m. and 6 p.m. That same year, the Finley ranch had twenty-three acres in hops, eight acres in apples, a prune orchard, and thirty-three acres in hay which yielded 132 tons. This was considered an enormous crop for a dry year.[8] One of Harrison and Livonia's granddaughters, Helen Alice (Finley) Comstock, commented in later years, as she wrote her recollections of growing up on the ranch, "When hop-picking time was over Grandpa drove alone in his buggy to the Exchange Bank and carried home bags of gold and silver coins with which to pay the pickers. No one in those days paid by check."[9]

The Finley ranch used Chinese and Japanese laborers to help with the crops. The Chinese originally came to California during the Gold Rush. They provided much of the unskilled labor required when the railroads were built, but also worked in lumber camps and quicksilver mines. In Sonoma County they worked in the fields and as domestics for some of the more affluent residents. During the depression years of the 1880s they were subjected to much persecution, but the hardy survived and by the late 1890s, as the depression subsided, the Chinese became a part of the community and had even started their own "Chinatown." The Japanese immigration to Sonoma County began just as the Chinese problems subsided. Ernest L. Finley, through his newspaper, is credited with lending a supportive hand to the integration of the Japanese into the community.[10]

However, pressure was still exerted on farmers to use American, rather than oriental, workers. The Finleys suffered two catastrophic years when they gave in and hired Americans.

One year Grandpa succumbed to their demands and hired workers through the organization. It was a terrible failure. The plants were not properly planted; the string trellises were not tied properly. The wires were not hooked in place on the poles and many acres of hops fell to the ground. It was a miserable harvest. The next year "boss Jap" H. Matashuma whom we called "Martin" was back with his crew of Japanese workers. In late August or early September, just before harvest, our barn and the barn of 2 neighbor hop farmers were set on fire—burning hay—equipment and in our case 2 horses and 2 mules which was a terrible loss. Fortunately dad had turned several mules and horses out to pasture the night before.[11]

On 9 March 1916 the Finley ranch became the scene of an incident related to a Tong War which had erupted in San Francisco. Hom Hong, who was the boss of Finley's crew of workers, was a much respected member of the Bing Kong Tong Society. That year the Hop Sing and Suey Sing Tongs ganged up against the more powerful Bing Kong Society.[12] Helen (Finley) Comstock recalls this period of time:

Wilson Ebenezer Finley and his bride, Alice Hudson, 1895

We had Japanese to plant and "string up" our hops and Chinese to weed the fields. The Jap Cabin was on the creek and the China Cabin was in a grove of pine trees near where Larkfield is now. The two groups never mingled. Hom Hong was the boss of 7 Chinese who lived in the cabin and weeded the fields. On a Sunday in March 1916 when the coolies were doing their weekly chores about the cabin 3 Chinese arrived in a taxi cab. Hom Hong was chopping kindling on a chopping block when one of the new arrivals, Willie Yee, fired 5 pistol shots thru the head and heart of Hom Hong. He then turned to the 6 surviving work-

Harrison Finley with his granddaughter Helen Alice, ca.1899.

CHRISTINE (SLOAT) FAUX COLLECTION

ers and said, "There's one shot left for anyone who testifies against us." Then he threw the pistol into the hop field. The frightened workers refused to identify the killers and it took many weeks and careful strategy on the part of the DA's office to catch and convict them but eventually they all went to San Quentin.[13]

Wilson Ebenezer Finley, named for his maternal great-grandmother and grandfather, and the only boy in the family, was the first to marry. He married Alice Hudson on 28 November 1895. Alice was a third generation native of Sonoma County, the daughter of Mr. and Mrs. Cornelius Hudson, and was born on their Porter Creek ranch in the Mark West area. Wilson and Alice lived out their lives on their fifty-two acre ranch which Wilson inherited from his father, the majority of which consisted of a prune orchard.[14] The family historian, Helen Alice, was their second oldest daughter. Born in 1899, she was old enough to remember the 1906 earthquake.

We both [she and her sister Frances] remember well the 1906 earthquake - the chimneys down, the spilled pans of milk in the pantry. We thought our little brother Mervyn was pulling down things in the pantry and cried, "Mama, make him stop." After the earthquake Grandpa's orange grove resembled a revival encampment - many acquaintances and relations arrived from San Francisco and stayed all summer - Dad and the hired men put up tents for them in the orange grove and Grandma and the girls had to do the cooking. Grandma was a very hospitable person but I remember a little grumbling about some of the ladies being lazy.[15]

Helen further describes some of her other early childhood memories.

Mark West Springs was a favorite resort for San Francisco people who came by train (N.W.P.) to Fulton and were met and taken to the resort by a 4 horse stage coach. As children we loved to see the coach go by. On holidays it always had flags flying from its staff. Burkes Sanitarium was just a mile north and east of us on Mark West Creek. It was a very popular health spa and much social life was centered there. I can remember ladies and well dressed gentlemen playing croquet on the grounds in front of the wide covered veranda which ran across the front of the building. They also ran a coach to Fulton to pick up visitors but it was not so spectacular as was Mark West Springs.

Gradually the daughters of Harrison and Livonia also married, the first in 1902 when Mattie Zoe married Claude Coates, and marriages continued through 1917 when Eliza Belle married James Simcoe. All of the girls married except for Mary Frances (Molly) who died in 1893. At the time of their father's death in 1917 Mattie was living in Hanford, Lucy in Stockton and Livonia in Oakland.[16] However, they all eventually moved back to Sonoma County.[17]

When Harrison Finley died on 5 July 1917, his son-in-law Grant Laughlin, who was an attorney, was appointed administrator. A lengthy probate file had a number of interesting items tucked away in it. The price of hops had not been good for the past few years and Harrison had held onto both his 1915 and 1916 crops. That was one good thing about hops. You could bale them and store them in the barn until things improved, if you could afford to do that. His inventory showed a total of 1,580 bales of hops from those two years and another projected 650 bales for 1917 that were still growing in the field. Under personal property, the 1,580 bales were given a value of $15,000, by far the largest item in his inventory. Earlier that year he had mortgaged the farm and taken a $50,000 loan from the Petaluma National Bank,[18] probably betting he could hold out until the price of hops improved.

One of the claims against his estate was that of Fong Yew and Chong Kee for labor during the period 1 January 1917 to 5 July 1917; in the amount of $1,513.[19] Apparently the Finley ranch weathered the earlier attacks revolving around the employment of Chinese and the Tong War the year before.

The listing of his inventory reflects what you would expect a prosperous farmer to have at that time; five mules, one horse, two big wagons, one surrey, one light spring wagon, one orchard truck, eight plows of various description, five harrows, four cultivators, one corn sheller, two cows, one bull, 200 hop baskets, 500 hop sacks, 1,700 prune trays, 500 prune boxes, fifteen cords of wood, and other farm implements.

When the estate was finally settled on 13 February 1919, a decree of distribution was filed which gave Livonia one undivided half and each of their six children an undivided one-twelfth interest in the Finley ranch.[20] The market value of the estate, at that time, was $52,518.27.[21] The land was divided roughly in proportion to the decree of distribution, and deeds were drawn up within a few days.[22]

Lavonia Finley with her grandchildren, Frances, with arms around her grandmother, and Helen Alice, ca.1900

Livonia went on for another twenty-four years after the death of Harrison, living out her life of ninety-seven years in the home she and Harrison had bought in 1888. Born in Morgan County, Missouri, 9 June 1844, the daughter of William Sanford and Matilda (Phillips) Ray, she came to California in 1852 with her mother and grandfather, Andrew Phillips. They settled in Ione, Amador County and that was where she met her husband of fifty-five years. She died 14 December 1941.[23] Ernest L. Finley's *History of Sonoma County* says of her:

> There was always time in Mrs. Finley's life for the purely feminine pursuits—needlework, quilting and the construction of hooked rugs. In evidence of her industry, each son and daughter cherishes a hooked rug made by Mrs. Finley at odd moments when no imperative duty claimed their mother's attention. She gardened in a joyous way, and kept the dooryard bright with blossoms, sometimes making a little patch in which to raise favorite vegetables, but during these later years of her life has given up occupations that quickly drain her vitality.[24]

One cannot help but notice the similarities between the lives of John and Keziah and that of Harrison and Livonia, and that both are diametrically different from that of William Asa and Sarah Finley. The first and the third Finley families to arrive in Sonoma County were farmers, although their use of the land to build a life for themselves and their children was different. They both had large families. Most of their children remained in Sonoma County.

———— 💥💥💥 ————

CHAPTER FOUR

EARLY VIRGINIA BEGINNINGS

All three of the Finley families who settled in Sonoma County prior to 1900 can trace their earlier beginnings to Augusta County, Virginia, in the late 1730s. John and William Asa shared a common ancestor in John Finley (?-1782), who lived on the South River of the Shenandoah from about 1737 or 1738 until 1765. Harrison Finley's ancestor, another John Finley (?-1791), lived just fifteen miles away on the Middle River of the Shenandoah. It was only a few years earlier that the flow of Scotch-Irish into the Valley of Virginia began. The area where they settled, in and near Beverley Manor, had been patented to William Beverley and others, a tract containing 118,491 acres in the Shenandoah Valley. The earliest deeds recorded there were in 1738.

The Scotch-Irish were among many Europeans who left their homeland because of religious persecution. Both John Finleys in Augusta County were active in establishing and supporting their religious convictions. Both baptized children at Tinkling Spring during the period 1740-1749. John of South River was an original commissioner and later an elder in that church. John of Middle River later switched his alliance to Brown's Meeting House which was built nearer his home.

Much of the story of early Augusta County is told in chapter 5 as it relates to the life of John Finley of South River. However, the early history of the American Presbyterian Church is also important to understand the life of our ancestors. Early in the century, there was a schism in the church which caused two factions known as the "Old Side" and the "New Side." Their differences were not over doctrine, but rather with the proper methods of promoting religions. The Old Side was more conservative and associated with the Synod (governing body) of Philadelphia, while the New Side associated with the Synod of New York.[1] Philadelphia had been the first Synod to be organized in 1717 and its member Presbyteries (ruling body of ministers and elders) included Philadelphia; New Castle, Delaware; Long Island, New York; Snow Hill, Maryland. The Donegal Presbytery in Lancaster County, Pennsylvania, was added in 1732.[2]

The Old Side leadership centered in the Donegal Presbytery, with John Thomson, Richard Sankey (his son-in-law), Robert Cross, and James Anderson taking the lead. John Caldwell appeared on the scene in 1733 as an elder in the Donegal Presbytery. At the meeting of the Donegal Presbytery on 11 April 1738, Caldwell presented a petition which marked the beginning of Presbyterianism in the Colony of Virginia. He, and many of his Presbyterian friends, were preparing to migrate to the "back parts of Virginia," and his supplication stated, in part:

> . . . in behalf of himself [Caldwell] and many families of our persuasion, who are about to settle in the back parts of Virginia, desiring that some members of the Synod may be appointed to wait on that government, to solicit their favour in behalf of our interest in that place . . .[3]

Governor Gooch of Virginia cooper-

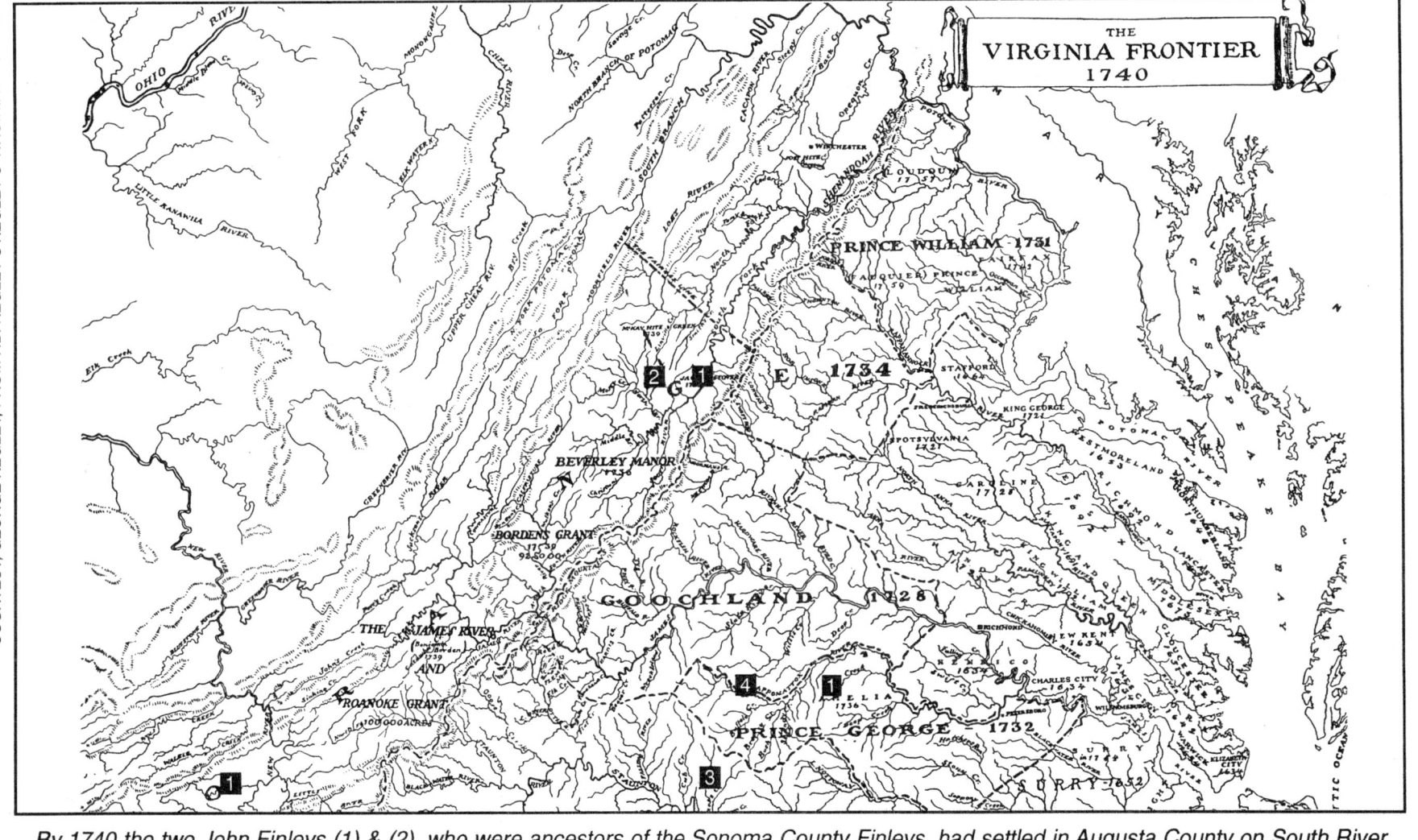

By 1740 the two John Finleys (1) & (2), who were ancestors of the Sonoma County Finleys, had settled in Augusta County on South River and on Middle River. John Caldwell (3) was firmly planted on Cub Creek in what is now Charlotte County. The Reverend John Thomson (4) was still officially in Pennsylvania at Chestnut Level but made trips into the "back parts" of Virginia. Reverend Thomson actually lived at the Buffalo Settlement in what is now Prince Edward County, between 1744 and 1751.

ated in this venture in return for certain conditions. The settlers had to promise to abide by the "Toleration Act" of England, which permitted dissenters to establish their own meeting houses (not church, a term reserved for the Church of England) which were properly registered and licensed. His motives were to establish a frontier line some distance from Williamsburg and he had confidence these people were, "firm, enterprising, hardy, brave, good citizens and soldiers."[4]

According to Wilson, "This strategic move was not only of paramount importance to Virginia Presbyterianism, but also to the extension of the Colony of Virginia—for it seems to be the key that unlocked the floodgates to unlimited emigration from Pennsylvania and Ireland."[5]

JOHN CALDWELL

John Caldwell, with his wife, Margaret (Phillips), arrived in New Castle, Delaware on 10 December 1727 from Antrim, Ireland, with their five children and other relatives. John, son of Joseph and Jane (McGhie) Caldwell, is said to have been born about 1683 in Donegal and married 4 June 1703 in County Derry. The most recent and well documented history of this branch of the Caldwells traces this line back four more generations to William Caldwell, who lived in Straeton, Ayrshire, Scotland, in the late 1500s and in Ennis Killen, County Fermanagh, Ireland in the early 1600s.[6] After their arrival in America, John and Margaret lived first at Chestnut Level, Lancaster, Pennsylvania, where John became actively engaged in the affairs of the church, serving as an elder.

John Caldwell apparently did some scouting of territory before the actual move was made. The territory he covered later provided the foundations for meeting houses at Cub Creek, Charlotte County (formerly Lunenburg, formerly Brunswick); Buffalo and Walkers in Prince Edward County; and Hat Creek and Concord in Campbell County. Caldwell settled at Cub Creek with a reported thirty-three heads of families.[7] The group formed by Caldwell, often referred to as Caldwell's Settlement, was the first Presbyterian congregation in Virginia south of the James. Their ministers were itinerant preachers either from Europe or the north, from whence they came. In between, Elder Caldwell gathered his flock for prayer and instruction. It was no great surprise that their first visiting ministers were Rev. James Anderson (1738) and Rev. John Thomson (1739) from Donegal Presbytery.[8] When Lunenburg County was formed from Brunswick in 1746, both John and his son, William, were named justices of the peace of the first county court. Son, David, later became a justice when Charlotte was formed from Lunenburg in 1764.[9]

John Caldwell died at Cub Creek 6 October 1750 and is buried there in the church cemetery, as are his sons William, Thomas, and David. Early researchers of John Caldwell and his immediate family are in conflict as to which of Caldwell's sons was the father of Mary Caldwell, who married John Finley, but this researcher tends to favor the line of argument that Mary's parents were Thomas and Mary Jane (Parks) Caldwell. We do have this citation carried down among Finley researchers.

> Eliz. Mounts' Bible is still in existence and on fly leaf written by her dau., Jane Ann [Finley] Smith, is statement [apparently addressed to next gener-

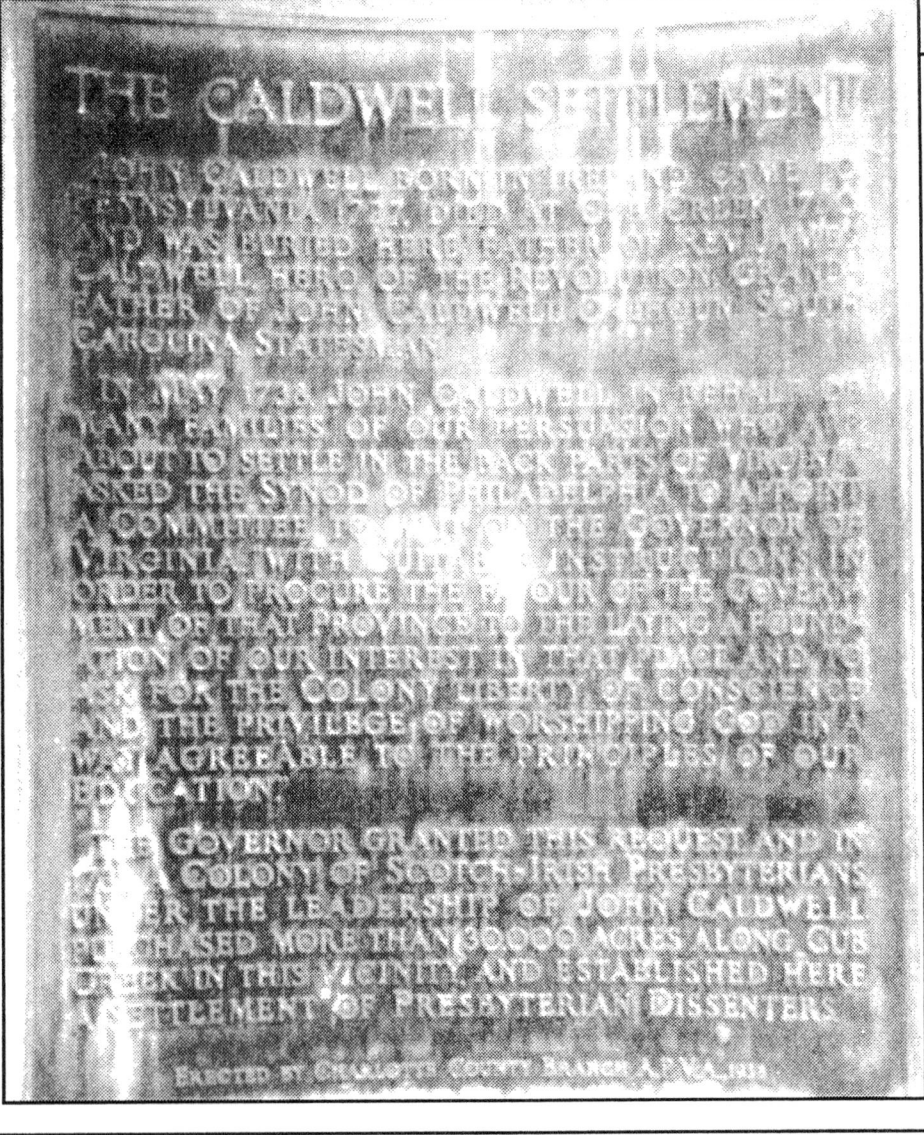

VERNE HOFFMAN COLLECTION

Caldwell's settlement on Cub Creek was the first Presbyterian congregation in Virginia south of the James River. The Caldwell Settlement marker reads:

John Caldwell born in Ireland came to Pennsylvania 1727. Died at Cub Creek 1750 and was buried here. Father of Rev. James Caldwell, hero of the Revolution. Grandfather of John Caldwell Calhoun, South Carolina Statesman.

In May 1738 John Caldwell in behalf of the back parts of Virginia asked the Synod of Philadelphia to appoint a committee to wait on the Governor of Virginia with suitable instructions in order to procure the favour of the Government of that Province to the laying of a foundation of our interest in that place and to ask for the Colony liberty of conscience and the privilege of woshipping God in a way agreeable to the principles of our education.

The Governor granted the request and in 1738 a Colony of Scotch-Irish Presbyterians under the leadership of John Caldwell purchased more than 30,000 acres along Cub Creek in the vicinity and established here a settlement of Presbyterian Dissenters.

ation]: "Your grandfather was David Finley and he married Elizabeth Mounts his father was John Finley who married Mary Caldwell, a cousin of Martha Caldwell who was the mother of the famous Statesman John C. Calhoun." [unpublished data in D.A.R. Library, compiled & certified by Maj. Albert Finley France.][10]

Independent research by this writer has confirmed that David Finley and Elizabeth Mounts did indeed have a daughter, Jane Ann, who married Edmund Smith. Their story is reported in the next chapter.

REVEREND JOHN THOMSON

When John Caldwell opened the flood gates that encouraged the immigration of the Scotch-Irish into Virginia, he was living in Lancaster County, Pennsylvania, and was a member of the Chestnut Level Congregation where the Reverend John Thomson was minister. Caldwell was a few years older than Thomson, but Thomson had migrated to America ten years before Caldwell.

John Thomson was born about 1689 in Ulster, entered the University of Glasgow 1 March 1706 where he obtained his master of arts degree and was licensed by the Ulster Synod meeting at Antrim 23 June 1713.[11] At that time, his family probably consisted of his wife (name unknown), his daughter, Esther, and other relatives. They arrived in Yorktown, Virginia, about 1713 or 1714, but soon moved north to New Castle-on-the-Delaware. Some reports have him arriving in New York in 1715. He sought assistance from the Presbytery of Philadelphia meeting at New Castle in finding a position and was ordained by the Presbytery in April 1717. From then until September 1729, he served as pastor at Lewes, Delaware, and also provided some services at Snow Hill, Maryland. He took an active part in the affairs of the church and served as moderator both of the Presbytery of New Castle and the Synod of Philadelphia. On 20 September 1722 when he was re-elected moderator of the Synod, he became the first person in the history of the church to be elected twice to this highest office of the church in this country. He was concerned about orderly government in the church and was directly responsible for laws which today are still a part of the constitution of the church.

Signature courtesy, Patrice McElwain, from Madison E. McElwain's FAITH AND WORKS AT MIDDLE OCTORARA SINCE 1727.

During the period from 1729 to 1733 he divided his time among four Pennsylvania communities, Newcastle, Nottingham (Lower Octorara Congregation), Fishing Creek (Middle Octorara Congregation), and Drumore (Chestnut Level Congregation). As the Scotch-Irish pushed to the interior, it became necessary to form the new Presbytery of Donegal, which included those congregations in Lancaster County. Reverend Thomson was elected first moderator at their organizational meeting on 11 October 1732, at the Donegal Meeting House. Financial support for religious efforts was always a problem. Pledges of support which had been made to him at Middle Octorara were not forthcoming and eventually his services there were terminated.

This led to a full-time pastorate at Chestnut Level in 1733, which lasted

VERNE HOFFMAN COLECTION

The Cub Creek Church marker states:

Here in 1738 the Caldwell Settlement established its place of worship. The first building was a log meeting house which was used until 1820, when the present church was erected.

At Cub Creek Meeting House October 13,1774 Hanover Presbytery decided to establish two schools of higher edcucation, one in the County of Augusta, one in Prince Edward or Cumberland. Rev. Caleb Wallace, then pastor of Cub Creek Congregation, a native of Charlotte County, author of the petition of 1776 to the Virginia Assembly for the establishment of religious freedom, later Justice of the Court of Appeals of Kentucky, was a member of two committees appointed by Presbytery to raise funds for these schools. From this action came Washington College, now Washington & Lee University and Hampden-Sydney College.

Ministers for the First Hundred Years

James Anderson - John Thomson -
William Robinson - John Blair -
Samuel Davies - Visiting Evangelists,
1738-1753

(Others Listed)

Middle Octorara Church, established in 1727, Lancaster County, Pennsylvania called Reverend John Thomson as their first regularly installed pastor.

until 1744. Reverend Thomson was elected clerk and served on various committees to take care of business matters, examine candidates for the ministry, determine bounds of certain congregations, secure funds, and otherwise manage such matters related to the conduct of the Donegal Presbytery. These were still formative years; financial problems continued and the "Old Side" vs "New Side" controversies continued. In 1734 he wrote *The Poor Orphans Legacy*[12] which was published by Benjamin Franklin. This was apparently prompted by the death of his wife, mother of his twelve living children. Reverend Thomson married Mary (McKean), widow of Thomas Reid, a justice of the peace and Presbyterian elder at Octorara. There was one child by the second marriage, Hannah.

At the meeting of the Donegal Presbytery on 4 April 1739, Reverend Thomson made a suggestion that the church should erect a public school or seminary of learning. As a result he was encouraged to pursue his idea and was appointed to a committee for this purpose. When his idea came to fruition, he was chosen to serve on the original board of directors. This later became the University of Delaware and its charter of 1769 specifically names Thomson as one of the founding fathers. His activities and his writings consistently pointed to a special interest in missionary encouragement and an educated ministry.

It was, of course, during this time that John Caldwell and other members of his congregation became interested in "the back parts" of Virginia and Reverend Thomson, too, took an interest in the early migration plans of his parishioners. When Tinkling Spring was being formed, the members of that group asked Reverend Thomson to become their pastor. His daughter, who had married John Finley, had recently settled there and Finley was active in the affairs of that congregation from its beginning. Reverend Thomson asked for his release from Chestnut Level to go to Tinkling Spring on 30 October 1739, but was refused. However, Thomson continued to serve the Virginia communities of Winchester, Staunton, Opekon, Rockfish Gap, and Cub Creek in Brunswick (now Charlotte) County, Buffalo and Walkers in Amelia (now Prince Edward) County, and Hat Creek and Concord in Campbell County. Finally, when he again requested leave from Chestnut Level, on 4 April 1744, approval was given and he settled at Buffalo in what is now Prince Edward County, the Scotch-Irish stomping grounds which John Caldwell had helped prepare.

According to one biographer, this is where:

> . . . he spent the happiest and possible also the most useful years of his life. The old dissensions were behind him. In his new community the families led by John Caldwell and those who later came were decidedly pro-Thomson. There he labored in a peaceful, despite its being a pioneer, settlement. But he loved pioneering, for his spirit was . . . 'to press on into regions that had as yet been unreached, and to organize churches.' In the opinion of the present writer, this Virginia community was chosen by Thomson for such labors because therein and nearby lived

COURTESY, STUART BROWN, PRESIDENT OF VIRGINIA BOOK COMPANY, FROM CARTMELL'S SHENANDOAH VALLEY PIONEERS AND THEIR DESCENDANTS

Opekon Memorial Church was one of the early churches where Reverend John Thomson preached while he was still a pastor at Chestnut Level, Pennsylvania.

many families who were close of kin to members of his congregation in Pennsylvania.[13]

The Reverend Richard Sankey, Thomson's son-in-law, was among those who had preceded him to Buffalo. Together they continued to serve the interests of the larger Synod in Philadelphia and the Donegal Presbytery, trying to resolve the differences between the "Old Side" and the "New Side" factions. Towards this end, Reverend Thomson participated in deliberations in Philadel-

Hampden-Sydney College in Prince Edward County, established in 1776, was outgrowth of an early Presbyterian school for boys which Reverend Thomson helped establish. Thomson's son-in-law, the Reverend Richard Sankey, was a member of the original board of trustees. This drawing shows the campus in the early 1800s. The buildings in the foreground are those originally built in 1775-76.

phia in May 1745. The Donegal Presbytery, on hearing the report, on 19 November 1747 authorized Reverend Thomson and others to "act with full powers in ecclesiastical matters in Virginia." Reverend Richard Sankey was directed to keep them informed.

Reverend Thomson is also credited with having a hand in the establishment of a school for young men in Prince Edward County. This is said to be the forerunner of Hampden-Sydney College, where Reverend Richard Sankey was a member of the original board of trustees in 1776. During his tenure at Buffalo, Reverend Thomson traveled to Augusta County where, on 4 January 1748, he baptized his grandson, John Finley's son, George, in a ceremony at Tinkling Spring.

In the spring or summer of 1751, Reverend Thomson made his final move to North Carolina and settled near Centre Church in Anson County (later Rowan, later Iredell). He is said to have been the first minster of any denomination to preach in that region. His parish contained about 314 square miles. He died there sometime within the year following 27 May 1752, the date of his last

COURTESY, PATRICE McELWAIN, FROM MADISON E. McELWAIN'S FAITH AND WORKS AT MIDDLE OCTORARA SINCE 1727

THE REV. JOHN THOMSON
C. 1690 — 1753
PIONEER PRESBYTERIAN PREACHER
TEACHER AND WRITER
GRADUATE OF U. OF GLASGOW
ADVOCATE OF THE ADOPTING ACT 1729,
PROBABLY THE FIRST MINISTER TO
PREACH IN THAT BECAME CONCORD
PRESBYTERY.
BURIED IN THIS ENCLOSURE

A monument in memory of Reverend John Thomson was erected in the Old Baker Graveyard in Iredell County, North Carolina. It reads:

"The Reverend John Thomson, c.(1690-1753). Pioneer Presbyterian preacher, teacher, and writer. Graduate of U. of Glasgow. Advocate of the Adopting Act of 1729. Particularly the first minister in what became Concord Presbytery. Buried in this enclosure."

attendance at the Synod meeting. He is said to have been buried under the floor of his cabin, a short distance from the home of his son-in-law, Samuel Baker. Reverend John Thomson was the author of many papers and doctrines for the church during his lifetime. Particular acknowledgments should be made of his *Explication of The Shorter Catechism* and his *Articles of the Church of England*.

Within this framework of early Virginia beginnings we can see the influences that must surely have affected the John Finley of Augusta County who lived along South River. He was the ancestor of John Finley of Bodega (1823-1910) and William Asa Finley of Santa Rosa (1839-1912) and was a son-in-law of both the Reverend John Thomson and of John Caldwell.

———— ❦❦❦ ————

CHAPTER FIVE: ANCESTORS AND DESCENDANTS OF JOHN FINLEY (1823-1910)

John Finley[1] (? – 1782) was the ancestor of the first two Finleys who settled in Sonoma County. He most likely arrived in America as a child, during the Scotch–Irish immigration of the early part of the eighteenth century. The earliest records found for him were in Beverley Manor, Augusta County, Virginia, in 1738.[2] He had come to Virginia from Pennsylvania with his two brothers, William and Robert, just a few years after the movement of Scotch–Irish to this area was started by John Lewis.[3] While we do not have a date of birth for him, we do know that he had five children born between 1740 and 1749. From this, one would assume that he was a fairly young man when he settled in Beverley Manor, possibly born not later than 1710.

His first wife was a daughter of the Reverend John Thomson, her given name unknown. John took an active role in establishing Tinkling Spring Meeting House, a Presbyterian congregation for the Scotch–Irish settlement in and around Beverley Manor. In the first action recorded, John Finley was appointed one of five commissioners charged with purchasing property on which to build their meeting house and collecting money to pay a minister. His brother William was one of the signers of this act, dated "August ye 14th 1741." However, as early as 1737, the people of Beverley Manor had petitioned the Donegal Presbytery to establish a meeting house. As a result a Christian Society called "The Triple Forks of the Shenando Congregation," was formed. Their first request was for the services of Reverend John Thomson:

> The Christian Societies in the back part of Virginia on September 5, 1739, united in presenting a supplication to the Presbytery of Donegal for the ministerial services of Rev. John Thomson, Chestnut Level pastor, as an "Itinerant Preacher to Virginia."[4]

However, the Donegal Presbytery refused Thomson's petition to release him from Chestnut Level, where he was stationed at that time, and the Reverend John Craig was assigned in his place.[5]

A site to build the first log structure was selected about five miles southwest of where the Finleys were living:

> A cool spring of water—issuing from beneath a rock, gathering into a pool from which man lives, overflowing into a stream by which the plains are made alive—is a delightful work of nature. The earliest pioneers in the Valley of Virginia found a bold spring, whose emerging waters made a musical sound upon the cavernous rocks, and they called it the tinkling spring. The church, located near this spring and named for it, is like "a spring of water welling up to eternal life" for multitudes who have passed this way.[6]

The first sanctuary was twenty–four by fifty feet, with a simple interior. "The floor was the ground over which the sanctuary was constructed. The pews were backless hand–made benches, probably small logs split with the smooth–hewn surface up and supported

The Tinkling Spring Log Meeting House, as it is described in the church minutes, from a painting by Anne C. Brown.

At left, seating arrangement and pew rent of the first Tinkling Spring Meeting House.

by wooden legs driven into auger holes . . . the meeting house was without heating facilities."[7]

The Tinkling Spring Commissioners posted their first notice for payment on the log building on 12 November 1744, calling for twelve shillings per family. The congregation was divided into three quarters, with John Finley heading one quarter. This was an administrative device for organizing and collecting money from the parishioners. John's brothers, William and Robert, were both listed as members of his quarter at this time.[8]

Those must have been busy years in the settlement of Augusta County. Population of the territory, authorized as Augusta County, was estimated at 2,500 in 1742, including about 500 persons in the bounds of the Tinkling Spring Congregation. The first court of law was established in late 1745 and John Finley [Finla in the records] was among those who took the oath of office on 30 October that year. The Augusta County Court was located at "Beverley's Mill Place," now Staunton, contrary to advice of local citizens who were ordered to view the land offered by William Beverley. Prior to that time, Augusta County citizens

Tinkling Spring was supported by the membership and the call for the first payment was posted on the Meeting House door on 12 November 1744. Administratively, the collection of dues was divided among three men, one of whom was John Finley. A monument to these first subscribers is standing today in front of the Fellowship Hall.

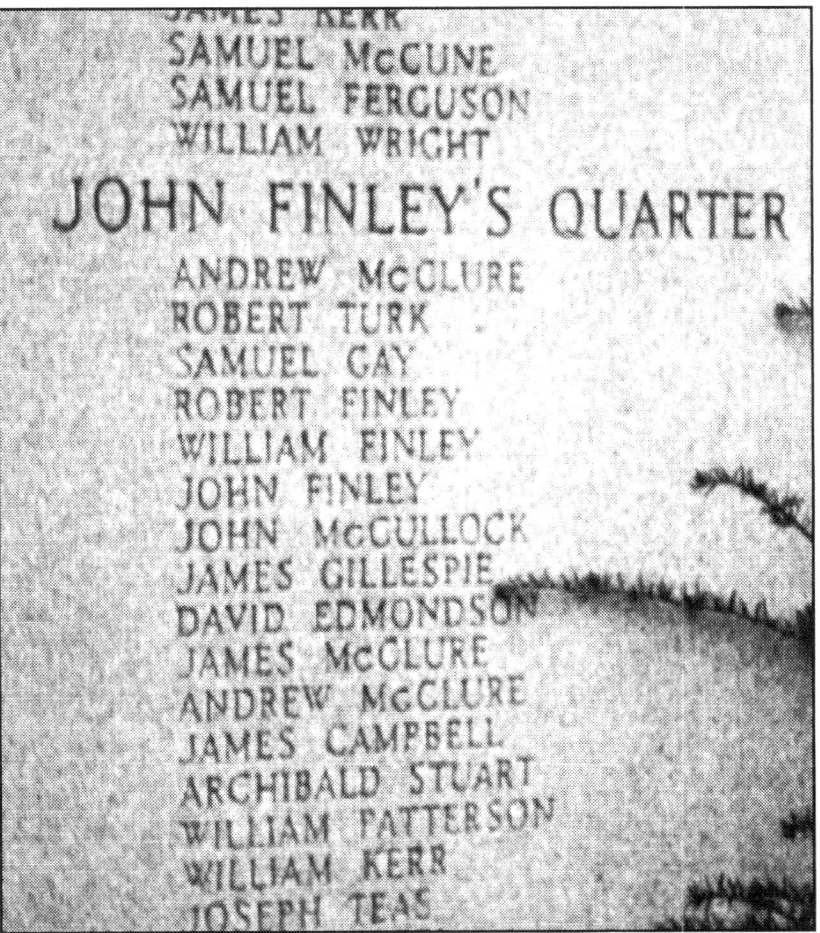

John Finley, along with his brothers, William and Robert, lived together on the 892 acre parcel on South River labelled "George Robinson" from 1746 on. Prior to that they lived on the adjacent property labelled "Charles Dalhouse." Tinkling Spring Meeting House was located on a 110 acre tract conveyed to the trustees by William Thompson in November 1747.

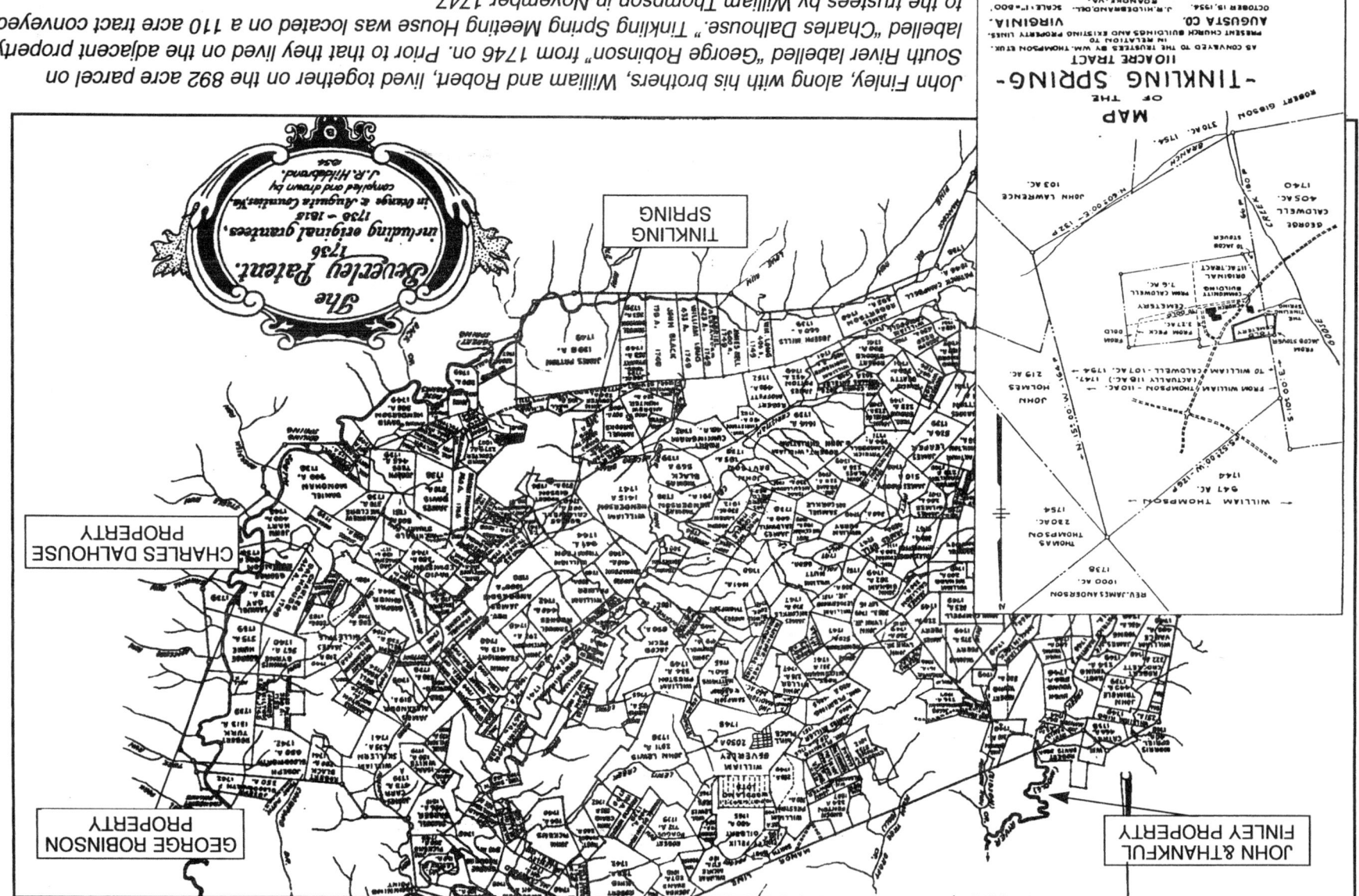

were served through the Orange County Court—and John Finley had been a justice there as well.⁹

An early road order showed that the Finleys operated a mill, "A Road be cleared from Finley's Mill to the Tinkling spring and thence to McCords Mill That John Finley and Archibald Stewart, John Christy and Robert Cunningham oversee the Same."¹⁰ John and his family had been living on property near South River adjacent to the property he bought in 1746, 892 acres purchased from George Robinson, directly on South River. By then John and his wife had at least two children and brother William had at least three.¹¹ Presumably the three brothers were living close together. Four years after the purchase of the Robinson property, formal deeds were drawn up in which John split his property into equal thirds and sold two of them to his brothers, William and Robert.¹²

In 1748 John was made an elder of Tinkling Spring, a position he held until about 1764.¹³ Between 1740 and 1749, the only years for which Tinkling Spring baptismal records are available, John and his wife had at least four, and possibly, five children; Elisabeth, William, James, George, and possibly another James

Scotch–Irish settlers built mills to grind wheat and corn. This is McDonald Mill near Lexington, Virginia, but it was probably fairly typical of those found in Augusta County.

(christened 26 March 1749). These are the children listed by Wilson as belonging to one of the two John Finley families in the area, the other being the John Finley family on Middle River. However, John's first wife died prior to 22 May 1750 when he divided his 892 acres and deeded two portions to his brothers. At that time, John's wife was named Mary, and while we do not know the given name of his first wife, we do know it was not Mary, since the Reverend John Thomson had another daughter named Mary who was living at that time. Son George was baptized on 4 January 1748 by his grandfather, Reverend John Thomson. One might speculate that Reverend Thomson may have made the trip from Prince Edward County to Augusta County to baptize the last child of this daughter.

John's second wife was Mary Caldwell, whose cousin Martha Caldwell was the mother of John Caldwell Calhoun. What is known about the Caldwells is discussed in the previous chapter.

The people of Augusta County lived

in relative harmony until the beginning of the French and Indian War in 1755. Augusta County men were then called upon to strengthen the lines at the frontier, but were reluctant to leave their families without protection against the Indians. When George Washington made a tour of inspection in 1756, in and around Staunton, Augusta County, his evaluation was that, "the militia are under such bad order and discipline, that they will go and come when and where they please, without regarding time, their officers, or the safety of inhabitants, but consulting solely their own inclinations."[14] Through all this John Finley, as a representative of Tinkling Spring, continued actively in the cause of the church, attending special meetings of the presbytery at Rockfish Meeting House beyond the Blue Ridge in 1759 and in Prince Edward County in 1760.[15] At the next meeting of the presbytery, held at Tinkling Spring on 1 April 1761, the Reverend Richard Sankey of Buffalo, in Prince Edward County, son–in–law of Reverend John Thomson, was "continued" as moderator of the group.[16] Tinkling Spring continued to be a favored meeting place and the Reverend John Craig also often served as the moderator.

However, problems mounted after the end of the French and Indian War in 1763. Craig's original mission included serving the Stone House just north of Beverly Manor, as well as Tinkling Spring, with the understanding that he would become a full time pastor for whichever could first afford his services. At the spring meeting held 5 May 1763 at Tinkling Spring, the Stone Meeting House asked for a separation from Tinkling Spring, with a decision deferred until the next meeting.

At the fall meeting of the presbytery in Cumberland County, 3 October 1764, the first item of business, following "Suplications for Supplies,"was that:

> Mr Craig is dismissed from the Tinkling Spring, and sustains the pastoral relation as to the Congregation of Stone meeting House only.

John Finley, who was the elder representing Tinkling Spring at this meeting, put in a request for a supply assignment at Tinkling Spring. None was made except, ". . . ministers in Augusta County, are left to their own discretion, in supplying." Mr. Craig preached his farewell sermon at Tinkling Spring in November 1764.[17]

Wilson, in discussing post war problems of the French and Indian War, summarized the situation succinctly:

> Tinkling Spring people, with Rev. John Craig as their pastor, pioneered in the practice of religious freedom in the Colony of Virginia . . . . Her men, though reluctant in aggression, were invaluable in defense against Indian cruelty. They were among the stalwart leaders that turned the tide in the frontier phase of the French–British struggle out of which grew the short–lived English rule over America. Tinkling Spring's first quarter of a century of service left her a changed and weakened meeting house group. Alexander Breckenridge, James Patton, John Preston, Archibald Stuart and John Lewis were dead by this time; John Finley, an active elder, disappears from the record, probably transferring his efforts to Brown's Meeting House; and families now removed entirely, or in part, were the Breckenridges, Lewises, Prestons, Campbells, Bells, Thompsons and others.[18]

Wilson, who published his book in 1954, probably made the same assumptions that earlier Finley researchers made

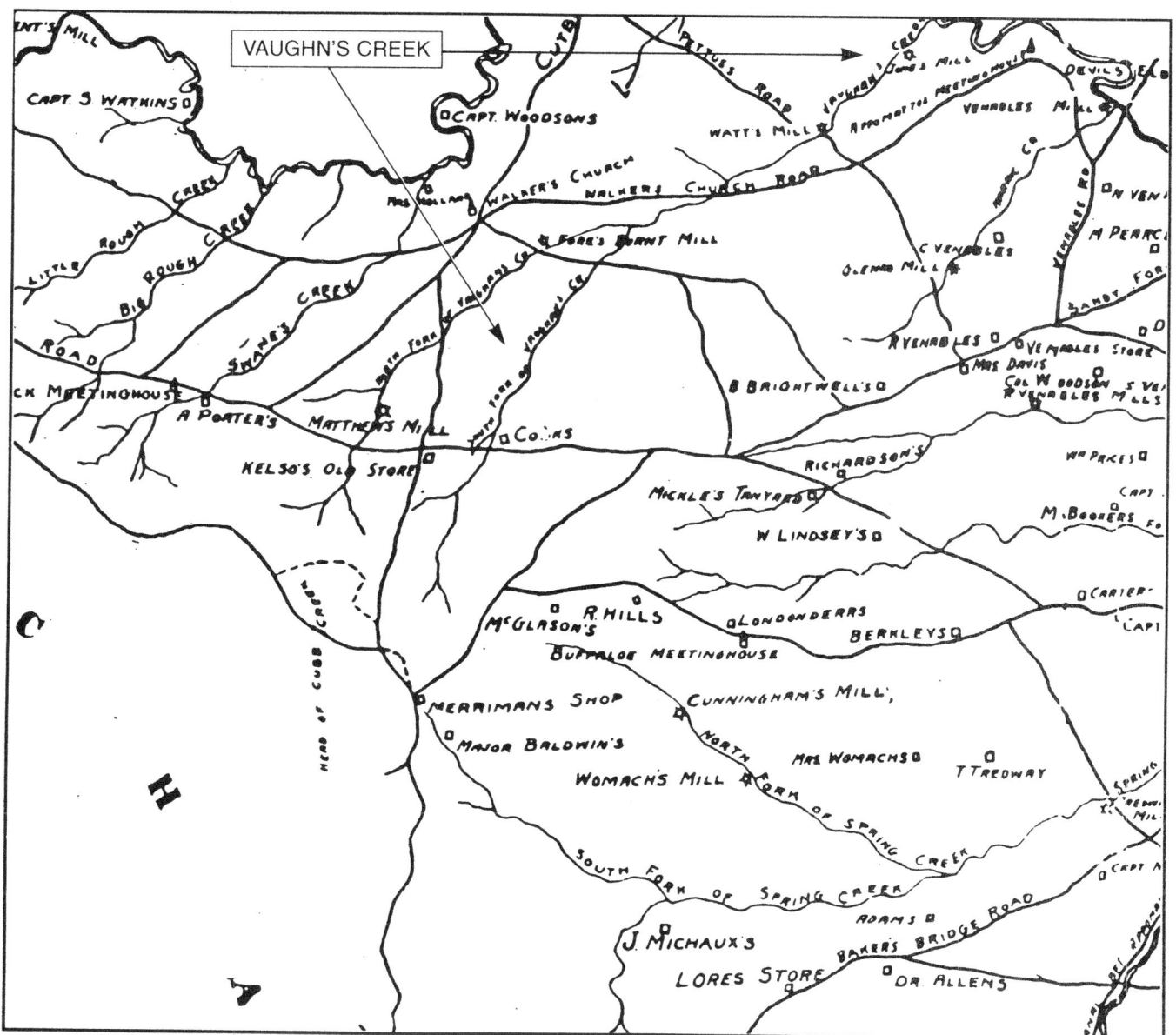

Vaughan's Creek, a tributary of the Appomattox River which is the dividing line between Prince Edward County and Buckingham County, was the home of John Finley and his family from 1765 until 1773.

and did not realize there were two distinct contemporary John Finleys in the area. The John Finley who showed up in the records of Brown's Meeting House was the John Finley who lived on Middle River, not the John Finley who lived on South River (see discussion in chapter 7).

One can imagine the feelings of dismay which probably overcame John after devoting a good twenty–five years of his life to the building of Tinkling Spring. He sold his remaining interest in the Robinson property, 297 acres, to his brother William in March 1765.[19] It is not surprising that he chose to go to Prince Edward County. This was another Scotch–Irish Presbyterian settlement adjacent to that of John Caldwell and one which Reverend John Thomson had helped develop. John was related by marriage to both the Thomsons and the Caldwells, and while neither were living at the time, his first wife's brother–in–law, Reverend Richard Sankey, was still actively engaged in church work in Prince Edward County. In fact, John's daughter, Elisabeth, had been living with the Sankeys before John made the move and until her marriage in January of 1764.[20] John purchased 400 acres on Vaughan's Creek on 15 June 1765 from Jacob and Honour Garrett,[21] and his son William bought 430 acres on Vaughan's Creek from John Caldwell on 19 August 1765.[22] Just where this John Caldwell fits into the family in unknown, but he was most likely related to John Finley's second wife, Mary Caldwell.

John and his family lived in Prince Edward County for only about seven years and then moved on to Reed Creek area in Montgomery County, now Wythe, Virginia. What prompted this move is unknown, but again he was moving into territory where other family and friends had located. There were two James Finleys already living there and it is strongly suspected that the elder James was a younger brother of John. Reverend Thomson's oldest daughter, Sarah, was living there with her second husband, William Sayers, who was also active in the affairs of the local Presbyterian Church at Reed Creek. George Breckenridge, son of Alexander, who had also been one of the original commissioners of Tinkling Spring, was nearby. John settled on a 327 acre parcel on Sally Run, waters of Reed Creek, which he bought from John McFarland in November 1773.[23] Six years later, John and "Meary", his wife, drew up articles of agreement giving their property to sons, David and Samuel, in exchange for life care. John died sometime prior to 19 August 1782, when the court ordered a deposition be taken of Mary to testify the document they drew up in 1773 was done according to his wishes.[24]

All of the children of John Finley by either marriage have most likely not been identified. However, we do have proof of three children by his marriage to Mary Caldwell, including David, who is the ancestor of the John Finley who first settled in Sonoma County:

+2	i.	David[2] Finley, born 1 June 1754,[25] probably in Augusta County, Virginia.
3	ii.	Samuel Finley, named heir with his brother David to his parent's plantation in Montgomery County in 1779, which they jointly sold in 1792. At that time both David and Samuel were "of Mercer County, Kentucky."[26] In 1785 a Samuel Finley signed a petition for the grant of land for a town site in Lincoln County.[27] In 1789 a Samuel Finley signed a petition

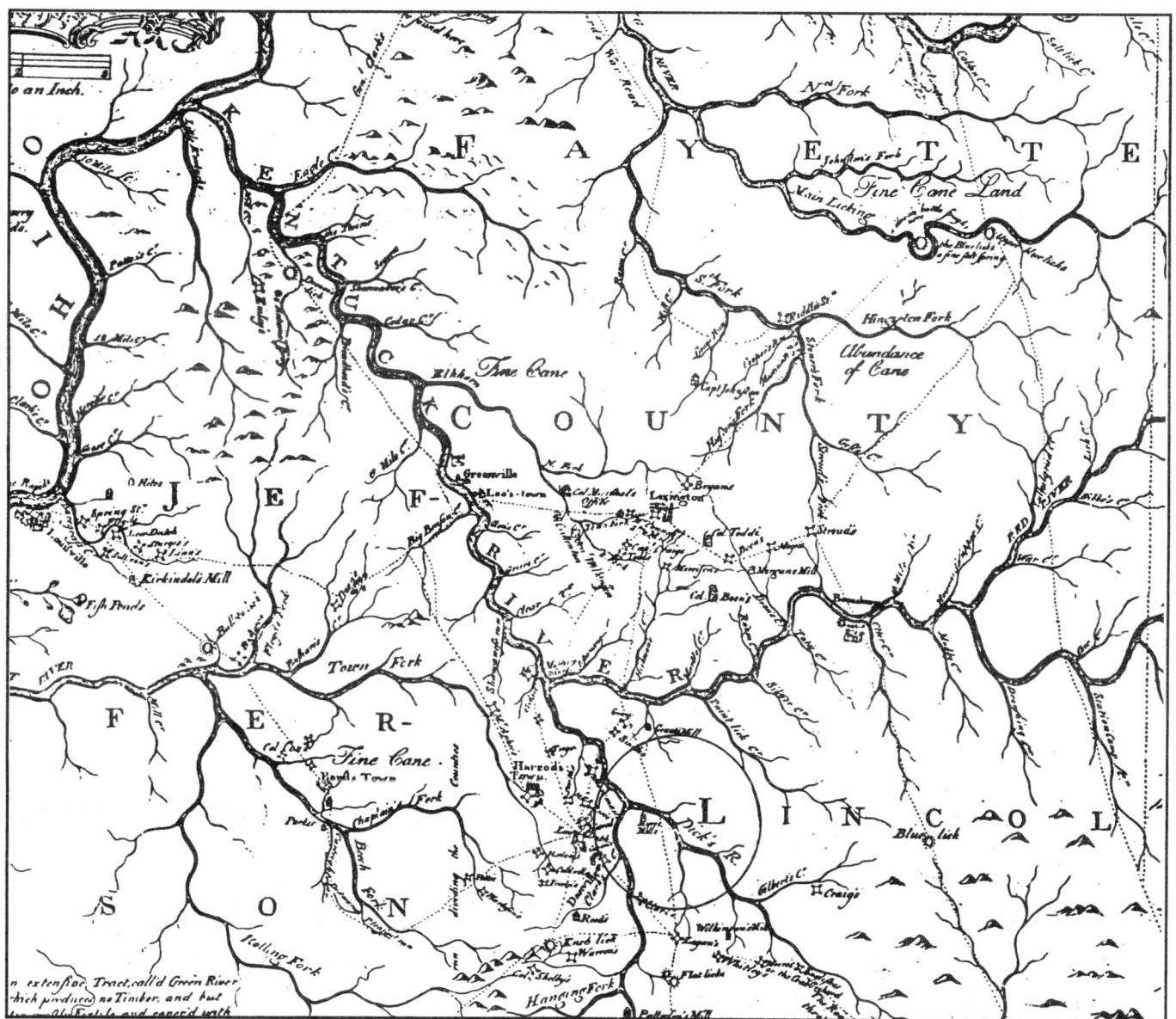

This early map of Kentucky, prepared in 1784, was drawn from "actual Observations" and shows the main waterways in relation to the Ohio River. The Dicks River, where David Finley settled, is a tributary of the Kentucky River which flows into the Ohio.

The fort at Boonesborough, the first in Kentucky, was built in 1775. Daniel Boone, along with thirty axemen, cut their way through the wilderness and established the now famous Wilderness Road, which began at the Long Island of the Holston. Both a David and a James Finley were listed among the early settlers of Fort Boonesborough (French Tipton Papers, Kentucky Room, Eastern Kentucky University Library). However, it is not known for certain that this is the same David Finley who settled along the Dicks River.

COURTESY, PARKE ROUSE, JR., FROM HIS *VIRGINIA: THE ENGLISH HERITAGE IN AMERICA*

David's route from Wytheville, Virginia, to Kentucky, is shown on this map. His property in Kentucky was along the Dicks River, a tributary of the Kentucky River, near Danville. This route, known as the Wilderness Road, was an extension of the Great Philadelphia Wagon Road and was blazed westward through Cumberland Gap into the Kentucky and Tennessee territories after 1774.

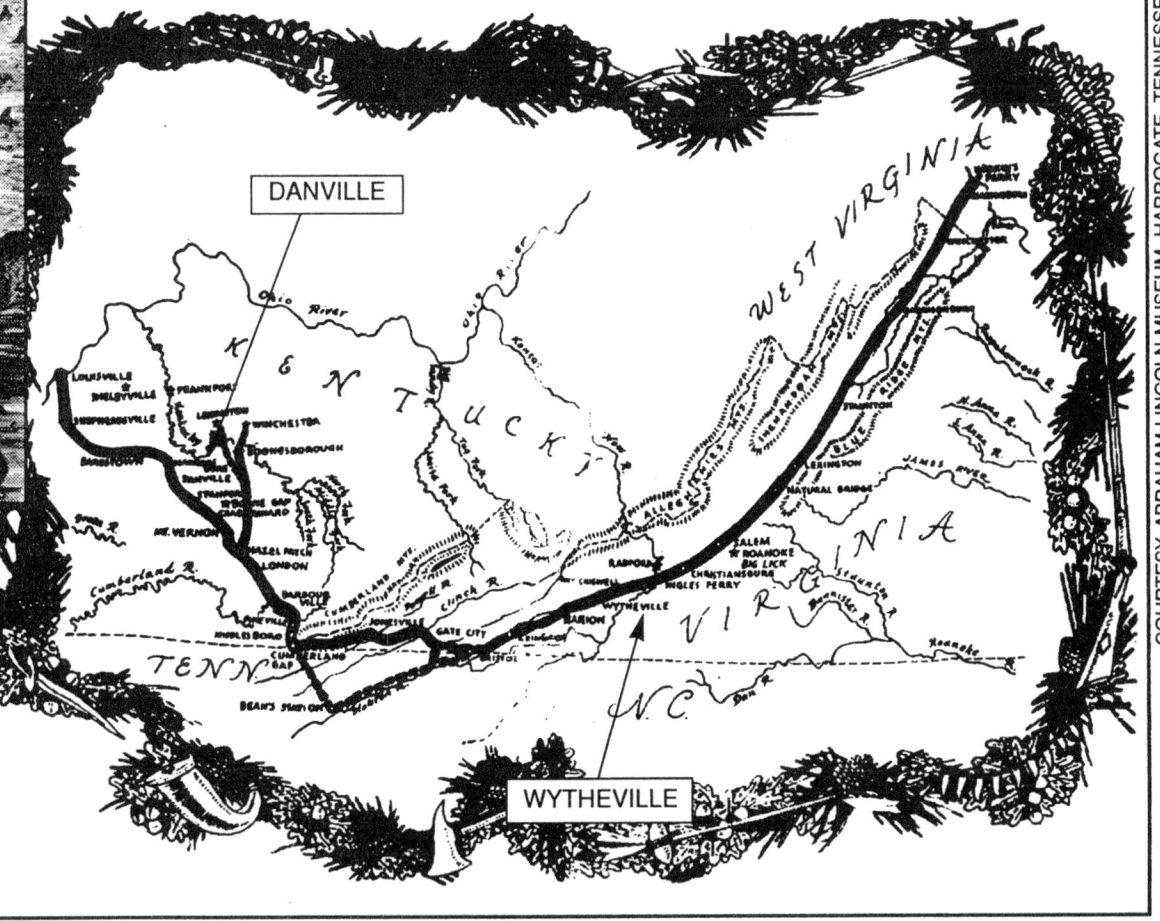

COURTESY, ABRAHAM LINCOLN MUSEUM, HARROGATE, TENNESSEE

PAGE 54

Harry Fenn engraving of Cumberland Gap, 1872

for the repeal of the Act of Separation. David Finley also signed this petition.[28]

In 1795 and 1796, Samuel Findley appeared on the Madison County tax list.[29] In 1796 a Samuel Finley was ordained as a Presbyterian minister in Madison County.[30] He appeared on the Lincoln County tax list from 1797, at least through 1811.[31] In 1801 he bought 100 acres in Lincoln County.[32] Evidence of his presence in Lincoln County continues at least through 1822, when the Reverend Samuel Finley served as President pro tem of Centre College in Danville.[33] It is tempting to believe this Samuel Finley is David's brother, and perhaps he is. The one disquieting fact is that in the 1810 census of Lincoln County he is placed in the twenty–six to forty–five age group, too young to have inherited property in 1779.[34] Perhaps the above records include more that one Samuel Finley.

+4 iii. Thomas Finley, born 11 February 1757, probably in Augusta County, Virginia.[35]

GENERATION TWO

2. David[2] Finley (John[1]) was born 1 June 1754, probably in Augusta County, Virginia, and died 19 April 1848 in Orange County, Indiana.[36] He married Elizabeth Mounts, daughter of Matthias and Mary Mounts, sometime prior to 10 February 1781.[37] Elizabeth was born 4 January 1763 and died 9 January 1835 in Orange County, Indiana.[38]

David was first found in Montgomery County records in 1773 when the New River tithables list "John Finley and sons David and Thomas."[39] Then, on 30 March 1779, he and his brother Samuel were deeded 327 acres by John and Mary Finley in exchange for life care.[40] Shortly after that, on 26 October 1779, he appeared in court to claim land he had staked out along the Dicks River in what later became Garrard County, Kentucky.

David Finley this day appeared and claimed a right of settlement and preemption to a tract of Land lying on the N.E. side of Dicks River about 3 or 4 Miles below the mouth of Falling Creek including two small Springs by building a Hut and raising a crop of Corn on the premises in the year 1776. Wm Frazer contested the claim by Joseph Frazer and alleged that the said Frazer has a prior improvement to the said land. Sundry Witnesses were sworn and examined in consideration of which the Court are of the Opinion that the said Finley has a right only to a pre–emption of 1000 Acres of Land including said improvement and that a Certificate issue for same and that the said Finley recover of the said Frazer his Costs.[41]

The records for David show he obtained a warrant for his 1,000 acres on 10 March 1780, while the survey date was 5 April 1781 and the grant date was 14 January 1784.[42]

It is not known precisely when David made the physical move permanently to Kentucky. Apparently it was not uncommon for many early settlers to claim their land, return to Virginia after putting in a crop of corn, and return to Kentucky later. The frequency of Indian raids in this area of Kentucky, through at least 1783, made it extremely hazardous to live in the area unless protected by a fort or stockade. Also David and Samuel were obligated to care for their aging parents and, as shown above, John died sometime before 19 August 1782. Prior to his move to Kentucky, David served with his brother Samuel in Captain Jehu Stephens's Company of the Montgomery County Militia. Since Stephens was promoted to colonel in 1781, David's service had to precede that date.[43] In addition, while David was listed, along with James, Samuel, Thomas, and William Finley in the 1782 tax list for Montgomery County, his record showed no tithes, slaves, horses or cattle,[44] suggesting he had moved on by that date.

In all likelihood, David was living in Kentucky prior to 10 February 1781, for on that date his wife, Betsey Finley, and her sister, Polly Collier, made a deposition concerning the death of their father, Matthias Mounts. Mounts had been killed by "the limb of a tree" and his body was taken to Downing's Station, in the immediate neighborhood of David's property on the Dicks River. After the death of Elizabeth's father, her mother, Mary Mounce, was appointed administrix. Apparently, the settlement was not handled in a manner to suit all heirs. A

David outlived four of his own children. He had already made provisions for all of them except Jefferson, his youngest son, who died at the age of twenty-four leaving three small children. According to David's wishes, his estate was divided equally among Jefferson's children.

lengthy set of papers is on file, including depositions and a quitclaim to Betsey and her sister, Polly, by their brother John. The final document involves a court case dated 17 June 1805 in which David Finley and Betsey, his wife, along with Moses Collier and Polly, his wife, are plaintiffs against Henry Mounts.[45] David did his share of defending the new frontier. The year 1782 was particularly bad and Indian attacks continued throughout the summer. In August 1782, Caldwell's attack on Bryan's stockade, barely thirty miles away, with fifty selected Tory Rangers and 300 Indians, was the last straw.[46] In November, David joined 1,050 mounted riflemen in a successful siege against the Shawnee. He served as a private in the company of Captain James Downing, whose daughter, Martha, later married David's son Samuel.[47] In 1788 David was recommended ensign in Captain George Scott's Company.[48] While these, together with his militia experience in Montgomery County, are the only documented service, family tradition also credits him with having served at the Battle of Cowpens[49] and at the massacre of Crab Orchard.[50]

David joined in petitioning the General Assembly of Virginia on at least two occasions to try to improve the lot of frontier living. In 1783 he was a signer, with other inhabitants of Lincoln County, in requesting laws dealing with better military protection, care of orphans, civil marriage, and stray stock.[51] In 1789 he signed a request for the repeal of the Act of Separation saying, "it was not the will of the good people of said District that the same should be erected into an independant state."[52]

On at least one occasion, in addition to his suit with his wife mentioned above, he went to court to provide bail for James and John Downing in a suit brought against them by James

Smith, whose son, Edmond, later married David's oldest daughter, Jane Ann.[53] Smith apparently did not hold this against David since he referred to him in his will as a "good and faithful" friend and named him, along with others, as an executor and trustee.[54]

In 1782 the Forks of Dix River Baptist Church was established on land owned by David and Elizabeth,[55] and they were among early members of the church. This was unusual for a strongly Presbyterian family, but it may have been because of the proximity. In 1785 David and Elizabeth sold the 300 acre portion of their original grant, where the Church was located, to William Downing, older brother of John and James Downing. Two years later, the Finleys sold another 300 acre piece of the original grant to Robert Singleton.[56] In 1792 David had 300 acres on Silver Creek in nearby Madison County surveyed[57] and the grant was made about a year and a half later, 9 May 1794.[58] In 1808 they also sold 24 7/8 acres to Arthur Thompson of Mercer County.[59]

Tax records exist in Garrard County[60] for David from 1797 through 1811, showing continuous residence during that period of time.[61] David and Elizabeth and most of their family then moved on to Orange County, Indiana.

David Fin(d)ley patented land at the land office at Jeffersonville in what is now Orange County, Indiana, from October 1811 until April 1819. This land was available under an Act of Congress providing for sale of lands of the United States in the territory northwest of the Ohio and above the mouth of the Kentucky River. His eight patents totaled 1,266.38 acres.[62] On 15 August 1817, he and Elizabeth deeded gifts of 160 acres each to five children: Samuel, Jesse, Mary Maxwell, Cyrus, and Harvey.[63] In addition, Samuel bought another 160 acres from his parents.⁶⁴ That, alone, totals 960 acres! Only two other land records were found for David during his lifetime. In 1819 he received an additional federal land grant for 110 acres⁶⁵ and in 1830 David and Elizabeth deeded 20 acres to their daughter, Elizabeth, and her husband, John H. Sneed, for $1.⁶⁶

In 1834, at the age of almost eighty, David wrote his will.⁶⁷ He provided first for his wife, Elizabeth, and second, for the education of the heirs of his son Jefferson, deceased. Specifically, he wanted any "over pluss of rents after giving to my wife what she may think proper and sufficient for her support," to be used to pay tuition until the two girls "shall each have two years [of education] . . . and Samuel three years." He stipulated that his executors should not sell his land until the youngest of Jefferson's children came of lawful age. At that time Jefferson's children, Josephine, Samuel, and Elizabeth, were to receive the proceeds of the sale. Son Cyrus, and son–in–law, Joseph Maxwell, were appointed executors. His own children were left $1 each, "in as much as I have equally divided," to them. His wife, Elizabeth, died less that ten months later, on 9 January 1835.⁶⁸

David still had a few good years ahead of him and in October 1845, at age ninety–one, he drew up an agreement with his son Cyrus.⁶⁹ In the agreement, David leased his land, the southwest and northwest quarters of section three, to Cyrus until 9 April 1851, when his granddaughter Elizabeth would become twenty–one. He also turned the notes he owned from the sale of personal property over to Cyrus. Cyrus, in turn, promised to care for David and provide a comfortable living for him. He also agreed to 1) provide a year of school for David's grandchildren, Samuel and Elizabeth, Jefferson's two youngest children; 2) pay taxes on the leased land; 3) rotate the crops, planting corn one year and grain the next; 4) not destroy timber more than necessary for use of the farm; 5) not box or fence any sugar trees south of the most southern field; and 6) enclose the graves of his parents and his brother, Jefferson, with a brick wall.

David lived two and one–half more years after his agreement with Cyrus, succumbing on 19 April 1848, at the age of almost ninety–four.⁷⁰ In keeping with David's wishes, Cyrus continued caring for David's land until Jefferson's youngest child, Elizabeth, was twenty–one years of age. Cyrus then offered the property (described as the west half of section three in township two north, range one east, less 20 acres, presumably 300 acres) for sale. Samuel, Jefferson's son and one of David's principle heirs, purchased the property for $2,700.⁷¹ The final settlement of David's estate was made 27 August 1851.⁷² Named were his sons and daughters, or their heirs, as follows:

John Findley
Jane Smith
Edmund Findley
Samuel Findley's heirs
Jesse Findley
Harvey Findley's heirs
Polly Maxwell's heirs
Elizabeth Sneed
the executor [Cyrus Findley]

Each was allotted $1 as provided in the will. The remaining estate, valued at $2,663.70, was divided equally among Jefferson's children, Samuel and Elizabeth Finley, and Josephine Fisher.

Known children of David and Elizabeth (Mounts) Finley are as follows:

5   i.   John[3] Finley born probably about 1782/1784, probably in Lincoln County, Virginia (now Garrard County, Kentucky). Because the name is so common and there were a number of John Finleys in Kentucky and Indiana, very little is known for sure about this son. A John Finley appears near David on the Garrard County tax lists beginning in 1797,[73] possibly a nephew. In 1805 a second John Finley appears near David owning no land and recurs in 1806, 1807 and 1809, still owning no land,[74] probably David's son. In the 1820 census of Indiana, John Finley age twenty-six to forty-five, is living next to David Finley in Lawrence County (Lawrence County was formed from OrangeCounty in 1818).[75] These are the only records that can reasonably be expected to be those of David's son.

+6   ii.   Jane Ann Finley, born 9 November 1785, Lincoln County, Virginia (now Garrard County, Kentucky).[76]

+7   iii.   Edmund Finley, born about 1787,[77] in Mercer County, Virginia (now Garrard County, Kentucky).

+8   iv.   Samuel Finley, born 14 February 1790, in Mercer County, Virginia (now Garrard County, Kentucky).[78]

+9   v.   Jesse Finley, born 17 May 1792,[79] Mercer County, Virginia (now Garrard County, Kentucky).

+10   vi.   Harvey Finley, born 11 February 1795, Mercer County, Kentucky (now Garrard County).[80]

+11   vii.   Mary (Polly) Finley, born 9 June 1797 in Garrard County, Kentucky.[81]

+12   viii.   Cyrus Finley, born 25 November 1799 in Garrard County, Kentucky.[82]

+13   ix.   Elizabeth Finley, born 8 February 1802, Garrard County, Kentucky.[83]

+14   x.   Jefferson Finley, born 16 May 1805,[84] in Garrard County, Kentucky.

4. Thomas[2] Finley (John[1]) was born 11 February 1757, probably in Augusta County, Virginia.[85] He married (1) about 1792, Jeanne Gibert, daughter of Jean Louis Gibert, probably in Abbeville, South Carolina.[86] He married (2) sometime before 1797, Sarah (McLane) Stedman Pettigrew.[87] He married (3), Jane Clark, on 20 December 1808.[88] Thomas died probably late in 1831 in Abbeville, South Carolina.[89]

Thomas was first found in Montgomery County, Virginia, in 1773 on the list of tithables with his father, John, and brother David.[90] On 12 September 1782, he claimed 140 acres on Sally Run, Montgomery County, (survey date, 13 January 1783) adjacent to property that had been owned by his father, John, then deceased.[91] His illegitimate son, Reuben Jefferson, was born 31 March 1783 to Catherine Kinder.[92] Soon after this birth, Thomas moved to South Carolina. Catherine Kinder married Andrew Swallow in the Spring of 1785 and Reuben was reared by his mother and Swallow.[93]

Little is known of Thomas's life in South Carolina, but his will left significant information. His will, written in 1823 in Abbeville, South Carolina, and probated 2 January 1832, showed he had become a wealthy land owner and possessed many slaves.[94] The appraisement of his estate listed twenty-three slaves and was valued at $8,935.40.[95] His will was unique in a number of ways. Basically, he left the bulk of his estate to his wife, Jane, and stated specifically that she should get his negroes named Finda, Tom, Jude, William, Caroline, Willey, and Rose, along with "all my other negroes." After her death, all property was to go to his son "Reuben Finley of the State of Tennessee, Wheelwright, whose mother's maiden name was Catherine Kinder . . . on the following conditions . . . that he emancipate all the female children of my two negro women, Hanny and Jinney or cause them to be sent to the State of Indiana or Ohio where the laws of the State will liberate them. The said female children are to be set free as they respectively arrive at the age of twenty-five years and all their children with them should they have any, as it is my wish and desire to put a stop to the slavery of the race of negroes belonging to me in future." He requested Reuben to erect marble headstones for himself and Jane and gave their respective birth dates . . . 11 February 1757 and 8 November 1765. He also directed Reuben to enclose his grave and his wife's "with a stone wall of five feet high with a shutter to the door of some durable materials, and that spot of ground to be reserved and never conveyed away with the tract of land." He further bequeathed to his niece Ann Finley his "negro boy Franklin . . . and . . . negro girl Peggy." Peggy was to be set free at age twenty-five and Franklin was not to be bartered or sold out of the family "where I trust he will be well treated." Thomas Finley Mitchel, son of Francis Mitchel, was to receive his "negro boy Robert." The death of Reuben Finley prior to that of Thomas's wife, Jane, created some problems, as will be seen in the following account of Reuben.

The child of Thomas Finley and Catherine Kinder was:

+15   i.   Reuben Jefferson[3] Finley, born 31 March 1783, Montgomery County (now Wythe), Virginia.

The only known child of Thomas Finley by his first wife, Jeanne Gibert, was:

16   i.   John Lewis[3] Finley, born 7 November 1795, Abbeville, South Carolina.[96] He died in Columbia, on 7 September 1814, at the age of eighteen, while in his junior year at South Carolina College (now University of South Carolina).[97]

GENERATION THREE

6. Jane Ann[3] Finley (David[2], John[1]) was the eldest daughter of David and Elizabeth (Mounts) Finley, born 9 November 1785 in Lincoln County, Virginia, now Garrard County, Kentucky.[98] She is also the only one of the children to have lived out her life in Kentucky. She died 12 May 1871 and is buried in the Burnt

Tavern Graveyard at Bryantsville.[99] Jane Ann married on 15 May 1801,[100] Edmond Smith, born about 1779, the son of James and Magdalene (Woods) Smith.[101] Edmond predeceased Jane Ann by more than twenty years, having died prior to 15 December 1848.[102]

Edmond's father, the Reverend James Smith, was a Separatist Baptist minister who came to Kentucky from Virginia in 1779, about the same time the Finleys and Downings arrived. James, together with his brother, Henry, and sons, John and William, built a station, or fort, called Smith's Station. It later became known as Smithtown, now Bryantsville. Edmond was only six months old when the family moved to the Dicks River area.[103] The Smith home was inherited by Edmond, who replaced the original log structure with a brick building around 1798-1800, and it became a tavern. The name, Old Burnt Tavern, was derived from two fires, in which the dining room was saved and added on to. Edmond, Jane Ann, and their son, David Finley Smith, operated the noted tavern which was an important stopping–place for stagecoach and horseback travelers from the North on their way to Crab Orchard Springs, Danville, Nashville, and Florence, Alabama. Here families stopped, ate, and slept overnight while they rested from long and tiresome stagecoach trips. Prices for lodging and refreshments at Burnt Tavern in the 1830s and 1840s included: breakfast 25¢; dinner 37^{1}/$_{2}$¢; supper 25¢; night's lodging 12^{1}/$_{2}$¢; whiskey per half pint 12^{1}/$_{2}$¢; cider per quart 6^{1}/$_{4}$¢; peach brandy per quart 12^{1}/$_{2}$¢; wine, rum or cognac brandy per half pint 25¢; beer per quart 12^{1}/$_{2}$¢; and hay, grain and stablage for horse overnight 37^{1}/$_{2}$¢. Burnt Tavern also served as a mail stagecoach stop in the mid–1830s.[104]

Jane Ann is the earliest family member for whom photographs have been found, along with two of her sons, Merrill and Edmund Finley Smith. Edmond's will, proved in 1848 named, in addition to Jane Ann, seven children (listed below with others), and four grandchildren, Mary Smith, Mary Virginia Smith, Presley Talbot, and Charles Talbot. Executors were Jane Ann and their oldest son, Harold F. Smith.[105] During the Civil War, the Smiths were Southern in their sympathies. However, they were located between two Union camps, Camp Dick Robinson and Camp Nelson, and the officers of both camps used the tavern for their entertainment, to the inconvenience of its owners. It was in Federal possession for the greater part of the war, with the exception of the time of Bragg's invasion of Kentucky and his retreat from Perryville, where the largest battle of the war in Kentucky was fought. According to one historian, the period during which this tavern existed was one of the most exciting of the history of Garrard County. He says, "A volume could be written about its guests, [among them Jenny Lind, the 'Swedish Nightingale,' and Henry Clay], pleasure seekers, statesmen, men of business and travelers of every kind, so rich it is in legend and story."[106]

Jane Ann lived through these exciting times to the age of almost eighty–six. She is buried in the Burnt Tavern Graveyard at Bryantsville.[107] The tract of land on which Jane Ann and Edmond lived remained successively in the possession of their descendants until 1944, when it was sold by Mrs. Bourbon Dawes.

Known children of Jane Ann (Finley) and Edmond Smith are as follows:[108]

17   i.   Harold F.[4] Smith, born 1803; mar-

18	ii.	ried Catherine Brown. Almira Smith, born 1806; married Rice.
19	iii.	Merrill Smith, born 1809; married Hannah Burnside.
20	iv.	Elizabeth F. Smith, born 26 November 1811; married John G. Talbot, 11 August 1829; died 23 May 1843.
21	v.	Mary Jane Smith, born 1814; married Nathan L. Smith.
22	vi.	Sally Ann Smith, born 1816; married Bowie.
23	vii.	Edmund Finley Smith, born 20 September 1819; married Mary Myers, January 1835.
24	viii.	David Finley Smith, born 1821; married (1) Martha Kemper, (2) Mrs. Pauline Kennedy; died 1881.
25	ix.	Anna Maria Smith, born 1825; died young.
26	x.	Josephine Peachy Smith, born 1827; married Simon Drake.

7. Edmund[3] Finley (David[2], John[1]) was born about 1787[109] in Mercer County, Virginia (now Garrard County, Kentucky). He married Catherine sometime prior to 17 June 1819,[110] and probably before 1810.[111]

Most of what is known about Edmund had to be reconstructed from census and land records. No records were found for him in the Dicks River area, suggesting he had moved out

Jane Ann (Finley) Smith and her husband, Edmond, owned and ran this tavern, built about 1797–1800. During the mid-to-late 1830s, Burnt Tavern served as a terminal for a four-horse stage coach between that point and Danville, eight miles away. According to Calico, "It was probably from [this] coach that Jenny Lind, the 'Swedish Nightingale,' traveling and touring America, alighted and sang on the cliffs of Dick's River as legend has it."

before the rest of the family went to Indiana. In addition, 1850, 1860, and 1870 census records give the birthplace of John Findley, probably his oldest son, as Tennessee about 1810.[112] Tennessee records have been searched to no avail. The earliest record of any kind found for Edmund was a land entry on 9

Jane Ann (Finley) Smith –
(1785–1871)

Merrill Smith, son of Jane Ann
and Edmond Smith – (1809 – ?)

Edmund Finley Smith, son of Jane Ann
and Edmond Smith – (1819–1882)

KELTON SMITH COLLECTION

April 1813 for 160 acres (Range 2E, Township 2N, Section 10, SE quarter) in Washington County, Indiana. On 16 January 1818 an entry was made for the SW quarter adjacent to him by H. [Harvey] Findley.[113] Edmund and Catherine, his wife, sold forty acres of their property on 17 June 1819.[114] They were not found in the 1820 Indiana census, nor have they been found elsewhere that year. However, in 1830 they were found in Wayne County, Missouri, not far from his brother Jesse.[115] By 1840, they had moved on to Van Buren County, renamed Cass County in 1849, Missouri.[116] Bates County was formed from portions of Cass, Van Buren, and Jackson Counties in 1841 and it is here that some of his nephews, sons of Samuel, are found in 1850.

However, by 1850 Edmund and Catherine had moved on and were found living in the home of Lewis Findley in Hopkins County, Texas.[117] In Cass County, Missouri, there were sufficient land records to identify two additional probable sons of Edmund and Catherine. In 1845 and 1848, David and Margaret A. Finley, his wife, sold property. In 1852 Lewis Finley and Letitia, his wife, and Edmund and Catherine, each sold two parcels.[118] In the 1840 census, David Findley was living next door to Edmund in Missouri.[119] In the 1850 census, Edmund and Katherine [Catherine], aged sixty–three and sixty–five, were living with Lewis and Lettecia [Letitia], aged twenty–five and thirty–five; nearby were David and Margaret Findley, aged

PAGE 64

thirty–five and thirty–two.[120] No further information is available on Edmund. Probable sons of Edmund and Catherine Finley include the following:

+27   i.   John[4] Finley, born about 1810 in Tennessee.
+28   ii.   David Finley, born about 1815 in Missouri.
+29   iii.   Lewis S. Finley, born about 1825 in Missouri.

8. Samuel[3] Finley (David[2], John[1]) was born 14 February 1790 in Mercer County, Virginia, now Garrard County, Kentucky.[121] He died 15 September 1835 in Macon County, Illinois, at the age of forty–five.[122] On 9 May 1809, he married Martha (Patsy) Downing, daughter of Captain James and Nancy Downing, a long time friend and neighbor of David Finley.[123] Martha was born 18 January 1788,[124] probably in the Dicks River area of Kentucky. She died 15 November 1832,[125] probably in Orange County, Indiana. Samuel's second marriage was to Rachel Black on 21 November 1833 in Macon County, Illinois.[126]

Shortly after the marriage of Samuel and Martha, the young couple moved to Orange County, Indiana. Samuel served in the Indiana Territory Militia during the War of 1812 in the same unit with his brother Jesse.[127] Samuel was found as a private on the payroll of Paddack's 5th Regiment, Captain Charles Busey's for the period 18 February to 19 March 1813, for which he received $8, one month's pay. In 1817 Samuel and Martha received a gift of 160 acres from his parents, who made like gifts to four other siblings.[128] At that same time, Samuel bought an additional 160 acres adjacent to the property that was gifted to him (SW quarter in Range 1E, Township 2N, Section 2) for $500.[129] Samuel and Martha (Patsy) lived in Orange County where most, if not all, of their eight children were born. When Martha died 15 November 1832, at the age of forty–four, she left Samuel with children ranging in age from three years to nineteen years. Martha may have been the victim of cholera for about this time an epidemic swept through the Upper Lost River area where they lived.[130] (Samuel's brother Harvey had died in May of 1832, and Harvey's wife and two of their children died in July and August of 1833.)

Samuel and his children moved to Decatur, Macon County, Illinois, where he married Rachel Black on 21 November 1833.[131] Less than two years later, Samuel died at the age of forty–five, leaving five minor children.

Samuel left a will and there are many court records concerning the disposition of his property and the guardianship of his minor children.[132] His will, written in July 1835, about two months before his death, divided his property equally among his wife and his children, except that his son James was to receive "one certain yellow filley now one year old past." In the event Rachel remarried, his property was then to revert to his children and be divided equally among them. His list of goods and chattels contained fifty–nine items, including household furnishings, tools, oxen, calves and cows, sheep, hogs, horses, and farm supplies including three bees stands and bees. Total value was appraised at $585.12. He owned a total of 360 acres, which had been entered at the land office at Vandalia,[133] Illinois. Two parcels were timber land four miles from Decatur, a third was prairie land. Total land value was set at $1,600.[134] Alvin, Samuel's eldest son, was the executor for his estate.

Apparently, some difficulty arose in the division of the

Samuel received a gift of 160 acres in Orange County, Indiana, from his parents "in consideration of love and good will."
15 August 1817. Samuel's will (above, right) divided his property equally among his heirs, except that his son James was given "one certain yellow filley now one year old." This "equal division" set the stage for later conflict among the heirs.

This Indenture Made this fifteenth day of August in the Year of our Lord One thousand eight hundred & seventeen by & Between David & Elizabeth Tarkly of the State of Indiana & Orange County of the one part & Samuel Tarkly of the same place, Mississippi, that the Said David & Elizabeth Tarkly for and in consideration of the love & good will which we bear to our Son Samuel Tarkly have given and granted & by these presents doth freely clearly & absolutely give, grant, convey & confirm unto the said Samuel Tarkly, the South East Quarter of Section thirteen two in Range No. One East of the Second Principal Meridian containing One hundred and sixty acres be the same more or less. To have and to hold the said Quarter Section of Land & all my part & parcel thereof with the appurtenances unto the said Samuel Tarkly, his heirs & assigns forever, free & clear from all incumbrances & claims whatsoever. In Testimony whereof we the said David & Elizabeth Tarkly have hereunto set our hands & affixed our seals, the day & year just above written.

David Tarkly (seal)
her
Elizabeth X Tarkly (seal)
mark

State of Indiana Orange County ss
October 1817
List of his Landers
and delivered in the presence of

This day David Tarkly and his wife personally before me Edward Miller
and [jurat] acknowledged the within
Deed of Conveyance to Samuel Tarkly to be their Act and Deed the said
Elizabeth firstly being examined separate and apart from her said husband
Did declare that she freely relinquished, her right and title of dower.

I Samuel Tarkly of the County of Sharon and State of Illinois, do hereby make this my last Will & Testament revoking all others:

1st. I will that all my Just Debts be paid.

2nd. I will that the remainder of all my real and personal Estate be equally divided between my wife Rachel and my Children, Except as hereafter specified.

3rd. I will that my son James have one certain yellow filley now one year old as his equal share.

4th. I will that the equal part of the real Estate which my wife Rachel shall be by this my last Will and Testament shall be at the time of her decease to be equally divided between my Children: and if she my wife Rachel shall hereafter intermarry the real Estate begin bequeathed to her shall revert to my Children to be equally divided between them at the said time of her intermarrying.

5th. I appoint ____ to be the Executors of this my last Will &c.

Given under my hand this fourteenth day of July AD 1835.

Samuel Tarkly
Testator

property, for on 29 August 1836, John Finley (Edmund³, David², John¹) and his wife, Mahala, Samuel's oldest daughter, petitioned the court for the division of Samuel's property.¹³⁵ In September, commissioners were appointed to divide the property.¹³⁶ On 3 November 1836, the commissioners reported to the court that "the said lands and tenements cannot be divided without manifest prejudice to the proprietors of the same." Final resolution of the matter is not given in the existing records of Macon County.

Nor did the matter of the guardianship of the minor children of Samuel go smoothly. Josephus Hewett was appointed guardian for minor children Jefferson, James, John, Samuel, and Elizabeth on 19 September 1836.¹³⁷ On 25 March 1837, the minor children's brother Alvin, was appointed their guardian and offered bond in the amount of $2,600 jointly with Randall Davis.¹³⁸ Apparently, that arrangement was not permanent, for on 16 June 1837, a similar document was presented naming Alvin guardian, but the bond, in the same amount, was made jointly by Alvin and Jacob Black, presumably kin to the widow Finley.¹³⁹ However, the widow, Rachel (Black) Finley married Hugh McCully in August,¹⁴⁰ and on 18 October Hugh and Rachel McCully summoned Alvin to court, claiming he, as guardian for the children, owed Rachel $50 for the care of the minor children. An inventory of the services she provided included such items as making two pair of pantaloons, several shirts, two pair of socks, two bed quilts, and one domestic sheet; washing and mending; and furnishing "victuals and drink at sundries times" for seven months between 15 September 1835 and 1 May 1836. The itemized list totaled $53 and a judgment was entered in favor of the plaintiff. Alvin filed an appeal, and the McCulleys were ordered to appear in May 1838.¹⁴¹ However, Alvin died before the appointed date,¹⁴² and Henry Snyder was officially appointed guardian on 3 November 1838.¹⁴³

One other item of interest was found in Samuel's probate records. Jacob Black testified on 14 March 1840 that John Finley and Mahala, his wife (formerly Mahala Finley); Jefferson Finley; and James Finley; heirs of Samuel Finley, "are no longer residents of Illinois, but reside in the state of Missouri.¹⁴⁴"

Known children of Samuel and Martha (Downing) Finley include:¹⁴⁵

30   i.   Mahala⁴ Finley, born 22 May 1811; married her first cousin, John Fin(d)ley, son of Samuel's brother Edmund, 25 December 1831. After their suit involving the division of her father's property in 1836, and sometime before 1840, they moved to Missouri, taking her younger brothers Jefferson and James with them. Since Jefferson and James appeared in court in Macon County in January and April of 1838 to choose Henry Snyder their guardian, that narrows the time of the move to Missouri. Attempts to find either court records or death records involving Mahala have failed, but by 22 March of 1840, Mahala's husband, John, had married Sarah Masters in Jackson County, Missouri.¹⁴⁶ Family tradition, as related by Ethel Work Balmer, grand-

daughter of this John Fin(d)ley and Sarah Masters, says Mahala and John had nine children,[147] however, nothing has been found to substantiate this.

+31   ii.   Alvin Finley, born 9 October 1813 in Orange County, Indiana.

+32   iii.   Nancy J. Finley, born 25 February 1816 in Orange County, Indiana.

33   iv.   Jefferson Finley, born 25 April 1818 in Orange County, Indiana; married Frances Foe, 1 February 1838 in Macon County, Illinois. Shortly after that, they went to Missouri with John and Mahala Findley. Nothing further is known of Jefferson.

34   v.   James Finley, born 20 January 1821 in Orange County, Indiana. Went to Missouri with his older sister Mahala and brother Jefferson sometime between 1838 and 1840. A James Finley married Caroline Masters, 21 May 1840, in Jackson County, soon after John Findley married Sarah Masters.[148] It is tempting to believe that this is the James Finley who married Caroline Masters, but no proof has been found. In 1845 in Cass County, he was appointed guardian for his brother Samuel, then aged nineteen; David Findley, most likely his cousin and younger brother of brother-in-law John, acted as surety.[149] About five years later, on 24 April 1850, James bought thirty-three acres[150] from Samuel, which he had entered in Bates County in 1847 (Bates County was formed from Cass, Van Buren and Jackson Counties in 1841; Cass County was organized as Van Buren County and renamed Cass in 1849). In the 1850 census that year, James, aged twenty–eight was found living alone not far away from his younger brother John, his wife, Kesia, and their two children.[151] It is possible that James went to California along with his brothers John and Samuel. Four deeds of purchase were found for a James Finley between 15 November 1855 and 28 February 1859 in Rancho Canada de Pogolimi in Sonoma County. Geographically, this is quite near the Bodega Rancho where John and Samuel settled in 1852. The last entry for James was the sale of his property 17 August 1859.[152]

+35   vi.   John Finley, born 5 June 1823 in Orange County, Indiana.

+36   vii.   Samuel Finley, born 6 March 1826 in Orange County, Indiana.

+37   viii.   Elizabeth Finley, born 13 April 1829 in Orange County, Indiana.

9. Jesse[3] Finley (David[2], John[1]) was born 17 May 1792, Mercer County, Virginia (now Garrard County, Kentucky).[153] He

probably died before 1870 and in Dunklin County, Missouri.[154] Jesse married Rachel Colglazure, on 20 July 1815, probably in Washington County, Indiana.[155] She was born 28 December 1788 in Westmoreland County, Pennsylvania, the daughter of Jacob Colglazure who later moved to Washington County, Indiana.[156] Rachel probably died between 1850 and 1860, in Texas.[157]

Jesse served in the Indiana Territory Militia during the War of 1812 in the same unit with his brother Samuel.[158] He was found on the payroll of Paddack's 5th Regiment, Captain Charles Busey's Company, as a private for the period 18 February to 19 March 1813, and 16 April to 15 May 1813, for which he received $16, two month's pay. However, this does not agree with a later application for bounty land that Jesse made, 5 August 1853, while living in Greenville, Hunt County, Texas. In that document, he stated he enlisted in June 1814 and served for one year. He was mustered in at Paoli and discharged at Vincennes, but had lost his certificate of discharge.[159]

In 1817 Jesse and Rachel received a gift of 160 acres from his parents, along with like gifts to four other siblings.[160] They were still living in Orange County in 1820,[161] but by 1830 had moved on to Wayne County, Missouri, where they were living near his brother Edmund.[162] The move was probably made between March 1827, when son Edmond, was born, and October 1829, when Joseph Jefferson was born, if the 1850 census in Hunt County, Texas correctly states the respective birth places of their sons Edmond and Joseph Jefferson.[163] However, the 1900 census for Edmond states he was born in Missouri,[164] so the family could have made the move a couple of years earlier. Unfortunately, the Wayne County Courthouse burned in 1854 with all land records, so it is impossible to get information on their land holdings. In 1840 Jesse was found in Stoddard County, Missouri,[165] adjacent to Wayne County. By 1850 they had gone on to Hunt County, Texas, where he, along with sons Milton, George, Edmond, Joseph J., and Marion, and brother Edmond and his son John, all settled in Mercers Colony.[166] Each received from Charles Fenton Mercer and Associates, known as the Texas Association, a certificate issued either 6 or 7 May 1850. Married men Jesse, Milton, George, Edmond, Sr., and John received certificates for 640 acres; single men Edmond, Jr., Joseph J., and Marion received certificates for 320 acres each. The description of a 320 acre survey done for Jesse the next month, places his property on Lake Fork Creek of the Sabine River.[167] By the time the 1850 census was taken, Jesse, Rachel, and their unmarried sons owning Mercers Colony certificates, were found living together, with married sons William, Milton, and George living nearby.[168] However, by the time the 1860 census was taken, Jesse had moved to Missouri and was living in the home of David and Margaret Finley in Dunklin County.[169] By 1870 Jesse had disappeared from the home of his son David, and has not been found elsewhere. Presumably, Rachel died between 1850 and 1860 when Jesse moved to Missouri, and Jesse died between 1860 and 1870, although no proof of this has been found to date.

Known children of Jesse and Rachel (Colglazure) Finley include:[170]

+38   i.   William[4] Finley, born 6 March 1816, in Indiana, probably Orange County or nearby.

+39   ii.   Milton Finley, born 6 February 1818 in Indiana, probably Orange County or nearby.

+40	iii.	David Finley, born 1 September 1819 in Orange County, Indiana.
41	iv.	Samuel Finley, born 22 May 1821 in Indiana.
+42	v.	Elizabeth Ellen Finley,[171] born 10 March 1823 in Indiana, probably Orange County or nearby.
+43	vi.	George W. Finley, born April 1825 in Indiana, probably Orange County or nearby.
+44	vii.	Edmond Finley, born 27 March 1827[172] in Indiana or Missouri.[173]
+45	viii.	Joseph Jefferson Finley, born 5 October 1829 in Missouri, probably Wayne County.
46	ix.	Marion Finley, born 16 August 1830 in Missouri, probably Wayne County. He received a certificate for 320 acres in Mercers Colony on 7 May 1850.[174] Marion married Arminda Kerbo, 17 April 1862 in Hopkins County.[175]
47	x.	Mary Elizabeth Finley, born 11 March 1833, probably in Wayne or Stoddard County, Missouri.

10. **Harvey[3] Finley** (David[2] John[1]) was born 11 February 1795, Mercer County, Kentucky (now Garrard County).[176] He died 26 May 1832 at the age of thirty–seven and is buried in Trimble Cemetery.[177] Harvey married Elizabeth McKinney, born 1 May 1790, daughter of David and Margaret (Wallace)

McKinney,[178] 24 January 1816.[179] Elizabeth died 3 August 1833 at the age of forty–three and is buried near Harvey in Orange County, Indiana.[180]

Harvey was one of five children of David and Elizabeth to receive a quarter section of land gift from his parents in August 1817.[181] They are listed in the 1820 census in Washington County.[182] After Harvey's death in May 1832, his brother Cyrus was appointed guardian to his seven infant children.[183] In July and August of the next year, 1833, two of Harvey's children, David and Elizabeth Ann, and his wife, Elizabeth died.[184] That was the time of a cholera epidemic in Washington County which swept down into the Upper Lost River Valley where the family lived.[185] With five premature Finley deaths, including Samuel's wife, Martha, during a fifteen month period, it seems likely cholera could have been the cause.

Over the next nine years, the guardianship of Harvey and Elizabeth's children changed several times, but Cyrus was involved in all but the final assignment for William, if not as guardian, then as surety. On 10 February 1835, Joseph Maxwell, Cyrus's brother–in–law, was appointed guardian of the remaining five orphans of Harvey and Elizabeth.[186] On 8 May 1843, Cyrus was reappointed guardian of Thomas, Mary, and William, and William Montgomery was appointed guardian of Margaret.[187] On 12 August 1844, Cyrus was again appointed guardian of Mary Jane, and David McKinney was appointed guardian of William.[188]

Known children of Harvey and Elizabeth (McKinney) Finley include:[189]

| 48 | i. | Eliza Ann[4] Finley, born 5 February 1817; |

49	ii.	James Harvey Finley, born 31 March 1820; died 11 January 1860, buried in Orleans Cemetery.[191]
50	iii.	David M. Finley, born 18 December 1822; died 20 July 1833, buried in Trimble Cemetery.
51	iv.	Thomas Jefferson Finley.
52	v.	Margaret Emily Finley, born 9 August 1825; married William Montgomery 5 October 1842;[192] died 24 January 1870, buried in Trimble Cemetery.[193] Known children of Margaret Emily and William Montgomery include:[194]

        a. Ida Beatrice Montgomery, died 18 March 1863; buried in Trimble Cemetery.
        b. Louise J. Montgomery, buried in Trimble Cemetery.
        c. Theofilus Montgomery, born 27 February 1845; died 15 February 1866, buried in Trimble Cemetery.
        d. William F. Montgomery, born 14 August 1846; died 30 January 1879, buried in Trimble Cemetery.
        e. female Montgomery, born about 1849.

53	vi.	Mary Jane Finley, was licensed to marry Thomas W. Riley,[195] 7 November 1844.
54	vii.	William Alexander Finley,[196] born 5 January 1831; married Elizabeth C. Lewis 21 December 1854;[197] died 2 June 1870.[198]

(preceding entry continues: died 22 August 1833, buried in Trimble Cemetery.[190])

11. Mary[3] (Polly) Finley (David[2], John[1]) was born 9 June 1797 in Garrard County, Kentucky.[199] She died 4 October 1842 in Orange County, Indiana, at the age of forty–five. She married Joseph W. Maxwell, probably in Orange County, Indiana, prior to 15 August 1817,[200] for on that date she and Joseph received a gift of 160 acres from her parents.[201] Joseph W. Maxwell, son of James and (Browne) Maxwell, was born 11 March 1795 in South Carolina. He died 26 January 1881 in Lawrence, Douglas County, Kansas, where he had been living with daughters Martha Jane Lindley and Mary Elizabeth Newlin.

Both Mary and her future husband had moved to the Lost River area of Orange County with their families in 1811. The impression we get of Joseph is one of a "solid citizen." He served with the Rangers to quell the Indians. He also served as a justice of the peace for many years. In 1832, when Mary's brother Cyrus was appointed guardian for the children of their brother Harvey, Joseph acted as surety.[202] In 1835 Joseph became guardian of the five living orphans of Harvey and Elizabeth.[203] Mary (Finley) Maxwell was one of four children who predeceased her father, for reference to "Mary Maxwell's heirs" is made in David's final settlement.[204] After Mary's death, Joseph remarried and had six more children. In 1866 he moved to Howard County, Indiana, and in 1878, to Lawrence, Douglas County, Kansas, where he lived with his daughters as noted above. Children of Mary (Finley) and Joseph Maxwell, all born in Orange County, include:[205]

55	i.	Almira[4] Maxwell, born 1 December 1816;

JOSEPHINE WILLIAMS COLLECTION

Almira (Maxwell) Tucker (1816 –?)   America Ann (Maxwell) Jeter (1822 – ?)   Martha Jane (Maxwell) Lindley (1823 – ?)

married John W. Tucker, 26 September 1833, Orange County, Indiana.[206]

56   ii.   Eliza Jane Maxwell, born 9 October 1818.; married Cyrus B. Collier, 24 July 1834.

57   iii.   James David Maxwell, born 14 February 1820; died 22 November 1831 in Orange County.

58   iv.   America Ann Maxwell, born 25 January 1822; married William O. Jeter, 24 January 1850 in Orange County.[207]

59   v.   Martha Jane Maxwell, born 23 September 1823; married Alfred Lindley, 9

January 1845, Orange County;[208] died after 3 November 1866.

60   vi.   Louiza Maxwell, born 25 September 1825; married Jonathan Dixon, 6 March 1845, Orange County;[209] died after 7 September 1882.

61   vii.   Mary Elizabeth Maxwell, born 23 January 1828; married Mahlon H. Newlin, 15 January 1846.[210]

62   viii.   Joseph Jefferson Maxwell, born 3 July 1830; married Martha Jane Smith, 29 October 1852 in Paoli, Orange County; died 12 May 1919 in Los Angeles,

Joseph Jefferson Maxwell (1830–1919) *George Washington Maxwell (1832 – ?)* *Cyrus Maxwell (1835–1873)*

63	ix.	George Washington Maxwell, born 4 October 1832. He was in New Mexico Territory in 1880 at Blazer's Mill.
64	x.	Cyrus Maxwell, born 2 January 1835; died 13 March 1873, Orange County.[211]
65	xi.	Sarah Brown(e) Maxwell, born 16 September 1838.
66	xii.	John Tucker Maxwell, born 1842.

12. Cyrus[3] Finley (David[2], John[1]) was born 25 November 1799 in Garrard County, Kentucky. He died 31 January 1874.[212] He was David's only son to remain in Orange County, Indiana, California.

and survive him. He married Rachel Downey on 17 December 1818.[213] Rachel was born 15 September 1795 and died 10 August 1856, probably in Orange County.[214] Both are buried in Green Hill Cemetery in Orleans, Orange County.

At the time of his marriage, Cyrus had already received a gift of 160 acres from his parents.[215] He was the one who assumed the family responsibilities when his brother Harvey died in 1832 leaving seven young children.[216] He was the one who made the somewhat unique agreement with his father in 1845 to take care of David's property and responsibilities.[217] And Cyrus was the one who carried out his father's wishes, administered his estate, and reported the final settlement in 1851.[218] Cyrus outlived his own three sons James, David, and leaving no widow, But leaving Eliza J Lee his child; and Cyrus E Finley his grand child and the only child of Merrell Finley Dec'd who was the Son of decedent and who died before the decedent, And leaving also as his grand children Ellen R Mahan and Merrell F Finley who are children of David Finley, Dec'd who was a Son of decedent and who died before the decedent,, And leaving also as his grand children Eliza Turley and Martha Mahan who are children of James Finley Deceased who was a Son of decedent and who died before decedent

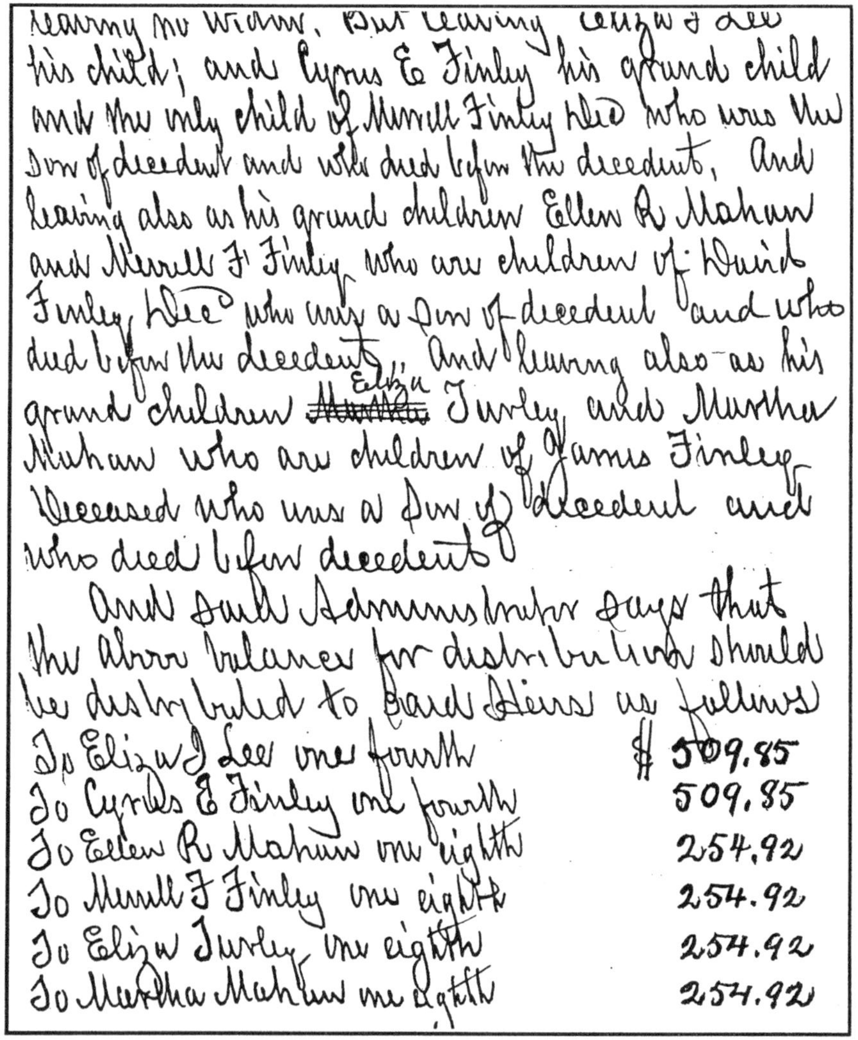

And said Administrator says that the above balance for distribution should be distributed to said Heirs as follows

To Eliza J Lee one fourth $ 509.85
To Cyrus E Finley one fourth   509.85
To Ellen R Mahan one eighth   254.92
To Merrell F Finley one eighth   254.92
To Eliza Turley one eighth   254.92
To Martha Mahan one eighth   254.92

Cyrus did not leave a will, but his executor, Gilead Lee, husband of Cyrus's only surviving child, Eliza Jane, carefully defined the relationships of all heirs, as shown here.

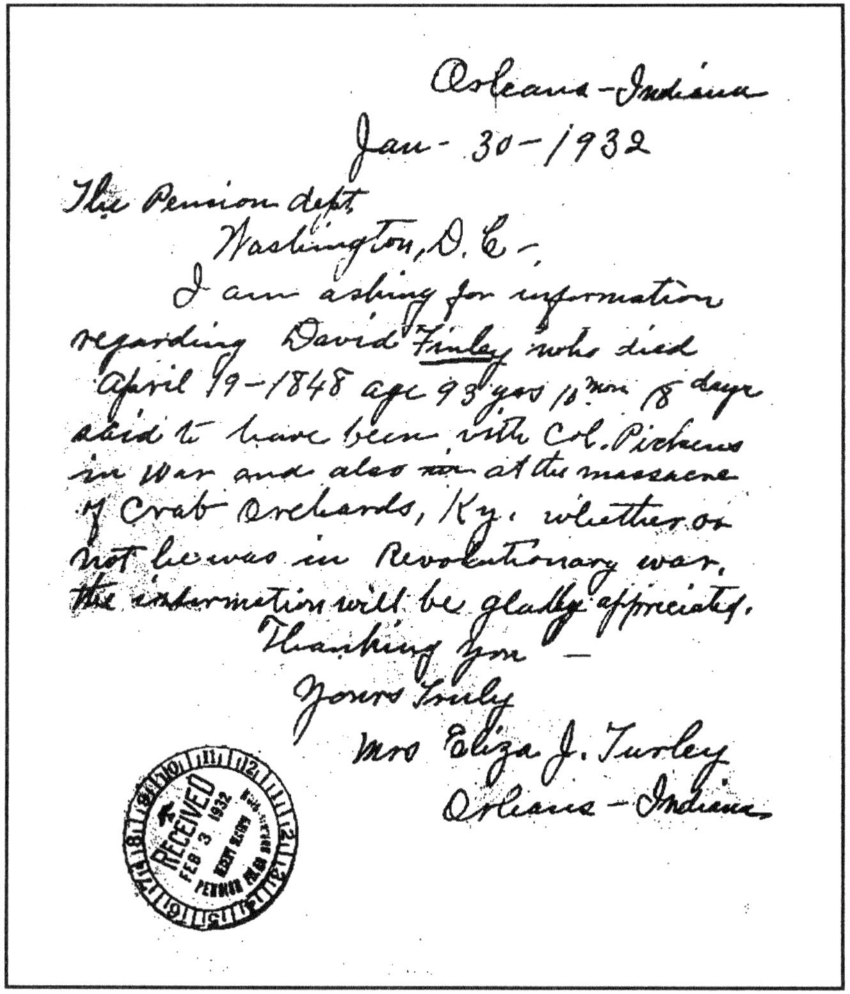

Orleans - Indiana
Jan - 30 - 1932

The Pension dept.
Washington, D.C.,

I am asking for information regarding David Finley who died April 19 - 1848 age 93 yrs 10 mon 18 days said to have been with Col. Pickens in War and also was at the massacre of Crab Orchards, Ky. whether or not he was in Revolutionary war, the information will be gladly appreciated.

Thanking you —
Yours Truly
Mrs Eliza J. Turley
Orleans - Indiana

Eliza Turley, one of Cyrus's grandchildren named as an heir, was apparently a family historian. This letter from Eliza, addressed to the Pension Department, Washington, D.C., was found misfiled under another David Finley in the National Archives' Revolutionary War Pension files.

Merrill, so when Cyrus died intestate, his son–in–law, Gilead P. Lee, was appointed executor.[219] Named in his settlement were Eliza J. Lee, daughter; Cyrus E. Finley, grandson, and son of Merrill Finley, deceased; Ellen R. Mahan and Merrill F. Finley, grandchildren, and children of David Finley, deceased; Eliza Turley and Martha Mahan, grandchildren, and children of James Finley, deceased. Known children of Cyrus and Rachel (Downey) Finley, all most likely born in Orange County, Indiana, include the following:[220]

67	i.	James[4] Finley, born 31 March 1820; married Amanda Johnson about 1847; died 11 January 1860,[221] buried at Green Hill Cemetery, Orleans. Their children included:[222]
		a. Eliza J. Finley, born about 8 June 1848; married Benjamin F. Turley, 19 March 1868 in Orange County;[223] died 16 February 1941.
		b. Martha Finley, born about 1853; married Worth Mahan, 13 January 1870 in Orange County.[224]
68	ii.	David Finley, born 24 August 1821; married Elizabeth Tegarden, daughter of John and Lucinda (Irvine) Tegarden, 30 September 1847;[225] died 19 July 1854, buried at Green Hill Cemetery, Orleans.[226] Their children, all born in Orange County, included:[227]
		a. Rachel E. Finley, born 21 November 1848[228] in Orange County; married John W. Mahan.[229]
		b. Lucinda E. Finley, born 10 October 1850; died 2 February 1855,[230] buried in Green Hill Cemetery, Orleans.
		c. Ellen R. Finley.[231]
		d. Merrill F. Finley, born 6 January 1853; died 27 August 1893/1896,[232] buried in Green Hill Cemetery, Orleans.
69	iii.	Merrill Finley, born 25 March 1827; married Sarah Marilda Wright, 4 January 1849;[233] died 28 July 1856, buried at Green Hill Cemetery, Orleans. Their children, all born in Orange County, included:[234]
		a. Cyrus E. Finley, born 25 October 1850; married Mary (Nannie) J. Monyhan, 27 March 1870 in Orange County.[235]
		b. Gilead E. Finley, born 18 December 1852; died 6 January 1865, buried in Green Hill Cemetery.
		c. Henry L. Finley, died 26 July 1856, buried in Green Hill Cemetery.
		d. Eliza J. Finley, born 5 February 1855; died 5 September 1856, buried in Green Hill Cemetery.
70	iv.	Eliza Jane Finley, married Gilead P. Lee, 16 September 1851.[236] Their children included:[237]

ROBERT MORTON COLLECTION

Gravemarker of Elizabeth (Finley) Sneed,

a. Sarah M. Lee.
b. Merrill S. Lee.
c. Carrie B. Lee.

13. Elizabeth[3] Finley, (David[2], John[1]) was born 8 February 1802, Garrard County, Kentucky, and died 25 September 1889 in Bloomington, McLean County, Illinois.[238] She married John Holman Sneed, son of John and Sarah (Johnson) Sneed, 2 September 1817, in Lancaster, Garrard County, Kentucky.[239]

Apparently, the Sneeds remained in Garrard County for a while after the Finleys had moved on to Indiana, for they are found there in the 1820 census.[240] However, on 28 June 1830, David and Elizabeth Finley, Elizabeth Sneed's parents, deeded twenty acres of their land in Orange County, Indiana, to the Sneeds.[241] The Sneeds are also listed in the 1830 census of Orange County as living near David and Elizabeth.[242]

The known children of Elizabeth (Finley) and John Sneed are:[243]

71	i.	John A.[4] Sneed, born 14 July 1818; died October 1818.
72	ii.	Harvey F. Sneed, born 26 September 1819; married Clarissa Kersey; died 15 April 1872.
73	iii.	Almira Sneed, born 8 January 1822; married S. Haley; died 4 November 1854.
74	iv.	Henry C. Sneed, born 26 May 1824; died 1863, buried at Ft. Snelling, Minneapolis, Minnesota.
75	v.	Benjamin Sneed, born 2 May 1826; married Elizabeth Boyd; died 27 June 1859.
76	vi.	Isabella H. Sneed, born 29 October 1828; married John Dunks; died April 1871.
77	vii.	John A. Sneed, born 10 December 1830; married Elizabeth Day; died 4 June 1877.
78	viii.	Sarah E. Sneed, born 10 January 1833; married Fletcher Wilson; died 2 October 1854.
79	ix.	James B. Sneed, born 10 March 1835; married (1) Julia Taylor in 1864, (2) Tamar Hawkins; died 30 May 1894.
80	x.	Mary J. Sneed, born 5 April 1837; married William McCoy; died 3 January 1899.
81	xi.	David F. Sneed, born 10 August 1839; married Alice Hebden; died 18 August 1891.
82	xii.	Nathan Sneed, born 25 May 1842; married Adelaide Cannon.
83	xiii.	Rufus Sneed, born 25 October 1844; married (1) Nohi Lechene, (2) Fannie Fridley.

14. **Jefferson³ Finley** (David², John¹), was born 16 May 1805,²⁴⁴ in Garrard County, Kentucky. He died 19 November 1829, probably in Orange County, Indiana.²⁴⁵ He married Miriam Brooks, 27 December 1825 in Orange County, Indiana.²⁴⁶ She was born 5 November 1803 in Kentucky, the daughter of John Clark and Hannah (Sharrow) Brooks and died 12 December 1848, probably in Orange County.²⁴⁷ After the death of Jefferson, Miriam married Andrew Tegarden in September 1832. He was born 15 March 1802, the son of Basil and Annie (Todd) Tegarden of Shelby County, Kentucky.²⁴⁸

Jefferson, David and Elizabeth's youngest child, died at the age of twenty-four, leaving three young children. David made these three grandchildren his major beneficiaries (see details above in discussion of David and Cyrus). Jefferson was the first person to be buried in the Finley Cemetery in Orleans, Orange County, Indiana. Although his wife, Miriam Brooks, remarried after his death, she is buried beside Jefferson in the Finley Cemetery. The children of Jefferson and Miriam (Brooks) Finley are:

+84	i.	Josephine⁴ Finley, born 20 January 1827²⁴⁹ probably in Orange County.
+85	ii.	Samuel Finley, born 10 July 1828²⁵⁰ in Orange County.²⁵¹
+86	iii.	Elizabeth F. Finley, born 10 April 1830²⁵² probably in Orange County.

15. **Reuben Jefferson³ Finley** (Thomas², John¹) was born 31 March 1783 in Montgomery County, Virginia, now Wythe County, the son of Thomas Finley and Catherine Kinder.²⁵³ He died on 9 August 1837 in Overton County, Tennessee.²⁵⁴ Reuben married Nancy (McCully) King in Hawkins County, Tennessee, on 7 May 1807.²⁵⁵

Reuben was reared by his mother and Andrew Swallow, whom she married in the spring of 1785. Swallow saw Revolutionary War service, both in Pennsylvania where he was born, and in North Carolina and Virginia, after his move to Montgomery County, around 1780. After Catherine Kinder and Andrew Swallow were married, the family moved to North Carolina and then to Overton County, Tennessee. He was living in Overton County in September 1832 when he made application for a pension. In those papers, Reuben is listed as the oldest child. They stated his birth date as 2 March 1783, somewhat at variance with existing Bible records.²⁵⁶

In November 1814, Reuben was drafted in Hawkins County for the War of 1812, and was discharged at Knoxville, 14 May 1815. He was a sergeant under Captain Slaten in a Regiment commanded by Colonel Baley of General Colter's Brigade.²⁵⁷ Sometime between the birth of daughter Rhoda in September 1818 and the birth of daughter Polly in January 1821, the family moved to Overton County. Reuben obtained land grants in Overton County between 1825 and 1839 totalling 250 acres.²⁵⁸

After the death of Reuben's father, Thomas, in December 1831, Alexander Hunter, executor of the estate, apparently tried to locate Reuben. A letter written by Hunter, dated 19 June 1833, explained he had made inquiries of the deceased's brother in Kentucky, to no avail. However, word apparently did reach Reuben for he wrote to the Ordinary at Abbeville Courthouse to make his whereabouts known. Hunter invited Reuben to visit his stepmother, Jane (Clark) Finley, in Abbeville, and expressed the opinion that she might be willing to give him some of her property before her death. "She has more property than is really useful to her at present. She sometimes adressed a desire that youd move here & live near her."[259] Whether Reuben made this visit is unknown. However, Reuben never saw any of the property his father left him for he died soon after, on 9 August 1837, at the age of fifty–four,[260] and Thomas's widow, Jane (Clark) Finley, was still living at that time. The confusion that ensued is continued in the section on Reuben's son Thomas Milton Finley. Nancy lived for some years after Reuben's death , and on 16 August 1852, she made a deposition for the purpose of claiming bounty land to which she was entitled for his service in the War of 1812.[261] She received a warrant for eighty acres. When a new act of Congress was passed in March 1855, she reapplied for additional bounty land to which she might be entitled.[262] Thus she was still alive and still a widow on that date, 23 June 1855. The children of Reuben Jefferson and Nancy (McCulley, King) Finley were:[263]

+87   i.   Thomas Milton[4] Finley, born 16 November 1808, Hawkins County, Tennessee.

88   ii.   Isaac Newton Finley, born 6 June 1811, Hawkins County, Tennessee; married Elizabeth Conaster, 25 December 1835, Overton County, Tennessee; died 30 August 1890, Overton County.

89   iii.   William Orville Finley, born 16 January 1814, Hawkins County; died 1 November 1832, Overton County.

90   iv.   Granville Huston Finley was born 16 June 1816 in Hawkins County, Tennessee.[264] On 3 April 1851 he married Mary Maxey in Jackson County, Tennessee.[265] At some time after the death of his brother Thomas Milton, he continued the quest for the family legacy, and just prior to his marriage, 4 March 1851, he received a letter from Alexander Hunter urging him to get everything in order so that the estate could be settled.[266] Finally, on 15 May 1851, Granville received a letter from Hunter instructing him to bring papers to meet with the Court of Equity the second Monday in June.[267] Final settlement is not apparent from the existing records. Granville was a doctor and served the Confederate cause during the Civil War.[268] He died September 1862.[269]

91   v.   Rhoda Finley, born 15 September 1818, Hawkins County, Tennessee; married Robert Oakley, 4 January 1838, Overton County; died 21 February 1890, Overton County.

92   vi.   Mary Ann (Polly) Finley, born 29 January 1821, Overton County; married Ahi Deck, 2 April 1846, Overton County.

93   vii.   Jane (King or Katherine) Finley, born 18 February 1823, Overton County; married William Walker; died 19 September 1891 possibly in Arkansas.

94   viii.   Reuben Jefferson Finley, born 2 May 1826, Overton County; married Henrieta Lora Walker, 2 June 1846. He was a Confederate soldier in the Civil War. He

		was shot by three Yankee bushwackers and died 26 January 1865, Overton County.
95	ix.	Nancy Ann Finley, born 5 March 1833, Overton County; died 29 September 1849, Overton County.

GENERATION FOUR

27. John[4] Fin(d)ley (Edmund[3], David[2], John[1]) was probably the eldest son of Edmund and Catherine Finley. He was born about 1810 in Tennessee.[270] He married his first cousin Mahala Finley, daughter of Samuel, on 25 December 1831[271] probably in Orange County, Indiana. He married, second, Sarah Masters, on 22 March 1840 in Jackson County, Missouri.[272] He married, third, Elizabeth Finley, youngest sister of Mahala, his first wife.[273] John died 7 August 1871 in Tulare County, California, the result of a gunshot wound.[274]

John and Mahala moved on to Decatur, Macon County, Illinois, about the time Mahala's father, Samuel, and her younger siblings went there, or shortly thereafter. At least, John and Mahala, are prominent in the court cases of Macon County when it came time to settle Samuel's estate in 1836. On 29 August 1836, John and Mahala petitioned the court for the division of Samuel's property.[275] There was also a John Finley who was an administrator of the estate of Daniel Porter, with inventory made 17 March 1836,[276] as well as a number of court cases involving a John Finley, during this general time period.[277] However, they were gone before March 1840, since Jacob Black made a statement to the effect that "John Finley and Mahala his wife (formerly Mahala Finley), Jefferson Finley, and James Finley, heirs of Samuel Finley, dec'd, of the County of Macon are not residents of this state but reside in the State of Missouri."[278] Mahala disappeared from the records about this time when John married Sarah Masters.

John Findley, 1810-1871

MICHELLE YAHNIAN COLLECTION

An exhaustive search was made to try to determine what happened to Mahala, to no avail. Ethel Work Balmer, granddaughter of John, claims Mahala died and that John and Mahala had nine children.[279] Since John and Mahala were married in December 1831, nine children would have been pushing the limits, unless there was at least one set of twins.[280] However, no supporting documents have, as yet, been found concerning Mahala's disappearance or any indication of children they may have had.

While there were eight John Fin(d)leys in the 1840 Missouri census index, there was only one whose profile seemed to satisfy what was known about this John Finley. He was in Boone Township, Van Buren County, in the general neighborhood of Edmund and his son David.[281] However, the oldest female in the household was fifteen to twenty, and Sarah would have been about twenty-four years old. Also living in the household were three males twenty to thirty, one female under five and one female five to ten. The males could easily be accounted for as being John himself, born about 1810, and Mahala's two younger brothers, Jefferson, born 1818, and James, born 1821.

Jefferson had married Frances Foe on 1 February 1838 in Macon County, Illinois.[282] While her birth date is not known, she would need to be only two or three years younger than Jefferson to be in the age category fifteen to twenty. It is, of course, possible this is not the John Finley of interest.

John and Sarah were found in Hunt County in 1850, not far from Jesse and Rachel (Colglazure) Finley.[283] They had five children, ranging in age from two to nine. Birthplace of the three oldest children was given as Arkansas, placing the family there for about the period 1841 to 1846. However, a part of northern Texas extending to the Sabine River and the headwaters of the Trinity River was once claimed by Arkansas. This area of Texas was formerly Miller County, Arkansas. The boundary dispute was not settled until 1838 when the lands south of the Red River were assigned to Texas.[284] According to a published biography of William J. Findley, son of John and Sarah, he was born along the Sabine River 22 February 1851.[285] In addition, John's uncle Jesse Finley, was also placed on Lake Fork Creek of the Sabine River by a survey done in June 1850.[286] That, coupled with the fact that Hunt County was formed in 1846 from Fannin and Nacogdoches Counties, makes one wonder if John and Sarah really moved or whether they were just living within the disputed area.

Also living in their household in 1850 was Elizabeth Finley, age twenty-one, Mahala's youngest sister, who was destined to be John's third wife. It is not known precisely when John and Sarah parted, nor when John and Elizabeth married. However, John and Sarah's son William was born 22 February 1851,[287] and a daughter Mary was born about 1852,[288] while John and Elizabeth's first son, David, was born about 1855/1856. According to the 1860 census, David was born in Texas, but the 1870 census gives his place of birth as Arkansas.[289] This also lends credence to the theory that the Finleys were living within the disputed area. By 1860, both John and his new family, and Sarah and her family, were living near each other in Los Angeles County, California.[290] John's daughter Julia Ann, by Sarah, then about sixteen, had married Moses Hart and they were also living close to John and Elizabeth.[291] On 6 April 1865, John bought 700 acres in Drumm Valley, Tulare County, California.[292] It was about this time that John's surname consistently took on the spelling "Findley." By 1870, John and Elizabeth had five children, ranging in age from one to fourteen.[293] The next year, on 7 August 1871, John was shot and killed.[294] There are extensive records in Tulare County for John Fin(d)ley both in Probate Court and in a local history.[295] A synopsis follows:

On 10 August 1871, the Visalia Weekly Delta, carried the following:[296]

HORRIBLE MURDER

We understand that Mr. John Findley, an old resident and a well known citizen, was murdered at his residence on Monday evening last. The old man was at home, in bed, when, just as the moon was rising, he heard someone call for him in the direction of the dooryard fence. He arose and went to the fence, some three rods from the door, when two men came up out of the creek bed, from the other side, and when within a few feet, one of them discharged what seems to have been a double-barreled shotgun in Mr. Findley's head, and leaving the brains scattered about the dooryard. Whatever of clues there may be to this fiendish act, is a matter that we feel bound to forebear discussing for the present.

The Tulare County Coroner moved very quickly. A jury of six persons[297] was assembled on 9 August and statements were obtained from John's widow, Elizabeth, and their oldest daughter, Catherine.[298] Elizabeth testified that on the night her husband was killed she heard him talking to someone about a sick horse. She asked who it was and John replied that he talked like Thomas Woody. Elizabeth heard the voice and stated she believed it to be Tom Woody. She heard her husband ask who else was present and the answer was "A boy." She heard two gunshots and ran out to find her husband deceased. Catherine's testimony included the following:

> That on the night of the 7th inst. I woke up and heard mother inquiring of father who he was talking to; he said the person talked mighty like Tom Woody. I heard father say, you talk mighty like Tom Woody. You are not allowed over here. The man said, yes sir. I saw two persons on horseback close up to the fence; they looked like well-grown men; father asked them where they come from; one of them said from the Old Mill Road; father asked them how they got off the Old Mill Road in here; the man did not answer this last question . . . Immediately after the last question and answer, there were two gunshots fired, and father fell dead. I believe that I could tell whose voice it was that was talking with father. I am almost certain that it was Tom Woody.[299]

The coroner's jury stated:

> We, the undersigned jurors impaneled to hold an inquest upon the body of a man killed at John Findley's residence, find that the deceased is John Findley; that he is a native of the State of Tennessee and that he is 61 years old, and that he came to his death on the night of the 7th inst. at his own residence, by a gunshot or gunshots in the head of some person or persons unknown to this jury. We find the homicide was done with criminal intent.

A grand jury investigation followed and in the County Court of Tulare on 11 November 1871, Thomas Woody and George Reeves were accused and indicted for the murder of John Findley. The trial took place during 1872 and 1873. Woody entered a plea of not guilty, but was convicted of murder in the first degree and sentenced to death. The case was appealed; the jury returned a verdict of second degree murder, and Woody was sentenced to State Prison for twenty-five years. Reeves entered a plea of not guilty, and, on motion of the District Attorney, was discharged.

John had written his will 29 August 1868.[300] In it he excluded his children by his former marriage and left everything to Elizabeth and her children, justifying it by saying, "I have made and accumulated nearly all my present property by and with the assistance of my present wife." He also named Elizabeth executrix and guardian of the children. However, if she remarried, then she would lose her right to guardianship and another "proper administrator and guardian" should be appoined.

Settlement of his estate began on 4 September 1781 when Elizabeth made a statement in court as to his family. They included: "John Findly, Julia Ann Hart, Nancy Work, William Findly and Mary Hart, by his first wife." Her own children included David, fourteen; Catherine, eleven; Elizabeth, nine; Samuel, five; Harvey, two; and Jefferson, three months. On the same date, James Boyd signed a statement concerning the personal property of John. He left cattle, horses, hogs, and improvements on public lands, notes, accounts, debts, etc. Total

Gravestone of John Findley, Chrisman Ranch, Boyd's Grade, Tulare County, California.

value was set at about $14,401. However, a detailed inventory prepared two weeks later, set the value of the property at $22,941.18. About two months later, on 7 November, John Findley, half brother of Elizabeth's children, petitioned the court for a legal guardian to be appointed for the minor children. Interestingly, his petition states that "Samuel Findley of the County of Sonoma in this state is now busily engaged in collecting the money belonging to said infant children and as petitioner is informed and believe is sending the same out of this county beyond the jurisdiction of the court and think there is reason to fear the said infants will lose most if not all their property by reason thereof." In 1871, there were two Samuel Finleys listed in the Great Register of Sonoma County. One was Samuel Joseph, brother to Elizabeth. The other was Samuel

Emanuel, Elizabeth's nephew and son of her brother John.[301] Whichever Samuel was referred to in the petition, it appears to have been a family matter with Elizabeth's family interceding. Reason leads one to conclude that it was Elizabeth's brother Samuel, who went to her rescue. The petitioner urged that a resident of Tulare County be appointed guardian to Elizabeth's minor children. This included, in addition to himself, his brother William and his sister Mrs. William Work. On 23 November, Elizabeth petitioned the court as executrix saying:

> That said deceased and family at the time of his death resided in the foothills in Tulare County and so removed from School facilities that the education of said minor children had been greatly neglected. That in order to get said children to some place convenient to School she has been obliged to remove from her said home in the foothills and establish a residence elsewhere.

Because of the necessary expenses incurred, she further asked for $125 per month out of the proceeds of the estate due her and her children, until the final settlement of the estate. Her request was approved. Elizabeth filed the final account of her administration on 3 March 1873. At that time the total value of the estate was $23,291.18. She also stated that while she had been appointed both executrix and guardian of her minor children, more recently, and at her request, her brother John, of Sonoma County, had been duly appointed guardian by the Probate Court of Sonoma County on 10 February 1873. Meanwhile, in January 1872, Elizabeth bought 160 acres in Sonoma County near her brothers John and Samuel.[302] On 23 March 1873, Elizabeth married Franklin Hutchinson in Tulare

County.

Known children of John and Sarah (Masters) Findley include:[303]

96	i.	John[5] Finley, born about 1841 in Arkansas.[304] As eldest son of this family, it was he who tried to protect the interests of his full brothers and sisters in the petition mentioned in the preceding section.
97	ii.	Julia Ann Finley, born 18 December 1843[305] in Arkansas; married Moses Hart 15 July 1859;[306] died 21 January 1908, Kern County, California.[307] Moses Hart was born 1 December 1833 in Conway County, Arkansas, the son of Josiah Hart.[308]
98	iii.	Edmund Finley, born about 1846 in Arkansas.[309] Edmund is not listed as an heir of his father, so probably preceded him in death. In fact, he is not living with his mother in the 1860 census, so possibly died before that time.
99	iv.	Nancy Caroline Finley, born 13 May 1849 in Texas;[310] married Will Work in 1864;[311] died November 1923 in Mt. View, Fresno County, California.[312]
100	v.	Martha Finley, born about 1848 in Texas.[313] She is said to have died on the way from Texas to California, about 1857.[314]
+101	vi.	William J. Finley, born 22 February 1851, Sabine, Hunt County, Texas.[315]
102	vii.	Mary Finley, born about 1852.[316]

Children of John and Elizabeth (Finley) Findley include:[317]

103	i.	David[5] Finley, born about 1855/56.
104	ii.	Catherine M. Finley, born 1 October 1859, San Bernardino, California;[318] married William Alburtus Akers, 12 September 1874 at Squaw Valley, Fresno County,[319] California; died 4 December 1942 in Coalinga, Fresno County. Several pages of biographical material are given in Hull's *And Then There Were Three Thousand*. (See end notes for complete reference)
105	iii.	Elizabeth Finley, born about 1862 in California; married (1) Seaborn N. (Zebe) Lashley, 25 April 1876 in Centerville, Fresno County, California; (2) Frank Humphrey after March 1883.[320]
106	iv.	Samuel F. Finley, born about 1864 in California; married Emma Chambers.[321]
107	v.	Harvey Finley, born about 1869 probably in Drumm Valley, Tulare County, California. He married Minnie Hunsaker, daughter of George and Nancy Ann Hunsaker.[322]
108	vi.	Jefferson Finley, born June 1871, probably in Drumm Valley, Tulare County,

California. He was only two months old when his father died.

28. David[4] Finley (Edmund[3], David[2], John[1]) was born about 1815 in Missouri.[323] David was first found in the 1840 census in Van Buren County, Missouri, living next door to his parents. At that time there was one female, age twenty to thirty, and one female under five years living in his household.[324] David and Margaret A., his wife, sold property in Cass County in 1845 and 1848.[325] In 1850 they were found in Hopkins County living near Lewis and Lettecia Findley.[326] David and Margaret were founding members of the Harmony Presbyterian Church at Mt. Zion in 1849.[327] From the 1850 and 1860 census,[328] it is possible to partially construct their family.

Their children included:

109	i.	Rachel[5] Finley, born about 1838 in Missouri.
110	ii.	John Finley, born about 1842 in Missouri.
111	iii.	Katherine Finley, born about 1846 in Missouri.
112	iv.	Marlena Finley, born about 1851 in Texas; married John N. Harris in Hopkins County, 11 September 1868.
113	v.	Harvey Finley, born about 1853 in Texas.
114	vi.	Thomas Finley, born about 1855 in Texas.

29. Lewis[4] Finley (Edmund[3], David[2], John[1]) was born about 1825 in Missouri.[329] He married Leticia Wade, 13 April 1849 in Hopkins County, Texas. They were also founding members of the Harmony Presbyterian Church at Mt. Zion.[330] They were found in both the 1850 census of Hopkins County[331] and 1860 census in Hunt County.[332]

Known children include:

115	i.	Edmund[5] Finley, born about 1850 in Hopkins County, Texas.
116	ii.	Nancy Finley, born about 1852 in Texas.
117	iii.	Mary Ann Finley, born about 1855 in Texas.

31. Alvin[4] Finley (Samuel[3], David[2], John[1]) was born 9 October 1813 in Orange County, Indiana,[333] and married Hannah Black, 12 November 1835 in Macon County, Illinois.[334] He died in 1838 at about twenty-six years of age.[335] Alvin was the eldest son when his father died in September of 1835. As related above in his father's probate records, he had a somewhat stormy time settling his father's estate and providing for his underage siblings, before his own premature death. Further information on Alvin is fragmentary. Correspondence with the Macon County Circuit Court Clerk indicates a probate file exists for Alvin, but the file papers are missing.[336] Court abstracts also list, in June 1839, the case of *The President, Directors and Company of the State Bank of Illinois vs. Jacob Black, Jr.,*[337] *and Hannah Finley, Administrators for Hannah Finley and Mary Elisabeth Finley, heirs at law of Alvin Finley, deceased.*[338] From this, one would conclude that Alvin and Hannah (Black) Finley had one child:

118	i.	Mary Elisabeth[5] Finley, probably born

Nancy J. (Finley) Braden, 1816-1886

Nancy Caroline Braden, 1839-1855, eldest daughter of Nancy J. (Finley) Braden

Julia Ann Braden, 1848-1926 and Isaac McReynolds, 1838-?, wedding picture.

between 1836 and 1838, probably in Macon County, Illinois.

32. Nancy J.[4] Finley (Samuel[3], David[2], John[1]) was born 25 February 1816 in Orange County, Indiana.[339] She married George Marbern Braden, son of Irish immigrant, Samuel, and Nancy (Young) Braden,[340] 26 December 1833 in Decatur, Illinois.[341] Nancy and George appear in the 1840 census of Macon County with one son and one daughter under five years of age.[342] George died 15 November 1853.[343] Nancy moved to Sonoma County, California, near her younger brothers John and Samuel, and she married George G. Gager there 25 March 1860.[344] Nancy and George are found in the 1860 and 1870 census of Sonoma County living near Nancy's brothers John and Samuel.[345] Nancy died 15 September 1886 at The Dalles, Wasco County, Oregon.

Known children of Nancy J. Finley and George Braden all born in Decatur, Macon County, Illinois, include:[346]

119   i.   Samuel R.[5] Braden, born 25 January 1835. Lived in Duncans Mills, Sonoma County, California, where he served as constable from 1875 to 1879.

120   ii.   Nancy Caroline Braden, born 29 October

1839; married Francis Cunningham, Decatur, Macon County, Illinois, April 1855.

121 iii. William James Braden, born 27 April 1842; died 18 March 1884, Dufur, Wasco County, Oregon; buried Obarr plot, Odd Fellows' Cemetery, The Dalles, Wasco County, Oregon.

122 iv. Elizabeth P. Braden, born 14 December 1844; married John Parker, 10 December 1864; died 22 July 1890, Petaluma, Sonoma County, California.

123 v. Julia Ann Braden, born 20 August 1848; married Isaac McReynolds, 11 November 1864, Sonoma County, California.

124 vi. Almyra J. Braden, born 11 November 1851; married Thomas A. Barnett, February 1868, Sonoma County, California; died 7 November 1876.

35. John[4] Finley (Samuel[3], David[2], John[1]) was born 5 June 1823 in Orange County, Indiana.[347] He married Keziah Head, 5 September 1844; she was born 14 January 1828 in Tennessee.[348] Keziah died of tuberculosis 8 November 1903 in Graton, Sonoma County, California.[349] John died 29 November 1910 in Graton, Sonoma County.[350] They are buried at Spring Hill Cemetery, Sebastopol, Sonoma County.[351]

John and Keziah are one of the three early Sonoma County Finley families whose story is told in chapter 1.

Children of John and Keziah (Head) Finley include:[352]

+125 i. Samuel Emanuel[5] Finley, born 20 February 1846, Arkansas or Missouri.

126 ii. James William Finley, born 17 January 1848, Arkansas or Missouri; died 17 July 1850, probably in Bates County, Missouri.

+127 iii. John Jay Finley, born 30 May 1850, probably Bates County, Missouri.

+128 iv. Henry Head Finley, born 17 April 1852, probably Bates County, Missouri.

+129 v. Nancy Caroline Finley, born 4 May 1854, Irish Hill, Sonoma County, California.

+130 vi. Elizabeth Finetta Finley, born 11 January 1858, English Hill, Sonoma County, California.

+131 vii. James Preston Finley, born 18 January 1860, Bodega, Sonoma County, California.

132 viii. Marenda A. Finley, born 18 January 1860, Bodega; died 18 January 1860, Bodega.

+133 ix. Jefferson Davis Finley, born 10 July 1862, Bodega.

+134 x. Andrew Jackson Finley, born 21 July 1863, Bodega.

+135 xi. William David Finley, born 30 October 1866, Bodega.

136 xii. Martha E. Finley, born 31 October 1868, Bodega; died 11 November 1868, Bodega.

+137 xiii. Alvin Wesley Finley, born 18 August 1870, Bodega.

36. Samuel Joseph[4] Finley (Samuel[3], David[2], John[1]) was born 6 March 1826, in Orange County, Indiana.[353] He married Prudence Brians, daughter of Jackson Brians,[354] probably in the late 1840s.[355] She died probably in 1870. He married, after Prudence's death, Mrs. Maria Wilkes of Tulare County, California, 14 December 1871.[356] Samuel died 22 July 1876 in Guerneville, Sonoma County, the result of a gunshot wound.[357]

Samuel was about six years old when his mother died and the family moved to Decatur, Illinois, and only nine years old when his father died. After a series of adoptive parents in Decatur, as reported in the section on his father, he was adopted by his brother James, in Cass County, Missouri, in 1845.[358] In 1847, as soon as Samuel was of age, he claimed Federal land, thirty-three and one-fourth acres (Range 22, Township 39, Section 11) in Bates County, for which he paid $41.[359] It was probably about this time, or soon afterwards, that he married Prudence Brians. The first census in which they are found, 1860 in Sonoma County, California, gives the birthplace of their two oldest children, Martha, ten, and Washington, eight, as Missouri.[360] On 4 April 1850, they sold their property to Samuel's brother James, for $100.[361] According to a biographical sketch on his son the Honorable James Buchanan Finley, Samuel Joseph was attracted by the California gold rush of 1849. He traveled by way of the Panama Canal and engaged in mining for a short while. In 1851 he returned for his family and brought them across the plains via the Platte River.[362] They settled in Bodega, Sonoma County, in 1852, where they were found in both the 1860 and 1870 census living near brother John, and his family.[363] In 1861 Samuel was elected constable of Bodega Township.[364] There he raised his family, farmed, and raised stock,[365] except for a few years in Nevada, until Samuel met his untimely death 22 July 1876 in the streets of Guerneville at the hands of Hiram Epperly. This event gave Sam the dubious distinction of being the first homicide committed in Guerneville.

Local newspapers carried a number of conflicting reports of his shooting. One of the two most popular beliefs was that one of Sam's sons owed money to Hi Epperly, Sam's assailant; that Epperly "threatened to have notices printed all over the county about the young man not paying his bill."[366] The other theory was that the two men had exchanged hard words about a horse trade several days before the shooting.[367] The account of the actual shooting also varied from one report to another. *The Sonoma Democrat* printed the following:

> Sam Findley abused him [Epperly] with high words for spoiling the reputation of his young boy, and told him as soon as he was able he would pay him. On the evening of the killing, Epperly, while under the influence of liquor, hunted Findley all over town, and finally called him out of Rube Williams' saloon. Findley said he would be out as soon as he had finished his game of cards. Epperly then dared him to come out. He stepped out and told Epperly that he did not have anything, but he Epperly could shoot if he wanted to. Hi called out I have no pistol, and slipped up and fired the fatal shot which sent one of his fellow creatures to his grave. On demand of a citizen our brave constable, Tom Pippin, was afraid to arrest the guilty party, and only after repeated demands was prevailed upon to do so. After being shot, Findley pulled out a small pocket knife and ran after his assailant and cut him slightly in one or two places upon the breast.

Another account, from parties who claim to have witnessed

the difficulty, is that the parties had sharp words through the day about the matter in controversy, and that Findley dared Epperly to meet him halfway in the street; that Epperly advanced halfway and Findley then dared him to come all the way across, which he did, with a pistol in his hands. It is said that Findley then jumped at Epperly and attempted to knock his pistol arm up and at the same time cut him with his pocket knife. About this time the pistol fired; Findley stood a few seconds and fell dead at Epperly's feet, shot through the heart.[368]

James F. Oliver, Samuel's son-in-law, apparently was one of the concerned citizens who sought the arrest of Epperly, and not being satisfied with the local constabulary, sent for the Sonoma County sheriff. This clearly added more fuel to the fire for Sheriff Joseph Wright was called upon to justify his interference in what some considered the jurisdiction of the local Guerneville law enforcement group.[369] In the same issue, there was a response from T.U. Pippin, the Guerneville constable.[370] Before the matter was over, there appeared two more articles by James F. Oliver and an editorial that was signed simply, "JUSTICE."[371]

A somewhat different version of the story of how Sam Finley met his death is given by John Schubert in the *Journal of the Sonoma County Historical Society*. According to that source, trouble had been brewing between Epperly and Finley for several weeks over Sam's bar tab at Epperly's saloon and he did not want Sam in his bar. The day of the shooting, Sam had been drinking and playing "Pedro" at Williams's saloon across the street. Finley was being vocal about his problems and said he had "tried to get a fight out of him [Epperly], and told him he was too big a coward to fight." Sam, according to this source, " had a turbulent character, more so when under the influence of alcohol." Upon hearing this and other threats made during the day, Epperly went to Williams's saloon and said, "Wash Finley [Sam's son] stole my horse and Sam Finley is accessory to it." The owner of the saloon told Epperly his horse was "up on the range." Williams successfully convinced Epperly to leave. A short while later, Sam went looking for Epperly and the taunting between the two began again. Epperly had a pistol, Sam had a pocket knife—Sam lost.[372]

It is difficult to reconstruct the family of Samuel Joseph Finley. One article states, "Finley will be buried today at Pleasant Hill Cemetery by the side of his wife.[373] He leaves a family of seven children. Five days ago word came that the eldest son S.W. Finley had been found by the roadside in Tehama Co. with his neck broken by a fall from his horse."[374] In a biography of his son James Buchanan Finley, the following is stated, "Mrs. Finley, who died in Santa Rosa, was the mother of ten children, seven of whom are living. Those besides James B., are: Alvira, who is now Mrs. C.F. Richardson, of Tucson; Samuel W., who is engaged in freighting at Naco, Ariz.; George T., who is living at Lordsburg, N.M.; Alice, who is married to Arthur Oman, of Palestine, Tex.; John L., who is a mining engineer in Sonora, Mexico; and Martha, who is now the wife of James F. Oliver, of Helena, Mont."[375] The census records of 1860 and 1870 show the following household members with their ages and place of birth:

	1860[376]		1870[377]	
S.J. Finly	45	Ind.	45	Ind.
Prudence	40	Ind.	40	Ind.
Martha	10	Mo.		
Washington	8	Mo.		

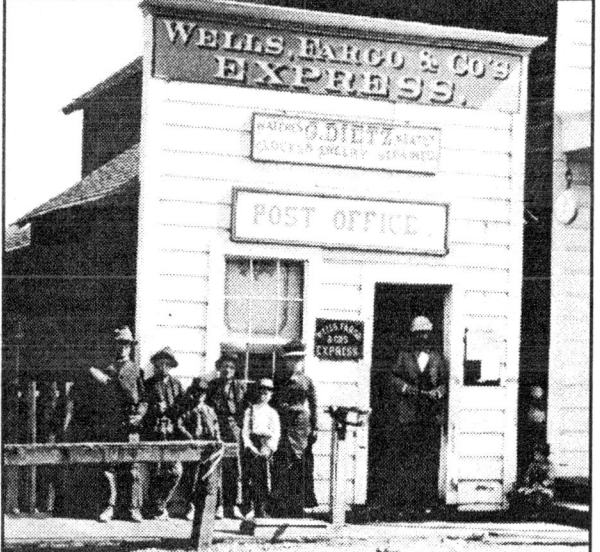

Guerneville, in the heart of Sonoma County's redwoods, was laid out in 1865 by George W. Guerne who built and ran the first sawmill in town. Still a lumber town, in 1875, here are a few scenes showing how Guerneville looked, just the year before Sam Finley was shot. Above is Hiram Epperly's Saloon, which belonged to Sam's assailant. Top right is the John Folks Hotel and right is the Wells Fargo Office.

PHOTOS BY JOSEPH P. DOWNING, COURTESY OF THE HEALDSBURG MUSEUM

Samuel W.		15	Cal.
James (B.)	6 Cal.	13	Cal.
Victoria	4 Cal.		
Elvira		12	Cal.
Nancy V.		6	Cal.
John L.		5	Nev.
Thomas		3	Nev.
Prudence		1	Nev.

Prudence preceded Samuel in death not long after the birth of her last child, Prudence. A marriage record was found in Tulare County for S.J. Findley of Sonoma County and Mrs. Maria Wilkes, 14 December 1871.[378] This was during the period when Samuel's youngest sister, Elizabeth, was settling her husband's estate after his death. Samuel was named in those probate records [see section on John[4] Fin(d)ley (Edmund[3], David[2], John[1])]. Note in the census records that none of the birth dates are what might be expected ten years later. In support of this obvious problem, in 1900 Elvira was found living in Pima County, the wife of Charles F. Richardson, and her birth date is given there as August 1862.[379] Also it would appear middle names may have been used in either 1860 or 1870. Is the George T. in the biography the same as Thomas in the census? Is the Alice in the biography, Prudence in the census? Clearly, these various records contain a great deal of misinformation. Considering these problems, here is a list of probable children of Samuel Joseph and Prudence (Brians) Finley:[380]

+138   i.   Martha[5] Finley, born about 1850 in Missouri.

139   ii.   Washington Finley, born about 1852; died July 1876 in Tehama County, California, in a fall from a horse.[381]

140   iii.   Samuel Washington Finley, born about 1855 in California.

+141   iv.   James Buchanan Finley, born 22 November 1856 in Sonoma County, California.[382]

142   v.   Victoria Finley, born about 1856 in Sonoma County; probably died before 1870.

143   vi.   Elvira Finley was born August 1862 in Sonoma County, California.[383] She married Charles F. Richardson of Tucson, Arizona, probably before 1880. Living with them in the 1900 census in Tucson was a daughter, Beryl, born January 1881 in California and a son, Charles F., born 1883 in New Mexico.

144   vii.   Nancy V. Finley, born about 1864 in Sonoma County, California. She is not mentioned as a living sibling to James Buchanan in his 1901 biographical sketch.

145   viii.   John Lee Finley, born about 1865 in Sonoma County, California. Listed in biography of brother James as a mining engineer in Sonora, Mexico, in 1901.

146   ix.   George (Thomas?) Finley, born about 1867 in Sonoma County, California. Listed in biography of brother James as living in Lordsburg, New Mexico, in

147 x. Prudence (Alice?) Finley, born about 1869. Married Arthur Oman, listed in biography of brother James as living in Palestine, Texas, in 1901.

37. Elizabeth[4] Finley (Samuel[3], David[2], John[1]) was born 13 April 1829 in Orange County, Indiana.[384] She married her first cousin John Fin(d)ley, son of Edmund and Catherine Finley, in the early 1850s.[385] After John's death in 1871, she married Franklin Hutchinson, 23 March 1873 in Tulare County, California.[386] Elizabeth died 17 March 1883 near Centerville, Fresno County.[387]

The youngest member of her family, Elizabeth was only three when her mother died and six when her father died. Her succession of adoptive parents after Decatur is less clear than that of her older brothers. Whether she ever lived in Missouri or not cannot be documented, however, it seems likely she did. Her first appearance is in the 1850 census of Hunt County, Texas, living in the home of her cousin John Finley, who had first been married to Elizabeth's oldest sister, Mahala.[388] John and his second wife, Sarah (Masters), then thirty-four, had five children ranging in age from two to nine years of age. Elizabeth was twenty-one. Some time between 1851 and 1856, cousin John and his second wife, Sarah, reached a parting of the ways, and John married Elizabeth. In 1860 John and Elizabeth were found living in Los Angeles County, California, with their two children aged five and one year; John's second wife, Sarah (Masters) Finley, was living nearby.[389] In 1870, John and Elizabeth were found living in Tulare County, California.[390] John was shot and killed 7 August 1871 by Tom Woody, a brother of his daughter-in-law Ellen Woody, who had married his son William, his youngest son by Sarah Masters.[391] Details are recorded in the probate records of Tulare County and are treated more extensively in the section on John Findley, above. In January 1872, Elizabeth bought 160 acres on Estero Americano in Sonoma County, near her brothers John and Samuel.[392] In November her brother John made application for the guardianship of her children[393] and he was appointed guardian in February 1873.[394] Shortly thereafter, Elizabeth married Franklin Hutchinson in Tulare County.[395] Less than three months later, Elizabeth and her new husband sold their Sonoma County property to John Finley.[396] Brother John officially continued as guardian for her children through February 1891, when the last entry was made in a large probate file.[397] The Hutchinsons lived in Squaw Valley, Fresno County.[398] Elizabeth died in 1883 shortly before her fifty-fourth birthday, at the ranch home of her daughter Elizabeth Lashley, near Centerville in Fresno County. She was buried at the Kings River Cemetery and Centerville Cemetery in Fresno County.[399] Children of Elizabeth and John Findley (Edmund[3], David[2], John[1]) are listed under his entry.

38. William[4] Finley (Jesse[3], David[2], John[1]) was born 6 March 1816,[400] in Indiana, probably Orange County or nearby. He married Elizabeth about 1841 and they were found living next door to Jesse and Rachel in Hunt County, Texas, in 1850.[401] They were clearly residents of Hunt County by 1846 since William was found on the Poll List for that year.[402] William died before 9 April 1855, when Elizabeth married Elias Dorris.[403]

Known children of William and Elizabeth Finley include:
148 i. Eliza C.[5] Finley, born about 1842 in Texas.

| 149 | ii. | Manna Finley, born about 1844 in Texas. |
| 150 | iii. | David M. Finley, born about 1848 in Texas; married Phoebe Hodges in Hopkins County, Texas, 23 September 1875.[404] |

39. Milton[4] Finley (Jesse[3], David[2], John[1]) was born 6 February 1818[405] in Indiana, probably Orange County or nearby. He was first found on public records in Hunt County, Texas, in 1846 when he appeared on the Poll List that year.[406] He married Orinda Davis in Hopkins County, 6 December 1847.[407] Milton was issued a certificate for 640 acres in the Mercer Colony on 6 May 1850.[408] They are listed in the 1850 census in Hunt County[409] and in Hopkins County, Texas in 1860.[410] Milton and Orinda (Davis) Finley had the following children:

151	i.	Jesse[5] Finley, born about 1849 in Texas.
152	ii.	Philena Finley, born about 1852.
153	iii.	Polly Finley, born about 1860.
154	iv.	Aaron Finley, born about 1860.

40. David[4] Finley (Jesse[3], David[2], John[1]) was born 1 September 1819[411] in Orange County, Indiana. He married Margaret McDaniel about 1841.[412] She died about 1865 of small-pox, and David married Julia Hite of Tennessee the next year.[413] He died 17 October 1884 in Dunklin County, Missouri.[414]

According to one historian, David moved to Dunklin County, Missouri, about 1834.[415] Since he would have been only about fifteen years old, this implies that perhaps his parents, Jesse and Rachel, found in Stoddard County in 1840, lived in that part of the county that became Dunklin County in 1845.

David and Margaret were found in Dunklin County in the 1850 and 1860 census.[416] In 1860 David's father, Jesse, age sixty-nine, was living with them. According to one historian, Margaret and three of their four children died of smallpox about the close of the Civil War, the other child having died prior to this time.[417]

David and Margaret (McDaniel) Finley had the following children:[418]

155	i.	William[5] Finley, born about 1842 in Missouri; died about 1865.
156	ii.	Moses Finley, born about 1844 in Missouri; died about 1865.
157	iii.	Jesse Finley, born about 1846 in Missouri; died February 1860.
158	iv.	Eliza Finley, born about 1848 in Missouri; died about 1865.

David and Julia (Hite) Finley had the following children:[419]

| 159 | i. | David Edwin[5] Finley, born about 1868 in Missouri. |
| 160 | ii. | Ellen Finley, born after June 1870, probably in Missouri. |

42. Elizabeth Ellen[4] Finley (Jesse[3], David[2], John[1]) was born 10 March 1823[420] in Indiana, probably Orange County or nearby. She married Merit Branom (Branum), born 18 February 1820, New Madrid County, Missouri, on 1 December 1842.[421] He died 24 January 1900, Cumby, Hopkins County, Texas. She was a founding member of the Harmony Presbyterian Church at Mt. Zion. Elizabeth Ellen died 14 March 1904 and is buried with her

husband in Cumby Cemetery, Hopkins County.[422] Elizabeth Ellen (Finley) and Merit Branom had the following children, all born in Hopkins County:[423]

161   i.   Mary (Polly) Ann[5] Branom, born 17 August 1843; married 18 October 1861, William Wesley Young;[424] died 15 July 1915, Oakland Community, Hopkins County, Texas.[425]

162   ii.   William J. Branom, born 7 November 1844; married (1) Nancy A. Chaffin, 27 July 1865,[426] (2) Sarah Francis Griffith; died 8 October 1935 in Hopkins County.[427]

163   iii.   Rachel Elizabeth Branom, born 29 October 1846; married Dr. J.E. McFarlin on 12 August 1875;[428] died 14 October 1900, Cumby, Hopkins County.

164   iv.   Albert Branom, born 30 January 1848; married (1) Sarah M.E. Ward 16 December 1874,[429] (2) Belle Kennemer Weaver; died 2 May 1938, Cumby, Hopkins County.

165   v.   Joseph Harvey Branom, born 17 June 1849; married Susan Thereda Butler on 27 February 1879;[430] died 19 June 1929, Branom Community, Hopkins County.[431]

166   vi.   Julia Ann Branom, born 7 November 1850; married Henry E. Smith 15 May 1869;[432] died in Antlers, Pushmataha County, Oklahoma, 31 August 1940.[433]

167   vii.   Eliza Jane Branom, born 18 March 1852; married James R. Ingram 2 October 1887;[434] died 23 October 1945, Austin, Travis County, Texas.[435]

168   viii.   Victorine Branom, born 2 January 1854; married Norman A. Gillis 3 September 1874;[436] died 30 September 1910, Cumby, Hopkins County.

169   ix.   Tecumpseh C. Branom, born 13 December 1856; married Mattie Welch in Paul's Valley, Oklahoma; died 22 April 1935, Cumby, Hopkins County, Texas.[437]

170   x.   Milton Branom, born 13 December 1857; married Beulah Newell 27 April 1885;[438] died 16 December 1937, Cumby, Hopkins County.[439]

171   xi.   Malona Ellen Branom, born 5 January 1860; died 13 February 1905.

172   xii.   David Merit Branom, born 23 June 1862; married Mary Rue Moore 27 January 1898;[440] died 11 January 1930, Commerce, Hunt County, Texas.[441]

173   xiii.   Lucy Ardena Branom, born 29 June 1864; died 28 April 1946, Cumby, Hopkins County.

43. George W.[4] Finley (Jesse[3], David[2], John[1]) was born April 1825[442] in Indiana, probably Orange County or nearby. He married Jane (Jinny) Odell, daughter of Simon Odell, on 12 March 1848 in Greenville, Hunt County, Texas.[443] He was issued a certificate for 640 acres in Mercers Colony on 6 May 1850.[444] In the

1850 census, they were living next door to brother Milton.[445] George died intestate in October 1853 in Hunt County at the age of about twenty-eight. The petition to administer his estate is dated 10 October 1853; he left considerable property.[446]

George and Jane (Odell) Finley had one child:

174	i.	Elizabeth[5] Finley, born about 1848 in Texas.

44. Edmond[4] Finley, (Jesse[3], David[2], John[1]) was born 27 March 1827[447] in Indiana or Missouri.[448] He received a certificate for 320 acres in Mercers Colony, Texas, on 7 May 1850.[449] He served in the Texas 23rd Confederate Cavalry, Company I, from the later part of 1861 to April 1865.[450] Edmond married Mary (Polly) Ann Kerbo in Hunt County, Texas, about 1863.[451] In 1876, they obtained a land grant of 160 acres.[452] Edmond and Polly had nine children and lived out their lives in Hopkins County. Edmond died 4 November 1917[453] in Ruff, Hopkins County, and is buried beside his wife, who died 6 January 1921, in Pleasant Grove Cemetery, Hopkins County. Children of Edmond and Mary (Polly) Ann (Kerbo) include:[454]

175	i.	Mary Ellen[5] Finley, born 10 October 1864; married J.B. McDonald.
176	ii.	Joseph Jefferson Finley, born 14 April 1866 in Texas; married Easter Hill; died 21 September 1917.
177	iii.	Frances Elizabeth Finley, born 10 February 1869;[455] died 8 June 1941.
178	iv.	Laura Ann Finley, born 7 August 1870;[456]
		died 11 September 1943.
179	v.	Emma Ardena Finley, born 22 May 1872; died in infancy.
180	vi.	Lucy Lavenia Finley, born 24 February 1874 in Texas; married Edward Sampson Sloan 12 June 1892;[457] died 9 April 1947 and is buried at Pleasant Grove Cemetery, Hopkins County.
181	vii.	Nancy Ada Finley, born 10 August 1878, Hopkins County; married Chester Clyde Ross on 15 July 1911; died 14 November 1967 and is buried at Ridgeway Cemetery, Hopkins County.
182	viii.	David Merrit Finley, born 30 March 1880, Ruff, Hopkins County; married Mary Lillie Stewart, daughter of Edward M. and Martha A. (Burns) Stewart, 13 October 1907; died 8 June 1932 and is buried at Pleasant Grove Cemetery, Hopkins County.
183	ix.	James Otis Finley, born 26 July 1882; married Kate Johnson 23 June 1901 in Hopkins County;[458] died 1951.

45. Joseph Jefferson[4] Finley (Jesse[3], David[2], John[1]) was born 5 October 1829[459] in Missouri, probably Wayne County. He married Nancy Southerland, 5 February 1857 in Hopkins County, Texas.[460] Joseph Jefferson died of throat cancer 14 June 1899 in Sonoma County, California.[461]

Joseph Jefferson is first found in public records when he received a certificate for 320 acres in Mercers Colony near

Greenville, Hunt County, Texas, 7 May 1850.[462] He is also shown as a member of his parent's household that year.[463] A Jeff Finley is listed as a member of Company D, 13th Texas Cavalry which was organized at Greenville, Hunt County, in October 1861, under Captain J.G. Stevens, and was disbanded in 1864.[464] However, there is some question as to whether this is the same person as the Joseph Jefferson who was found in the 1860 census living in Bodega Township, Sonoma County, California,[465] near his cousins John and Samuel Finley, sons of Samuel. There is little doubt that the Joseph Jefferson Finley found in Sonoma County is the son of Jesse and Rachel (Colglazure) Finley. A book in the possession of descendants of Joseph's brother Edmond carries the following inscription:[466]

On 23 April 1866, he also served as a witness at a coroner's

> A. Present(ily?)
> By Joseph J. Finley
> Sonoma Co. California
> To his naim saik
> Joseph Jefferson Finley
> Hopkins Co
> Texas
> Oct the 19 1870
> Jo Finley

inquest, in Sonoma County.[467] A patent for fifty-eight and nineteen-hundredths acres is recorded for him in Sonoma County, Bodega Township, on 20 May 1872.[468] He sold this property on 18 April 1877[469] and bought property in Guerneville from T.J. Sutherland, possibly a brother-in-law, the next year.[470] The 1880 census showed Joseph Jefferson and his family living next door to the families of John Sutherland, age forty, and Thomas Sutherland, age forty-two, probably brothers of his wife, Nancy.[471] He lived the remainder of his life in Guerneville and a number of other land transactions are on the records there. In 1879, he approved a right-of-way to Sonoma County, beginning at Guerneville and running up Hulbert Canyon to a point known as Frances? Ridge on the land he owned.[472] On 17 March 1897, he sold a lot on the corner of Church and Main Streets in Guerneville to his three daughters; Sarah, then married to McClerry; Emma; and Ada for $450.[473] Today this is a prime location in downtown Guerneville. Joseph Jefferson appeared as a registered voter in Sonoma County from 1867[474] through 1898. His physical description, obtained from the Great Register of 1898, describes him as "5' 10", fair complexion, blue eyes, gray hair, right eye gone."[475]

Children of Joseph Jefferson and Nancy (Southerland) Finley include:[476]

184	i.	Mary E.[5] Finley, born about 1859.
185	ii.	Sarah J. Finley, born about 1862 probably in California; married McClerry.
186	iii.	Emma J. Finley, born about 1871 probably in California.
187	iv.	Ada V. Finley, born about 1875 probably in California.

84. Josephine[4] Finley (Jefferson[3], David[2], John[1]) was born 20 January 1827,[477] probably in Orange County, Indiana. She married James Fisher 20 January 1848,[478] shortly before the death of

her grandfather, David. When David's estate was settled in 1851, James Fisher received $887.90 on behalf of his wife.[479] Josephine died 29 March 1867 at the age of forty and is buried in Trimble Cemetery.[480] Josephine (Finley) and James Fisher had six children:[481]

188	i.	Miriam E.[5] Fisher, born about 1849.
189	ii.	Amanda Fisher, born about 1851.
190	iii.	John F. Fisher, born about 1854.
191	iv.	Lydia Fisher, born about 1857.
192	v.	Laura Fisher.
193	vi.	Clara J. Fisher.

85. Samuel[4] Finley (Jefferson[3], David[2], John[1]) was born 10 July 1828,[482] in Orange County, Indiana.[483] He married Elizabeth Elliott,[484] 7 December 1848,[485] five days before the death of his mother, Miriam (Brooks, Finley) Tegarden.[486] Elizabeth was born 5 March 1830 in Washington County, Indiana, daughter of Ludwell Elliott.[487]

Samuel's share of his grandfather David's estate, as one of three major heirs, was $887.90.[488] When the provisions of his grandfather David's will were settled in 1851, Samuel purchased, for $2,700, the entire 340 acre property David had owned.[489] He then deeded one-third of that property to Elizabeth Findley, presumably his sister, for $900.[490] All three transactions, Samuel's purchase, David's final settlement, and the sale to Elizabeth, took place on 27 August 1851. In 1889, Samuel and Elizabeth (Elliott) Finley sold the northwest quarter and part of the southwest quarter of their property to George W. Tegarden and the remaining part of the southwest quarter to two of their children Charles S. and Sarah J. Finley.[491]

According to one local historian, Samuel was a "Republican and a prominent and useful citizen."[492]

Samuel and Elizabeth (Elliott) Finley had ten children all born in Orange County:[493]

194	i.	Jefferson L.[5] Finley, born 25 April 1850.
195	ii.	Sarah J. Finley, born 11 February 1852.
196	iii.	William J. Finley, born 18 June 1854; married Eliza J. Edwards, 12 November 1872, Orange County.[494]
197	iv.	Susan Finley, born 27 January 1856; married William A. Hardman, 7 March 1886, Orange County.[495]
198	v.	Charles S. Finley, born 8 January 1858; married Mary J. Bishop, 26 December 1887;[496] died about 1936, buried in Orleans Cemetery.
199	vi.	Baby girl Finley, born 13 February 1860.
200	vii.	Preston T. Finley, born 25 March 1861.
201	viii.	Oliver P.M. Finley, born 24 October 1863.
202	ix.	Ulysses S.G. Finley, born 9 February 1868; died 17 May 1869, buried in Finley Cemetery, Orleans.
203	x.	Reed Finley, born 14 November 1869.

86. Elizabeth F.[4] Finley (Jefferson[3], David[2], John[1]) was born 10 April 1830,[497] probably in Orange County, Indiana. When her grandfather David's estate was settled in 1851, she received $887.90 and reinvested it immediately by purchasing one-third of his property from her brother Samuel.[498] She married William

R. Walker, 9 December 1853.[499] Elizabeth died 23 March 1882 at the age of fifty-one and is buried at Trimble Cemetery.[500]

Elizabeth (Finley) and William Walker had two children:[501]

204	i.	William H.[5] Walker.
205	ii.	Mary Walker.

87. **Thomas Milton[4] Finley** (Reuben Jefferson[3], Thomas[2], John[1]) was born 16 November 1808 in Hawkins County, Tennessee.[502] He married Lutecia Horne in Overton County, Tennessee, on 25 December 1832.[503] He died 30 September 1849 shortly before his forty-first birthday, in Overton County.[504]

After his father, Reuben, died in 1837, Thomas Milton took over the quest for property left to Reuben by his father. In a letter written to Thomas Milton by Jane (Clark) Finley, his step-grandmother, dated 20 December 1842, she refers to his having been in Abbeville. Apparently he had asked her if she wished to dispose of a part of her Negroes. Her answer was, "I believe not, they are much attached to me & would be exceeding loth to part [from?] me while I live, and as that by the course of nature cannot be long I think it my duty to gratify their wishes in that respect." She signs it, "I remain yours with affection till death."[505] In a letter from Alexander Hunter, executor, to Thomas Milton, dated 20 September 1845, he advises Thomas that the estate of Thomas, Sr., must remain undisturbed until after the death of Jane (Clark) Finley.[506] Scarcely a month later, on 26 November 1845, Jane Findley wrote her own will leaving nine Negroes to her sister Mary Mackey and her children; seven Negroes to her grandnephew, Thomas Findley Mitchell; and cash from sale of her estate also to Thomas Mitchell.[507] Three days later, she died.[508] Alexander Hunter immediately wrote Thomas Milton informing him of her death, saying, "there is no obstruction now in the way to prevent the heirs of Reubin Findley prosecuting their claims to the Estate of Thomas Findley decs'd."[509] If he knew of the will of Jane, he did not mention it. However, by March of 1846, Dr. Mitchell, presumably the grandnephew, had given written notice to Hunter not to disperse any funds and claiming his interest because of Jane's will. The matter was to be taken before the Abbeville Court of Equity, whose next meeting was the second Monday in June.[510] In May 1847, Thomas Milton petitioned the court in Abbeville concerning his interest in the estate of Thomas Finley. He listed himself as eldest son and administrator of Reuben Finley, deceased.[511] The estate was finally sold in February 1849 and Nancy Finley, Reuben's widow, received $25 from the estate in March 1849.[512] In September 1849, Thomas Milton Finley died in Overton County.[513] The story continues as brother Granville Huston takes up the pursuit of the legacy to his father, Reuben. (See Granville Huston Finley, under section on his father, Reuben Jefferson Finley (Thomas[2], John[1]).

Known children of Thomas Milton and Lutecia (Horne) Finley are:[514]

206	i.	Nancy J.[5] Finley, born 11 October 1833, Overton County, Tennessee; married Felix G. Osborne, 2 August 1872, Dallas County, Texas; died 12 August 1921, Dallas County, Texas.
207	ii.	Amanda M. Finley, born 11 April 1835,

		Overton County; married Jess Ramsey; died after 1908.
208	iii.	Reuben Oscar Finley born 11 April 1835, Overton County; died after 1878.
209	iv.	William Orville Finley, born 4 January 1837, Overton County; married Mary C. Alford, 22 February 1872; died 9 June 1895, Dallas County, Texas.
210	v.	Stephen Horne Finley, born 15 September 1838, Overton County; married Margaret L. Daniel, 23 April 1879, Dallas County, Texas; died 2 February 1912, Dallas County.
211	vi.	Sarah Ann Finley, born 25 January 1840; married James Carder, 20 September 1869; died 23 January 1924.
212	vii.	Lucy W. Finley, born 14 February 1842, Overton County; married Albert M. Roberts, Dallas County, Texas; died 20 October 1926, Dallas County.
213	viii.	Granville Houston Finley, born 8 February 1844, Overton County; married Fannie Daniel, 18 April 1875, Dallas County, Texas; died 21 March 1900, Buffalo Gap, Taylor County, Texas.

GENERATION FIVE[515]

101. William J.[5] Findley (John[4], Edmund[3], David[2], John[1]) was born 22 February 1851 near the Sabine River in Texas, probably in or near Hunt County. He married Ellen Louisa Woody 22 February 1869 at Sand Creek, now Orosi, Tulare County, California.[516] William died 15 November 1917 in Coalinga, Fresno County, and is buried at Smith Mt. Cemetery in Dinuba.[517]

When William was six or seven years old, he came with his family across the plains by ox team. According to one account, they had frequent trouble with the Indians.

The savages often attempted to stampede or run off their cattle, and even when they were driven away they managed to kill the animals. At times the emigrants, under protection of wagon stockades, fought long battles with their red-skinned foes, whose flintlock guns laid many a white man low. Ten of the party were killed by the Indians and Mr. Findley's sister Martha died on the way out.[518]

They first settled in Hackby Ford, Los Angeles County, where they started a cattle business, but moved shortly thereafter to Kern County.[519] It is not clear exactly where William spent the rest of his childhood, but presumably he lived with his mother, since his parents had divorced and his father was now raising another family. His father remarried before leaving Texas, but both families made the trip across country together. His father, John, relocated in Tulare County in 1865. It was only four year later that William, barely eighteen years old, married Ellen Woody in Tulare County. And it was only two and a half years later that Tom Woody, Ellen's brother, shot and killed John Findley, her father-in-law.

Little is known of the early life of William and Ellen Findley, but records do indicate they settled about 1907 on a homestead of 133 acres in Tulare County. A portion of this farm was planted in grain and the rest served as pasture land for livestock, which included both cattle and hogs.

The children of William and Ellen include:

+214 i. John Moses⁶ Findley, born 10 December 1871, Drumm Valley, Tulare County, California.

215 ii. William Jackson Findley, born 13 June 1874, Tulare County; married Ida (Gaster) Converse; died 16 August 1922.[520]

216 iii. Adeline Calla Findley, twin, born 10 December 1876, Tulare County; married Levi Dean; died 1946. Their children included:
   a. Forest Dean, born 1902; married Iola Lee in 1925; died 1945.
   b. Gilbert M.L. Dean; never married.

217 iv. Martha Alice Findley, twin, born 10 December 1876, Tulare County; married John Dean; died 1 September 1919. Their children included:
   a. Cleo D. Dean; married (1) Roland Weisner, (2) Richard Cruz.
   b. Maude Dean; married Wickland; no children.
   c. Jack M. Dean, born 26 August 1919; married Shizino (Judy) Mikami, 11 August 1957.
   d. Carl Dean.

William J. Findley, 1851-1917. William J. Findley's grave marker, Smith Mt. Cemetery, Tulare County.

+218 v. Ivan Walter Findley, born 9 September 1879, Sand Creek, Tulare County.

219 vi. Mary Elizabeth Findley, born 1882, Tulare County; married John Fred Kiner; died 1922. Their children included:
   a. Clarice E. Kiner, twin; married Charles Sumner.
   b. Elsie Kiner, twin; married (1) Clay Carr, (2) Bob Abbot.

c. Harold Kiner, never married.

d. Denzelle Kiner, married (1) Sonny Unisck, (2) John Mendes

e. Herman Kiner, married Inez Perviance.

220 vii. Lee Robert Findley, born 7 February 1883, Tulare County; married Minnie Robinson; died 8 September 1969. Their children included:

a. Melba Findley, born 1906.

b. Earl Frances Findley, born 19 May 1908, Orosi, Tulare County; married Rosemary Chorzas 11 January 1946.

c. Oswald Allen Findley, born 15 March 1910; married Dorothy Billingsly.

d. Kenneth Lee Findley, born 1912, Orosi; married Jessica.

e. Margarite Findley, born 1914, Orosi; married Lyn Dalstrum.

f. Cathel Findley, born 14 November 1915, Orosi; married Vearldeen Agnes Wirht.

221 viii. Muriel Rose Findley, born Tulare County; married (1) Smith, (2) Coleman.

222 ix. Ira Sylvester Findley, born 4 July 1887, Tulare County; married Doll Street; died 1 April 1966.

223 x. Nancy Jane (Daisy) Findley, born Tulare County; married (1) Tullie Daniels, (2)

Gordon Wilson.

125. Samuel Emanuel[5] Finley (John[4], Samuel[3], David[2], John[1]) was born 20 February 1846, probably in Bates County, Missouri; died 9 August 1917 in Petaluma, Sonoma County, California. He married Mary Jane Stanley, 2 August 1875. She was born 12 December 1855 and died 3 March 1934.[521] The eldest son of John and Keziah, Samuel was but six years old when the family made the trip by wagon train from Missouri to Sonoma County, California. He grew up on his parent's ranch near Bodega, helped with chores at home, and found jobs away when he was older. He was working in a sawmill in Gualala, Mendocino County, when he met and married Mary Jane Stanley. A few years earlier, on 20 August 1871, Sam's father had deeded him half of a 330 acre farm called the sheep ridge between Finley and Coleman Valley Creeks in Bodega.[522] Shortly after Sam and Mary Jane married, they decided to settle there. They lived on the west bank of Coleman Valley Creek and Sam worked in Joy Woods and other places, hauling logs with his oxen to local sawmills. Nettie McDonald, family historian, tells this story:[523]

In December 1895, Bodega County suffered one of the worst storms in its history. At Mary Jane and Sam's home a mudslide came down the hill and through the house. One of the children, little three-year-old Grace, was covered in the slide. She was miraculously saved with no ill-effects. They all moved to temporary quarters and very soon moved to Two Rock—a settlement near Petaluma, where Sam farmed and raised hay for market. When he retired, they moved into Petaluma.

Sam inherited two lots totalling 256.46 acres from the estate of his father in 1911.[524] After his own death, 9 August 1917, the 106-acre portion was sold to R.T. Kee for $2,000.[525] Mary Jane retained the remaining portion, 150.46 acres, until her death, 4 March 1934. This portion was bought in 1937 by Samuel's niece Ethel and her husband, George Pedrazzi.[526] Today it is held by a great-great-granddaughter of John and Keziah, Lorraine (Wilds) and her husband, Alfred Piazza, the only piece of the Finley estate still in the hands of descendants.

Their children included the following:

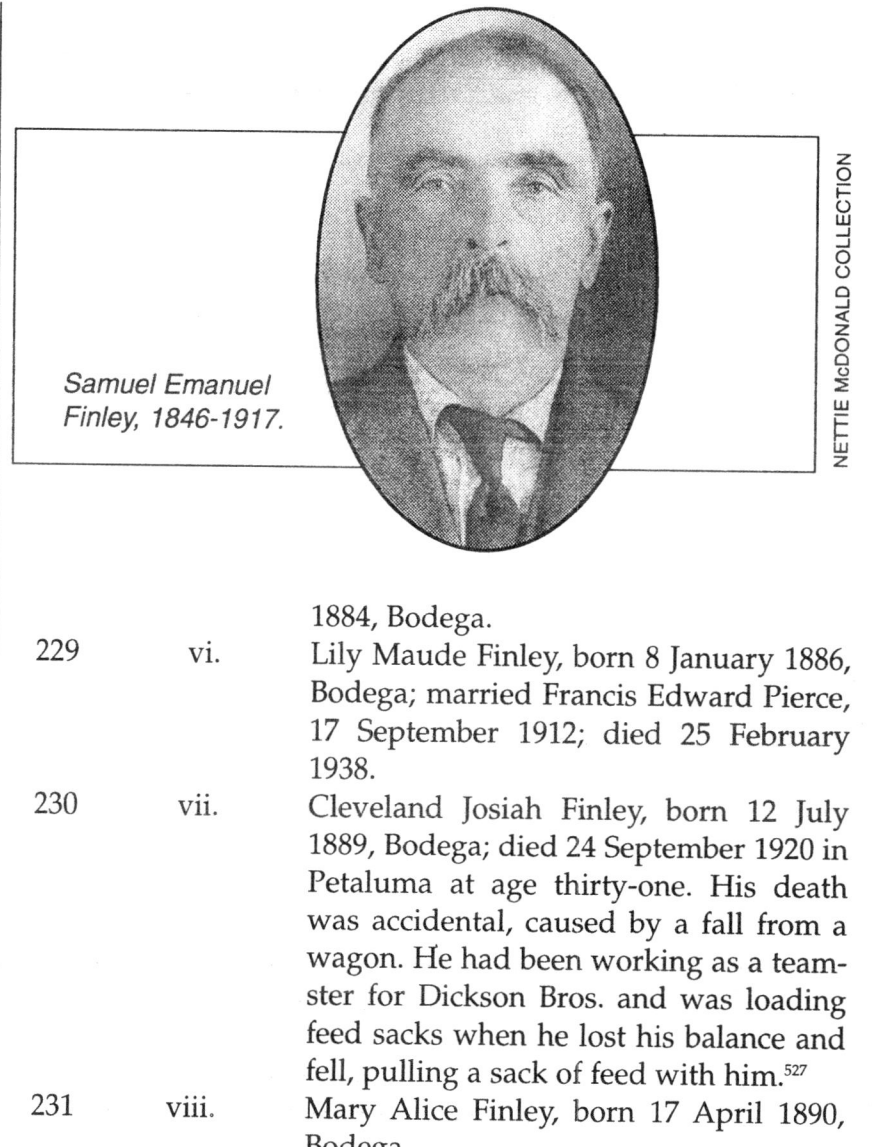

Samuel Emanuel Finley, 1846-1917.

224   i.   Eva Cential[6] Finley, born 4 July 1876, Bodega, Sonoma County, California; died August 1877, Bodega, buried at Spring Hill Cemetery.

225   ii.   James Franklin Finley, born 10 June 1878, Bodega; died 1959(?), Petaluma, Sonoma County, California, buried Petaluma Cemetery.

226   iii. Martha Elvira Finley, born 30 December 1880, Bodega; died 14 November 1928, Petaluma, buried Petaluma Cemetery.

227   iv.   Rollin Pierce Finley, born 9 October 1882, Bodega; married Mae Peacock, 25 June 1905; died 2 November 1963, Lakeside, San Diego County, California. They had at least one child, Alesia Vaneta, born 20 March 1910 in Freestone, Sonoma County, California.

+228   v.   Louis Emanuel Finley, born 7 February 1884, Bodega.

229   vi.   Lily Maude Finley, born 8 January 1886, Bodega; married Francis Edward Pierce, 17 September 1912; died 25 February 1938.

230   vii. Cleveland Josiah Finley, born 12 July 1889, Bodega; died 24 September 1920 in Petaluma at age thirty-one. His death was accidental, caused by a fall from a wagon. He had been working as a teamster for Dickson Bros. and was loading feed sacks when he lost his balance and fell, pulling a sack of feed with him.[527]

231   viii. Mary Alice Finley, born 17 April 1890, Bodega.

232   ix.   Grace Pearl Finley, born 12 February 1892, Bodega; died 7 November 1963, at her home, 310 Western Avenue, Petaluma. She is buried in Cypress Hill Memorial Park.

233   x.   Charles Wesley Finley, born 5 July 1894, Bodega; married Ira Kalen, 6 October 1936; died 2 February 1937.

234   xi.   Samuel Edward Finley, born 15 June 1896, Two Rock, Sonoma County; died 27 July 1896, Two Rock.

235   xii.   Willie Calvin Finley, born 15 June 1899, Two Rock.

127. John Jay[5] Finley (John[4], Samuel[3], David[2], John[1]) was born 30 May 1850, probably in Bates County, Missouri; died 19 March 1931, Bodega, Sonoma County, California; buried in Spring Hill Cemetery.[528] Nettie McDonald comments on John Jay:

John had a mental breakdown when he was still a young man and never fully recovered, though he was able to help with the work around the ranch. He was a very kind and gentle person and I remember him best for his concern for the safety of little children and animals—watching to see that they kept away from places where they could be hurt. He had his own place to live on the ranch, but he came to Nancy's and Henry's every day for his meals and they always looked after him.

128. Henry Head[5] Finley (John[4], Samuel[3], David[3], John[1]) was born 17 April 1852 in Bates County, Missouri and died 18 April 1918 in Graton, Sonoma County, California. Henry was an infant when his parents came by wagon train to California. He grew up on his parents' ranch near Bodega, went to school there, and worked with the family on the ranch.[529] As a young man he also worked in the nearby lumber mills, particularly Joy's Sawmill.

Henry never married, but after 1888 he made his home[530] on Coleman Valley Creek with his young widowed sister, Nancy, and her daughter, Clara. Also living with them were Clarence, Lulu, and Robertson (Rob) Head, children of another sister, Elizabeth Finetta (Nettie), who died the year before. They had a comfortable two-story home and ran the dairy, which was across the creek on the west bank. Henry also took outside jobs which included seasonal work for neighbors, work on the county road, and hauling lumber for Joy's Mill. Nettie McDonald adds:

Nancy's and Henry's home was a gathering place for all the family and friends. The long table in the dining room was stretched to seat a dozen or more at mealtime. They looked after their brother, John, who lived just down the road and he had his meals with them . . Nancy and Henry attended Shiloh Presbyterian Church in Bodega regularly and took part in all the church activities. Both had beautiful singing voices and sang in the choir. Family and friends gathered at their house after church for Sunday dinners and an afternoon of music and visiting.

Nettie also cites a letter written by Mrs. James McCaughey to her son Walter, dated 4 September 1892:

We held our church social yesterday (Saturday) at Finley's and had a nice time . . . It was something like a picnic . . . They had a nice croquet grounds and a large swing erected, also a hammock and all just before you go to Henry's house on the left on the other side of the creek in a lovely place under the trees.

They had every accommodation in the way of amusements. They carried the organ out and had nice exercises first. Then they had a delicious lunch and after that had games, races and all kinds of fun.

After the death of their mother, Keziah, in 1903, Nancy received the forty-eight acre fruit ranch in Graton. Together Henry and Nancy operated both it and the Coleman Valley Creek ranch, with help from the family. By 1915 Henry's health was failing, so his nephew Rob Head, and his family leased the Coleman Valley Creek ranch and ran it. Henry and Nancy divided their time between Coleman Valley and the fruit ranch.

Henry died at the fruit ranch on 18 April 1918. In his will, he left two-fifths of his Coleman Valley Creek property to Nancy and three-fifths to his brothers John, James, Jack, and Alvin.[531]

129. Nancy Caroline[5] Finley (John[4], Samuel[3], David[2], John[1]) was born 4 May 1854 at English Hill,[532] the first of John Finley's children to be born in Sonoma County.[533] She married Calvin Keithley, 3 February 1875 in Bodega. He died a year and a half later. Nancy lived to be ninety-nine years old; died 5 March 1953, and is buried in the Keithley lot at the Santa Rosa Rural Cemetery.[534]

Nancy grew up on her family's ranch and, along with her sister, Nettie, learned about housekeeping and homemaking. According to Nettie McDonald:

This included making almost everything the family needed in the way of clothing and bedding—preparing almost all the food they ate and helping to produce some of it. So they

Henry Head Finley, 1852-1918.

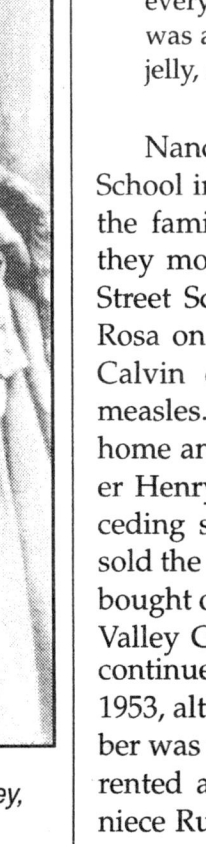

Nancy Caroline Finley, 1854-1953, and Calvin Harrison Keithley, 1848-1876, wedding picture.

learned how to sew their clothes; knit and crochet sweaters, socks, mittens, gloves, caps; to piece quilts and comforters; make mattresses and pillows from feathers and down plucked from the geese the family raised. They learned how to plant and tend a vegetable garden—the secret of raising turkeys and chickens—to make butter and cheese with the cream and milk from the dairy. In the summer they learned how to can fruit, make pickles, relishes, jams, and jellies. Blackberries grew in abundance all around the country and every one went berry picking. Fresh blackberry shortcake was a special treat, but plenty of the fruit also went into jam, jelly, and canning to store away for winter.

Nancy's husband, Calvin, had been a teacher at Potter School in Bodega, and they were married under the trees near the family home on Fay Creek. Shortly after their marriage, they moved to Santa Rosa where Calvin taught at the Davis Street School. Their only daughter, Clara, was born in Santa Rosa on 17 December 1875. The next year 6 September 1876, Calvin died from complications following a siege of the measles. Nancy and baby Clara moved back to her parents' home and lived with them until 1888 when she and her brother Henry set up housekeeping. Their story is told in the preceding sketch of Henry. After Henry's death in 1918, Nancy sold the fruit ranch to Oliver Winkler on 4 December 1920[535] and bought out her other brothers' remaining shares of the Coleman Valley Creek property where she and Henry had lived.[536] She continued to lease the property to Rob Head until her death in 1953, although the old homestead was torn down and the lumber was used to build a house on the ridge. In the 1920s, Nancy rented a house in Santa Rosa so that her grandchildren and niece Ruth Head (Rob's daughter), could live there while they went to high school. In her later years, she lived with her daughter, Clara, at Lone Pine Ranch, high up a mountain road between Santa Rosa and St. Helena. Her final years, when she needed nursing care, were spent in Stone's Rest Home on Davis Street in Santa Rosa.[537]

In 1948 Nancy, nearing ninety-four years of age, was featured in an article in the local newspaper for being the oldest native-born resident of Sonoma County—at least she was the oldest native-born white woman. A Wappo Indian woman named Mary Ely of East Windsor was nearing the century mark, but no one knew for sure just how old she was.[538]

The only child of Nancy Caroline (Finley) and Calvin Keithley was:

+236   i.   Clara C. Keithley, born 17 December 1875, Santa Rosa, Sonoma County, California.

130. **Elizabeth Finetta (Nettie)[5] Finley** (John[4], Samuel[3], David[2], John[1]) was born 11 January 1858 at English Hill, Sonoma County, California.[539] She married Albert Pike Head in Bodega, 12 December 1880, son of Robertson and Margaret Janetta (Thompson) Head. He was born 19 November 1858 in Byhalia, Marshall County, Mississippi and died 6 February 1935 in Bodega. She died 23 November 1887 in Santa Rosa, Sonoma County. Both are buried in the Santa Rosa Rural Cemetery.

Nettie learned all the homemaking skills along with her older sister, Nancy, the only two girls to survive in a family with eight brothers. Both the girls loved music, had lovely voices and played the organ. Nettie also enjoyed horseback riding.

Signatures of John Finley heirs are found in a deed of correction drawn up 13 May 1916.

She was preparing for a job as a dressmaker when she met and married Albert Head. The marriage took place at the home of her parents. The young couple lived for a while with Albert's parents on a sheep ranch in the hills near Santa Rosa, then rented a small place of their own with a vineyard. It was here their first child, Clarence Elmore, was born. For the next six years they moved about while Albert worked in the mills and took various seasonal jobs, some of which included working for Nettie's father on the Bodega dairy ranch. Two more children were born, Lulu Myrtle and Robertson Calvin. Nettie had never

Elizabeth Finetta Finley, 1858-1887, and Albert Pike Head, 1858?-1935, wedding picture. (above, left)
Clarence Elmore Head, 1881-1935, and May Lena Bruce, 1883-1959, wedding picture. (above, right) Clarence and May are the parents of
Nettie (Head) McDonald, who contributed heavily to the history of this branch of the Sonoma County Finleys.

been physically strong and had suffered from rheumatism even before her marriage. She died of intermittent fever on 6 November 1887, shortly before her thirtieth birthday. It was the death of Nettie that precipitated the alliance between her older brother, Henry, and her widowed sister, Nancy, to establish a household that could also care for Nettie's three young children.

The children of Elizabeth Finetta (Nettie) Finley and Albert Pike Head were the following:

237	i.	Clarence Elmore[6] Head, born 5 September 1881, Santa Rosa, Sonoma County, California; married May Lena Bruce, 26 March 1904; died 1 September 1935, Santa Rosa. May Lena was born 27 November 1883; died 6 April 1959. Both buried Evergreen Cemetery, Sebastopol, Sonoma County, California. They had one daugher, Nettie Mae Head, born 11 April 1906; died 19 February 1993, Sebastopol, Sonoma County, California.
238	ii.	Lulu Myrtle Head, born 30 December 1882, Santa Rosa; married Otis Edwin McKune, 12 September 1909; died 4 February 1955, Santa Rosa. Otis Edwin was born 10 January 1880; died 30 October 1969. Both buried Santa Rosa Oddfellows Cemetery.
239	iii.	Robertson Calvin Head, born 10 March 1887, Santa Rosa; married Lulu May Marsh, 23 November 1908; died 26 April 1970, Sebastopol; buried Evergreen Cemetery, Sebastopol. Lulu May was born 21 February 1887.

131. James Preston[6] Finley (John[4], Samuel[3], David[2], John[1]) was born 18 January 1860 in Bodega. He never married; he died 24 March 1934 in Bodega and is buried at Spring Hill Cemetery.[540]

Jim, as he was known, was one of twins. His sister Marenda A., died the same day they were born. As was the tradition, Jim went to school, helped his father and brothers on the ranch, and worked for other neighbors. When he was old enough, he also worked for the neighboring mills hauling out logs with teams of oxen. Eventually, he went back to the dairy and ranching business and, when his father died in 1910, he inherited eighty-four acres on Irish Hill. Jim was a music lover, played his "fiddle" for local dances, and joined in with the family entertainment at home. Among his favorite folk music was "The Irish Washer Woman" and "Turkey in the Straw."

A good deal of "land swapping" went on among the heirs of John Finley after his death. Jim's record of purchases and sales shows this fairly clearly. In 1915 he bought the 109.3 acre parcel on Salmon Creek from his brother Jeff,[541] and three years later he sold his original inheritance to R.T. Kee.[542] The next year, when his brother Henry died, he bought the 103.48 parcel from that estate.[543] This property had been inherited by the youngest brother, Alvin, who had sold it to Jeff, who had then sold it to Henry. A few months later, Jim added the 57.7 acre parcel that had been inherited by his brother John.[544] A few months later, on 24 February 1920, he purchased property near

NETTIE McDONALD COLLECTION

James Preston Finley, 1860-1934.

Bodega Bay.[545] The activity slowed down for a while, and then he sold his two larger parcels to D.M. Murray on 14 September 1929.[546] At this point he had just one parcel of 57.7 acres left, which he sold to his niece and her husband, Ethel (Finley) and George Pedrazzi, in 1931, retaining the right to use two acres for life.[547]

133. Jefferson Davis[6] Finley (John[4], Samuel[3], David[2], John[1]) was born 10 July 1862 in Bodega.[548] He married Caroline (Carrie) Anne McCready, daughter of Samuel and Jane (Boyd) McCready, on 30 July 1892 in Santa Rosa. Carrie was born 12 July 1871 in Bodega and died 22 May 1959 in Santa Rosa. They divorced sometime between 12 June 1914 and 29 March 1915.[549] Carrie married George D. McKinstry on 10 October 1916. Jeff died 26 January 1918 of pneumonia at the home of his daughter, Bessie Garloff, in Sonoma County, and is buried in Spring Hill Cemetery.

Little is known of Jeff's younger years but, presumably, he grew up on the ranch and participated in family activities and chores much as did his brothers and sisters. Jeff's inheritance from his father's estate was a parcel of 109.3 acres on Finley Creek. He also bought the parcel containing 103.48 acres which his younger brother, Alvin, had inherited[550] and then sold to his brother Henry three years later.[551] A few months later, in June 1915, he sold his original inheritance to his brother James.[552]

Jeff and Carrie had ten children:[553]

240	i.	Cecile Vienna[6] Finley, born 17 February 1894, Bodega; married Sam Hansen Sorensen, 4 August 1911, San Francisco. She celebrated her 100th birthday in 1994 at a Novato rest home, and died 12 February 1995. She had three daughters: Mae (Sorensen) Renati, Novato; Caroline (Sorensen) Fregulia Small, Petaluma; Edna (Sorensen) Durso, Vallejo.
241	ii.	Leora Martha? Finley, born 23 February 1895, Bodega; married William Matthews, 17 June 1915, Santa Rosa;[554] died 24 November 1972, Santa Rosa.[555] She had four other marriages: James H. Townsend, Andrew Elliot, James Lester, and Robert Linebaugh. Leora worked as a waitress and cook for many years and was a member of the Bartenders and Culinary Workers Union Local 770 in Santa Rosa. She had three children by her first husband: Florence (Matthews) Kneppler, Santa Rosa; George Matthews, Monterey; William Matthews, Phoenix.
242	iii.	Bessie Finley, born 9 June 1897, Bodega;

		married Walter W. Garloff, 24 May 1915, Sebastopol, Sonoma County;[556] died 17 January 1920, Richmond?, Contra Costa County, California.
243	iv.	Genevieve Finley, born 26 June 1898, Tomales, Marin County, California; married Henry R. Garloff, 24 May 1915, Sebastopol, Sonoma County;[557] died about 1974, Oakland?, Alameda County, California. Second husband Lineberg.
244	v.	Anita L. Finley, born 5 January 1900, Tomales, Marin County; married John W. Dei, 24 January 1916, Santa Rosa;[558] died 4 June 1963, Bodega. Both her marriage and death record refer to her as Annette. She died after a fire in her home which started possibly from a cigarette in her bedroom. She suffered second and third degree burns, and died of terminal bronchopneumonia at Sonoma County Hospital.[559]
245	vi.	Winfred Alberta Finley, born 26 July 1902, Bodega; died by drowning, 12 April 1917, Dixon, Solano County, California.
246	vii.	Henry Harrison Finley, born 18 December 1903, Bodega; died by drowning, 12 April 1917, Dixon, Solano County, California.
247	viii.	Lucille Harriett (Hattie) Finley, born 5 September 1905, Bodega; died 26 Feb-

Jefferson Davis Finley, 1862-1918, and Caroline Anne McCready, 1871-1959, wedding picture.

Potter School, built in 1873, and St. Teresa's Catholic Church, built in 1860, were two early landmarks of Bodega Corners. St. Teresa's still holds services. Potter School was first converted to an art gallery with living quarters above and later a restaurant was added. It is now a private residence.

ruary 1926, Santa Rosa; buried Evergreen Cemetery, Sebastopol. Never married; lived with her mother at 904 Beaver Street, Santa Rosa at time of death. She had been an office clerk at Cleveland Bros.; died of pulmonary tuberculosis.[560]

248   ix.   Lillian Eva Finley, born 19 May 1911, Santa Rosa; married (1) Ray Patterson, 31 December 1929; married (2) Carl Hodgson, September 1973.

249   x.   Albert Charles Finley, born 6 May 1912, Bodega; died 11 July 1936, Petaluma.

134. **Andrew Jackson**[5] Finley (John[4], Samuel[3], David[2], John[1]) was born 21 July 1863 in Bodega and died in Oakland, Alameda County, California on 28 May 1929.[561] He married Alfaretta Isadore Stemple, 27 April 1887, in Santa Rosa. She was born 21 January 1869 in Tomales, Marin County, California, the daughter of Henry Martin and Eliza Ann (Minear) Stemple. She died 17 July 1947 in Bodega. Both are buried in the Evergreen Cemetery in Sebastopol.

The tenth child of John and Keziah Finley, Andrew Jackson, was known to the family as "Jack." Like his brothers and sisters, he grew up on the homestead, went to local one-room schools, and worked on the family's dairy ranch. He was twenty-three when he married Alfaretta Stemple from the nearby community of Tomales. That was in 1887, and the next year, according to family tradition, they moved to Arizona where he worked on the railroad. His cousin James Buchanan Finley, son of his father's brother Samuel, had gone to work for Southern Pacific Railroad a few years earlier, and by 1888 he was working as a master repairman for the Tucson division between El Paso and Yuma.[562] It is assumed this was the tie that lured Jack to try his hand with the railroad. If they really did live in Arizona, it was only for a very short time since their first child, Leon Grover, was born in Orange County, California on 27 February 1888. Their second child, Vivian Gertrude, was also born there 24 January 1890.

In June of that same year, Jack and Alfaretta purchased twenty acres in Rancho Las Bolsas near Westminster, in what is now Orange County.[563] Curiously, the land was purchased from an S.J. Finley. While Jack had an uncle Samuel J. Finley, he was not still living in 1890. However, according to his biographical sketch, James Buchanan Finley had a brother named Samuel W. The possible relationship of the seller of the land to Jack and Alfaretta in not clear. The Finleys spent about four years in Southern California and during that time bought and sold two more pieces of property, all in township five.[564] The last piece of their property was sold in November 1892.

Jack and Alfaretta returned to the family homestead in Bodega for the next few years where their next two children, Ethel Agnes and Edward Leroy, were born. Then in the late 1890s, they moved to Weaverville, Trinity County, where Jack worked as a teamster, hauling provisions by covered wagon to the remote communities in the northern part of the state. Their last two children, Perry Elmo and Harold, were born in Trinity County. Finally, about 1902, the family moved back to the Bodega homestead and lived on the part of the ranch that bordered Fay Creek. Jack and his oldest son, Leon, now in his early teens, worked on the family dairy ranch and for neighboring dairy ranchers. Shortly before the death of his father, Jack built his home up on the sheep ridge. The sheep ridge is a 150.46 acre parcel of the original Finley homestead which Jack inherited from his father's estate in 1910.

Jack and Alfaretta continued to live the life they had mostly known, that of dairying and farming. Alfaretta helped by raising turkeys, pigeons, and guinea hens which she prepared for market in San Francisco. In 1928 they gave a ten-year lease to Jacob Smith of Healdsburg to erect a sawmill on one acre of their property.[565] The following year Jack died of a prostate obstruction [cancer?] at the age of sixty-five. His son Edward Leroy was appointed administrator of his estate. In addition to his real estate, Jack's personal property at the time of death consisted of fifty farm implements, thirteen cows, two horses, an automobile, seventeen shares of Central National Farm and

CARMEN J. FINLEY
COLLECTION

Andrew Jackson (Jack) Finley lived in Trinity County, California from about 1897 to 1902, where he hauled provisions to the remote communities in that area.

(clockwise from right) Andrew Jackson Finley, 1863-1929, and Alfaretta (Stemple) Finley, 1869-1947, about 1924.

Andrew (Jack) teaching granddaughter Carmen the finer points of dairy ranching, about 1929.

Andrew Jackson Finley family about 1903. Standing in back, left to right are Andrew (Jack), Vivian, Ethel, Leon (Leo), and Alfaretta; Edward (Roy) in front of his mother; infant Harold; and Perry sitting in front.

Andrew Jackson Finley, 1863-1929.

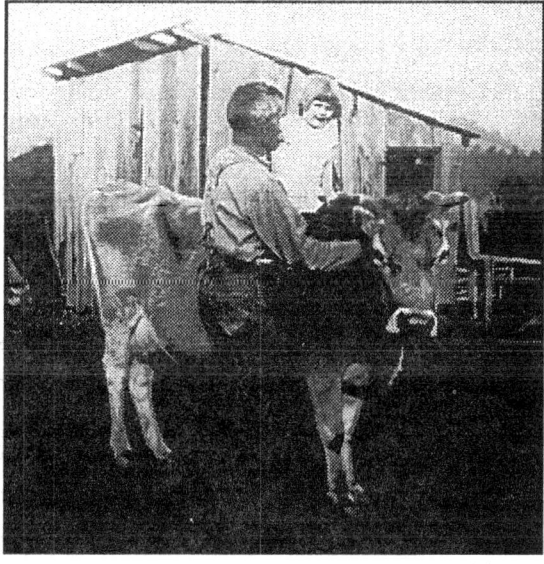

CARMEN J. FINLEY COLLECTION

Loan Association, two shares of stock in Verden Packing Company, and twenty shares of the Bodega Cooperative Creamery.

On 29 July 1930, Alfaretta married Henry Graff and moved to his poultry ranch in the Penngrove area. At that time she sold the sheep ridge property to her daughter Ethel and her husband, George Pedrazzi.[566] Within the recollections of this writer are a few memories of visits to Grandma Graff's new Penngrove home. She and Henry raised pigeons there, just as she had at the Bodega ranch, and she had a big feather bed where I slept on occasional overnight visits. Probably best of all, the Peterson chicken ranch was just across the road and they let me help when it was time to gather eggs! How long she remained with Henry Graff is a bit "fuzzy", but eventually she moved back to Santa Rosa, with frequent visits to the Bodega ranch to visit her daughter Ethel and husband. It was there she died of a heart attack in 1947 at the age of seventy-eight.

Their children included the following:

+250   i.   Leon Grover[6] Finley, born 27 February 1888, Westminster, Orange County, California.

+251   ii.   Vivian Gertrude Finley, born 24 January 1890, Westminster, Orange County, California.

+252   iii.   Ethel Agnes Finley, born 14 October 1893, Bodega, Sonoma County.

+253   iv.   Edward Leroy Finley, born 16 April 1896, Bodega, Sonoma County.

+254   v.   Perry Elmo Finley, born 28 October 1898,

255   vi.   Weaverville, Trinity County, California. Harold Finley, born 15 December 1901, Weaverville, Trinity County; died 16 January 1960, Santa Rosa, Sonoma County.

135. William David[5] Finley (John[4], Samuel[3], David[2], John[1]) was born 30 October 1866 in Bodega and died of an accidental gun shot wound 17 December 1890 at the age of twenty-three.[567] From a local newspaper:

Last Wednesday morning William Finley, son of John Finley of Bodega, accidentally shot and killed himself. He was leaving home for a hunt when his rifle was accidentally discharged, the ball entering his mouth and passing through his skull. He died soon afterward. The unfortunate man was 23 years of age.[568]

137. Alvin Wesley[5] Finley (John[4], Samuel[3], David[2], John[1]) was born 18 August 1870 in Bodega. He married Frances Gertrude Head, daughter of Robertson and Margaret Janetta (Thompson) Head, on 5 September 1901. She was born 13 May 1880 in Santa Rosa and died 4 March 1968 in Menlo Park, San Mateo County, California. Alvin died 27 November 1950 in Palo Alto, Santa Clara County, California.[569]

When his mother's health required a warmer climate, it was Alvin who accompanied Keziah to live for a period of time on an orange grove in the Santa Ana area of Southern California. Later Alvin attended Santa Rosa Business College, where he graduated as an accountant 30 November 1898. Soon after Alvin's marriage in 1901, his father bought the fruit ranch in

Graton where Alvin and his young bride lived with Keziah until her death in 1903. The main crop on the ranch was grapes, which Alvin sold to Asti Winery near Cloverdale. Their first child, Claude Thompson, was born in Graton in 1902. After Keziah's death, Alvin and Frances moved into Santa Rosa and ran the Waverly, a rooming house. He purchased this property in Benton's Addition in Santa Rosa from Josiah Kirkpatrick on 1 July 1904.[570] They soon moved to San Francisco and then to Point Richmond, where Alvin worked for Standard Oil Company. This is where they were living during the earthquake of 1906. The next year Alvin and his family moved to Ukiah, Mendocino County, where he worked at the Ukiah State Hospital and their second child, Florence Maurice, was born. Alvin and his family were still living in Ukiah when his father's estate was settled in 1911, and he inherited lot number four of the estate, 103.48 acres on the west side of Finley Creek. Alvin sold this property to his brother Jeff, and bought a dairy in Yam, now Atwater, Merced County. Here their third child, Madeline Bernice, was born. After the tragic drowning of young Florence, not yet three years old, they moved to Watsonville in 1913, where Alvin worked for Southern Pacific Railroad. He was later transferred to Santa Cruz, and then to San Jose, retiring in 1932. During the depression years Alvin and Frances, together with their youngest daughter, Madeline, and her family, combined households and moved to San Carlos. They later built a home in Palo Alto where they had a small orchard and lived there until Alvin's death in 1950.[571]

Their children included the following:

Alvin Wesley Finley, 1870-1950, and Frances Gertrude Head, 1880-1968, wedding picture.

256   i.   Claude Thompson[6] Finley, born 3 October 1902, Graton, Sonoma County; married Catharine Lorraine Gomez, 6 July 1920; died 7 March 1974, San Mateo County, California.

257   ii.   Florence Maurice Finley, born 2 November 1910, Ukiah, Mendocino County, California; died 30 August 1913, Merced

County, California.

258   iii.   Madeline Bernice Finley, born 11 July 1912, Winton, Merced County; married David Miner.

138. Martha[5] Finley (Samuel[5] Joseph[4], Samuel[3], David[2], John[1]) was born about 1850 in Missouri and came to Sonoma County, California, while still an infant. She married James F. Oliver about 1866.[572] According to census records, they moved from California to Nevada after the birth of their first child, where their second child was born about 1870. Their next three children were born in Missouri between 1872 and 1874; this apparently included one set of twins. They returned to California in time for the birth of the sixth child in 1876. It was Martha's husband, James, who took steps to bring Hi Epperly, her father's killer, to justice after the homicide in Guerneville. The Olivers appear in various mortgage records and promissory notes between September 1874 and May 1879, including foreclosures.[573] On 26 March 1880, James F. Oliver of Meadows Creek, Madison County, Montana, gave power-of-attorney to his uncle by marriage, Henry Finley, of Sonoma County.[574]

Known children of Martha (Finley) and James F. Oliver include:[575]

259   i.   Charles F.[6] Oliver, born about 1867 in California.

260   ii.   Mary E. Oliver, born June 1869 in Nevada.

261   iii.   John Oliver, born about 1872 in Missouri.

262   iv.   James Oliver, born about 1872 in Missouri.

James Buchanan Finley, 1856-1930

FROM ARIZONA TERRITORY, 1863-1912, A POLITICAL HISTORY

263   v.   Nellie Oliver, born about 1874 in Missouri.

264   vi.   William Oliver, born about 1876 in California.

265   vii.   Eva Oliver, born about 1878 in California.

141. James Buchanan[5] Finley (Samuel[5] Joseph[4], Samuel[3], David[2], John[1]) was born 22 November 1856 in Sonoma County, California.[576] About 1895 in Tucson, Arizona, he married Clara Letts. She was born March 1873 in Burlington, Iowa.[577] James Buchanan died 25 October 1930 and is buried at Forest Lawn Cemetery in Glendale, California.[578]

James Buchanan Finley grew up on his parents' ranch in Bodega and worked in local sawmills until he was twenty-one.

Shortly after the death of his father in 1876, he left the area. From 1877 until October 1882, he raised cattle and mined near Winnemucca, Nevada, then moved to Deming, Grant County, New Mexico. For several years he was a contractor and builder. Then he went to work for the Southern Pacific Railroad Company at Deming, as manager of the Pullman repair shop. He advanced through the company's Tucson repair division as foreman of the company's shops and master repairer for the Tucson Division, between El Paso and Yuma. He eventually became vice-president and general manager of Southern Pacific de Mexico. He retired 1 December 1925.[579] In 1896 he was elected to the Democratic ticket of the nineteenth legislative assembly, and in 1898 and 1900, to the territorial council of Arizona. During this time his opposition is said to have been largely responsible for the defeat of the women's suffrage bill. He also helped secure passage of the poll tax law.

James and Clara had only one known child:

266   i.   Clara Eva Finley.

GENERATION SIX

214. John Moses[6] Findley (William[5], John[4], Edmund[3], David[2], John[1]) was born in Drumm Valley, Tulare County, California, 10 December 1871. He married Martha J. Dean of Aukland, Tulare County, on 18 November 1896, in Visalia. John died 29 October 1931 and Martha died 26 March 1953. They are both buried in Smith Mountain Cemetery at Dinuba, Tulare County.

When John and Martha were first married, John was a farmer, raised cattle, and owned a small store in Drumm Valley. Before the depression years, the family moved into Orosi where John established a meat market, built a home, and grew grapes. During the depression they lost both their home and land. John and Martha made a new start in Visalia, where they had a small dairy.[580]

Their children included the following:

267   i.   Blanch B.[7] Findley, born 10 December 1897, Dunlap, Fresno County, California; married Frank Day, 24 December 1917 in Visalia.

268   ii.   Cecil M. Findley, born 9 April 1899, Aukland, Tulare County; married James D. Dean, 29 October 1917, Bakersfield, Kern County, California.

+269   iii.   Garold E. Findley, born 27 June 1905, Orosi, Tulare County.

270   iv.   Inez E. Findley, born 25 July 1907, Orosi, Tulare County; married Favel Runyon.

218. Ivan Walter[6] Findley (William[5], John[4], Edmund[3], David[2], John[1]) was born 9 September 1879 at Sand Creek, Tulare County, California. He married Susan M. Collier, daughter of Thomas and Amanda C. (Boyd) Collier on 10 August 1905. She was born 30 July 1882 in Tulare County and died 27 December 1945 in Visalia. Ivan died 8 March 1966 in Visalia. They are both buried in the Visalia Cemetery.

The life of Ivan and Susan is reflected through the recollections of their granddaughter, Michelle (Findley) Yahnian:[581]

Ivan Walter Findley, 1879-1966 and the Ivan Findley homestead, Tulare County.

They were good parents and grandparents. There was always someone—friends, family at their home. Everyone was always welcomed. They lived in a large two story home in the country. Everyone called them Dad and Mom. They attended church on Sundays and enjoyed going very much. My grandfather was a farmer and raised much of their own food. There was always a vegetable garden, fruit, and walnut trees, a blackberry patch, chickens, sheep, hogs, cows, grain, grapes. In the fall it would be time to get the animals ready to butcher. There was a large walnut tree in the side yard, where the animals to be killed were hung and ready to be put over the black iron pot to be scraped clean. There would be pickling done, curing hams, shoulders, chops, making of lard. The meat would then be hung to cure in the smokehouse. The black pot was also used for making soap, and on wash day for boiling the clothes. I can sit in my chair and see the black iron pot on the deck. Aunt Thelma had it for years and before she passed away she gave it to me and my sister. It really brings back memories (it must be 90 years old).

My grandfather loved going to Rodeos, and wore his brightest silk shirt when he went. I remember a really bright yellow one. He owned one race horse named Squaw. We also enjoyed going to Rodeos when we were small.

My grandmother had a lot of work to do, such as: canning, pickling, cooking, churned butter (we helped churn the butter), washing, ironing sewing, quilting. She had a quilting frame set up in the living room, and when she had spare time, she and her friends worked on quilts. In the summer we had water melons to eat. It was really fun, it was great when the cousins came to visit. In the winter taffy was made and pulled, it was so good.

Every May there was a Findley picnic at Mooney Grove Park. Everyone came and brought food, visited with all of the friends and family. I still have the tablets where everyone wrote their names.

Ivan and Susan had six children:

271	i.	Myrtle L.^{7} Findley, born 20 May 1906, Orosi; married Monte B. Hartline 11 October 1924, Hanford, Tulare County; died 14 April 1974, Visalia, and is buried in the cemetery there.
272	ii.	Aaron B. Findley, born 14 October 1907, Orosi; married Thelma Connelly, 10 November 1930, Visalia; died 30 October 1979.
+273	iii.	Byron F. Findley, born 1 November 1910, Drumm Valley, Tulare County.
274	iv.	Ruth Amanda Findley, born 21 November 1913, Sand Creek, Tulare County; married (1) Walter Ernest Massey, 8 October 1930, Hanford; (2) Erik Fresk. Children by her first marriage include:

    a. Marilyn Ruth Massey, born 4 October 1933, Visalia; married David Henry Boesch, 30 June 1950, Visalia.

    b. Marjorie Elaine Massey, born 20 March 1935, Visalia; married LaVoy Eugene Hughes, 30 October 1954, Tulare County.

275   v.   William Francis Findley, born 24 July 1916, Sand Creek; married Nan Cotton, 27 December 1936, Visalia. Their children include:

a.   Judith Lou Findley, born 5 March 1941, Bakersfield, Kern County, California.

b.   Kathleen Lea Findley, born 13 August 1945, Los Angeles.

c.   William Cotton Findley, born 5 March 1948, Los Angeles.

d.   Patrick Michael Findley, born January 1951, Los Angeles.

e.   Daniel Findley, born 6? March 1957?, Los Angeles.

276   vi.   Marian Ella Findley, born 5 September 1921, Visalia; married (1) 22 August 1941 Bruce Hardcastle, born 4 April 1920; divorced 28 August 1956; married (2) Basil Hudson Deceare. Children by her first marriage:

a.   Susan Ellen Hardcastle, born 5 September 1946, Visalia; married in Bakersfield, 16 October 1963, Joe Michael Batten, born 18 July 1945, son of Wesley and Dorothy (Freeze) Batten.

b.   Gregory Bruce Hardcastle, born 26 February 1948, Visalia; married Denise Jean Diffley, 12 September 1970, Barstow, San

Bernardino County, California. She was born 30 October 1948, Los Angeles, daughter of Joseph Lee and Florence (Doty) Diffley.

228. Louis Emanuel[6] Finley (Samuel Emanuel[5], John[4], Samuel[3], David[2], John[1]) was born 7 February 1884 in Bodega, Sonoma County, California. His early years were spent on the Finley homestead, his father's house being located on the sheep ridge between Finley and Coleman Valley Creeks. Following the mud slide of 1895, they moved to Two Rock, and then to Petaluma. Louie married Bessie Elizabeth Misselbrook, 24 April 1907, in Arcata, Humboldt County, California. She was born 15 April 1890, the daughter of William and Catherine (Brown) Misselbrook. They lived for a while at the site of his boyhood home in Bodega,[582] but moved to Eureka in Humboldt County after the birth of their third child. Louis died 25 April 1967 in Eureka. Bessie died 30 June 1969 in Eureka.

Their children included:

277   i.   Fred Louis[7] Finley, born 28 June 1908, Eureka, Humboldt County, California; died 1 March 1973.

278   ii.   Percy Edward Finley, born 31 October 1910, Petaluma, Sonoma County, California.

279   iii.   Irva Elizabeth Finley, born 27 March 1913, Bodega.

280   iv.   John Victor Finley, born 28 May 1915, Eureka; died 24 October 1956.

281	v.	Edith Mary Finley, born 25 May 1917, Eureka.
282	vi.	Earl Lester Finley, born 24 February 1919, Beatrice, Humboldt County, California.
283	vii.	Vivian May Finley, born 28 August 1923, Eureka.
284	viii.	Juanita Louise Finley, born 29 November 1931, Eureka.
285	ix.	Samuel Emanuel Finley, born 13 October 1934, Eureka.

236. Clara C.[6] Keithly (Nancy Caroline[5], John[4], Samuel[3], David[2], John[1]) was born 17 December 1875 in Santa Rosa, Sonoma County, California. She married Martin Tarwater 21 September 1905 at her grandparents' ranch in Graton. Martin was born 19 August 1876 and died 29 July 1948. Clara died 10 June 1973 in Santa Rosa at the age of ninety-seven.

Clara's father died before she was a year old, and her mother returned to live on the Finley homestead in Bodega. They lived with John and Keziah, Clara's grandparents, until 1888, when her Uncle Henry and her mother established a separate home on the property and took in her three cousins, Clarence, Lulu, and Robertson Head, whose mother had died the year before. When she was nineteen, Clara enrolled at McMean's Normal School in Santa Rosa, a teacher training institution. After graduation, she taught at the newly formed Joy School when it opened on 10 May 1901, where classes were held in a tent until the building was completed. The Joy School was located in the Bodega neighborhood and she taught there for two years.

Next, Clara taught at Tarwater School in the Mark West area north of Santa Rosa. While there, she met Martin Tarwater and they were married 21 September 1905 at her grandfather's fruit ranch near Graton. The newly married couple lived on the Tarwater Ranch in the hills east of Santa Rosa where they raised their family of five children.

Clara was a charter member of the Sonoma County Historical Society and wrote a number of articles for publication in their journal. She was the first real historian of this branch of the Finleys in Sonoma County. After the death of her husband, Martin, in 1948, she continued to live at the family ranch for some time. In later years she purchased a home in Santa Rosa at 1315 Olive Street. Clara died in 1973 at the age of ninety-seven years.

The children of Clara and Martin Tarwater included the following:

286	i.	Vernon Keith[7] Tarwater, born 19 December 1906; married Elizabeth Best, 15 April 1939.
287	ii.	Francis Calvin Tarwater, born 14 January 1909; married Mae Wallin, 2 March 1935. They had three children: Helen, Arlene Frances, Dolores.
288	iii.	Martin Raymond Tarwater, born 28 September 1910; died 5 September 1948.
289	iv.	Orville Glenn Tarwater, born 24 May 1913; married Ruth Burns, 18 February 1934.
290	v.	Marion Carroll Tarwater, born 27 March

Ethel Agnes Finley, 1893-1976.
DIANE STARKEY COLLECTION

Edward LeRoy Finley, 1896-1940.
CARMEN J. FINLEY COLLECTION

Perry Elmo Finley, 1898-1986.
CARMEN J. FINLEY COLLECTION

Leon Grover Finley, 1888-1919.
CARMEN J. FINLEY COLLECTION

Vivian Gertrude Finley, 1890-1973.
JACQUIE MARIE NAISH COLLECTION

1916; married Clarence Shaffer, 15 October 1934. They had three children: Jeanne (Shaffer) Purcell, Paradise; Judy (Shaffer) Trombetta, Bakersfield; Leonard Shaffer, Santa Rosa. Marion married (2) Glen Bessire, Healdsburg, California.

250. Leon Grover[6] Finley (Andrew Jackson[5], John[4], Samuel[3], David[2], John[1]) was born 27 February 1888 in Westminster, Orange County, California. He married Mary Elizabeth Kee, 3 October 1918 in Sonoma County.[583]

Leo, the eldest son of Jack and Alfaretta Finley, spent the first fourteen years of his life living with his family first in Southern California, then Bodega, then Trinity County. When the family finally settled on the old homestead in Bodega, he helped his father with the family dairy ranch and worked for neighboring dairy ranchers. Later he worked in the woods for Wade Sturgeon hauling lumber out of Coleman Valley. He married Mary Elizabeth Kee when he was thirty years old.

Leo died on 19 February 1919, only a few months after his marriage. He had prepared a will on 24 November 1918 leaving his wife $200 cash, saying that his property "is my separate property," and that he had obligations to his brother Perry and to his parents. He left his mother a Liberty Bond, face value $100. Everything else, both real and personal property, was left to his brother Perry, who was also named executor. However, Mary Elizabeth petitioned the court contesting the will. She pointed out that twenty-year-old Perry was underage and asked that she be appointed administrator. On 21 April 1919, the court ruled in favor of the widow. Leo's estate, estimated at $750 consisted of eight or nine cows, one calf, one bull, two

Leo Finley, Wade Sturgeon, and Roy Finley prepare to fall this giant redwood tree at Sugar Loaf, Coleman Valley, Sonoma County for the Sturgeon's Mill in Coleman Valley. Taken July 27, 1914.

Vivian Gertrude Finley, 1890-1973, and Jesse Wilds, 1877-1959.

horses, four hogs, a small lot of farming implements, household goods, and wearing apparel, plus cash in the Dairyman's Bank of Valley Ford in the amount of $208.[584]

251. Vivian Gertrude[6] Finley (Andrew Jackson[5], John[4],

Samuel[3], David[2], John[1]) was born 24 January 1890 in Westminster, Orange County, California. She died 9 July 1973 in Arcata, Humboldt County. She married (1) Jesse S. Wilds on 10 June 1908 in Sonoma County.[585] He was born 5 December 1877 in Lake County, California, the son of George Edward and Celesta Jane (Young) Wilds, and died 5 December 1959, Lake County. Vivian married (2) James Weston Williams, 14 January 1922 in Santa Rosa. He was born 12 December 1892, probably in Siskiyou County, California. He was the son of John Weston and Hannah Catherine (Harrison) Williams. John Weston Williams was a native of Ocracoke, Hyde County, North Carolina and served as a coxswain on the monitor Wyoming during the Civil War.[586]

Vivian and Jesse lived at the headwaters of Mark West Creek, a few miles north of Santa Rosa, where four children were born. Jesse worked for Grace Brothers Brewery delivering ice and later tended the bar at the Moose Club in Santa Rosa. About 1918 Vivian and Jesse separated and later divorced. The boys stayed with their father for a while, but eventually Ed, the oldest, went to live with his mother's sister Ethel, while Horace went to live with his Finley grandparents, both families residing in Bodega.

After Vivian's marriage to Jim Williams in 1922, they moved to Arcata, Humboldt County, where Jim worked in the local Barrel Factory. Their daughter, Jacquie Marie, was born there in 1926 and soon afterwards they moved back to Santa Rosa. Jim worked for a short time in the tire business, but this was depression time and they soon moved to the Dry Creek area just outside of Healdsburg, where Jim worked for various farmers plowing, pruning, and harvesting. He also worked sporadically for Grace Brothers Brewery in Santa Rosa. About

1936 they moved back to the Arcata area, living for a while on a chicken ranch at Bella Vista Hill. Here the entire family worked; Jim tending to farm needs, Vivian candling and cleaning eggs, while Jacquie Marie made up the cartons for the eggs to travel to market. After a year the family moved back to Arcata and Jim resumed his old position at the Barrel Factory, while Vivian went to work at the local hospital as a nurses' aide. They both remained in these positions until 1950 when Jim's health required him to retire. In order to find a drier climate, they moved to Salyer, in the Trinity Alps east of Arcata. Jim died 16 September 1962 at Salyer. Vivian remained in Salyer until 1968 or 1969, then returned to Arcata to live near her youngest daughter until her death in 1973.

Vivian and Jesse Wilds had four children:

291   i.   Edward Jackson Wilds, born 25 April 1909, Sonoma County; married Malfalda Celeste Albini 27 July 1931 in Santa Rosa.

292   ii.   William S. Wilds, born 5 October 1910 in Sonoma County; died 13 November 1948.

293   iii.   Horace E. Wilds, born 1 November 1911 in Santa Rosa; married Marguerita Alice Comer. She was born 7 February 1921 in Grant County, Oklahoma.

294   iv.   Edna Thelma Wilds, born 9 March 1913, Santa Rosa; married Wesley Embert Orr, 1 May 1931; died 23 January 1980 in Santa Rosa.

Vivian and Jim Williams had one child:

295   i.   Jacquie Marie[7] Williams, born 28 July 1926 in Arcata, Humboldt County, California. Marie, as she is now known, married (1) Roy Peter Wold, 27 November 1945 in Oakland, Alameda County, California. He was born 30 November 1921 in Wisconsin and died 21 March 1960 in Arcata. Marie married, (2) Joseph Naish. Joe was born 28 September 1925 in Nebraska. Joe died 29 June 1992 in Arcata.

Marie and Roy had six children:

a.   Roy Lee Wold, born 18 August 1946, Arcata; married (1) Nancy Gaethle, 29 May 1965; married (2) Anita Applegate.

b.   Arne J. Wold, born 12 April 1948, Arcata; died 24 February 1965, Sonoma County.

c.   Timothy Allen Wold, born 14 November 1951, Arcata; married Kim Roberta Keller, 20 August 1983, New Orleans, Louisiana.

d.   Terry Dean Wold, born 9 December 1953, Arcata; married (1) June Ramsey, April 1973; married (2) Patricia Peterson; married (3)

Linda McIntyre.

e. Curtis Lynn Wold, born 16 May 1955, Arcata; married Brenda Lynn Edwards, 18 April 1980, New Orleans, Louisiana.

f. Rick Layne Wold, born 25 October 1957, Arcata; married Teresa Marie Vahldick, 26 June 1982, Arcata.

252. Ethel Agnes[6] Finley (Andrew Jackson[5], John[4], Samuel[3], David[2], John[1]) was born 14 October 1893 in Bodega and died 8 June 1976 in Santa Rosa. Although she was reported to have married four times, none of her marriage records have yet been found. The purported list of husbands includes (1) Harold Roth, (2) Julius Mantua, died 17 October 1948, Alameda County,[587] (3) George Pedrazzi, died 21 May 1948, Sonoma County[588] and (4) Verner Hendren, born 25 March 1893, died 17 January 1974, Sonoma County.[589]

Ethel was, in fact, married to George Pedrazzi by 25 July 1930 since on that date, as Ethel Pedrazzi, she was deeded the sheep ridge by her mother, Alfaretta Finley, property where she was born and raised.[590] George and Ethel also bought the fifty-seven and one-half acre portion of the Finley estate inherited by James Preston Finley[591] and the 150.46 acres inherited by Samuel Emanuel Finley.[592]

Within the recollections of this writer, Ethel was one of the better known and most colorful of her generation of Finleys. My father, Perry, was Ethel's younger brother. Our family frequently went for Sunday outings to the ranch. It was often an adventure. Aunt Ethel would take me with her as she did her round of chores, and when those were done, there were other adventures and many things to explore. I have fond memories of picking mushrooms, flying kites, picking watercress at the spring, sneaking pickles out of the cellar's big pickle crock, picking raspberries in the back yard, and picking blackberries in the surrounding hills. And then at milking time I was allowed to wander freely in the barn to watch the operation, just as long as I remained out of way of a frisky cow's hind heels. But if I lingered too long, the scent of hay and other barnyard aromas would bring on a hayfever problem and the adventure was over. Ranch meals were hearty and always included mashed potatoes, green lettuce salad with wine vinegar dressing, and some kind of meat. Ethel was the only person I ever knew who kept a whole salami as a regular part of her larder and "Dago red" wine was always on hand for everyone. I remember when electricity finally came to the ranch, and not long after, the first indoor plumbing. The telephone was on a party line and listening in on the neighbors' calls was an accepted practice. As I reached high school age, Aunt Ethel took seriously my plans to go directly to the University of California at Berkeley, and upon my graduation from high school, she presented me with five crisp new $100 bills. During my five years in Berkeley, she also was a regular contributor to my college fund.

In 1909, at the age of fifteen, Ethel was baptized at the Church of the Assumption (Catholic) in Tomales, Marin County, California, along with her mother and three younger siblings.[593] Ethel, according to family tradition, had attended Healds' Business School in Santa Rosa and worked for a time as a bookkeeper for a local Cadillac dealer.[594] She is also had some nurses' training at Merritt College in Oakland. Most of her life, however, was spent on the ranch where she was born, and she seemed most at home there. She went deer hunting with the men and helped with the harvests, including baling hay. She milked cows, chopped wood, slaughtered the animals when needed, rode horseback, and in later years, bought and drove a jeep around the hills.

Ethel had no children of her own, but nurtured other members of the family both before and after me. During her marriage to Julius Mantua, she took in her nephew Ed Wilds after the divorce of his parents. He stayed with them until he completed his schooling at Ocean View School in 1923.[595] Sometime before 1930, Ethel had married George Pedrazzi and moved to the sheep ridge, where she had grown up. In the 1940s, her grandniece Lorraine Wilds, Ed's daughter, came to live with her. While living with Ethel, Lorraine met and married Alfred (Buck) Piazza. In 1948, a few years after George died, Ethel married Verner Hendren and went to live with him on his Coleman Valley ranch. Lorraine and her husband continued to live on the sheep ridge property. About 1956 or 1957, Ethel left Verner and moved back to the Finley homestead, living in a cabin at the foot of the hill leading to the sheep ridge. Lorraine's children, born in 1949 and 1953, came to live with her in the early 1960s. Ethel certainly filled a caretaker role as seen in earlier generations of the Finley family.

253. Edward Leroy[7] Finley (Andrew Jackson[5], John[4], Samuel[3], David[2], John[1]) was born 16 April 1896 in Bodega. He married Stella Potter 21 January 1922.[596] He most likely died 18 June 1940 at age forty-four at Livermore, Alameda County, California.[597] He is buried at the National Cemetery, the Presidio, San Francisco.

Not a great deal is known of Roy, as he was called. At the age of thirteen, he was baptized at the Church of the Assumption (Catholic), in Tomales, Marin County, along with his mother and three other siblings.[598] He was only eighteen when World War I broke out, and while he served in the war, no record of his service could be found. After the war and prior to his marriage, he worked for Wade Sturgeon in the woods of Sonoma County driving a bull team. Shortly after his marriage he worked as caretaker of the King Ranch in Cazadero.[599] Roy contracted tuberculosis related to his World War I experience, and spent his last years at the Livermore Veterans' Hospital. Apparently he had lived in Oakland prior to that and is listed in city directories at 3608 Emerson (1930), at 2486 82nd Avenue (1933), and at 526 35th (1934, 1937).[600] He was a member of the Oakland Chapter 7, Disabled American Veterans. Roy and Stella had no children.

254. Perry Elmo[6] Finley (Andrew Jackson[5], John[4], Samuel[3], David[2], John[1]) was born 28 October 1898 in Weaverville, Trinity County, California. He married Ardith Bernice Bobst on 30 April 1922 in Oakland, Alameda County. She was born 29 July 1904 in Healdsburg, Sonoma County, the daughter of Richard Milton and Jessie Maude (McFarling) Bobst. She died 14 January 1987 in Santa Rosa at the age of eighty-two. Perry died of pneumonia 12 February 1986 in Santa Rosa at the age of eighty-seven.

Although Perry was born in the northern part of the state, when he was four years old his parents returned by horse and wagon to the Bodega homestead, where his father was born and grew up, and which was just a few miles from the Tomales home of Perry's mother. There Perry began school and for

St. Teresa's Catholic Church in Bodega. Perry was an altar boy here. He was baptized, along with his mother and three of his siblings at the Church of the Assumption in Tomales, Marin County in 1909.

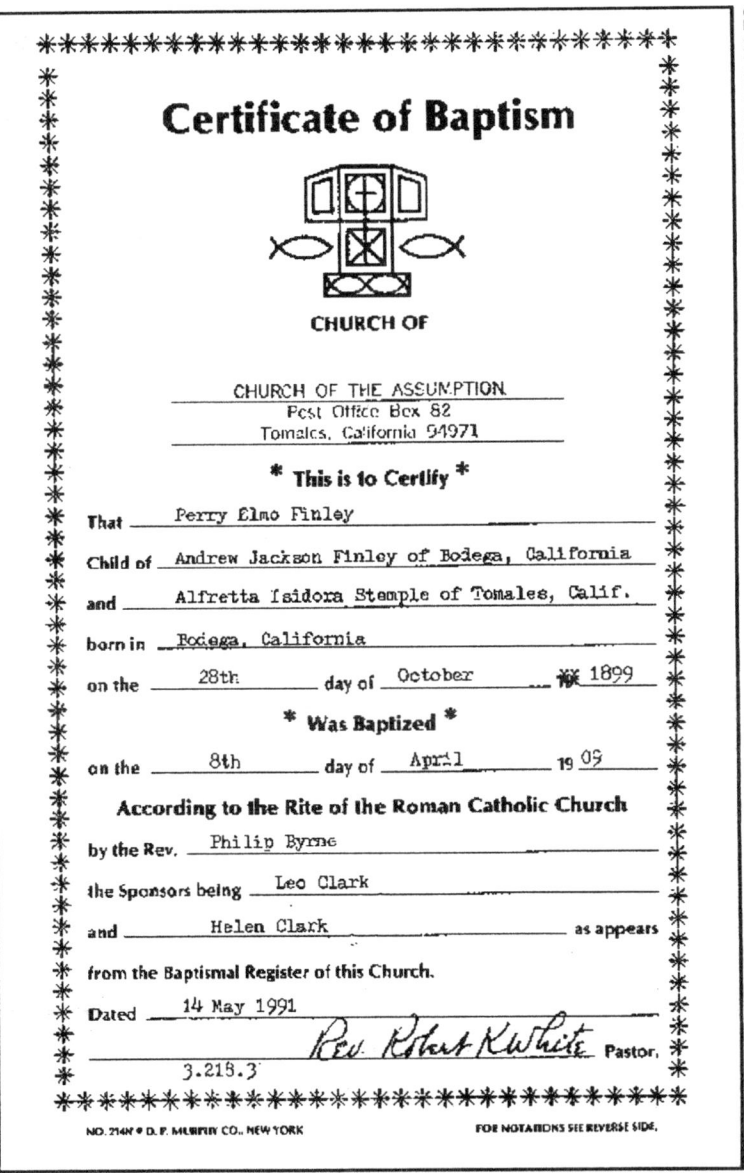

Certificate of Baptism

CHURCH OF

CHURCH OF THE ASSUMPTION
Post Office Box 82
Tomales, California 94971

* This is to Certify *

That ___Perry Elmo Finley___

Child of ___Andrew Jackson Finley of Bodega, California___

and ___Alfretta Isidora Stemple of Tomales, Calif.___

born in ___Bodega, California___

on the ___28th___ day of ___October___ 19 ___1899___

* Was Baptized *

on the ___8th___ day of ___April___ 19 ___09___

According to the Rite of the Roman Catholic Church

by the Rev. ___Philip Byrne___

the Sponsors being ___Leo Clark___

and ___Helen Clark___ as appears

from the Baptismal Register of this Church.

Dated ___14 May 1991___

___Rev. Robert K White___ Pastor.

___3.218.3___

NO. 214N • D. F. MURPHY CO., NEW YORK   FOR NOTATIONS SEE REVERSE SIDE.

almost eight years he attended four different one-room schoolhouses in this rural dairy community. The first of these, Bodega School, proved feasible only until the first winter rains came. Then he and his three brothers and sisters found they could not find a way to cross the swollen waters of Salmon Creek and were allowed to change to Potter School in the town of Bodega proper. This meant about a three mile hike to and from school. When Perry was about eleven years old, the family moved from their home on Fay Creek up to the sheep ridge, the property his father inherited the following year when grandfather John died.

Moving to the sheep ridge property caused another change in school districts for Perry and his brothers and sisters. They now had to trek only two miles across the hills to Ocean View School. At this time the majority of the school population was made up of Finleys, three from Perry's own family and five from his Uncle Jeff's family.

Shortly after the move, when Perry was twelve years old, he went to work for his cousin Clarence Head on his dairy ranch for $15 per month plus his room and board. He worked there for about a year and attended Joy School. Then he returned to his own family to help them on the sheep ridge and returned to Ocean View School.

At the age of fourteen he quit school and went to work full time for his father and other dairy ranchers in the neighborhood, hauling lumber and doing ranch work. He did this kind of work until 1918, with his range of pay rising to $50 per month. In 1918, at age twenty, he began driving the local route for a Bodega butcher shop. This involved driving a Ford pickup truck loaded with meat to different communities in the northwest section of Sonoma County. His route included going to Bodega Bay and along the Pacific Coast Road to Jenner, then back through Duncan's Mill and Monte Rio, or back through Willow Creek. Camp Meeker, Occidental, and Freestone were also frequent stops. One circle trip from start to finish probably was thirty miles or so and served twenty to twenty-five customers. He called on individual ranchers along the way, and since this was a heavily saturated Italian area, it was necessary to learn some of the language, especially the names of the cuts of meat and amounts of money. In later years he recalled that at this time the best steak sold for 25¢ a pound and an entire oxtail could be had for 15¢. He drove the butcher route for three years and it was during this time that he met his future wife, Ardith Bernice Bobst, at a dance in Camp Meeker. When they decided to marry, she was influential in getting him to move to Santa Rosa and find a job that would offer greater security.

In 1922 Perry went to work as a deputy for the Sonoma County Sheriff's office, with a starting salary of $100 per

Perry Finley, the young hunter, shown here about age 14.

CARMEN J. FINLEY COLLECTION

CARMEN J. FINLEY COLLECTION

(clockwise from upper left:)

The Finley Family: LeRoy (Roy) and Stella Finley; Edna Wilds; Alfaretta (Stemple) Finley; Ardith and Perry Finley; Harold Finley; and Horace Wilds holding Carmen Finley; about 1929.

Perry Finley holding daughter, Carmen, about 1929.

Five mechanics and a bookkeeper took care of the Sonoma County equipment in 1930. Perry at far left.

PAGE 130

month. This position brought him in contact with the Sonoma County Garage where he began to develop interests and skills in the garage work done to maintain county equipment. He went to work at the garage the next year and worked there until his retirement in 1966, a total of forty-three years. During that time he became garage foreman and supervised the maintenance of fleets of county-owned automobiles and heavy equipment. This often necessitated his having to travel anywhere in the county to make repairs. During the 1930s, in the summer when school was not in session, this writer recalls with fond memories his invitations to pack a lunch and go with him.

During Perry's early years on the ranch, he developed interests in hunting, fishing, and the outdoors that remained with him all his life. Steelhead from the ocean would come up the creeks where he lived while growing up. He caught his first steelhead at about age six. Hunting quail, squirrels, and cottontails were also a way of life and part of the business of helping to feed the family. His mother tried to put his first shoes on him when he started school, but he quickly learned to take them off and hide them along the way, and would return to pick them up before going home.

During his adult years deer hunting was a continuing interest and his three-week vacation each year was always devoted to this sport. He hunted with the same close set of hunting partners for a period of over fifty years. Most years included a three week stay at a cabin near Cloverdale owned by his close hunting partner, Dick Violetti. Each year his family put in a request for him to make venison jerky, but we only got it once every three or four years. Other life-long interests were raising pigeons and breeding dogs for hunting. For over fifty-five years he kept detailed records on each of his pigeons and knew their

Perry's pigeon trophies from the Redwood Empire Pigeon Club, 1950-1961.

productivity. During the 1950s and 1960s he was an active member of the Redwood Empire Pigeon Club, and in 1952 his bird "Snow White" took grand champion of the show for King pigeons at their annual exhibit at the Sonoma County Fair. He also won awards in 1959, 1960, and 1961 for best utility and best King birds.

A more detailed sketch of the lives of Perry and Ardith Finley was prepared under the auspices of the Finley McFarling Scholarship Fund at Sonoma State University in 1991.[601]

Perry and Ardith (Bobst) Finley had one child:

+296 i. Carmen Joyce[7] Finley, born 9 March 1926, Santa Rosa, California.

GENERATION SEVEN

269. Garold E.[7] Findley (John Moses[6], William[5], John[4], Edmund[3], David[2], John[1]) was born 27 June 1905 in Orosi, Tulare County, California. He died 1 September 1992 at the age of eighty-seven. He married Mary DeMello on 10 October 1928 in Visalia, California. She died there 7 May 1995.

Mary (DeMello) Findley was interviewed by niece, Michelle (Findley) Yahnian, in February 1995, shortly before her death. From her comes the following information.[602]

Garold and Mary met when his family moved next door to the DeMellos in Visalia. Garold was an outdoors man. When he was a small boy he went with his father on cattle drives to Fresno, Coalinga, and other areas of the San Joaquin Valley. He liked rodeos, calf roping, and going to the livestock sales yard where he worked at times. He collected Indian artifacts and antique farm machinery. Garold and Mary were farmers. When they were first married, Garold worked for other ranchers in his area. He finally bought his own farm at Munson, a small community between Visalia and Dinuba. They raised cotton and lived there for fifty-four years. Mary took care of their children and in later years had a catering business. About 1990 they sold the farm and bought a home in Orosi, where Garold died two years later.

Their children include:

297   i.   Beverly Findley, married William Pattee, 14 August 1948. Their children include:
       a.   Debra Renee Pattee, born 16 September 1951; married Dean Priest, 10 November 1978.
       b.   Carol Ann Pattee, born 5 May 1956; married Casey Johnson, 17 August 1974.
       c.   Jane Lucille Pattee, born 8 January 1961.

298   ii.   Carolyn Jane Findley, married (1) James Harness. They had one child:
       a.   Marc Garold Harness, born 28 February 1954; married 4 December 1972 Sarah Rodrequiz.
       Carolyn Jane Findley married (2) Robert Agnew. They had one child:
       a.   Robert Lee Agnew, born 22 June 1961.

299   iii. Mary Lou[8] Findley, married Steven Biswell, 17 August 1968. Their children include:
       a.   Jana Michelle Biswell, born 22 November 1973.
       b.   Jason Tren Biswell, born 13 June 1976.

273. Byron F.[7] Findley (John Moses[6], William[5], John[4], Edmund[3], David[2], John[1]) was born 1 November 1910 in Drumm Valley, Tulare County, California. He married Dorothy Marie Williams on 27 June 1931 at Hanford. She was the daughter of William E. and Nettie Sarah (Eaton) Williams and was born 7 July 1914 in East Highland, California. Byron died 13 September 1982 in Visalia and is buried in the cemetery there.

Michelle (Findley) Yahnian gives the following information

about her parents:[603]

Byron F. Findley and Dorothy Marie Williams met while in their early teens at a young people's meeting at the church they attended. At this time my father was a professional boxer, but at my mother's insistence he gave up the sport for her. He did have some instances where he defended his honor and several men over the years were treated to his left handed knock out punch. He also listened to all of his favorite sports on radio, and TV. His two sons were in sports also, so he attended many of their games.

Growing up he worked before and after school on the family farm. There were plenty of chores. After marriage he worked for a family friend on his dairy. He eventually went into farming for himself full time. He bought and sold several farms over his lifetime. The last farm he owned until he sold it around 1980.

He and my mother made a trip to Australia. She wasn't in good health and passed away in 1981. My father, brother and my brother's son, made a trip to Australia and my dad passed away one month later in 1982. My father farmed cotton, alfalfa, walnuts, potatoes, melons, and also vegetables for the household. He was a very intelligent businessman, he helped anyone who asked for help of any kind. He helped several of his former farm workers to own their own farms. My father loved going to the Findley picnics. I don't think he ever missed one. He had a sense of humor that we all miss very much. We still quote most of his quips and stories. My mother was an excellent cook, sewed beautifully, canned fruit, jellies, raised rabbits and chickens (show chickens) and wrote a few songs, and did oil painting. I have many of her pictures in my home.

Byron and Dorothy Findley had four children:

300   i.   Michelle R.[8] Findley, born 6 January 1933, Visalia; married Dodd Yahnian, 24 November 1954. They have three children:
- a.   Dodd Steven Yahnian, born 4 November 1955; married Ann Barsamian.
- b.   Janet Lynn Yahnian, born 3 January 1959; married Jonathan Chilingerian.
- c.   Marc A. Yahnian, born 14 January 1963.

301   ii.   William B. Findley, born 27 January 1935, Visalia; married Carolyn Lehman, 10 September 1955. They have three children:
- a.   Robin Leigh Findley, born 6 January 1959, Visalia; married Yvonne Ennulate. She was born 22 August 1959 in Frankfurt, am Main, West Germany.
- b.   Carrie Lynn Findley, born 8 April 1961, Visalia; married Alastair Lawrence Haire. They are currently (1993) living in Wee Waa, N.S.W., Australia.
- c.   Natalie Lynette Findley, born 21 May 1965, Wee Waa, N. S. W., Australia; married Adrian Schwager.

302   iii.   Jeanne M. Findley, born 14 September 1936, Visalia; married Joseph E. Vanoni, 8 March 1966. They have four children:
- a.   Maria Kathleen Vanoni, born 9 December 1966, Visalia.
- b.   Joseph Attilio Vanoni, born 11 December 1968, Prineville, Oregon.
- c.   Brenda Jeanne Vanoni, born 28 January 1971, Prineville, Crook County, Oregon; married Robert Greene, 3 November 1990. He was born in Bakersfield, 26 October 1963.
- d.   Antonia Renee Vanoni, born 20 December 1976, Bakersfield, Kern County, California.

303   iv.   Richard I. Findley, born 12 August 1939, Visalia; married Lee Ann Council, 25 April 1964. They have two children:
- a.   Amy Findley, born 5 December 1967.
- b.   Richard Ivan Findley II, born 2 September 1970.

296. Carmen Joyce[7] Finley (Perry Elmo[6], Andrew Jackson[5], John[4], Samuel[3], David[2], John[1]) was born 9 March 1926 in Santa Rosa, California. She married Joseph Hayes Hunter 20 December 1956 in Santa Rosa; they divorced in 1968.

This writer has childhood memories of a home in Santa Rosa where she was nurtured with love, respect, and individu-

ality. My mother tried her best to develop all the talents expected of a young girl in the 1930s and a young lady in the 1940s. This included lessons in dancing, music, cooking, and sewing. However, I failed to take interest in any of these except music.

From an early age, both parents worked. Once I started Burbank School, after school hours I would walk to the Wildwood Dairy where my Mother worked. This was conveniently located next to the public library, where I spent many happy hours under the tutelage of the childrens' librarian, Dagney Juell. She had taught me how to write my name, even before I entered school, so I could get a library card.

At about age eight, I began taking piano lessons, soon to be followed by flute lessons. My music teacher, George Trombley, was also conductor of the Santa Rosa Symphony Orchestra. In December 1938, when his orchestra was scheduled to perform on Santa Rosa's new radio station, KSRO, his two regular flautists could not perform and he selected me to replace them. The local newspaper carried this paragraph in its article about the performance:

Of the orchestra of forty people assembled under the baton of George Trombley, special acclaim was accorded 12-year-old Carmen Finley of Santa Rosa, youthful musical prodigy, who carried the entire flute part throughout the concert.[604]

When I entered high school the next year, I became a regular member of the symphony orchestra and continued until my graduation four years later.

I always loved school and, as a child, never considered any career other than education. As I went through the grades, my focus changed. At first I wanted to be an elementary teacher, then a junior high teacher, and finally a high school teacher—which I eventually did become.

Realizing that my educational goals would be a financial strain on my family, I began early to build my own college fund. Picking prunes and hops was a way of life for those of us who were too young to do anything else. When I got old enough, my list of odd jobs included working in the public library, delivering milk for the Wildwood Dairy, ushering and cashiering at two local theaters, and working in a local frozen food plant. Between three college semesters I worked at *The Press Democrat* newspaper business office as well as in classified and display advertising. All of these jobs, in addition to a scholarship, family assistance, and part-time work on campus, helped me realize my educational goals at the University of California at Berkeley. Working at the Men's Faculty Club on campus, was an education in itself. Of the men who regularly sat at my table, Ernest O. Lawrence was my most favorite. It was not until years later I discovered that he was a Nobel Prize winning nuclear physicist who established the Lawrence Berkeley and Livermore Labs for nuclear research. Tucked away in another corner of the dining room was a table reserved for the "boys" from the radiation laboratory up on the hill. Of this group, J. Robert Oppenheimer was a regular, but my recollections of him were not nearly so favorable as those of Lawrence. It wasn't until sometime later the world recognized him as the person who directed building the first atomic bomb. My recollection of Governor Earl Warren, future Chief Justice of the Supreme Court, who attended a meeting in our special banquet room was one of embarrassment. I had failed to recognize him and did not serve him first!

Mathematics had become the focal point of my interest

Carmen poses for Library Week photo for Dagney Juell, children's librarian, Santa Rosa Public Library, about 1933.

while still in high school, so working in the statistics lab[605] and correcting assignments for math classes at college fit in very well with a curriculum heavily saturated with mathematics. After receiving a B.A. degree in 1947 and a secondary teaching credential the following year, I accepted my first and only teaching position, at Porterville Union High School in Tulare County, California. It took just three years of teaching algebra, geometry, and general math to convince me that this routine would not be an exciting career over the long run.

Indecision sent me back to college for an M.A. degree, but an earlier course in educational measurement and evaluation

CARMEN J. FINLEY COLLECTION

Carmen, age 36, Director of Research and Data Processing, Sonoma County Schools, 1962.

helped me decide to study at Teachers College, Columbia University, where Robert L. Thorndike, son of measurement pioneer, Edward L. Thorndike, was on the staff. During this year I took several statistics courses, including two from Helen M. Walker, then head of the statistics department, who was influential in furthering my interest in this area. At the time she was writing one of the first texts on statistical inference and her students suffered through a draft copy of her text where our main function was to help catch typographical errors. At the end of the year she offered me a position as her lab assistant. However, one year of starvation in New York City was enough.

That fall I began a fifteen-year career with the Sonoma County Superintendent of Schools Office in Santa Rosa as a psychometrist and assistant to their school psychologist. One of my first assignments included the administration of a county-wide testing program, which led me to develop a more efficient automated scoring system. Following completion of a school

psychologist and a general administration credential, I was promoted to Director of Research and Data Processing and expanded our data processing system to include other pupil personnel services and some accounting functions. Ultimately, our center became one of ten state-wide systems providing pupil personnel services to all northern California coastal counties.[606]

During a half-year sabbatical leave in 1959-1960, I began work on a Ph.D. degree in measurement and evaluation, which was completed in 1962 at Teachers' College, Columbia University. At this time I was greatly influenced by Robert L. Thorndike and Irving R. Lorge, who became members of my dissertation committee, with Thorndike as chairman. While taking a data processing course from Dr. Lorge, he encouraged me to enroll at Watson Laboratory[607] for an additional computer programming course. This was my introduction to computer programming in machine language and began an interest which has continued into retirement. That experience at Watson Lab was also a very sobering one since my class included a number of gifted high school students who ran circles around the rest of us. By this time, membership in honorary societies included Sigma Xi, Kappa Delta Pi, and Pi Lambda Theta.

While still employed by the Sonoma County Schools Office I decided to try my hand at college level teaching, and during the summer of 1963 I taught courses in vocational testing and statistics at Sonoma State College at Rohnert Park in Sonoma County. During the summer of 1964, when I taught educational measurement and statistics as an Associate Professor at the University of Rochester in New York, I was offered a permanent position there, but declined. In the mid-1960s, I was offered a position of Dean of Women at Santa Rosa Junior

College, but after much soul searching, I decided against it. My interest and training in educational research was greatly enhanced in the summer of 1965 when I was selected to attend a special summer training session held by Julian B. Stanley at the Laboratory of Experimental Design at the University of Wisconsin at Madison. Stanley was pioneering in the area of experimental design for educational research at that time and, in true researcher style, had selected fifteen predoctoral students and fifteen postdoctoral students to participate in his intensive summer training program.

In 1968 I took a year's leave of absence from the Sonoma County Schools Office to work with Frank B. Womer, Director of the National Assessment of Educational Progress (NAEP), then in St. Paul, Minnesota, to assist in the development of a national testing program. As my interest and involvement in this project grew, so did my wish to remain longer than my year's leave. This forced me to sever my ties with the Sonoma County Schools.

Before joining the NAEP staff, I was selected, as one of ten United States educational researchers, to attend a month long European Seminar on Learning and the Evaluation Process. This was held at Skepparholmen, Hasseludden, Sweden just outside Stockholm where we were joined by ten European educational researchers. Headed by John B. Carroll, noted linguist, this experience added a new dimension to my understanding and appreciation of the evaluation process and international problems. In our lighter moments, I recall a number of parties in which we sampled libations brought by our European counterparts from their countries, accompanied by Carroll's extemporaneous piano selections.

Following my return from Sweden, the National Assessment project office was moved to Ann Arbor, Michigan, where I became Associate Staff Director, as well as Director of Exercise Development. During this time, the first actual assessment of a national sample of ages nine, thirteen, seventeen, and young adults was made. The next year when the Federal Government took over funding and changed the governing body of the project, I made the required move to Denver, Colorado.[608] But the project had vastly changed from its developmental days, and after having lived in four apartments in as many years, I was ready to return to California, and a sunnier climate. However, in retrospect, my four years with NAEP were undoubtedly the most professionally rewarding of my entire career. I not only learned first hand about the problems and intricacies of large scale testing programs, but was able to observe master educators, sampling statisticians, and evaluators at work.[609]

In 1972 I accepted the position of Principal Research Scientist at the American Institutes for Research (AIR), a non-profit private research "think tank" in Palo Alto, California.[610] While there, I worked on a variety of projects where my measurement skills were required. I assisted in obtaining a contract to revise the Medical College Admissions Test which I then directed for the first year. During my last six years at AIR, I directed one of ten National Technical Assistance Centers for Title I Evaluation, working through state departments of education to teach local school district personnel how to evaluate their federally funded Title I programs.[611]

During 1974-75, while still working at AIR, I worked with the San Mateo County Schools office on the development of evaluation materials for the California State Department of Education that were eventually published by Educational Testing Service in Princeton, New Jersey. In 1976 I taught a

Carmen Finley in retirement, with friends Kenneth Vance and Frank Womer, visiting a Malaysian home, 1992.

research course in the Counseling Department at Sonoma State University in Sonoma County. During the mid-1970s, I was founder and president of Educational Evaluation, Inc., a private company which developed tests for local school districts in the San Francisco Bay Area.

During my professional career, I served on the editorial and review boards of numerous professional organizations and journals, which included serving as president of the California Educational Research Association in 1966-1967.[612] In addition, I have published approximately fifty studies, plus a monograph on NAEP, and two abbreviated scales for screening exceptional children. During the 1970s, I was a consultant in test develop-

ment for numerous states and was listed in Who's Who in America, Who's Who in American Women, and Who's Who in American Education.

In 1983, after thirty-five years as a career woman, I retired and returned to my birthplace, Santa Rosa, California. During my first year home I enrolled as a student at Sonoma State University as a computer science major. This led to the purchase of my first personal computer, which meshed nicely with an interest in my family history that began in 1979. I joined the Sonoma County Genealogical Society and have served as president, vice-president, chairman of the Special Projects Board, and a member of the editorial board of their publication. Following credentialing as a Certified Genealogist, I agreed to chair the Family History Writing Contest sponsored by the National Genealogical Society. As of this writing, I have published six articles on various genealogical problems found in the study of my own family.

At Sonoma State University, I established a scholarship program and a trust which will eventually provide for the Finley-McFarling Chair in History. Continued involvement with SSU includes serving as a volunteer for their Development Office and as a board member of the Academic Foundation. Other community activities include serving as a former board member of the Sonoma County Museum, a former advisory committee member to a Catholic Charities project serving caretakers of brain injured adults and, currently, as membership secretary of the Sonoma County Historical Society

But there has been time for play as well as work in retirement. Although extensive travel was required during my working years, there was never time to stop off and enjoy the sights. Since retirement I have been able to enjoy a more relaxed travel style and have taken both Elderhostel and individualized trips, which have included Europe and the Far East, as well as the United States and Canada.

SUMMARY

This branch of the John Finley family certainly lived up to a phrase descriptive of the Scotch-Irish, that they were people "who constituted the skirmish line of civilization." John and Mary (Caldwell) Finley were among the earliest settlers in the Shenandoah Valley of Virginia. Their sons, David and Samuel, were in Kentucky in the late 1770s or early 1780s, years before that area attained statehood. David, with much of his family intact, pushed on to Indiana by 1812, four years before that area attained statehood. From there on, the family split. David's sons Jesse and Edmund forged ahead to Missouri between 1820 and 1830, early in the statehood of that area. Samuel went to Illinois about 1832 and died there a few years later, but a number of his children went on to Missouri between 1840 and 1850. Again the family branched, with Jesse and Edmund and a number of their children going on to Texas, probably in the early 1840s; Texas attained statehood in 1845. Several of Samuel's children made their way to California by 1852, just three years after the Gold Rush and two years after California became a state.

At least two of the sons of Jesse and Edmund relocated in California. John, son of Edmund, went to Southern California in the early 1850s; Joseph Jefferson, son of Jesse, joined his cousins in Northern California at least by 1860.

John Finley (1823-1910), son of Samuel and a primary subject of this work, was the first Finley settler to remain in Sonoma County where he spent the remaining fifty-eight years of his life. Starting as a potato farmer in the Bloomfield area, he went on to acquire a 1,000 acre dairy ranch where he and Keziah raised a large family and provided for the needs of their children in times of adversity.

CHAPTER SIX

ANCESTORS AND DESCENDANTS OF WILLIAM ASA FINLEY (1839-1912)

William Asa Finley and the John Finley who settled in Bodega shared the same ancestor, John Finley(?-1782), a first generation Scotch-Irish immigrant who arrived in America in the early part of the eighteenth century. However, their immigrant ancestor was married twice. William Asa Finley was the great-great-grandson of the earlier John Finley by his first wife, a daughter of the Reverend John Thomson, given name unknown. John Finley of Bodega was a great-grandson by his second wife, Mary Caldwell. The story of John Finley, the immigrant, as told in chapter 5, is one of heavy devotion to the development of Presbyterianism in early colonial Virginia.

Children of John and (Thomson) Finley include, so far as they are known:

+2	i.	John[2] Finley, born about 1738/39, most likely in Augusta County, Virginia.
+3	ii.	Elizabeth Finley, baptized by Rev. John Craig 18 January 1740/41, Tinkling Spring, Augusta County, Virginia.
+4	iii.	William Finley, baptized by Rev. John Craig 30 January 1743, Tinkling Spring, Augusta County, Virginia.
5	iv.	James Finley, baptized by Rev. John Craig 8 March 1747, Tinkling Spring, Augusta County, Virginia.[1]
+6	v.	George Finley, baptized by Rev. John

Thomson 4 January 1748, Tinkling Spring, Augusta County, Virginia.

A second James Finley, said to have been born to this John Finley, cannot be definitely identified as the son of Thomson or of Mary Caldwell (and it is assumed Wilson was correct in his grouping of the children into separate John Finley families).

7	vi.	James Finley, baptized by Rev. John Craig 26 March 1749, Tinkling Spring, Augusta County, Virginia.

GENERATION TWO

2. John[2] Finley (John[1]) was probably born about 1738/39, most likely in Augusta County, Virginia.[2] He died in Augusta County between 6 July 1807, the date he wrote his will, and 28 December 1807, the date his will was proved.[3] He married Sarah Steele, daughter of Samuel and Martha (Fulton) Steele, probably about 1767/68.[4] Sarah outlived John by about ten years. She wrote her will 11 May 1816 and it was proved in court January 1818.[5]

John, Jr., the eldest son, was only about ten years old when his mother died. His father had remarried at least by 1750. He spent his formative years living in the South River area of Beverley Manor while his father was actively engaged in the formation of the Tinkling Spring Meeting House. By the time the family moved on to Prince Edward County in 1765, John, Jr., was a young adult. Presumably he remained with the family until they moved on to Montgomery County about 1772/73, although there is no proof of this. When the court records for Prince Edward County were examined, one interesting entry involved a John Finley. It stated:

> September 1767, The King against John Finley for Misbehaving. Ordered that the said Findly do give bond in the sum of £12.5.0 with one good surety in the Penalty of £6.5.0 to be bound of their respective goods chattels lands and tenements to our said lord the King, bonded but upon this condition that if he the said Fenly shall keep himself of good behavior toward all his Majesty leige Ropa(?) for twelve months and one day next ensuing that this recognizance to be said and that he be committed to the goal of this said county until he find such security and pay costs.[6]

Since there is a strong possibility that both John, Sr., and John, Jr., were living in Prince Edward County at that time, it cannot be said with certainty whether it was father or son who went afoul of the law. Nothing further was found to explain the circumstances or eventual outcome. When the family decided to move on in 1773, the younger John decided to return to Augusta County.

John's first purchase of land was made 18 August 1773 in Augusta County, when he bought 100 acres from his sister and brother-in-law, the James Gillespys.[7] Actually, the Gillespys sold him a portion of what James had inherited from his father, near the old homestead where John had grown up.

John was a wheelwright, so identified by the tax lists of the 1780s.[8] He and Sarah took in at least two children as appren-

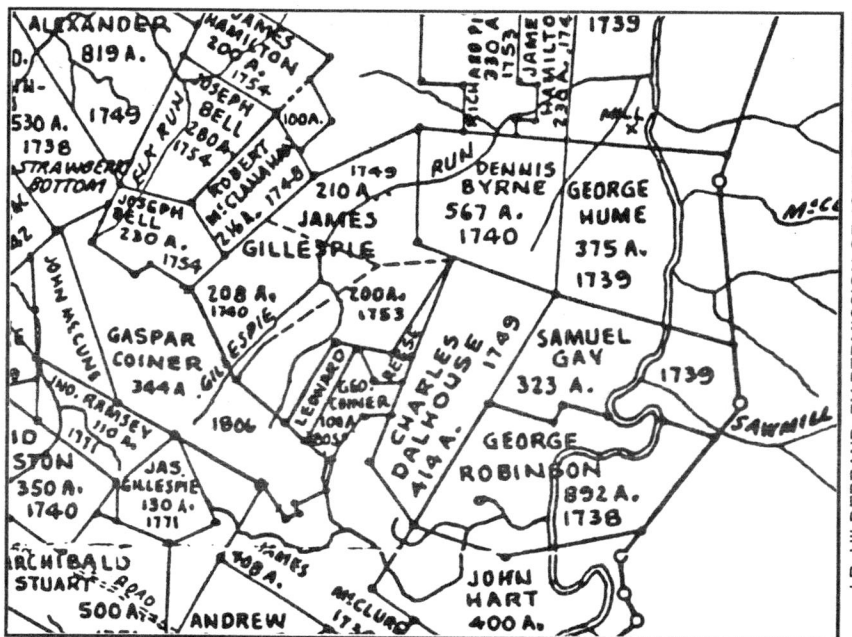

Note proximity between George Robinson property purchased by John Finley, Sr., and that owned by James Gillespie.

tices, and this helped further identify him separately from other John Finleys still living in Augusta County. On 24 January 1775, Matthew Gleaves, son of Matthew Gleaves, deceased, bound himself to John as an apprentice to learn the trade of wheelwright.[9] The Gleaves had been living on South River prior to 1771 when Matthew Gleaves, Sr., died and his brother, William, was appointed guardian for Esther and Matthew, Jr. Uncle William soon moved off to Montgomery (later Wythe) County where his own daughter, Esther, eventually married Asa Finley, John's nephew through his brother William.[10] Matthew Gleaves, Jr., eventually brought suit against John for not living

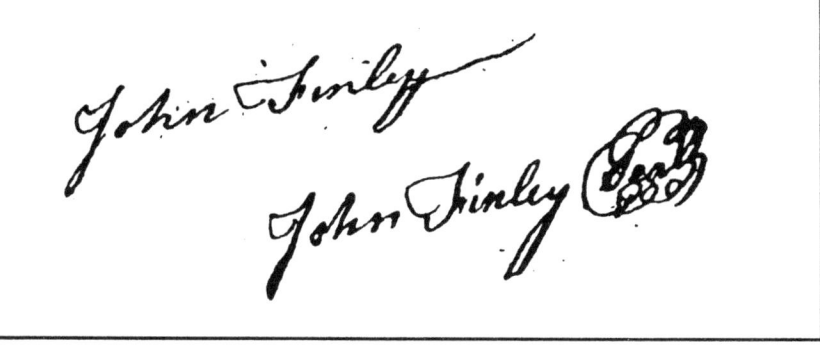

The 1775 document in which Matthew Gleaves was apprenticed to John Finley, wheelwright, contains the original signature of John, along with Matthew, his uncle William, and others who were witnesses. Twenty years later, Margaret Mooney was apprenticed to John to "learn the business of spinning knittin sewing and other housework as is Customary." Compare the signatures.

up to his part of the agreement. While the complaint is not dated, an attached paper dated 14 June 1793 states John's intent to obtain a deposition from James Gillespy, then living on Little River, waters of the Holston.[11] How the matter was resolved was not found in court records.

A second apprentice was Margaret Mooney, who at age four was bound to John to learn "the business of spinning knittin sewing and other houswork as is Customary," until she was eighteen years old. She came to the Finley household on 2 June 1795 from the Overseers of the Poor when her former custodian, Jacob Berrier, died.[12] She had not yet reached eighteen when John died in 1807, but she was provided for in his will saying, "I allow that something may be done for Peggy Mooney."[13] Some interesting family clues surface in the will of John's son William, in 1836, as to Peggy Mooney's fate. William, obvious-

ly unmarried, provides for his sister Sarah; brother John (now residing in Kentucky); sister Jane Frazer (now residing in Ohio); Margaret Mooney (who is residing with me); and Francis Marion Finley, son to Margaret Mooney.[14]

When John's father died in 1782 the laws of primogeniture were still in force, thus the eldest son was entitled to his father's real property. However, the elder John had made arrangements through articles of agreement for the property, 327 acres on Salley Run, waters of Reed Creek, to go to David and Samuel, sons of his second wife, in exchange for life care.[15] In order to honor the intent of this agreement it was necessary for John, Jr., to deed this property back to David and Samuel. This transaction was actually carried out in June and August of 1792 by William Findley of Wythe County to whom John, Jr., had given power-of-attorney.[16]

John, identified in his will his wife, Sarah, three sons, and three daughters listed below, in the order named in his will. Sarah, who died some ten years later, named the three daughters, but only one son, William. The older sons who had inherited property from their father were then living in Scott County, Kentucky. Birthplace of the children is not known, but is most likely Prince Edward and/or Augusta County.

+8	i.	Samuel Steele[3] Finley, born about 1769, probably in Prince Edward or Augusta County, Virginia.
+9	ii.	John T. Finley, born probably in Prince Edward or Augusta County.
10	iii.	Sarah (Sally) Finley, born about 1773, most likely in Prince Edward or Augusta County; died 17 April 1851, Augusta

		County; buried at Tinkling Spring.[17]
11	iv.	William Finley, born about 1780, most likely in Augusta County; died 28 November 1836, Augusta County, buried at Tinkling Spring.[18]
12	v.	Margaret Finley, born most likely in Augusta County; married John Hutchison, son of Robert Hutchison, 2 June 1793 in Augusta County.[19] Prior to her father's death, about 1796, Margaret, her husband, her sister Jean, and Jean's husband, moved to Bourbon County, near Paris, Kentucky, where they remained until about 1806. Then they moved to Greene County, Ohio, because they opposed slavery.[20] Margaret and her sister Sally, inherited land on the Dicks River in Kentucky.[21]
13	vi.	Jane/Jean (Jinney) Finley, born most likely in Augusta County; married William Frazier, 1 April 1794, in Augusta County.[22] She inherited a lot in Waynesboro, near the family homestead, but apparently made a trade with one or more of her other siblings (see sister Margaret, above).

3. **Elizabeth**[2] **Finley** (John[1]) was baptized at Tinkling Spring on 18 January 1740/41.[23] She married James Gillespy, in Prince Edward County, in January 1764.[24] James was born about 1730 and came to America from Ulster, Northern Ireland, the son of

This power-of-attorney, given by John Finley of Augusta County to William Finley of Wythe County, establishes the link between the Sally Run property of his father, John, and his half-brothers David and Samuel.

James, Sr., and Jennet Gillespy.[25] James's and Elizabeth's places and dates of death have not yet been established, but their last known residence was on Little River, waters of the Holston, in what is now Blount County, Tennessee.[26]

Elizabeth was eight or nine years old when her mother died. By the time she was ten or eleven her father had remar-

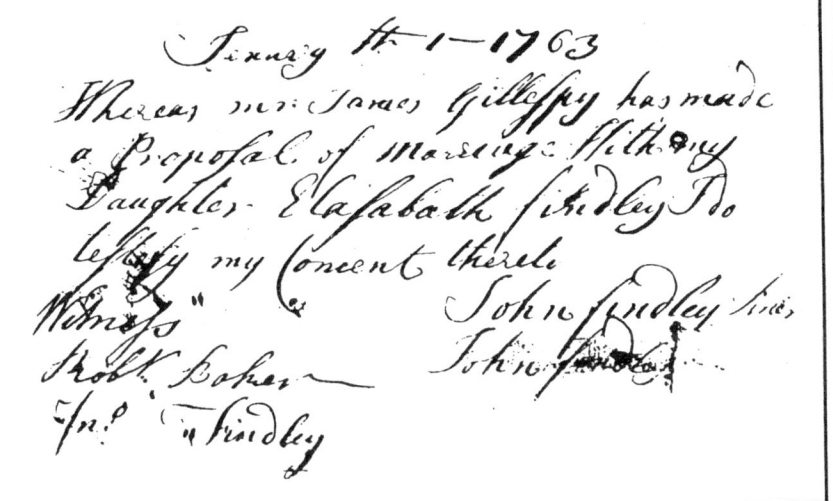

Permission for Elizabeth to marry James Gillespy was given by her father 1 January 1763. The note states, "Whereas Mr. James Gillespy has made a Proposal of marriage with my Daughter Elizabeth Findley I do testify my concent thereto." It is signed by John Findley, Senior, and witnessed by Robt. Baker and Jno Findley.

ried and was still deeply immersed in the affairs of Tinkling Spring. The James Gillespy family lived nearby (see Hildebrand's map), and James Gillespy, Sr., was also an Elder at Tinkling Spring and very active in the affairs of the church. James Gillespy, Jr., whom she eventually married, was the proverbial "boy next door." However, two or three years before their marriage, Elizabeth went to live with her aunt and uncle, Rev. Richard and Sarah (Thomson) Sankey, in Prince Edward County.[27] Elizabeth and James were married in Prince Edward County in January 1764. Her father, John, Sr., signed his consent and the document was witnessed by another John Finley, pre-

sumably her brother, and by Robert Baker, presumably her uncle by marriage.[28]

The young couple returned to Augusta County to live. James Gillespy, Sr., wrote his will 5 September 1768 and died the next year.[29] James, Jr., inherited the "plantation he now lives on with the half of the great Meadow. . . ." James and Elizabeth sold 100 acres of their property to Elizabeth's brother, John, on 18 August 1773.[30] On 22 August 1787, the Gillespys sold their remaining 300 acres on South River to Michael Coyner of Cumberland County, Pennsylvania.[31] It was then that James Gillespy, Jr., along with his brothers, John and William, went to a sparsely settled wilderness of the Indian Territory of North Carolina, State of Franklin. The State of Franklin existed from 1784 to 1788. It was originally North Carolina territory ceded to the United States to satisfy a debt. This area later became the Tennessee Counties of Caswell, Sevier, and Blount. William settled on the south side of the Holston River a few miles below where Little River joined the Holston, now in Blount County at the Holston College Cemetery in Louisville. James and John settled a few miles to the north.[32]

The names of the children of James and Elizabeth (Finley) Gillespy were provided by three Gillespie descendants.[33]

14	i.	Male[3] Gillespy, died 12 September 1792, Blount County, Tennessee.[34]
15	ii.	Jane Gillespy.[35]
16	iii.	Mary Gillespy, born 26 April 1770, Augusta County, Virginia; married Major James Houston, son of Samuel and Elizabeth (McCoskey) Houston, 16 April 1791.[36] Children included Esther Jane,

		Esther (Hettie), Lucinda C., Mary Finley, Phoebe M., Elizabeth Gillespie, Samuel Finley, Martha, Melinda Gillespie, Sidney N.
17	iv.	James (Smoking Jimmy) Gillespy, born 2 September 1772, Augusta County, Virginia; married Eleanor Cowan, daughter of William and Jane (Walker) Cowan. Children included John Finley, William Cowan, James, Ellen Jane, Campbell.
18	v.	Elizabeth Gillespy.
19	vi.	Sarah Gillespy.
20	vii.	Ann Gillespy.

4. **William² Finley (John¹),**[37] was christened 30 January 1743 at Tinkling Spring, Augusta County, Virginia.[38] He died in Wythe County, Virginia, between 15 December 1801, the date he wrote his will, and 9 February 1802, the date his will was proved.[39] He married (1) Mary Pettus, daughter of Dabney and Elizabeth (Rodes) Pettus,[40] before 1775.[41] She disappeared from the records sometime between 10 July 1787[42] and 15 January 1800.[43] He married (2) Judith. Judith later remarried Thomas Holsey before 14 January 1806.[44]

About 1765, when William was in his early twenties, his family moved from their home on South River in Augusta County to Prince Edward County. He bought 430 acres on Vaughn's Creek from John Caldwell[45] 19 August 1765.[46] Since William's step-mother was a Caldwell, one would assume the Finleys settled in Prince Edward County to be near their relatives.

William most likely married sometime after his arrival in

The Gillespy's move to the Little River area of the Holston is documented by John Finley's statement made in the Matthew Gleaves case. The document states, "You please to take notice that Intent to Take the deposition of James Gilespy in that dist.[?] now pending in the County Court of Augusta betwixt Matthew Gleaves plantiff & myself defendant at the said Gilaspy's own House on little River a water of the Holston in the New Teritory - on monday the 22nd day of July next betwixt the Hours of 12 o'clock & five in the Evening. To Mr. Archibald Stewart Atty for Mathew Gleaves, signed, John Findley, dated June ye 14th 1793." Note that this signature of John Finley is not expected to match the previous signature samples because this document is a copy made by a court clerk, not the original.

Our Fore-Fathers

Copied from a letter written by Uncle John P. Finley of Kentucky Dated January 25th 1854 To Uncle Asa H Finley Esq.

About the year 1700 my Great Grand Father Emigrated from Ireland to America with eight Sons. and settled in the State of Pensylvania;—One of this sons John by name who was my Grand Father settled in Augusta County Virginia; he had eight Sons and three daughters;—his son William was my Father and your Grand Father;—he settled in Prince Edward County Virginia, and lived there a few years, and then moved to Wyth County Virginia and died there in the year 1802;—leaving behind him four Sons and four Daughters; his sons moved to Christian County Kentucky. Asa Finley who was your Father moved from Christian County Ky to Missouri in 1818, and settled in Saline County where he lived till his Death in April 8th 1853.

This brief family history, written by William's son John Pettis Finley and copied by Newton Gleaves Finley in 1870, corroborates the movement of William's father, John Finley—from Ireland to Pennsylvania; to Augusta County, Virginia to Prince Edward County; and finally to Wythe County, Virginia.

Prince Edward County. At least we know from census records that his son, William, Jr., born before 1775, was the eldest of the male children.[47] His mother, Mary (Pettus) Finley, had a brother, Stephen, living nearby, who purchased land from John Finley on 20 July 1772.[48] Few records exist for William in Prince Edward County, but they are sufficient to show that he remained in that location after the departure of his father and brother George, about 1772/73. In September and October 1773, William acted as assignee for John Finley in a suit against Thomas and Stephen Wood.[49] George, however, appeared on his own behalf when he sold his property 20 December 1773.[50] In May 1774, William exercised a power-of-attorney for George in a suit against Stephen and Edward Wood, John Fielder, and Josiah Cole.[51] William signed a petition on 24 September 1776 in support of American independence.[52] He also appeared in land transactions in Prince Edward County 16 August 1781 and 8 May 1784.[53] Shortly after that, on 24 August 1784, he bought 165 acres in Montgomery County (later Wythe) from Samuel Montgomery.[54] He had 162 acres on the Cove, adjacent to his own patent land, surveyed 11 February 1785. This was survey #20 and was "by virtue of an entry on a treasury warrant of 500 acres No. 13145 dated 3rd August 1783 assd to him James Clerks Att."[55]

William first appeared in Montgomery County court records in 1785, when he served on a jury of inquest.[56] He also appeared a number of other times in court records, but always as a juror or to testify for others (except as noted below).[57] When they sold their last piece of property in Prince Edward County, fifty acres to Joseph Fore, 10 July 1787, he and his wife, Mary, were referred to as "of Montgomery County."[58]

William Finley was given power-of-attorney 27 August

1784 by David and Samuel Finley in Lincoln County, in order to sell the property on Salley Run they had inherited from their father.[59] On 24 January 1792 he was given power-of-attorney by John Findley of Augusta County. William Finley, Jr., witnessed this document.[60] William, Sr., acted as attorney for them 12 June 1792 when John Finley of Augusta County deeded the 327 acres on Salley Run to David and Samuel.[61] He also took care of the transaction when David and Samuel sold this property to William Finley, Jr., on 14 August 1792.[62]

On 9 September 1794, William Finley deeded two slaves, "Negro woman Nan," and "Negro boy Martin," to his loving daughter Elizabeth Montgomery of Wythe County.[63] While William did not name an Elizabeth in his will, it seems most likely that she was his oldest daughter. Other Williams living in the

---

William's son, Dabney, by his first wife, Mary Pettus, claimed five slaves for himself and his brothers and sisters, Rhoda, Margaret, John Pettus, and Asa. These slaves, Sal, Mourn, Hanna, Amy, and Spencer, were those, or the progeny of those, that belonged to Dabney's mother at the time of her marriage to William Finley.

area (his own son, and the son of Capt. James Finley), would not have been old enough to have had a married daughter. In addition, a handwritten manuscript handed down in subsequent generations through son John Pettis Finley, states that William had four sons and five daughters.[64]

As noted earlier, William's wife, Mary, disappeared prior to 15 January 1800. On that date, their son, Dabney, then living in Lee County, brought suit against his father to claim slaves, or their progengy, owned by his mother at the time of their marriage. William had sold six slaves, Caty, Abby, Rachel, Sarah, Joseph, and Charles, "from the stock whereof," and he still possessed five slaves, Sal, Mourn, Hanna, Amy, and Spencer, who either were, or were issue of, Mary Pettus's slaves. Those five slaves were transferred to his children named in the claim, Dabney, Rhoda, Margaret, John Pettus, and Asa.[65] The wording in this document, "the right to said slaves . . . passes to the children of the said Mary formerly Mary Pettus," seems to indicate that Mary was not living as of this date. This did not leave William destitute for he named five additional slaves in his will, Hagar, Ned, Sampson, Reubin, and Harry.

William wrote his will 15 December 1801 and it was proved 9 February 1802.[66] The only evidence of his second marriage to Judith is found in this will. He provided that his lands be divided into four parts, as equally as possible. One part was to go to his wife, Judith. On her decease or remarriage, that property was to go to their daughter Mary Ann, and the child, Sally Milton, "with which my wife is now pregnant." A second parcel of his land was left to his son Esau (Asa), while the remaining parcels went to Mary Ann and Sally Milton. Other children named in the will were William, Rhoda, Margaret, and John Pettis. The daughters received mares; William received his

father's blacksmith tools; John Pettis received cash after the settlement of debts. Of the three slaves which he still possessed at the time of his death, Hagar, Ned, and Sampson, one went to his wife, one to Esau, and the other was to be hired out to provide for his wife and her young children. Interestingly, Dabney, the son who claimed five slaves the year before, was not named in the will, nor was Elizabeth, who had received two slaves in 1794.

William's executors were his wife, Judith, and "my friends William Finley, Samuel Crockett and Robert Adams."

Children of William and Mary (Pettus) Finley include:[67]

+21	i.	William[3] Finley, born before 1775, Prince Edward County, Virginia.
22	ii.	Elizabeth Finley, born probably 1775/ 1776, Prince Edward County, Virginia; married Montgomery.
+23	iii.	Dabney Finley, born 22 November 1777, Prince Edward County, Virginia.[68]
24	iv.	Rhoda Finley, married 1 September 1803, Joseph Barron in Wythe County, Virginia.[69]
25	v.	Margaret (Peggy) Finley, married 16 September 1802, William Gleaves in Wythe County, Virginia.[70]
+26	vi.	John Pettus Finley, born 1780/1785, probably in Montgomery County, Virginia.
+27	vii.	Asa Finley, born about 1788, Montgomery County, Virginia.

Known children of William and Judith Finley include:

28   i.   Mary Ann Finley, married 4 April 1821, George W. Nye, in Wythe County, Virginia.[71]

29   ii.   Sally Milton Finley, born 1802, Wythe County, Virginia.

6. George[2] Finley (John[1]), was baptized 4 January 1748 at Tinkling Spring by his grandfather, Rev. John Thomson.[72] He died before 19 December 1817, the date when his son, Obediah, took inventory in Wilson County, Tennessee.[73] He married (1) Jane Fulton, daughter of Thomas Fulton before 28 April 1769 in Prince Edward County, Virginia.[74] He married (2) Mary Gaines, daughter of William Gaines of Lincoln County, Virginia (later Mercer County, Kentucky), 29 June 1786.[75]

George was most likely the last son of John Finley by his first wife, a daughter of Rev. John Thomson. His father had remarried by 1750. He was about seventeen years old when the family moved to Prince Edward County. His marriage a few years later is documented by the deed for 200 acres sold to him by his father-in-law, Thomas Fulton.[76] His property was on Vaughn's Creek, where his father and brother, William, had bought land four years earlier.[77] When George sold this 200 acres on 20 December 1773, his wife, Jane, relinquished her dower rights.[78] Nothing else is currently known of Jane or of their children.

Apparently, George was the first of the three Finleys who held property in Prince Edward County to move on to Montgomery County (later Wythe).[79] He appeared on the tax lists there in 1772 and 1773 (Captain Doack's list), where two adult James Finleys were already living.[80] This was within a few miles of where his father, John, settled and was first found on the tax lists in 1773, along with his half-brothers David and Thomas.[81] It seems that George did not remain for long in Montgomery County. At least he did not appear on the tax list of 1782, which is the next year available.[82] Nor were any land records found for George. However, George Finley acted as a witness to a deed between David and Mary Doack to Robert Doack, a transaction of 150 acres on Evans Creek, a branch of Reed Creek.[83] In addition, a George Finley was found listed among participants in Dunmore's War of 1774, from Fincastle County, and Fincastle was the county from which Montgomery was officially created in 1776.[84] Also, during this time period both John and George Finley signed a petition from the "western part" of Fincastle to divide the county so that the petitioners could more easily attend court.[85]

The next ten years or so are a void for George. He does not appear in Montgomery/Wythe County records after 1774. However, a George Finley then appears in the Dix River area of Kentucky, where David and Samuel, his half-brothers, moved from Southwest Virginia. Some caution must be exercised in assuming the George Finley who lived from about 1786 to about 1805 or so, near David Finley, is the same we have traced above. There were several George Finleys living in Kentucky during this period of time and they have not been satisfactorily sorted one from another. However, another George Finley who lived in nearby Madison County has been shown to be the son of a John Finley who lived on Coddle Creek and Rocky River in Cabarrus County, North Carolina.[86] Most of their records can be separated from one another. Another George Finley who left a will in Logan County in 1810, has been shown to be the son of John and Thankful (Doak) of Middle River, Augusta County.[87] There is also a George Finley associated with the Finleys in Jefferson County.[88] The spelling of their surname evolved to Fenley. This leaves various George Finleys who appeared in Bourbon, Fayette, Harrison, Nelson, and Woodward Counties unaccounted for. One or more of the Georges may have moved about and may account for these other records. However, if we confine our analysis to the George Finley living nearest David Finley, the following records emerge. (Note that records appear in Lincoln, Mercer, and Garrard Counties, as county lines were being established. David Finley records are also found in all these locations, even though he did not physically move).

29 June 1786 - George Finley marries Polly (Mary) Gaines of Lincoln County, Virginia, (later Kentucky).[89]

3 October 1797 - George Finley buys 100 acres on Dicks River in Lincoln County from Jesse Helton.[90]

1802 - George Finley appears on Garrard County tax records with 100 acres on Dicks River in Garrard County; David Finley nearby.[91]

18 February 1805 - George and Polly Finley sell 100 acres on Dicks River in Garrard County.[92]

1809 - Mary Finley sues George Finley for divorce in Mercer County.[93]

4 March 1809 - George Finley of Wayne County, Kentucky, places personal property with Wm. Gaines in Mercer County, in trust for George's wife, Mary.[94]

19 December 1817 - Obadiah Finley, son of George and M. Gaines Finley, takes inventory of estate of George Finley, deceased, in Wilson County, Tennessee.[95]

10 February 1818 - Obadiah Finley accounts for sale of personal property of George Finley, deceased, in Wilson County, Tennessee.[96]

Three marriage records in Mercer County identify daughters of Mary Finley, as Mary, Lucinda W., and Sally Finley.[97]

The divorce proceedings in 1809 between Mary (Gaines) and George state they had been married about twenty-two years, had nine children, and that he had abandoned her, having been gone for more than four years. Her father had been helping support her along with "her own exertions."[98] As a result of this action, George subsequently placed his personal property in trust with Mary's father, William.

It is interesting, however, to note that the last mentioned document above shows that Obediah sold George's belongings consisting of three horses, a saddle and bridle, along with a pair of saddle bags, a bell, and two books for a total of 119.12^1/_2$. The accounting was approved in court 2 March 1818.[99]

The following seems like the most probable identification of seven of their nine children:[100]

+30   i.   Obediah Gaines[3] Finley, born 24 May 1787,[101] probably in Lincoln County, Ken-

> To the Honorable the Circuit Court for Mercer County setting in Chancery — Humbly complaining sheweth unto your Honors your Oratrix Mary Finley — That your Oratrix intermarried with a certain George Finley about twenty two years ago, that she continued to live with her sd Husband untill she had nine Children and during that time performed all the duties of a faithful & loving wife. That her sd Husband George Finley who she prays may be made a defendant to this her bill, not regarding the endearing ties which ought to have induced him to have used every exertion for the support of your Oratrix & her Children — has left your Oratrix & Children

Not often seen in early records, this record of divorce proceedings brought by Mary Gaines against George Finley served to establish that they had nine children.

TENNESSEE STATE LIBRARY AND ARCHIVES
NASHVILLE 3, TENNESSEE

February 21, 1963

Mrs. Paul Heple
222 Douglas Ave
Salinas, California

Dear Mrs. Heple:

In reply to your letter of February 14th, that has been referred to me.

Please note: Official registration of births and deaths in a state agency, did not begin until 1914; therefore I would have to know what county or town in which these people lived, while in Tennessee, before I could begin to search the records. There are ninety-five counties.

I do not find a marriage for George Finley in Wilson Co. Tenn. 1802-1840, but find the following in Wilson Co. Tenn.
An inventory of the personal property of GEORGE FINLEY decd. taken the 19th day of Dec. 1817 by me Obediah G. Finley adminstrator, four heads of horses, one saddle, one pair of saddle bags, one bridle, one bell, two books, one note on hand on Isaac Crabtree for fifty dollars, dated 25th June 1813 doubtful, one note on Thomas Bouton for seven pounds ten shillings dated 10th May 1776, doubtful, one note on Joseph Brady for fifteen dollars dated 1st March 1817 doubtful, a receipt given by J. Talbot Esqr. for the collection of a bond on Charles Lynch for one thousand dollars in which saml Johnston is interested all of which is doubtful. Cash came to my hands $250
    O.G. Finley Admr.
    Dec. 19th, 1817

George Finley's Inventory
State of Tennessee
Wilson County Court   December term 1817
The foregoing inventory was exhibited in open court and ordered to be recorded
The same recorded Jan 20th, 1818
Test John Allcorn Clerk, of Wilson County, Court.

Sincerely,
Hermione D. Embry (Mrs. Chas. A.)
Genealogical Reference Librarian

George's inventory was taken in Wilson County, Tennessee, in 1817, by his son Obediah.

tucky.

+31 ii. George Finley, born 15 February, 1789, Lincoln County, Kentucky.[102]

32 iii. Lucinda W. Finley, born 23 December 1794, Kentucky; died 16 November 1874 Farmersville, Tulare County, California; married William Harrison Pennebaker, 24 September 1818, Mercer County, Kentucky.[103] He was born 19 November 1788 in Kentucky; died 7 April 1874, Farmersville, Tulare County,[104] California. Their children included Mary Ann, George Finley, John Hearst, Catherine B., Emeline, Lucinda, Lucinda Prechus, William Gaines, Sarah Ellen, and Samuel.

33 iv. Mary Finley, born about 1796, Kentucky; died 21 April 1882, Putnam County, Indiana;[105] married Joseph Denny, 30 May 1814, Mercer County, Kentucky.[106] He died in 1873, Putnam County, Indiana.[107]

34 v. Sarah (Sally) Finley, born 12 January 1799, probably in Garrard County, Kentucky; died 7 February 1877; married (1) Samuel W. Pennebaker, 4 October 1819, Mercer County, Kentucky.[108] Sarah married (2) Rev. John Wiseman.[109]

35 vi. Ann Finley, born 24 May 1801, probably in Garrard County, Kentucky; died 13 August 1857; married Robert H. Greene.

36 vii. Catharine Kitty Bruce Finley, born 24 May 1803, probably in Garrard County, Kentucky; died 14 January 1882, White County, Tennessee; married (1) William F. Brewster, 19 July 1821; married (2) Robert H. Greene after death of sister Ann.

GENERATION THREE

8. Samuel Steele[3] Finley (John[2], John[1]) was born about 1769, probably in either Prince Edward or Augusta County. He died 21 December 1833 in Scott County, Kentucky[110] There is some question as to whether he married (1) Mary Tate, daughter of John Tate, 20 September 1796 (date bonded) since there may well have been two eligible Samuel Finleys in Augusta County on this date.[111] By 1815 his wife was Martha_____.[112]

Samuel is cited in Augusta County records a number of times before his move to Kentucky. In 1789, he was a witness for Samuel Steele when he wrote his will.[113] Samuel served as surety for his sister Jean when she married William Frazier in 1794.[114] He may have served as an ensign in the militia, Infantry, 2nd Battalion, 32nd Regiment in 1796, although the other Samuel may have been the one to which this referred.[115] In 1801, he served as surety when William Finley and Sally Ramsey, daughter of Andrew Ramsey, were bonded to marry. That record carries a notation that William and Samuel were cousins.[116] Then again, he served as surety for his cousin Anne Finley when she married James Shannon in 1802.[117] Also in 1802 he served as a witness for James Steele when he wrote his will,[118] and for another John Finley.[119]

In addition to the obvious ties between Finley cousins noted above, Samuel was related to the William Finley for whom he provided surety since their mothers were sisters. Samuel's mother, Sarah Steele, was daughter of Samuel and Martha (Fulton) Steele, while William's mother, Martha Steele, was also a daughter of Samuel and Martha.

1807 was a turning point in the life of Samuel Finley. That year, his father died leaving him property in Kentucky. Land on both the N. Elkhorn and Green Rivers was mentioned.[120] Soon after their father's death, Samuel and his brother, John, moved to Kentucky. They were located in Scott County.[121] Samuel appears in the 1810 census with two males under ten, two males twenty-six to forty-five, and one female twenty-six to forty-five.[122] This suggests that brother John may have been living with Samuel initially. It also suggests that since Samuel is head of household, he was married and the two young boys were his. The next documented proof of Samuel and Martha's presence in Scott County is found in a fragmented deed, undated, but following a deed dated December 1810.[123] Then on 7 June 1813, Samuel and his wife deeded property in Augusta County to William Finley.[124] In 1817 a deed was found to Samuel and Patsy Finley from Benjamin Bradford (James Hogan's preemption) on the N. Elkhorn bordered by Gregg, Finley, and Spoon.[125] By 1820, there were five children living in Samuel's household.[126]

The date of Samuel's death, 21 December 1833, was found in notes handed down through several generations of descendants. Some confirmation is found in the court records of Scott County. On 20 January 1834, John (S. or T.) Finley was granted administration of the estate of Samuel Finley, deceased.[127]

Known children of Samuel and Martha Finley include the following:[128]

37   i.   Samuel Thomson[4] Finley, born 2 August 1815, Bourbon County, Kentucky; died 24 January 1879, Palmyra, Marion County, Missouri; married Ellen Bryan, daughter of Samuel Bryan of Fayette County, Kentucky. His obituary also refers to him as "Capt."[129] A Thomson Finley is mentioned in the inventory and appraisement of John (S. or T.) Finley, 11 September 1837 in Scott County, Kentucky, possibly, the nephew.[130]

38   ii.   Martha Jane Finley, born 11 October 1819; married Robert M. Hathaway, 7 April 1840;[131] died 7 April 1842.

9. John T.[3] Finley (John[2], John[1]) was born probably in the late 1760s or early 1770s either in Prince Edward or Augusta County, Virginia.[132] He died before 11 September 1837 in Scott County, Kentucky.[133] His wife is known only as Elizabeth.[134] They were probably married in Kentucky shortly after 1820.

When his father died in 1807, John inherited land in Kentucky on the N. Elkhorn and Green Rivers. John went to Kentucky with his brother Samuel shortly afterwards, as noted above. John was not found in the 1810 Scott County census, but was most likely living with his brother Samuel since two males age twenty-six to forty-five were shown in his household. The earliest land record found for John was undated, but it immediately preceded one dated 1811, when he and his wife, Elizabeth, sold to Samuel Gregg, land on the N. Elkhorn bordering Hogan's preemption and Bradford's line, which he had inherited.[135] In 1822, they sold another twenty acres bordering land of Bradford and Samuel Finley, to Lewis Thomson.[136] John was enumerated in the 1820 census and was shown with three children under ten years of age.[137]

No will was found for John, but there are lengthy papers showing the settlement of his estate, the first dated 11 September 1837. His son Benjamin Franklin (Frank) Finley was appointed administrator, along with W.S. Hood (unknown relationship). These were helpful in confirming family relationships.[138] In addition, on the same day, Elizabeth Finley, widow of John S. Finley, assigned her property, by deed of conveyance, to James H. Finley and Benjamin Franklin Finley along with slaves Westley, Milley, and Aia and her three children. In return, Elizabeth received three promissory notes of $500 each, to be paid the 11th day of September in 1838, 1839, and 1840.[139] The final settlement, presented in April Court 1839, showed a balance of $2,279.74, of which Elizabeth received her third. The remainder of $1,521.83 was to be divided among four heirs, each receiving $380.46 less costs, or $375.32.[140]

The children of John and Elizabeth Finley include:

39	i.	James H.[4] Finley.[141]
40	ii.	Benjamin Franklin (Frank) Finley, born 8 February 1816, Scott County, Kentucky; died 25 June 1862, Scott County;[142] married Susan Graves, 10 September 1845, in Scott County.[143] She was born 16 Novem-

ber 1830 and died 15 February 1888.[144] He was an Elder at the Cherry Spring Presbyterian Church.[145] They had at least nine children,[146] three of whom died in infancy: Joseph Finley, the eldest, who died 18 December 1942 at the age of 89;[147] Ida Finley Crosswaith; Lillian Finley; Bettie Finley Cantrell, who died 20 February 1879; Mattie Finley Neale who moved to Sedalia, Missouri; and William G. Finley, born 1857, died 1896, married Lucy Hall.

41	iii.	Joseph Walker Finley, died between 16 October 1843 and May 1844, probably in Scott County.[148]
42	iv.	Maria J. Finley,[149] married Wesley Rozell, 3 July 1839 in Scott County.[150]

21. William[3] Finley (William[2], John[1]) was most likely born in Prince Edward County, Virginia, before 1775, according to the 1820 census of Christian County, Kentucky, referenced above. He died in Christian County between 26 August 1823, the date he wrote his will, and 3 November 1823, the date his will was proved.[151] He married Nancy Barron,[152] probably in Wythe County, probably in the early 1800s.[153] She disappeared from his household between 1810 and 1820.

As his legacy from his father, William received a set of blacksmith tools. William and his brothers Dabney, John Pettus, and Asa moved to Christian County, Kentucky shortly after the death of their father. In fact, Dabney and John Pettus may have gone a bit earlier as their first grant survey dates were in 1799, while the earliest survey dates for William and Asa were in

1803. Dabney was, by far, the heaviest investor, having claimed a total of 2,987 acres in eleven different grants between 1799 and 1808. William claimed 400 acres on the west fork of the Red River, with a survey date of 20 November 1803.[154] Dabney and Asa also claimed land on the Red River, but John claimed land on Little River and Clear Creek.

William appeared in the 1810 and 1820 census in Christian County, near his brothers.[155] However, the number of children living in his household in 1820, seven males and seven females, are not accounted for in his will, which names four males and three females. The possibility exists that some of those living with him in 1820 may not have been his. Never-the-less, his will, which was written 26 August 1823 and proved 3 November 1823, does give some information on the family structure. His wife, Nancy, was not named in his will. Ely (Eli) is identified as his oldest son, and William A. is identified as his second son. He named daughters Betsey, Nancy, and Polly, and refers to his two younger sons, Walk and Jerome.[156] William A. was required to care for the girls until they married and to raise the two younger boys, since he had more than his share of his father's estate. By comparison to his brothers, William did not fare as well during his rather brief lifetime, but he did own three slaves; Jo was bequeathed to William A.; Hagar to Polly; and Stephen was to be hired out for a period of five years. His will also indicated he was a wheelwright, for his tools were bequeathed to Eli. His executors were Edward Bradshaw; his brother John P.; and his son Eli. The partition of his estate was recorded 6 September 1824.[157]

Known children of William and Nancy (Barron) Finley include:

43	i.	Eli[4] Finley, born before 1806, Wythe County, Virginia.
44	ii.	William Adam Finley, born 26 May 1806, Wythe County; died 25 October 1867, Saline County, Missouri.[158]
45	iii.	Elizabeth (Betsey) Finley, married John W. Estes.[159]
46	iv.	Nancy Finley, born Christian County; married Hardy Holman, according to Stout.[160]
47	v.	Mary (Polly) Finley, born Christian County; married 27 November 1829, Thomas Hutchinson, Christian County.[161]
48	vi.	Walker H. Finley, born about 1818, Christian County;[162] Prairie Junction, Missouri;[163] married Mary L. Wallace;[164] died 20 December 1899.
49	vii.	Jerome Finley.[165]

23. Dabney[3] Finley (William[2], John[1]) was most likely born in Prince Edward County, Virginia, 22 November 1777.[166] He died in Nelson, Saline County, Missouri, 24 March 1843.[167] He married Mary Lewis, daughter of Col. Aaron and Sarah Mary (South) Lewis, 23 July 1800. She was born 14 May 1781, probably in Kentucky; she died 22 March 1865.[168]

Dabney was first located in public documents 15 January 1800, when he brought suit against his father to recover slaves owned by his mother at the time of their marriage.[169] Dabney was living in Lee County at the time. His father, William, had already sold six "from the stock whereof," namely, Caty, Abby,

> This day Asa Finley, Administrator of Dabney Finley decd made annual settlement with the court, and he is credited as follows towit—
>
> By Vou— No. 1— Amt. paid Asa Finley— 2458.94
> 2 - " " Philander Finley 2458.94
> 3 - " " P. H. Finley 2458.94
> 4 - " " P. D. Finley 2458.94
> 5 - " " Thos. P. Finley 2458.94
> 6 - " " Robt. Crocket 2458.94
> Voucher No. 7 - " " Rhoades Marshall 2458.94
> 8 - " " Hugh Crocket 2458.94
> 9 - " " Jas. Campbell 2458.94
> 10 - " " Jno. R. Hancock 2458.94
> making in all the sum of $24589.40

Each of Dabney's children received a substantial inheritance.

Rachel, Sarah, Joseph, and Charles. Slaves Rachel, Sarah, and Joseph went to Dabney. William still held Sal, Mourn, Hanna, Amy, and Spencer. The suit questioned whether William was entitled to them or whether ownership should pass to the children of his first wife, Mary Pettus. To settle the suit, William transferred ownership in a deed of gift. Interestingly, Dabney's brother William, who was named in his father's will, was not included in this transaction, nor was Dabney included in his father's will.

Dabney went on to amass a considerable fortune. He and his brother John Pettus were the first of the children of William and Mary Finley to stake out and survey land in Christian County, Kentucky. On 27 October 1799, Dabney had 200 acres on the West Fork of Montgomery Creek surveyed; John P. did likewise on McFarland's Fork on 30 September 1799.[170] Between then and 24 September 1807, Dabney surveyed an additional 2,682 acres in Christian County on Montgomery Creek, the West Fork of Red River and Muddy Fork of Little River.[171] He also bought and sold considerable property while living in Christian County. Between 29 December 1803 and 3 March 1842, twenty-eight grantor and grantee deeds were found naming Dabney, involving around 5,000 acres. Total cost was about $3,000, while total receipts were about $9,000, a tidy profit for those days.

It is not known precisely when Dabney moved to Saline County, Missouri. However, on 21 November 1823, he traded 200 acres in Christian County for seven quarter-sections of land in Missouri.[172] He was counted in the 1810 and 1820 Christian County census[173] and the 1840 Saline County, Missouri census,[174] but was found in neither place in 1830, although his sons Brutus and Filander were located in Boone County, Missouri in 1830.[175] The 1840 census record showed Dabney owning ten slaves.

According to Stout, as noted above, Dabney died 24 March 1843. Technically, he died intestate and on 8 May 1843, his brother Asa was granted letters of administration in Saline County.[176] The extent of his estate is indicated by securities required in the amount of $40,000. It was noted in his probate records that Dabney had made a will but failed to have it witnessed, therefore, the Court would not admit it to probate. The heirs, all of whom where of age or married, entered into an agreement among themselves that carried out the intent of Dabney's will.[177] On 15 May 1844, Asa made an annual settlement to each of Dabney's children in the amount of $2,458.94, for a total of $24,589.40.[178] Final settlement showed he left an estate of just under $30,000.[179] In the final settlement, his widow, Mary, received $1,800. Also benefiting from his estate was the Board of Foreign Missions, the American Colonization Society (see discussion under his brother John Pettus Finley), and the American Bible Society, each in the amount of $100.[180]

Known children of Dabney and Mary (Lewis) Finley include:[181]

50   i.   Philander[4] Finley, born 22 September 1801, Christian County, Kentucky; married 3 September 1823, Mary T. Harris; died 2 February 1875, Saline County, Missouri. Philander has probate records on file.[182]

51   ii.   Sally Finley, born 17 November 1803, Christian County, Kentucky; married 1 May 1822, Christian County, Eli E. Finley, her first cousin, son of William and Nancy (Barron) Finley.

52   iii.   Brutus William Finley, born 6 May 1806, Christian County, Kentucky; married 8 November 1827, Sarah Adams; died 7 March 1880, Saline County, Missouri.

53   iv.   Virginia Finley, born 17 March 1808, Christian County, Kentucky; married 11 April 1829, Christian County, John R. Hancock.

54   v.   Margaret A. Finley, born 8 March 1810, Christian County, Kentucky; married 29 July 1830, Christian County, James Campbell; died 28 July 1846 in Wyoming while on wagon train trip to Oregon with brother-in-law, William Campbell.

55   vi.   Porus Dabney Finley, born 19 February 1812, Christian County, Kentucky; married 6 February 1839, Boone County, Missouri, Nancy Crockett; died 5 December 1860, Saline County, Missouri. He has probate records on file.[183]

56   vii.   Thomas B. Finley, born 15 November 1813, Christian County, Kentucky; married Rhoda Finley, his cousin (daughter of Asa and Esther (Gleaves) Finley).

57   viii.   Rhoda Finley, born 17 April 1816, Christian County, Kentucky; married 12 November 1840, Saline County, Hugh Crockett.[184]

58   ix.   Mary E. Finley, born 4 December 1818, Christian County, Kentucky; married 2

		November 1837, Saline County, Missouri, Rhodes Marshall.[185]
59	x.	Hester Finley, born 26 May 1821, Christian County, Kentucky; died 29 July 1829.
60	xi.	Narcissa Finley, born 30 June 1824 Christian County, Kentucky; married 3 November 1842, Saline County, Missouri, Robert Crockett;[186] died c1870.

26. **John Pettus[3] Finley** (William[2], John[1]) was born 1780/1785,[187] probably in Montgomery County, Virginia. He died in Christian County, Kentucky, between 16 July 1860, the date of his will, and 21 January 1861, the date his will was proved.[188] He married Hester Clarke, 26 November 1805, in Christian County.[189] She disappeared from the household between the 1830 and 1840 census.

John Pettus and his brother, Dabney, were the first to have lands surveyed in Christian County, Kentucky, John's being 200 acres on McFarland's Fork which was surveyed 30 September 1799.[190] He surveyed an additional 100 acres on 30 March 1803, 400 acres on 8 August 1806, both on Little River, and another 70 acres on Clear Creek 15 January 1810.[191] Between 9 February 1807 and 1 July 1819, he appeared as grantor or grantee on nine deeds in Christian County.[192]

John Pettus Finley became heavily involved in the establishment and support of the Cumberland Presbyterian Church at Salubria. The first house of worship was the Finley schoolhouse, which was used in common with other denominations. He later deeded it to the church and, in his will, John provided quite handsomely for the church. He left $100 outright to the Bible Society. In addition, he directed his executor to deposit the remainder of his estate in a bank, after providing for his heirs, with the annual interest to go to the Cumberland Presbyterian Church for twenty years. At the end of that time the principle was to go to the General Assembly to be used for missionary work, either at home or in foreign areas where they could best advance the Savior's causes.[193]

He was also quite involved in the American Colonization Society. The primary mission of this society was, apparently, to free slaves and return them to Liberia. He left $50 directly to the society "to remove some of the Africans to Liberia." He also made elaborate provisions designed to encourage his own slaves to take advantage of the society's goals. He states, "My will is that my servents shall be free to go to Liberia or as many of them as are willing to gou [go] after they are hired out for the space of five years to humane men. . . ." He further directed his executor to pay back to them one-fourth of what was received for hiring them out. This was to be used so that "they may enjoy some of the good things here on earth and to learn how to economise and use their money. . . ." He also provided for a way for all his slaves to pool their money so that each could have at least $500, and if the money fell short of that mark, the difference was to be made up from his estate. All of this, however, was conditional on their being willing to go to Liberia. According to a local historian of Christian County, the name of the person heading the American Colonization Society at that time was John Pettus.[194] This John Pettus, son of William Overton Pettus, is said to have come from Louisa County, Virginia, was born 9 September 1778 and died 7 January 1849,[195] hence was a contemporary of John Pettus Finley and most likely related through his mother's side of the family, probably being a cousin.

John Pettus Finley's death in Christian County, Kentucky, occurred sometime between 16 July 1860, the date of his will, and 21 January 1861, the date his will was proved.[196] From his will, it is clear that John Pettus Finley had been a financial success in his lifetime. The inventory of his estate showed the following assets:[197]

certificates/notes	$10,240.45
crop of tobacco, 10,000 lbs.	400.00
corn, 150 barrels	450.00
other crops	276.50
8 slaves,[198] ($400 to $1000 each)	5,700.00
misc. household	697.05
TOTAL	**$17,764.00**

He directed his executor to sell off all his property, five parcels containing 605 acres. The money was to be distributed to his grandchildren, as follows: $1,066 each to Sarah Jane, George C., John P., Melissa, and Amanda Finley, children of his son Milton, then living in Morgan County, Missouri; $1,200 each to Hester C. and James D. Ware, grandchildren, living in Texas. He also established a scholarship at Cumberland College for the benefit of his grandsons John P. Finley and/or James D. Ware. However, if they did not wish to take advantage of it, it was to go to any young man "who is Candidate for the ministry in the Cumberland College and Cumberland Presbyterian."

The provisions for his own children are less clear. He directs his executor to:

> . . . sell it [one share in the Henderson & Nashville Railroad] or what ever will be best for the Children who are of the following names, To Wit, William Y. Moore, now living in Missouri I have paid him off and his receipts is filed away in my will marked No. one, Hester M. Finley I have paid her off and her receipt filed away in my will marked No. two, and Margaret Finley I have paid her off and her recept filed away in my will marked No. three, And two notes my son ous [owes] me and for his satisfaction ammounting to twelve hundred and eighty three dollars and 22 cents marked Number fore and five. But I do not charge his Children with interest in said notes for they were truly unfortunate in his lost.

A marriage record does exist for Margaret Finley and William Y. Moore, 18 October 1832, in Christian County,[199] so it would appear that the above paragraph identifies two of his daughters, Margaret S. (who married William Y. Moore) and Hester M. He also identified five of his grandchildren as children of Milton Finley. The surname of two other grandchildren being Ware, a third daughter must have married a Ware. There also exists a brief two page family history, prepared by Asa Wallace Finley, nephew of John Pettus, and son of John's youngest brother, Asa. In it he states that, "Uncle John's children moved out to Missouri in an early day also and settled near my father. Their names were John, Milton, Dabney, and Clark. They had but one sister her name was Susan."[200] Stout, on the other hand, identifies two children, Milton Ogden and Hester Finley as children of John Pettus Finley.[201] An analysis of the census records of the members of the John Pettus Finley household for 1820, 1830, and 1840 gives us a fairly good picture of the composition of his family.

If all the children listed in his household were his, it would appear that John Pettus Finley had six sons and three daugh-

AGE	1820[202]		1830[203]		1840[204]
	M	F	M	F	M
<5					1
5-10			1		
<10	3	1			
10-15				2	
10-16	3				
15-20			2		
20-30			1		1
26-45	1	1			
40-50			1	1	
50-60					2

ters. Perhaps Asa Wallace Finley named only those children who were living at the time of his history, or only those who moved to Missouri. In either case, it would appear the most probable children of John Pettus and Hester (Clarke) Finley are as follows:

61   i.   John[4] Finley.

62   ii.   Milton Ogden Finley, married Mary Wear.

63   iii.   Dabney B. Finley; married Lucy B. Anderson, 5 November 1840, Christian County, Kentucky.[205] Dabney wrote his will 12 September 1840 and it was probated 2 October 1843.[206] Lucy B. Finley married Oliver C. Smith on 29 October 1850.[207]

64   iv.   Clark Finley.

65   v.   Margaret S. Finley, married William Y. Moore, 18 October 1832.[208]

66   vi.   Hester M. Finley.

67   vii.   Susan, or unnamed daughter, who married Ware and lived in Texas in 1860.

68   viii.   Unnamed son.

69   ix.   Unnamed son.

27. Asa[3] Finley (William[2], John[1]) was born about 1788,[209] most likely in Montgomery County, Virginia. He died 8 April 1853 in Saline County, Missouri.[210] He married (1) 18 August 1806 in Wythe County, Esther Gleaves, daughter of William and Elizabeth (Turk) Gleaves of Wythe County.[211] She died about 1 March 1839 in Saline County, Missouri.[212] Asa married (2) an unidentified woman by whom he had three children. He married (3) Sarah Ann Hodges 24 February 1847 in Saline County.[213] Sarah married Coleman Jeffress of Chariton County, Missouri, on 5 February 1855.[214]

Asa, the youngest of his family, struck out with his brothers for Christian County, Kentucky, at an early age. His earliest survey, 400 acres, was made 30 August 1803 on Buck Grove. He surveyed additional 100 and 150 acre parcels on the West Fork of the Red River on 16 January 1805 and 26 September 1807, respectively. Again on 16 June 1812 he surveyed another 125 acres on the West Fork of the Red River.[215] Only three deeds were found for him in Christian County, all sales totaling over 1,000 acres.[216] The last deed, executed 17 September 1818, showed Asa and his wife, Esther, living in Cooper (later Saline) County, Missouri. This is consistent with a family sketch written by his grandson Newton Gleaves Finley,[217] which he extracted in great part from a letter written by John Pettis Finley to Asa Wallace Finley (Asa's son) dated 25 January 1854.

Very little is known of Asa after his move to Missouri, except that he was very successful. According to a family sketch left by his son, Asa Wallace Finley, Asa's wife, Esther, died about 1 March 1839. This is consistent with the 1840 census which shows only two females, aged ten to fifteen and twenty to thirty in Asa's household.[218] He is also shown with eight slaves at that time, indicating he was fairly well off. After the death of his brother Dabney, in May 1843, he was empowered as administrator and granted letters of administration.[219]

His marital status after the death of Esther in 1839 is not clear. A marriage record exists for Asa and Sarah Hodges, 24 February 1847, in Saline County.[220] The 1850 census shows Asa, age sixty-two; Sarah, twenty-seven; Harrison D., eight; Helen C., seven; Henrietta, four; and a male child one month old.[221] One would assume that there was another wife between Esther and Sarah since Harrison D., Helen C., and Henrietta[222] were born after Esther's death and before Asa married Sarah. However, no certificate for this marriage has been found in Saline County.

Asa Finley wrote his will 11 December 1847, shortly after his marriage to Sarah.[223] He provided quite handsomely for her and his younger children. His older children, by Esther, had already received money and property which was accounted for in his will as follows:

Eliza and William B. Wear - $2,078 already received, receives more to total $3,000.

James W. Finley - $2,803 plus negro man Plim to total $3,200 already received, no additional legacy.

Rhoda (daughter) and Thomas B. Finley - $2,053.50 already received, receives more to total $2,500.

Asa W. Finley - $2,730 plus negro boy Clark to total $3,203 already received, no additional legacy.

Mary Jane McCorkle - $2,500 already received, no additional legacy.

Provisions to his "younger children" included the following:

Harrison Decatur Finley - $3,500 in property and cash, plus enough to give him a "good classical education."

Helen and Henrietta Finley - $3,000 each, plus enough to give them a "good plain education."

The younger children were also given the opportunity to have three slaves each instead of their cash equivalent, if they so chose. The girls were to receive 200 acres each, selected by the County Court, the value to be deducted from their total inheritance. All younger children were to be supported from the farm until they reached maturity.

His wife, Sarah, was to receive the interest on $1,000 annually, plus a Negro girl named Emily, plus farm stock and household furniture, and all the use of slaves, Wash, Eli, Nancy and her children, Polly Ann and Shadrick, who were to be kept on the farm to support his family. On her death or remarriage, the benefits were to be distributed to his children in proportion to their other inheritance. In the event Sarah had a child or children (which she did), they were to receive benefits patterned after those given to his other "younger children." He also left $100 to his great-grandson Asa Jameson, son of Janis Jameson and Jane Ware.

Four slaves, Green, Boce, Henry, and Hardin were either to be hired out or sold and the money deposited to earn interest until the youngest child reached maturity. At that time his total remaining holdings were to be sold and distributed among his heirs.

He appointed his son-in-law, William B. Wear, and son, James W. Finley, executors.

Known children of Asa and Esther (Gleaves) Finley include:

70 i. Eliza[4] Finley, born about

A substantial part of Asa's estate was comprised of the slaves he owned. While it is difficult to get an exact count of the number of his slaves at his death, this document is typical of the way in which a value was assigned to individual slaves.

1811, Christian County, Kentucky.[224] She married William B. Wear probably by 1827. Children included Mary, Finley, George, Margaret, William, Elizabeth, Susan, Francis, Louisa, Ellen, and Wallace.[225]

+71   ii.   James Washington Finley, born 13 October 1813, Christian County, Kentucky.[226]

72   iii.   Rhoda Finley, born about 1816,[227] probably in Christian County, Kentucky. She married her first cousin, Thomas B. Finley (son of Dabney Finley).

73   iv.   Asa Wallace Finley, born 3 January 1822,[228] Saline County, Missouri.

74   v.   Mary Jane Finley, born about 1825,[229] Saline County; married H.B. McCorkle, 14 October 1841,[230] Saline County. Their children included William, Elizabeth, Eliza, Archibald, and probably others.[231]

Known children of Asa and his second wife include:

75   i.   Harrison Decatur[4] Finley, born about 1842,[232] Saline County.

76   ii.   Helen C. Finley, born about 1843,[233] Saline County; married William S. Gaines before 7 April 1864,[234] probably in Saline County.

77   iii.   Henrietta Finley, born 4 January 1846, Saline County; married William B. Roy, before 4 January 1846,[235] probably in Saline County.

The only known child of Asa and Sarah Ann (Hodges) Finley is:

78   i.   John P.[4] Finley, born 1850,[236] Saline County. He was named in Asa's estate papers, and his guardian, Thomas J. Thorp, made final settlement on 5 July 1871.[237]

30. **Obediah Gaines[3] Finley** (George[2], John[1]) was born 24 May 1787, most likely in Lincoln County, Kentucky. He died 22 March 1871 in Lebanon, Wilson County, Tennessee.[238] He married (1) 26 February 1811, Mary Lewis Johnson, born 20 August 1791, died 14 February 1830, daughter of Jesse Johnson;[239] (2) Sarah Ann Johnson, sister of his first wife; (3) Bettie A. Wasson, 16 April 1861 in Wilson County, Tennessee.[240] The latter died 18 February 1883 in Lebanon.

Obediah lived in the general area where he was born, at least in the early 1800s, having purchased a lot in Stanford, Lincoln County, Kentucky, on 14 May 1808.[241] He sold it 4 July 1809 to John F. Bell for a tidy profit.[242] Soon, however, he moved on to Tennessee. He served in the War of 1812 as a private in the Company of Captain B.Q. Marles of the Tennessee Militia, having enlisted 19 December 1813. He was discharged 20 February 1814.[243] Obediah, as the administrator of his father's estate, took inventory 19 December 1817[244] and reported on the sale of property 10 February 1818.[245]

Children of Obediah and his first wife, Mary (Lewis)

Gaines, taken from the family Bible of Foster Gaines Finley, include the following:

79	i.	Jesse G.[4] Finley, born 17? November 1812; died 6 November 1904, Lake City, Florida.
80	ii.	Napoleon B. Finley, born 30 December 1814; died 25 September 1826.
81	iii.	William M. Finley, born 11 October 1816.
82	iv.	Mary Eliza Finley, born 15 September 1818; died 2 October 1821.
83	v.	John B. Finley, born 18 June 1820; died 1868.
84	vi.	Foster G. Finley, born 22 March 1822; married 17 July 1845, Altamire G. Taylor, born 10 October 1826; died 14 May 1893, daughter of Isaac and Margaret Taylor. Children included Isaac Taylor Finley, born 20 June 1847; Mary Luella Finley, born 1 December 1852; Margaret Taylor Finley, born 16 January 1856; William M. Finley, born 10 November 1857; Charles D. Finley, born 11 November 1860; Obadiah G. Finley, born 1 October 1866.
85	vii.	Sarah A. Finley, born 15 November 1823; died 1888.
86	viii.	Mary Eliza Finley, born 4 December 1826; died 1857.

31. George[3] Finley (George[2], John[1]) was born 15 February 1789 in Lincoln County, Kentucky.[246] He died 3 November 1851 in Perry Township, Monroe County, Indiana.[247] He married Frances (Fanny) Hancock, daughter of William and Martha (Patsy) Hancock, 1 March 1812, probably in Jackson County, Tennessee.[248] She was born 5 January 1796[249] in Laurens County, South Carolina, and died 9 January 1875 in Perry Township, Monroe County, Indiana.[250] Both George and Frances are buried at the Mount Salem Cemetery in Perry Township.[251]

Soon after their marriage, they moved to Overton County, Tennessee, where they were found in the 1820 census.[252] By 1830 they had moved on to Monroe County, Indiana, where they lived the remainder of their lives.[253] George wrote his will 8 August 1850, naming wife, Frances, executrix. It was proved 13 November 1851.[254]

Children of George and Frances (Hancock) Finley include the following:[255]

87	i.	Martha Finley, born 5 February 1813 in Overton County, Tennessee; died 17 September 1834. She married Zebulon Smith, 21 June 1831 in Monroe County, Indiana. They had one child, Martha Jane Smith.
88	ii.	Rufus Finley, born 22 December 1814 in Overton County, Tennessee; died 2 January 1847 in Mississippi while on a business trip. He married Nancy Mitchell, 5 November 1835.
89	iii.	William Finley, born 29 October 1816 in Overton County, Tennessee; died 11 June 1836.

90	iv.	Mary Gaines Finley, born 1 May 1818 in Overton County, Tennessee; died in 1905. She married William P. Sharpe, 2 September 1840 in Monroe County, Indiana.
91	v.	Bluford Finley,[256] born 20 March 1820 in Overton County, Tennessee; died September 1860, White County, Putnam County, Tennessee; married Adelaide Johnson, 30 December 1841, probably in Overton County. They lived out their lives there.
92	vi.	Almira Finley, born 5 December 1821 in Overton County, Tennessee; married John Horton 8 November 1840; died 25 December 1848 in Monroe County, Indiana.
93	vii.	Ann Finley, born 6 September 1823 in Overton County, Tennessee; married Wesley Stultz 17 November 1843; died March 1880 in Seward County, Nebraska.
94	viii.	Jane Finley, born 31 October 1824 in Overton County, Tennessee; died 5 September 1829, three months after moving to Indiana.
95	ix.	Sally Dillard Finley, born 8 October 1826 in Overton County, Tennessee; died 3 August 1901 in Harrodsburg, Monroe County, Indiana. She married Armstrong Carmichael, 13 March 1850. After Armstrong's death, she married Alexander Carmichael.
96	x.	Catherine Finley, born 27 November 1828 in Overton County, Indiana; died 14 August 1905; married John H. Strain in Monroe County, 13 March 1850. They lived first in Lawrence County, Indiana. Five years later they moved to Mahaska County, Iowa. After the death of her husband, 24 April 1874, she ran their 1,000 acre farm for the next twenty years, then moved to Oskaloosa, Iowa. Catherine and John had ten children.
97	xi.	Mariah Finley, born 1 May 1831 in Monroe County, Tennessee; died 6 May 1869 in Monroe County, Indiana; buried at Mt. Salem Cemetery, in Perry Township, Monroe County.[257]
98	xii.	Frances Jane Finley, born 7 February 1833 in Monroe County, Indiana. She married Monoah Hardin Sullivan 6 April 1854 in Monroe County; died 27 June 1897 in Custer County, Nebraska.
99	xiii.	David Finley, born 29 April 1834 in Harrodsburg, Monroe County; died 9 July 1863 at Vicksburg, Warren County, Mississippi. He married Julia Ann Dillman 21 May 1854 in Lucas County, Iowa. He fought in the Civil War, enlisting in Lucas County, Iowa. He died of sunstroke in Vicksburg immediately after the Battle of Vicksburg.

100	xiv.	George Finley, born 3 September 1836 in Harrodsburg, Monroe County; died 15 September 1846.
101	xv.	James Finley, born 24 June 1838 in Harrodsburg, Monroe County; died 17 August 1934 in Sargent County, Nebraska; married Matilda (Mattie) F. Nichols 5 December 1858. He served in the Civil War and afterwards moved to Sargent County, Nebraska. He was married three times, his third wife being the widow of his brother David, Julia Ann (Dillman) Finley.
102	xvi.	Infant daughter, twin to James Finley, born and died 24 June 1838.

GENERATION FOUR

71. James Washington[4] Finley (Asa[3], William[2], John[1]) was born 13 October 1813 in Christian County, Kentucky.[258] He died 2 May 1865 in San Jose, Santa Clara County, California.[259] He married (1) Margaret Jane Campbell, daughter of William and Sarah (McNary) Campbell, on 25 October 1838 in Calloway County, Missouri.[260] She was born 1 February 1820 in Muhlenburg County, Kentucky, and died 1 October 1852 in San Jose, Santa Clara County, California.[261] James married (2) Rebecca Ivy McCoy 4 May 1854 in Santa Clara County.[262]

James was about five years old when his family moved from Christian County, Kentucky, to Saline County, Missouri, in 1818.[263] He is first found there in census records in 1840[264] short-

ly after his marriage. The young family was living near James's cousins Pois (Porus Dabney) and Thomas B., sons of his Uncle Dabney, and Walker H. Finley, son of his Uncle William.[265] By 1850, the family had grown to six children, four sons and two daughters.[266] Their neighbors now included Philander, Brutus, and Porus Finley, sons of Uncle Dabney.[267] Two years later, in April, the James Washington Finley family, now with seven children under the age of thirteen, joined three other families[268] in a wagon train to San Jose, California. The total party numbered forty-four counting the necessary teamsters and cooks. A detailed account of their trip, which took five months, was written in retrospect by son Newton Gleaves Finley seventy years later and is reported in chapter 2.[269]

James's wife, Margaret, died the day they arrived in San Jose. He married Rebecca Ivy McCoy in 1854 and they started another family. James had inherited $3,200 and a Negro man, Plim, from his father's estate in 1853 and, presumably, that helped in establishing his own farm in Santa Clara County. The nature of his farming operation can be gleaned from the inventory included in his probate records. Listed were wheat, barley, and hay growing in the field. He also had, five horses, four cows, a wagon, and various farming tools. His wife's legacy was 239.63^{1}/_{3}$, while each of his ten children received $39.94.[270]

Known children of James Washington and Margaret Jane (Campbell) include the following, all born in Saline County, Missouri:[271]

| +103 | i. | William Asa[5] Finley, born 16 September 1839. |
| +104 | ii. | Newton Gleaves Finley, born 5 March 1841. |

Newton Gleaves Finley, son of James and Margaret, included this information giving vital data on his family in his history, "Our Fore-Fathers."

105   iii.   Sarah Esther Finley, born 28 September 1842. She married Rev. Joseph Emery.[272]

+106   iv.   John Pettis Finley, born 30 December 1844.

+107   v.   Hugh McNary Finley, was born November 1846 according to his brother Newton's records, but unconfirmed records from Oregon State University archives give his date of birth as 27 January 1847.

108   vi.   Ann Eliza Finley, born October 1848 according to her brother Newton's records, although her obituary gives 27 April 1849 as her date of birth. She moved to Corvallis, Benton County, Oregon, to attend Corvallis College (now Oregon State University), where her brother William was President. She married Dr. T.V. Embree, 13 February 1868, and they later lived in Lafayette, Corvallis, and Dallas, Oregon. She was living with her two sons, Clyde and Van, of Mount Hood, when she died 7 March 1925. They also had a daughter, Lillie, who married Guthrie and lived in Portland.[273]

109   vii.   James Benjamin Finley, born May 1850.

Children of James Washington and Rebecca (McCoy) Finley included the following, all born in Santa Clara County, California:[274]

110	i.	Thomas B. Finley, born about 1855.
111	ii.	Margaret E. Finley, born about 1857.
112	iii.	Joseph W. Finley, born 22 April 1860.
113	iv.	Reuben Edwin Finley, born 1 April 1862.
114	v.	Irving Hansen Finley, born 8 January 1864.

GENERATION FIVE

103. William Asa[5] Finley (James[4], Asa[3], William[2], John[1]) was born 16 September 1839 in Saline County, Missouri.[275] He died 18 July 1912 in Santa Rosa, Sonoma County, California.[276] He married Sarah Latimer, daughter of Robert A. and Malinda Latimer,[277] 8 August 1866 at Pacific Methodist College, Vacaville, Solano County, California.[278] Sarah was born in March 1848, probably in Arkansas.[279] She died 14 November 1937.[280]

William Asa and Sarah were the second of three early Finley families to arrive in Sonoma County in 1876. Their story is told in chapter 2:

Known children of William Asa and Sarah (Latimer) Finley were:

| +115 | i. | Ernest Latimer Finley, born 15 September 1870, Benton County, Oregon.[281] |
| 116 | ii. | Willie C. Finley, born March 1882, Santa Rosa, California.[282] |

104. Newton Gleaves[5] Finley (James[4], Asa[3], William[2], John[1]) was born 5 March 1841 in Saline County, Missouri.[283] He died 21 June 1933 in Campbell, Santa Clara County, California.[284] He married (1) Mary Elizabeth Hicks, 20 December 1866. She died in 1872; no issue.[285] He married (2) Kate Rowena (Minnie) Dozier, 4 August 1874 in Campbell. She was born 1 May 1848 in St. Louis, Missouri, the daughter of Lewis Fort and Cynthia (Carnes) Dozier. Rowena, as she was called, died 28 December 1926 in Santa Clara County and is interred with her daughter at Chapel of Memories, Oakland, California.[286]

Newton was only eleven years old when the family made the five-month trek by wagon train from Missouri to California, but the memoirs of that trip, written seventy years later, were amazingly detailed and a testament to his alertness in his eighties. The eight-page account, written in 1922, was preserved by family members and submitted to the Family History Center in Salt Lake City in 1981 by Dr. Alton Lovell Alderman.[287]

However, Newton's interest in recording information about the family surfaced much earlier in life. In 1870, when he was twenty-nine years old, he wrote *Our Fore-Fathers.* This was a five page document including a letter copied from one written by his Uncle John P. Finley of Kentucky, dated 23 January 1854. Some of this has already been reproduced.

Our Fore-Fathers confirms much of what has been independently discovered and written above about John Finley of Montgomery/Wythe County, and his son William. John Pettis Finley's (William[2], John[1]) grandfather was named John, and he settled in Augusta County. His father, William, settled in Prince Edward County and then moved to Wythe County, where he died in 1802. He also says John had eight sons and three daughters, while William had four sons and five daughters. This

means we have not identified two of John's daughters, but have accounted for all of William's children.[288] Newton later sketches a seven-generation family tree which shows John's father as having eight sons portrayed here.[289]

Newton, a farm laborer, was first found in California records in the 1860 census living with the rest of the family in Santa Clara County.[290] He attended Pacific University (now College of the Pacific) for two years, but left due to failing health.[291] His first marriage to Mary Elizabeth Hicks ended with her death in 1872. He married Kate Rowena (Minnie) Dozier in 1874, and the young family was still located in Santa Clara County in the 1880 census.[292] During much of that time he worked as salesman, yard foreman, and bookkeeper for the Pacific Manufacturing Company founded by his brother John Pettis Finley. However, Newton and Kate soon moved north to the Santa Rosa area where his older brother, William Asa, had relocated a couple of years earlier. Described as a "pioneer prune grower," by family members, this must have been a mecca for Newton. He had chosen the very location where Luther Burbank was conducting his plant breeding experi-

This seven generation family tree, sketched by Newton Gleaves Finley, documents earlier generations of this branch of the Finley line. Of special interest is the original generation comprised of eight sons. This is one of several indications that this earlier generation could be James and Elizabeth (Patterson) Finley, whose last known residence was in Franklin County, Pennsylvania.

(Above, left) Newton Gleaves Finley, 1841-1933.

(Above, right) Newton's maternal grandfather, William Campbell, 1793-1883.

JOHN C. FINLEY
COLLECTION

Prior to 1907, hearses were horse drawn.
J.P. Finley & Sons was the first undertak-
ing firm on the Pacific Coast to use a
motorized vehicle. The one shown here
(at right) is not the very first, but is one of
the fancier models.

(Above, right) John Pettis Finley,
1844-1924.

ments. Burbank is most often quoted by Santa Rosans from an early letter he wrote home describing the area . . . "I firmly believe from what I have seen that [this] is the chosen spot of all this earth as far as Nature is concerned . . .".[293]

Newton appeared in the Great Register of Sonoma County from 1884 through 1896, which gives his physical description in 1892 as "5'11" tall, fair complexion, gray eyes, brown hair, scar on left cheek."[294] About 1899, after their children completed high school, the family moved to Berkeley where both children graduated from the University of California at Berkeley (1902 and 1903).[295] About 1902, Newton moved back to Santa Clara County where he died in 1933. Rowena remained in Berkeley with her daughter, Edna. In November 1926, Rowena was hospitalized at Agnew State Hospital in Santa Clara, where she died 28 December of that year.

Newton Gleaves and Kate Rowena (Dozier) had two children:

117	i.	Edna Rowena[5] Finley, born 30 June 1875, Santa Clara County; died 16 March 1966 in Berkeley.[296] After graduating from high school, she took a teaching course and taught elementary school in Sonoma County.[297] She then attended the University of California at Berkeley, graduating in 1903. She remained unmarried and taught school in Berkeley for the remainder of her life.
118	ii.	Hugh Dozier Finley, born 22 December 1880, Santa Clara County; died 25 May 1960 in Berkeley, Alameda County, California.[298] He married Mary Bingham Latta 21 April 1919 in Philadelphia, Pennsylvania. They had four children: William L., Mary Dozier, Cynthiana, and Hugh. Known as Dozier, he graduated from the University of California, Berkeley, in Chemical Engineering and was Director of Research for Pabco Paint (later The Paraffin Companies) in Emeryville. He was a captain in the Army during World War I.[299]

106. John Pettis[5] Finley (James[4], Asa[3], William[2], John[1]) was born 30 December 1844 in Saline County, Missouri.[300] He died in 1924, probably in Portland, Oregon. He married Nancy Catherine Rucker, 20 April 1869, probably in Santa Clara County, California. She was the daughter of William Thornton and Veranda Rucker.[301]

John was about seven years old when the family went by wagon train from Missouri to California. Traveling on the same journey was his future wife, Nancy Rucker, who was the youngest member of the group making the trek. In 1860, at age sixteen, he was still living with the family in Santa Clara County and was listed that year as a farm laborer.[302] Shortly after his marriage, he founded the Pacific Manufacturing Company, a lumber and building concern in Santa Clara. A few years later he expanded and established a casket factory, which was the first industry of that kind on the coast. In 1887 he moved to Portland, Oregon and opened a branch of the casket company (Oregon Casket Company). He continued in the wholesale manufacturing business until December 1892, when he became a partner in the firm of Delin, River & Finley. By 1892 he became the sole owner and, when his son Arthur reached adulthood, the firm became J.P. Finley & Son. Between 1902 and 1908 he served as coroner of Multnomah County. He was active in community organizations and was a member of the Independent Order of Odd Fellows, the Ancient Order of United Workmen, the Knights of Pythias, the Artisans, the Woodmen of the World, the Knights and Ladies of Security, and the Elks. He was also active in politics and a supporter of the Republican Party.[303]

The children of John Pettis and Nancy Catherine (Rucker) Finley include:[304]

119	i.	Anna L.[6] Finley, married 7 September 1920, Frank A. Kenney.
120	ii.	Arthur L. Finley, born 1873, married Ina Craig of Portland. Their children include: John and Craig.
121	iii.	William Lovell Finley, born 1876, a naturalist, ornithologist and one-time Oregon State Game Warden. He married Irene Barnhart of California. Their two children were: Phoebe Catherine and William.

107. Hugh McNary[5] Finley (James[4], Asa[3], William[2], John[1]) was probably born in November 1846 in Saline County, Missouri. He died 24 April 1923 in Benton County, Oregon. He married Emma Cauthorn in 1872, presumably in Oregon. Emma was born 1852 in Missouri and died in 1921 in Benton County, Oregon. Both are buried at Crystal Lake Cemetery.[305]

Hugh was only five years old when the family made the trip from Missouri to California. He attended school in Santa Clara County, California. At the age of twenty-one he transferred to Corvallis, Oregon, where his brother William Asa was president of Oregon Agricultural College. Hugh graduated in 1871, one of six in the second graduating class of the college. Hugh remained at the college as professor and principal of the Preparatory Department for the next two years. During this time he married Emma Cauthorn, a classmate who graduated from OAC in 1872. The next year Hugh resigned his position at the college to accept the principalship of the public schools at nearby Shedd, Linn County. In 1876 he gave up his career in education and bought a 200-acre farm on the Willamette River, about six miles northeast of Monroe in Benton County. Here he had a prune orchard and a large grain warehouse capable of storing both his own and his neighbors' crops.

Hugh and Emma had four children, all of whom graduated from OAC.[306]

122	i.	Ross[6] Finley, born about 1774, probably in Linn County, Oregon.[307]
123	ii.	Edna Finley, born February 1876, probably in Linn County.
124	iii.	Ada Finley, born November 1883, Benton County.
125	iv.	Percy E. Finley, born October 1885, Benton County.

GENERATION SIX

115. Ernest Latimer[6] Finley (William Asa[5], James Washington[4], Asa[3], William[2], John[1]) was born 15 September 1870, Corvallis, Benton County, Oregon. He died 24 October 1942 in Santa Rosa, Sonoma County, California.[308] He married Ruth Woolsey, daughter of Frank and Sarah (Caldwell) Woolsey, 14 December 1912, in Santa Rosa.[309] She was born in 3 February 1890 in Portland, Oregon, and died 29 September 1973 in Santa Rosa.[310]

It is difficult to write "just a little bit" about Ernest L. Finley. The intent of this documentary is to focus on the three early Finley families who migrated to Santa Rosa, prior to 1900. This meant Ernest L. Finley's parents, primarily, but Ernest did come with them and it was prior to 1900.

Born in Corvallis, Oregon, in September 1870, he was barely two years old when his parents decided to return to California. During his early childhood years, both his parents were dedicated to, and actively involved in, the field of education. In later life he attributed his mother with having influenced his interest in writing and his father for having given him views that were broad and liberal.[311] No doubt his early home life also influenced his keen interest in music and the arts.[312] As early as 1879, a "musical instrument" was listed a part of his parent's taxable property. In 1881 and subsequent years, a "piano" was listed.[313] In 1884 at the opening of his father's Santa Rosa Ladies' College, Ernest played the piano accompaniment for an allegory presented by a cast of twelve young ladies. During another commencement, young Ernest played piano solos by Chopin and Shuloff.[314]

His interest in printing developed at a young age and was fostered by the possession of a small printing press which he used to print cards and handbills for both neighborhood and downtown events. When he was only twelve years old, Santa Rosa's first theater, the Athenaeum, was built at the corner of Fourth and D Streets. In addition to a 2,000 seat auditorium, it also had a Society Hall upstairs that was used for dances and it became the center of many of the town's activities.[315] Ernest became an avid fan of the shows that came to town. It was not long before his printing interests and his theater interests merged and he was printing the playbills and tickets for the Athenaeum shows. In 1890, by the time he was twenty years old, he was in the job printing business with Rufus Hawley at 529 Fourth Street.[316]

The next few years were formative ones for the business, seeing changes in partners and the establishment by 1895 of *The Evening Press*, an afternoon daily newspaper. Two years later the partners bought out the *Sonoma Democrat* and consolidated

This letter, written by Ernest to his father in 1875, has been preserved in the Oregon State University Archives.

the two under the name of *The Press Democrat*. By 1900 Ernest had bought out his partners and, at age thirty, was well on his way to becoming one of the most influential forces in Sonoma County history.

On 14 December 1912 Ernest married Ruth Woolsey, daughter of Frank and Sarah (Caldwell) Woolsey, in a ceremony at the Methodist Episcopal Church, South.[317] Ernest had been living with his parents at 1127 McDonald Avenue, but with his marriage, he and his young bride established a home at 714 Slater Street where they lived for several years before moving to 605 College Avenue.[318] These two homes were actually adjacent to each other, 714 Slater is still a well-kept home just one lot north of where Slater Street ends at College Avenue. The home at 605 College was on the corner of College and Slater next door to their previous residence. Today it is a parking lot for The Bike Peddler. Their final move to 1020 McDonald Street occurred in 1923, when they purchased the home from Henry P. and Elizabeth B. Hilliard.[319]

Ernest L. Finley championed many causes during his lifetime. An endorsement of women's right to vote, one of

The Press Democrat building, 1909.

Ernest L. Finley, 1870-1942.

COURTESY, THE SONOMA COUNTY LIBRARY

the first in the state, was no doubt related to his mother's keen interest and activities on this issue. His continuing interest in the arts merged with the development of electricity and the wireless. In 1921 he had a 400-foot antenna built from the bell tower of the fire station to the roof of his newspaper office. Before a gathering of some 700 people who stood in the street below, the first radio-transmitted opera ever sung in California was heard, preceded by the results of the Pacific Coast League baseball games. This was broadcast from the Fairmont Hotel in San Francisco.[320]

He developed a strong interest in agriculture, horticulture, and conservation and, in 1925, purchased a Jersey dairy farm and apple orchard in the Laguna District near Sebastopol.[321] Ironically, it was closed in 1975 "because stringent rules by the Water Quality Control Board made operation of the dairy uneconomical."[322] During the depression he fought to help prevent mortgage foreclosures against local farmers.

He was in at the beginning of the fight to build a bridge across the Golden Gate[323] and remained active throughout the fourteen-year battle. An often repeated comment of his, made to his circulation manager at a time when the paper was losing advertising accounts and subscriptions because of his stance on the bridge, was, "Damn the circulation! The bridge MUST be built!"[324]

When Leonard Howarth, a wealthy industrialist, died in 1930 and left $75,000 to the city of Santa Rosa, Ernest was one of several local businessmen entrusted with the disposition of the funds. Today Howarth Park embraces a spacious community park around Lake Ralphine complete with tennis courts, picnic, boating, fishing, and playground facilities.[325]

The 1930s brought other major changes to the community for which Ernest L. Finley was either directly responsible or a moving force. In 1937 he established the town's first radio station, KSRO, with the studio on the top floor of *The Press Democrat* building. His "Voice of the Redwood Empire," as he called it, was one outlet for his continuing musical interests. "Sunday nights were devoted to classical music 'The Ernest L. Finley Hour,' five hours of classical music, would endure for two decades after the founder's death in 1942."[326] He founded the Santa Rosa Symphony Orchestra and was a staunch supporter, providing one outlet for them with his new radio station.[327] He was, himself, an accomplished piano player. His daughter, Ruth, later commented, "He kept a piano upstairs at the old *Press Democrat* building and, at the end of a long day at work, he would sit down at the keyboard and play the piano all by himself, the refrains of his music filtering down through the offices and inadvertently serenading those still at work in the editorial rooms and printing department."[328]

In the mid-thirties he also helped establish the Sonoma County Fair Association. While county fairs had been held as early as 1859 in the county, it had been an off and on again affair until Ernest and other influential men of the day put it back together again. Pari-mutual betting on horse racing had just been legalized and was then combined with the agricultural aspects of the fair. He served as vice-president in 1937.[329]

In celebration of the completion of the Golden Gate Bridge, he compiled a *History of Sonoma County*. His methods were unique compared to earlier county histories that had been written. He hired three professional researchers and three competent writers to work with a twenty-six person advisory board.[330] The resulting 866-page history is still a standard work in Sonoma County.

His humanitarian efforts included a relentless campaign against infantile paralysis. He was instrumental is raising money through local fund drives to fight the disease and find a cure. "Days before his death, he personally urged foremost physicians to take active steps to obtain first-hand information about the Sister Kenny treatment for cure of infantile paralysis and bring such information back to Sonoma County."[331]

These are only a few of his many accomplishments. He was also instrumental in founding the Santa Rosa Junior College; served as Santa Rosa's postmaster for three years; served on the Santa Rosa Selective Service Board; was active in the California State Chamber of Commerce and Santa Rosa Chamber of Commerce, serving as president in 1909-1910; and was president of the Redwood Empire Newspaper Publishers' Association. He was a member of the Episcopal Church of the Incarnation, the Rotary Club, and the Santa Rosa Elks Lodge.[332]

Ernest Latimer Finley died 24 October 1942,[333] but his work and good deeds have lived on long after him. He had, during his lifetime, kept notes on many of the early Santa Rosans he had known and wrote some of his reminiscences in the diamond jubilee issue of *The Press Democrat*. His plans were to expand this into a book under the title *Santa Rosans I Have Known*. However, his death intervened. The publication of his book was done posthumously by friends and associates on the newspaper.[334]

His wife, Ruth Woolsey Finley, who had been secretary of *The Press Democrat Publishing Corporation* from 1920 to 1942, served the next thirty-one years as president and publisher. In addition, she became president of the Finley Broadcasting Company. She was both a businesswoman and a humanitarian. Her directive for *The Press Democrat* policy was, "It is to be hon-

est, independent and fair, and to support all the things that are good for this home city and area. Under no circumstances it is to be a bully—or is it to submit to being bullied."[335] Her special interests included the reestablishment of the Sonoma County Humane Society and she served as its president. For her activities there, she later received a certificate of commendation signed by President Richard M. Nixon. During the Korean War she was Sonoma County chair-

Ruth (Woolsey) Finley, 1890-1973.

man of the American Aid to the Korea Foundation for which she received a Certificate of Achievement. She served as a member of the Personnel Board to recommend a replacement for the county's retiring director of mental hygiene. Continuing work her husband had begun many years earlier, she was a long time active supporter of the Sonoma County Fair as well as the California State Fair. She received a plaque from the Western Fair Association, recognition which goes annually to a newspaper that gives major assistance in the promotion of fairs. When she died 29 September 1973, ownership of the Finley fortunes went to her son-in-law and daughter, Evert B. and Ruth Finley Person.[336]

In 1977 Ernest L. Finley was chosen as the entrant in the

California Newspaper Hall of Fame to join other such notables as M.H. and Charles de Young, Col. Harrison Gray Otis, and William Randolph Hearst.[337]

In 1985 the Ernest L. and Ruth W. Finley Foundation was formed by Evert B. Person, their son-in-law and only remaining tie to the family. A second foundation was formed at the same time, the Evert B. and Ruth Finley Person Foundation. The stated purposes and activities of the foundations are for the performing and visual arts, social services, and religious endeavors; to promote music; and provide scholarships and grants into human diseases and the study of journalism, engineering and the sciences. The nine years that have elapsed have seen the establishment of Finley Community Park in West Santa Rosa—a twenty-two-acre area that includes swimming pools, a gymnasium, weight-training and exercise rooms, meeting rooms, a kitchen, a large hall and a theater—a seven million dollar gift.[338] In addition, a challenge gift of three million dollars went to Sonoma State University for use in the performing arts. Another one million dollars went to the Luther Burbank Center; the Ruth Finley Person Theater commemorates this gift. Money from these foundations has also helped build playgrounds and aided youth organizations, supported Canine Companions for Independence, helped remodel the Church of the Incarnation, built a child-care center at St. Eugene's Catholic Church, supported the Santa Rosa Symphony, Redwood Gospel Mission, and the Summer Repertory Theater.[339]

Ernest L. and Ruth (Woolsey) Finley had a daughter and an adopted son:

+126 i. Ruth Finley, born 27 November 1916, San Francisco.

127 ii. Robert Woolsey Finley (adopted), who in 1975 lived in Carmichael, California with his son, James Christopher Finley. He has two daughters, Carolyn Elaine Finley, San Francisco, and Dana Annette Stockton, Sacramento.[340]

GENERATION SEVEN

126. Ruth[7] Finley (Ernest Latimer[6], William Asa[5], James Washington[4], Asa[3], William[2], John[1]) was born 27 November 1916 in San Francisco and died 15 May 1985 in Palo Alto, California. She married 26 January 1944 in Santa Rosa, Evert B. Person,[341] a native of Berkeley, born 1914.[342]

By the time she was born, Ruth's father was well established as Santa Rosa's leading newspaper publisher. She grew up in a atmosphere which included a strong interest in music and the arts. It is no surprise that she became an accomplished pianist, having majored in music at the University of California at Berkeley, with continuing study in New York City. She studied with Wager Swayne, Arthur Schnabel, Frank Mannheimer, Adolph Baller, Alexander Liberman, Elizabeth Simpson, and Harald Logan and made her debut as a concert pianist in San Francisco in 1950. In subsequent years she made a concert tour of Mexico and appeared as soloist with the Stockton, Napa, Oakland, San Francisco, and Santa Rosa Symphonies.[343] She also performed under Arthur Fiedler, then conductor of the Boston Pops. While touring Mexico, she performed on the National Radio Hour. Other radio performances were made both in New

Neat Tribute Paid Ruth Finley

Hal Garrott, music critic of the Monterey Herald, pays a fine tribute to Miss Ruth Finley, talented Santa Rosa pianist, who appeared Saturday evening in a Bach recital at the Hotel Del Monte. In describing Miss Finley's work, Garrott says:

RUTH FINLEY, PIANIST, WINS OVATION HERE

By HAL GARROTT

If the Bach Society continues to select such artists as Ruth Finley, the pianist who played in Hotel Del Monte last night, we predict success for the organization.

Miss Finley is a charming brunette, petite, with exquisite stage presence, and quite young. But, oh, how she can play. A local musician compared her with Fanny Bloomfield-Zeisler in her youth, and the comparison is just. Ruth Finley has the Zeisler vitality, brilliance and nervous quickness. She possesses great power, which she does not abuse for technical display.

On the musical side, this pianist's playing is colorful, possesses contrast and displays lyric beauty in such numbers as Respighi's "Nocturne" and the Gluck "Ballet Music" encore.

Ruth Finley will bear watching. Certainly she possesses fire as well as the technical equipment requisite to land her near the top of her profession.

York and in California and she once had her own radio program on KSRO, the local station established by her father.

She was vice-president of *The Press Democrat Publishing Corporation* and the Finley Broadcasting Company from 1944 to 1973 and took over as secretary and secretary-treasurer, respectively, at the death of her mother in 1973. Ownership passed to the Persons at that time. Evert B. Person joined both the family and their newspaper and radio business after his marriage to Ruth. He became co-publisher and secretary-treasurer of *The Press Democrat* and secretary-treasurer of the Finley Broadcasting Company at that time. He successfully saw the paper through many changes in the next forty years and eventually became publisher and editor-in-chief.[344] The Persons were actively involved in the Luther Burbank Foundation formed in 1975 to establish a per-

This newspaper article in The Press Democrat, Sunday, April 10, 1938, gives testimony that Ruth Finley was well on her way to an outstanding musical career in her early twenties.

forming arts center for the community. Together, with twelve other local couples, they formed a partnership to buy the Christian Life Center complex, then in bankruptcy, and this became the Burbank Center for the Arts. Ruth served as a member of the center's board of directors.

In other community and civic activities, Ruth served as a member of Sonoma State University's Advisory Board and the board of Visiting Home Care Service. She was president of the California

Ruth (Finley) Person, 1916-1985

Newspaper Publisher's Women's Group and was a charter member of the Etude Music Club of Santa Rosa and first president of the Symphony League. Ruth's father had founded the Santa Rosa Symphony Orchestra and the Persons continued to support it. In 1981 they donated forty acres of land on Mark West Spring Road, valued at $200,000, to the Santa Rosa Symphony Association, the largest single gift since its inception. She was also active in the Camp Fire Girls' activities and the Welfare League. She was a member of the Episcopal Church of the Incarnation, the Saturday Afternoon Club, Santa Rosa Golf and Country Club, San Francisco Metropolitan Club, St. Francis Yacht Club of San Francisco, Santa Rosa Ballet Guild, and Santa Rosa Memorial Hospital Auxiliary.

The Press Democrat was sold to the New York Times in May 1985, just prior to the death of Ruth. However the Finley support of the community continues in the capable hands of Ruth's husband, Evert Person (see discussion above under Ernest Latimer Finley).[345]

SUMMARY

Much of the same pioneer spirit seen in John's children by his second wife, Mary Caldwell, is also noted in his first family by a daughter of the Rev. John Thomson. Although his two eldest sons, John and William, both lived out their lives in Virginia, John in Beverley Manor and William in Wythe County, their children pushed on with the frontier. Daughter, Elizabeth, moved with the Gillespy brothers to Tennessee by 1787, and son, George, was in Kentucky at least by 1786, years before either area had gained statehood.

The next generation, children of John, Jr. and William, were in Kentucky in the first decade of the 1800s. Samuel and John (John^2, John^1) and William and John Pettus (William^2, John^1), lived out their lives in Kentucky. Dabney and Asa (William^2, John^1) pushed on to Missouri during the first quarter of the nineteenth century, about the time Missouri became a state. Dabney's daughter, Margaret, who married James Campbell, died while on a wagon train to Oregon in 1846. Asa's son, James Washington Finley, made the overland trip to California safely in 1852, although his wife died just as they arrived.

Another theme is noted, especially in the sons of William, and that was the ability to amass a considerable fortune during their lifetime. Dabney was clearly a heavy land speculator. At his death in 1843, the bond required of his administrator was set at $40,000. The 1840 census showed he owned ten slaves. John Pettus's estate in 1861 totalled just under $18,000 and he owned eight slaves at the time. He also made an elaborate plan whereby his slaves could become free men and earn their own passage to Liberia under the structure of the American Colonization Society. The appraisal of Asa's estate in 1853 totalled almost $32,000 and included four slaves. However, he had already given from $2,000 to $3,000 to each of his five older children.

Measures of financial and/or professional success are also seen in a number of Asa's grandchildren (sons of James Washington Finley). William Asa Finley (1839-1912) became the first president of what is now Oregon State College in Corvallis, Oregon. His son, Ernest Latimer Finley (1870-1942), developed the leading newspaper in Santa Rosa, California, *The Press Democrat*, established the first radio and TV stations; and left a multi-million dollar Foundation which recently donated $7,000,000 for the establishment of Finley Community Center and Park. John Pettis Finley (1844-1924), founded the Pacific Manufacturing Company in Santa Clara, including a casket factory, the first of its kind on the coast. In 1887 he moved to Portland, Oregon, where he continued manufacturing caskets and established the Finley Mortuary. The latter is still being operated by his descendants.

Members of both families of John Finley, Elder of Tinkling Spring in Beverley Manor, Augusta County, made significant contributions to the development of a young and developing America.

CHAPTER SEVEN

ANCESTORS AND DESCENDANTS OF HARRISON FINLEY (1836-1917)

Harrison Finley's probable great-grandparents John and Thankful (Doak) Finley, were also among the earliest settlers of the Shenandoah Valley in what is now Augusta County, Virginia, most likely having come from Pennsylvania. Like their early neighbors, they were Scotch-Irish Presbyterian farmers. John was also a wheelwright. From land records and other documents we can get some feel for his life in this early Virginia settlement. John and Thankful lived on Middle River, a branch of the Shenandoah. While his property is not shown on the settlement map of Beverley Manor, one can make a pretty good estimate of his location as being just across the manor line near the property of Robert Davis.

We cannot be sure whether John Finley and Thankful Doak were married in Pennsylvania or in Virginia. The Doaks were also early settlers in this region and it is possible that John and Thankful met after both families arrived in the area. Thankful's brothers Samuel and David Doak, had properties about ten miles due south of John's Middle River property. Her sister, Ann Doak, was married after the Doaks moved to Augusta County.

The first record found for John appeared in Augusta County records of 1 December 1740 when he received a patent for 183 acres "on a branch of Cathey's River called Finley's Branch" (now Middle River).[1] Since the actual receipt of a patent was the third step in a process that normally took several years, we can assume they were probably in that location by 1737 or 1738. On 15 October 1741, he received another patent

for 300 acres "on a draft of Cathey's River."[2] This property was described as being adjacent to land owned by Alexander Breckenridge, whose son George married Thankful's sister, Ann Doak, the next year.[3]

John sold his first patent, 183 acres, to Alexander Garden on 27 November 1749.[4] On 17 November 1767, John and Thankful deeded 179 acres of their property to their son George for five shillings. George, however, soon moved to Washington County about 170 miles to the southwest and sold his Middle River property to Robert and Margaret Clendenen for £16 less than five years after it was given to him.[5] The Clendenens, in turn, sold it back to John and Thankful three years later for five shillings.[6]

On 20 July 1768, John acquired another patent of 238 acres "on a branch of the middle River of Shanando adjoin to the land he lives on."[7] This same year he was named as one of the representatives and commissioners[8] of Brown's Meeting House and received two acres on Meadow Run, a branch of Middle River, from John and Margaret Brown.[9] North Mountain Meeting House (later Hebron), which was the church nearest the Middle River neighborhood, had originally been "Old Side" Presbyterian and held only sporadic services until the mid-1740s when the "New Side" revivalist Presbyterians stepped in. Brown, not pleased with this turn of events, joined with his neighbors to build a meeting house near his home. Brown's Meeting House officially opened its doors 16 February 1748.[10] This, perhaps, explains why John and Thankful's children were baptized at Tinkling Spring, some fifteen miles away, until

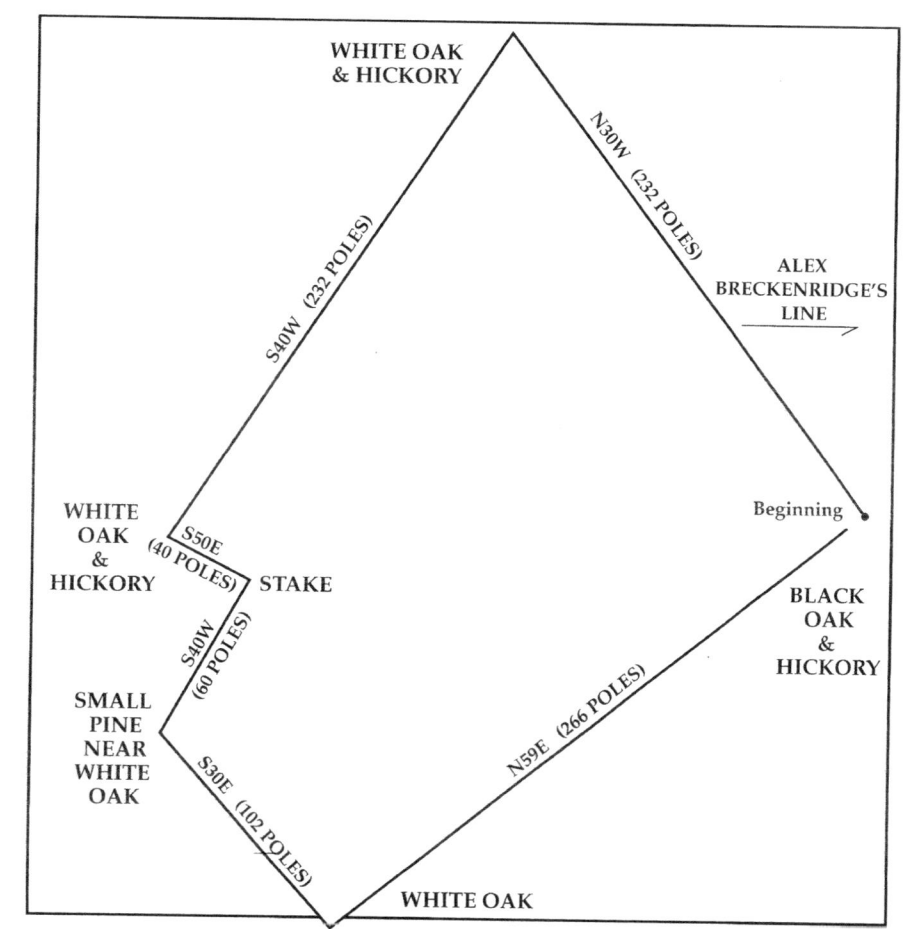

John Finley's patent for 300 acres, which he received in 1741, was adjacent to that of Alexander Breckenridge. The next year the Breckenridges became family as well as neighbors when Ann Doak, sister of Thankful (Doak) Finley, married Alexander's son George. The alliance between the Finleys and the Breckenridges continued a generation later when John and Thankful's son Robert married Sarah Breckenridge, daughter of George and Ann (Doak) Breckenridge.

John and Thankful (Doak) Finley lived west of Brown's Meeting House on Middle River. (Below), John and Mary (Caldwell) Finley lived east of Tinkling Spring Meeting House.

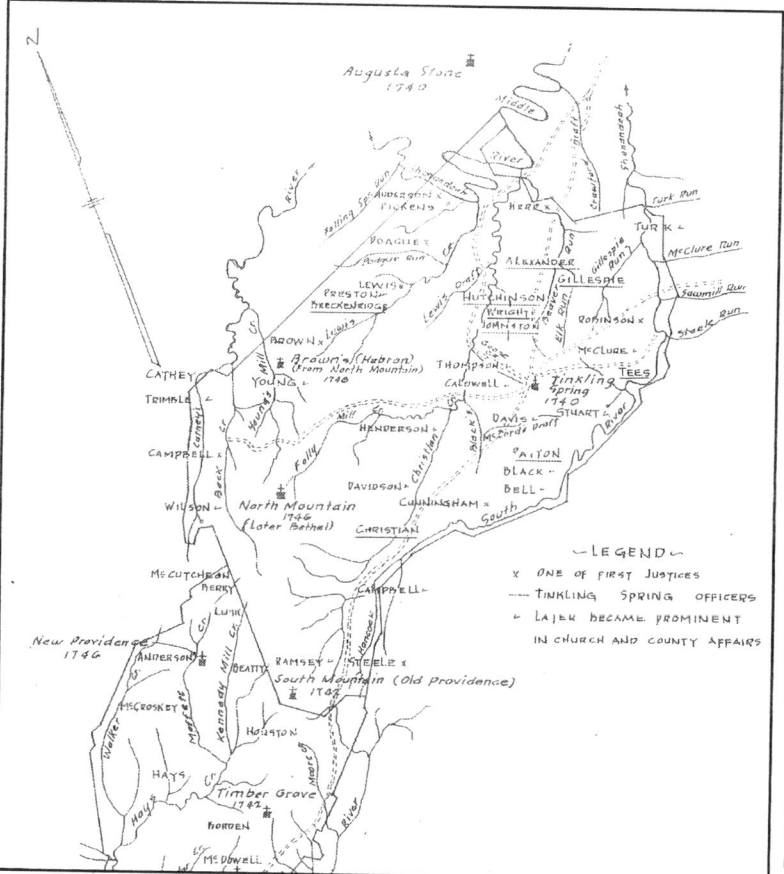

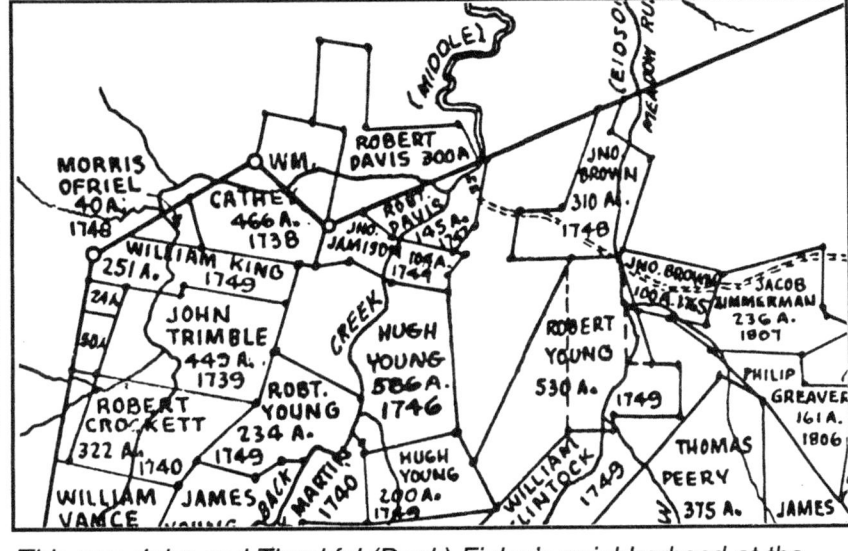

This was John and Thankful (Doak) Finley's neighborhood at the extreme northeast corner of Beverley Manor.

December 1746. The map of Beverley Manor and Borden Grant Meeting Houses reproduced here shows the relative distance between Tinkling Spring and Brown's Meeting House.

On 16 March 1773, John was bound, along with his neighbors William McPheeters, Jr. and George Berry, in the settlement of the estate of William McPheeters, Sr.[11] That same year, John and Thankful were both named in an accounting of Samuel Craig, who served as a guardian for John Black, orphan of Anthony Black. John received £5 and Thankful received £5 6s. for services or goods.[12] Three of the persons with whom John is associated in these documents, John Brown, Hugh Young, and John Trimble, can be found in the extreme northwestern corner of Hildebrand's map of The Beverley Patent. They lived either on, or close to, the Manor line and near Middle River.[13]

This gives us another good indication of the location of John and Thankful's property as being just outside the Manor line along Middle River.

John Finley appeared on the tax rolls during the periods 1777-1778 and 1782-1787, the only years for which lists were found. Until 1786 he was listed as the only tithable in his household. His 1786 entry read "Jno & David," while the 1787 entry read "self & son David."[14]

John wrote his will on 7 August 1791 naming in order; wife, Thankful; children, David, George, Robert, Margaret Shields, James,[15] John, Jean, and Thankful McKarter; and grandson John Trimble, son of Jean. David received the lion's share of the estate. Thankful received all household furniture except "one old bed and furniture," his Negro woman, Hannah, and a saddle and horse, with maintenance out of the estate willed to David. George, Robert, and Margaret Shields received five shillings each. James received £120 "with interest from this date," to be paid by David out of the estate. John was to receive one bed and furniture upon the death of Thankful. Jean was to receive a mare and Negro woman upon the death of Thankful, while her son, John Trimble, was left a saddle and bridle. Thankful McKarter was left six shillings. David, probably the youngest son, was also named executor.

It is interesting that John chose to divide his estate so unequally and no clues have really been found as to why this was so. Often, when the parents have already provided for their children, the children are left only nominal amounts in the will. This may have been the case here and is just not specified. We do know, however, that George received a portion of John and Thankful's property in 1767. Naming David as executor may have been a practical necessity as it appears all other male sons

> *[handwritten excerpt from will]*

John and Thankful's son was "James" not "Thomas."

Three key documents from early Augusta County records prove that it was John and Thankful Finley's son, James, not Thomas, who inherited, "one hundred and twenty pounds Virginia Currancy with interest from this Date [17 August 1791] to him and his heirs for ever to be payd by my son David out of the part I now will to him." This, no doubt, contributed to errors of interpretation made by earlier researchers who claimed John and Thankful's sons, John, Robert, and Thomas went to North Carolina.

Two versions of John Finley's will exist and are available through the office of the Augusta County Clerk. The original version contains the actual signature of John Finley. Another version, in a completely different handwriting, was prepared by a scribe. In the scribe's version, "James" was apparently read and transcribed as "Thomas."

An excerpt from John's original will, shown above, shows "Virginia Currancy," inserted between "shillings" and "to them." The insertion mark, which is directly above "James" makes it appear that the son's name could have been read as "Thomas." Unfortunately, the error made by the scribe was the one used by Chalkley in his transcriptions.

> *[handwritten excerpt from deed of trust]*

Further confirmation that it was "James" and not "Thomas" who was named in John's will is found when David settled his father's estate. In carrying out the intent of this portion of his father's will, David, who was named executor, made a deed of trust to his brother-in-law John Shields, "in Consideration of the Sum of one hundred twenty pounds which he the Said David Finley is Justly indebted to James Finley." This obligation further identifies the same time period for interest specified in John Finley's will. The name, "James," is clearly readable in this document.

one falling Leaf oval Table	1	10	
Seven Walnut Chairs	1	1	
two Split bottom ditto		8	
one check reel		4	
one Large wheel and one small wheel		13	
One small wheel 1/. Cans bottles 8. Chist 9/. one Box 1/.	1	2	
Puter £1.1.3, one dozen of Puines plaits 5/. Sundries 3..11	2	1	11
one spice Morter 9/. Hammer with sundries 1/. for Bottle 3/.			
Looking glass .. 2/		16	
two hackles 18/. Spoon 7/3 one mug Teapot 1.6		13	9
one Bed and furniture	4	5	
two sheats and Cwer how table Cloth two pillow Cases	5	17	6
Loom and tackle £2..5/ pails 5/ pots 1/4 hangings 9/ shovel tongs	4	11	
Cooper tools	2	10	6
four Bells 13/ two Mattocks 9/ Sadle & Bridle 15/. Iron wedges 5/	2	2	
Books £5 still vessels 14/ one Gun barrel £2..10	8	5	6
old vesals saddle bags 3/9 one sorrell Mare £7	7	3	9
Loom gear 6/ one woman saddle & bridle £1..17..6	2	3	6
two sutes of mens Cloath £4..12..6 one pair of sillyards 12/	5	4	6
one Great Coat 6/ one hat 6/ a parcel nott of Same Stuart tat	10	14	
a nott of a Book acct against David Finly of £19..6	19	16	
Small trunk two hooms and pockett Book		10	
Gold weghts 10/. one old still & worm £3..1..6	3	11	6
one dung fork 2/6 hay fork 2/ ten geese 1/6		19	6
	99	5	2

had left the area by 1791.

An appraisal of John's estate was made on 20 December 1791 by David McNair, James Wilson, and John Thomas, the same men who had witnessed his will. The total of his estate was £99 5s. 2p. including one slave, Hannah, valued at £12. The largest single entry was a book of accounts of David's totalling £19 16s.

It is not known how much longer Thankful lived. However, David sold his entire holdings on 1 October 1794 to John Johnston for £1,100 and moved on,[16] suggesting, perhaps, that Thankful had died prior to that time.

Known children of John and Thankful (Doak) Finley include the following, in the order named in John's will (except for David who is presumed to be the youngest male):

+2   i.   George[2] Finley, christened at Tinkling Spring, 30 January 1743.[17]

+3   ii.   Robert Finley, christened 21 April 1745, at Tinkling Spring.[18]

+4   iii.   Margaret Finley, christened 21 Nov-

The appraisement of John Finley's estate lists a set of cooper tools. This helps separate him further from the Finleys who lived on South River. In May 1746, court records state, "Robert Armstrong was appointed overseer of a road from Jennings Gap to Daniel McAnaires [McNair] thence to John Finla's cooper - thence to the Courthouse all tithes within four miles on each side to work the road." Jennings Gap is about six miles from the Middle River property of John Finley to the northwest, while the South River Finleys lived southeast of the Middle River community. The McNairs also lived in the Middle River area and David McNair, son of Daniel, was a witness to John Finley's 1791 will.

+5	iv.	ember 1746, at Tinkling Spring.[19]
		James Finley.
+6	v.	John Finley.[20]
+7	vi.	Jean Finley, married Joseph Trimble.[21]
8	vii.	Thankful Finley, married McKarter.
+9	viii.	David Finley.

GENERATION TWO

2. George[2] Finley (John[1]) was christened at Tinkling Spring in Augusta County, Virginia, 30 January 1743.[22] His wife, Jean/Jane, is first identified in a deed of sale on 17 March 1772.[23]

George's first appearance as an adult in Augusta County was on 17 November 1767 when, at age twenty-three, John and Thankful deeded to him 179 acres, "a part of John Finleys land he now lives on,"[24] for five shillings. Perhaps this was at the time of, or near, his marriage. Four and a half years later, George and Jane deeded this property to Robert Clendenen on 17 March 1772 for £16.[25] Although George and Jane were referred to as "of Augusta" at the time, this transaction probably signalled their intent to move on. This particular piece of property was resold back to John Finley by the Clendenens on 21 March 1775 for five shillings.[26]

On 25 January 1772, just prior to George's sale to the Clendenens, he had thirty-five acres on the south side of Middle River surveyed,[27] indicating he had already set in motion the application for a grant which was to come on 1 February 1781.[28] George and Jean/Jane held this property for almost eleven years and then sold it to David McNair on 20 December 1791.[29] This was helpful in positively identifying George and Jean/Jane Finley of Washington County as the same who received property from John and Thankful in 1767.

It appears that the George Finleys made the physical move to Washington County, Virginia, prior to 29 January 1777, for on that date he was ordered to be an appraiser in the estate of Edward Sharp.[30] Interestingly, Alexander Breckenridge was also named an appraiser. This might well have been George's cousin since George and Ann (Doak) Breckenridge did have a son Alexander.

George appeared regularly in Washington County Court Minutes from January 1777 through March 1784. He served on jury duty numerous times,[31] participated in the planning of new roads,[32] and served in various capacities in estate settlements involving Edward Sharp,[33] James Young,[34] Thomas McCullock,[35] Thomas Hill,[36] William Campbell,[37] James Mobley,[38] and William Grier.[39] On 18 June 1782, he was named along with others for selling liquor higher than the rates allowed by law, but the case against him was dismissed.[40] An orphan, Thomas Watson, was bound to George on 23 August 1782.[41]

George was clearly a Revolutionary War soldier. On 30 September 1777, he filed a claim for £2 15s. for a saddle he lost in an expedition against the Shawnee.[42] He was listed as a lieutenant in the Shawnee Expedition and in the Battle of King's Mountain.[43] He acted as commissary to the Washington County Militia and submitted vouchers in the sum of £2,570 3s. 5p. on 25 November 1777.[44] On 20 May 1779, he was recommended as a lieutenant in the Washington County Militia.[45] By 17 October 1792, George was being referred to as a captain.[46]

George was also active in political concerns of the times. On 17 January 1785, he was one of a number of petitioners to the Congress of the United States concerning the rights of citizens

COURTESY, SMITHSONIAN INSTITUTION

A Virginia rifleman of the Seventh Regiment in frontier uniform during the American Revolution. Drawing by Peter Copeland.

On the Virginia frontier settlers lived simply amid threat of Indian attack. Drawing by Thomas L. Williams.

COURTESY, PARKE ROUSE, JR., FROM HIS VIRGINIA: THE ENGLISH HERITAGE IN AMERICA

in his area and the proposal of a new state.[47] That same year, he also signed a petition to Patrick Henry, Governor of Virginia, concerning the adoption of a new militia law.[48] On 18 May 1786, George made a deposition at Abingdon concerning Arthur Campbell, a local magistrate, and the difficulty people were having paying taxes.[49]

The first survey made by George in Washington County was for 400 acres on the North Fork of the Holston in 1781. George's next surveys occurred on 27 and 28 May 1785 when he surveyed 370 acres on the East Fork of Wallace's Branch of the Holston and an 180 parcel on both sides of Wallace's Branch.[50] On 2 October 1786, George received his patent for 370 acres and was mentioned as having land adjacent to John Finley's patent of 312 acres on the headwaters of the East Fork of Wallace's Branch, waters of the North Fork of the Holston River.[51] George also received a patent for 180 acres on 6 June 1793.[52] George bought another 264 acres on the North Fork of the Holston from Patrick Watson on 14 October 1788.[53] George and Jean, his wife, began selling their land in 1795; three parcels of 127, 85, and 158 acres each went to Moses White, John White, and Joseph White.[54] Additional sales were found 15 March 1799, twelve acres to Hugh Miller, Sr.;[55] 21 October 1801, three parcels of 265, 44, and 56 acres to John Greenway;[56] and 5 July 1805, 180 acres to William Harley.[57] The 1805 deed indicated that George Finley was "of Kentucky." This turned out to be Logan County, Kentucky, where George was first recorded as a grantee on 14 June 1798, having bought 200 acres on waters of Clifty.[58]

Marriage records were found for two of George and Jean's three daughters. Betsy Finley married Peter Hay on 30 January 1794 and Rachel Finley married James Glenn on 2 February 1797.[59]

George Finley wrote his will on 22 August 1810.[60] In his will he named son-in-law James Glenn and daughter Rachel, his wife; son-in-law Peter Hay and daughter Elizabeth, his wife; son-in-law Hugh Orr and daughter Mary, his wife. George did not name his wife, so one would assume that Jean/Jane died sometime betweem 5 July 1805, the last date her name appeared on a deed, and 22 August 1810 when the will was written.

From 1814 to 1820, the last being dated 18 November 1819 and recorded 10 January 1820, seven land records were found for George Finley in Logan County. With one exception involving the settlement of a land dispute with John Washington,[61] all were deeds made "in consideration of love & for other good causes" to his three sons-in-law.[62]

Known children of George and Jean/Jane Finley included:

10   i.   Rachel[3] Finley, married James Glenn, 2 February 1797, in Washington County, Virginia.[63]

11   ii.   Elizabeth Finley, married Peter Hay, 30 January 1794, in Washington County, Virginia.[64]

12   iii.   Mary Finley, married Hugh Orr.

3. Robert[2] Finley (John[1]) was christened at Tinkling Spring in Augusta County, Virginia, on 21 April 1745.[65] According to one descendant, Alverta Brown Martin, he married Sarah Breckenridge, daughter of George and Ann (Doak) Breckenridge, in 1777. They were said to be living near her father's home in southwest Virginia at the time of their marriage.[66] While this record has not yet been found, George Breckenridge did name a daughter, Sary Findley, in his will.[67] Since George and Sarah's mothers were sisters, this would mean Robert and Sarah were first cousins.

Robert's life has been pieced together from existing histories and the primary evidence that has been found tends to support Martin's work to a greater extent than that given by France.

Robert is found in only two Augusta County documents. He signed as a witness when his brother, George, was given 176 acres by John and Thankful on 17 November 1767.[68] He was also named in his father's will in 1791 and was given five shillings.[69]

Ample support is found for his having lived in southwest Virginia, near George Breckenridge, in numerous documents found in Montgomery County. George Breckenridge's property can be fixed precisely about three or four miles northeast of Wytheville, by a settlement map of Wythe County, formed from Montgomery County in 1789.[70] Members of the Doak clan, Samuel, David, Robert, William, and John, lived about eight to ten miles due west of Wytheville. Robert Finley and George Breckenridge were both found on John Montgomery's list of persons who took the Oath of Allegiance in 1777.[71] On 8 April 1778, Robert was fined for refusing to go out to the Frontier after being called on.[72] On 5 May 1779, he served on jury duty, and again on 17 November 1780.[73] Robert Finley had a survey made on 27 March 1783 for 148 acres on Cove Creek, waters of Reed Creek. The description referred to a common line shared with Breckenridge.[74]

Martin claims that shortly after Robert and Sarah married, they "moved southward down the Valley of the Holston River to the western border of North Carolina. Amid many dangers and with the prospect of greater hazards, he cleared his land and built a home for his family in the center of the wilderness."[75] She claims they later went on to Blount County, Tennessee. While no records could be found for Robert between 1783 (last appearance in Montgomery County) and 1796 (first appearance in Blount County), a number of records were located for a Robert Finley in Blount County between 1796 and 1818.

On 12 September 1796, Robert Finley appeared in Blount County on a list from which a grand jury was chosen. On the same list were a number of familiar Augusta County names; James Gillaspy, John Gillaspie, George Berry, Robert Wilson, John Finley,[76] and Alexander Read.[77] The Gillespys were South River persons, James Gillespy having married Elizabeth Finley, daughter of John Finley the commissioner and elder at Tinkling Spring, not directly related to the Middle River Finleys.[78] George Berry was one of the commissioners appointed along with John Finley of Middle River, when John and Margaret Brown gave two acres of land to build Brown's Meeting House in March 1768.[79] George Berry and John Finley of Middle River were also bonded together in the settlement of the estate of William McPheeters on 16 March 1773.[80] James Berry was a witness on 1 October 1794 when John and Thankful's son David, sold the Middle River property left by John.[81] John Wilson was a witness to the will of John Finley of Middle River on 17 August 1791.[82] David Finley, son of John and Thankful, married Elizabeth Wilson, daughter of Joseph Wilson, on 10 March 1791.[83] James Wilson was one of the appraisers of the estate of John Finley of Middle River, 20 December 1791.[84] James and John Wilson were witnesses when John and Thankful's son George sold his thirty-five acre patent to David McNair, 20 December 1791.[85] Alexander Reid was the father-in-law of the

John Finley who left a will dated 2 February 1802 in Augusta County.[86] This John Finley was the son of Captain William Finley and they both lived on the Robinson property bought originally by John of South River in 1746.[87] However, the Reids were also found on Middle River.[88] It appears there was a neighborhood in Blount County which was comprised of a number of the Augusta County descendants, including persons who had lived on both Middle River and South River.

When Robert Finley was again called upon to serve on a jury in May 1801, other familiar Middle River names appeared—John Trimble and Wm. Young—along with South River Wm. Henderson.[89] On 25 November 1806, Robert was again called for jury duty.[90] Robert Finley received a grant for 271 acres on 1 October 1808.[91] This property on Nails Creek was sold 22 December 1818, to Alexander Shadden of Jefferson County, Tennessee.[92] The last record found was for the sale of 274 acres near the Blount and Sevier County line to James Finley, 21 June 1823. This was to satisfy a judgment obtained by Robert Finley on 6 March 1822 against Alexander Shadding.[93] Martin claims Robert and Sarah probably died a few years after selling the Nails Creek property and are buried in Eusebia Cemetery in Blount County. Efforts to find burial or cemetery records there have failed so far.

Martin claims the following children are those of Robert and Sarah (Breckenridge) Finley:[94]

13	i.	Thankful[3] Finley.
14	ii.	Sarah Finley.
15	iii.	John Finley.
16	iv.	Robert Finley, born 1780; married Mary

		Pickens, 18 February 1812; died Lee County, Iowa. Children include Margaret Jane, and Nancy Ann.[95]
17	v.	Ann Finley.
18	vi.	Margaret Finley.
19	vii.	James Finley, born September 1796 in Blount County, Tennessee; died 1 July 1874 in Brown County, Kansas. He married, 15 February 1816, in Blount County, Margaret Pickens, daughter of John and Letitia (Hannah) Pickens.[96] Margaret was born in the Elljoy section of Virginia (now Tennessee) near the middle fork of the Holston River, 12 September 1792. She died 28 August 1846. Their children included John, Robert, Jane, Sarah, James, and Lettie.

4. Margaret[2] Finley (John[1]) was born 21 November 1746[97] and christened at Tinkling Spring in Augusta County in December 1746.[98] She married John Shields, 26 June 1768, probably in Augusta County.[99] He was born 1740 in Virginia. He died probably in Amhurst or Nelson County, Virginia, before 17 September 1802, when Margaret relinquished her right to administer his estate.[100]

Margaret's legacy from her father's will was five shillings. Her brother David, named executor of John Finley's estate, conveyed to John Shields of Amhurst County two pieces of property on 2 September 1793.[101] This transaction was to provide for the inheritance of her brother James, who was to receive £120 plus interest from the date John Finley had written his will, the property to be sold at a later date. However, on 1 October 1794, David found a buyer for all of John's property including that transferred to Shields.[102] Presumably the legacy due to brother James was settled at that time although no documents were found to verify this. Nor were there any clues as to why James's legacy was settled in this manner rather than with him directly.

On 17 September 1802, Margaret Shields relinquished her right to administer the estate of her deceased husband to her son Robert Shields.[103] John Shields inventory was taken 20 December 1802, and was valued at £1,797 75s. 18p. Included in his inventory were seven adult named negroes and fourteen children; Betty and seven young children; Lavery; Nell and four children boy called Pompey; Eve and three children; Jack, and John.[104] On 3 June 1805, the settlement of John Shields's estate mentions widow, Margaret, and eight of their children; Thankful, Peggy, Robert, William, Alexander, Nathan, Rebecka Shields, and Rachel, wife of James Montgomery. At that time James and Rachel Montgomery, and Thankful and Peggy Shields released their undivided share in 247 acres on Hat Creek in Nelson County for £100.[105]

Children of John and Margaret (Finley) Shields, as given by McIntosh, nearly identical with Stout, include:

20	i.	Rachel[3] Shields, born 1 July 1769; married Col. James Montgomery, 13 September 1791, in Amhurst County, Virginia.
21	ii.	Thankful Shields, born 20 September 1770; married Charles Blount, 18 April 1808.

22	iii.	James Shields, born 9 March 1772, in Augusta County; died 9 September 1839, in Bowling Green, Kentucky; married Elizabeth Higginbotham, 2 March 1797 in Amhurst County. She was born 11 July 1778 in Amhurst County; died 7 September 1837 in Kentucky.
23	iv.	Elizabeth Shields, born in Amhurst County.
24	v.	Jane Shields, born 4 October 1773; married Nathaniel Harlow, Jr., 4 October 1805.
25	vi.	Margaret Shields, born 5 August 1775;[106] married Col. Samuel Alexander Doak, 28 May 1803, at Mt. Crawford, Rockingham County, Virginia.
26	vii.	John Shields, born 3 March 1777; died in Kentucky?
27	viii.	Robert Shields, born 7 February 1779; died in Kentucky?
28	ix.	David Shields, born 5 May 1781; married Elizabeth Smith, 1797 in Amhurst County.
29	x.	George Shields, born 1 December 1782; died at home of brother John in Kentucky.
30	xi.	William Shields, born 15 December 1784; died 1863 in Tennessee; married Mary Hampton Kenner; was a captain in War of 1812 from Tennessee under General Andrew Jackson.
31	xii.	Alexander Shields, born 15 December 1786; married in Tennessee Matilda Kenner, sister of Mary.
32	xiii.	Rebecca Shields, born 2 April 1788; married Stephen Carter.
33	xiv.	Nathan Shields, died after 17 September 1802.

5. James[2] Finley (John[1]) was the fifth child named in his father's will and was to receive "one hundred and twenty pounds Virginia Currency with interest from this date [17 August 1791]."[107] Unfortunately, both the transcribed copy of the will and Chalkley's published abstract incorrectly substitute THOMAS for JAMES.[108] However, James's legacy is protected in a subsequent deed of transfer between David, his brother and the executor of the will, and John Shields, their brother-in-law, until the money can be realized from the sale of the inherited property.[109] This clearly spells out JAMES as the legatee. James received a much larger share of his father's estate than did his brothers and sisters, George, Robert, Margaret, Jean, and Thankful, perhaps because they had already received something from their parents, although this is not specified in the will. However, it is not apparent as to why these arrangements were made with Shields rather than with James directly.

Very little about James can be proven from primary records. Earlier researchers mistakenly claim he was a captain in the militia in Montgomery County, Virginia, in 1781 and that he owned property there.[110] There were two James Finleys, father and son, in Montgomery County at this time, but they both left wills.[111] Neither of those wills include heirs that faintly resemble what is claimed to be James's children.

Earlier researchers claim he married Keziah Martin 16 May 1769 in Augusta County, and at least some of his children were born in Lincoln County, now Whitley County, Kentucky.[112] However, no marriage record could be found. The only James Finley who left records in Augusta County during this period of time was a James Finley who came from Cumberland County, Pennsylvania, to settle the estate of his brother Robert.[113] There does exist a will for a James Finley dated 15 December 1824, in Whitley County.[114]

This researcher, as of this date, has been unable to find documentation that ties the James Finley found in Whitley County to John and Thankful Finley of Augusta County. The will of this James Finley names wife, Keziah, and children William, James, Marry, Travis, Elizabeth, and Robert. A descendent of Robert adds John, George, Samuel, and Janet.[115]

6. John[2] Finley (John[1]) was the sixth child named in his father's will. According to Stout he was born 11 January 1742 and christened at Tinkling Spring 24 January 1742.[116] However, it seems strange that while the christenings of George, Robert, and Margaret could be verified in Tinkling Spring records, which give all baptisms between 1740 and 1749,[117] John's baptismal date could not be found. In addition, the deeding of property to George by his parents would tend to support the hypothesis that George was the eldest son.

Previous researchers are in conflict as to where John went after he left the homestead on Middle River. France claims he died in Lincoln County, North Carolina, in 1818, aged seventy-six years and two months and lies buried in Bethel Church graveyard.[118] An exhaustive study was made of the John Finleys in the southern North Carolina and northern South Carolina regions. There is no Bethel Presbyterian Church in Lincoln County, North Carolina. There is, however, a Bethel Presbyterian Church in York County, South Carolina, quite close to Lincoln County. No records for the burial of a John Finley during this time period were found, but other Finleys are buried there.

According to France, John had gone to South Carolina prior to 1766 with brothers Robert and Thomas, however it has been shown that "Thomas" was an error in transcription for "James" in the will of their father in 1791. A Robert Finley who died in 1791/1792 was found in Lincoln County. He left a wife, Isabella, and five minor children, John, James, Robert, Alexander, and Agness.[119] A bond was made by Robert Finley to John Reed on 15 March 1789 because:

> . . . on Jan. 7, 1772 John Reed & wife Martha made a deed for 300 ac to James Finley desc, and it wasn't good enough so John Reed was to make a new deed to Robert Finely (sic), heir of James Finley desc; now Robert Finley is to pay damages that may arise due to John Reed making a deed and then bond is void.[120]

This clearly rules out this Robert as a son of John and Thankful and therefore he is not the brother who is said to have accompanied John to the Carolinas. In addition, Robert's father, James, would have been too old to have been a son of John and Thankful.

No Johns or Jameses of proper age were found in Lincoln County for the period 1790 to 1820. However, during the time period 1790 to 1825, there were numerous John Finleys living in

Peter Fulkerson and his heirs, that he the said John Finley and his heirs the said ____ of land with all the appurtenances unto the said Peter Fulkerson and his heirs against all persons whatever will forever warrant and defend. — In Witness whereof the said John Finley hath hereunto subscribed his name and affixed his seal the year and day above written. Signed Sealed and delivered in the presence of

George Finley
Benj. Longley
James Logan
Jno White
George Clark

John Finley {LS}

At a Court held for Washington County November 20th 1792. This Indenture of bargain and Sale between John Finley of the one part and Peter Fulkerson of the other part was proven in court by the oath of John White, George Clark jr and Benjamin Longley subscribing witnesses thereto and Ordered to be recorded.

Teste. And. Russell DCWC

The preponderance of evidence indicates that the John Finley who lived adjacent to George Finley in Washington County, Virginia, for about eighteen years was George's brother, another son of John and Thankful (Doak) Finley of South River. John moved on to what is now Knox County, Tennesse, in 1792 having sold his Washington County property to Peter Fulkerson.
The deed itself describes John's land as running along "a line of George Finley's lands," and George Finley is one of the witnesses, as noted in this excerpt.

Chester, Fairfield, and York Counties, South Carolina, quite close to Lincoln County. All could be ruled out except the York County John Finley. All York County Finleys had gone before the 1820 census.[121] Earlier tax reports in which Finleys appeared in 1769, 1771, 1772, 1779, 1782, 1784, and 1790 showed no John, Robert, or James Finley anywhere near Lincoln County.[122] A James Finley did buy 300 acres on the south side of the Catawba River from John and Martha Reed of Tryon County,[123] on 7 January 1772.[124] However, he has been shown to be the father of the Robert Finley of Lincoln County. James was deceased by 15 March 1789 and Robert was deceased by 1791/1792. Hence, no sign of brothers Robert and James could be found in the general area where John was supposed to have relocated.

The brothers Robert and James, at least according to other researchers of their family lines, are found in Blount County, Tennessee, and Whitley County, Kentucky, where they lived out their lives. A good alternative hypothesis exists for John which places him in Knox County, Tennessee, quite near Robert and not very far from James. In addition, by 1794, his brother David had moved to Montgomery County, Kentucky, about 130 miles north of Knox County.

It has already been shown that his brother George relocated in Washington County, Virginia, where he lived from the mid-1770s to the early 1800s.[125] Living on the property adjacent to George was a John Finley, and his presence can be estimated from approximately 1774 to 1792. John's first appearance in Washington County Court records was 26 February 1777;[126] George's first appearance was on 29 January 1777.[127] This John is documented as having received a wound in the thigh in the Battle of Long Island Flats, a Cherokee Expedition in July 1776.[128] This John Finley, a Revolutionary War soldier, was too old to be George's son, and he was not George's father nor even of that generation, hence he was a contemporary of George. John was a witness when Thomas McCullough wrote his will, 9 October 1780,[129] and George served as security when the will was proved, 24 November 1780.[130] John received a grant for 312 acres on Wallace's Branch of the Holston adjacent to land of George Finley on 2 October 1786 the same day George received his grant.[131] According to Summers, John had settled on a 400 acre parcel on the North Fork of the Holston in 1774.[132] John sold his 312 acres on 31 October 1792 and was described at that time as "of Knox County, Territory South West of River Ohio."[133]

For the period 1792 to 1819, records for three different John Finleys were found in Knox County, Tennessee. Through an analysis of these records, two of these John Finleys could be eliminated as having come from Washington County.[134] The remaining John Finley was born before 1754.[135] He owned seventy-eight and a half acres in the District South of the French Broad and Holston Rivers,[136] and he gave power-of-attorney to David Finley in July 1819.[137] John of Middle River had a brother David.

At this point it is interesting to return to France to pick up another thread on the children of John Finley, son of the John who left the 1791 will in Augusta County. According to France, this John had a son William, born 11 April 1765, who died in Jefferson County, Tennessee, will dated 13 April 1818 and proved June 1819. One of William's daughters was Mary Finley who married Davy Crockett, 3 August 1806. Mary was born in 1788 in Tennessee and died there in 1814.[138] Much of this can be documented except the link between John and William. According to one biographer of Davy Crockett, commenting on his first wife:

The father and mother were William and Jean Finley; the daughter, Mary, nicknamed Polly. David obtained this second marriage license [earlier plans to marry had gone as far as getting a license but then faltered] at the Dandridge Courthouse on Tuesday, August 12, 1806, five days before his twentieth birthday.[139]

A will does exist for a William Finley, dated 3 April 1818, proved in Jefferson County, June Session 1819.[140] In his will he provides for "my daughter Mary Crocket's three Children, John, William & Polly." A picture of the grave of William Finley, father-in-law of Davy Crockett, is carried on the cover of a Jefferson County Cemetery booklet with the sub-title *South of the French Broad River and Dumplin Valley Sections*.[141] Jefferson and Knox County share a common border and John Finley of Knox County described above lived south of the French Broad River.

In summary, there are several pieces of circumstantial evidence supporting the hypothesis that John, son of John and Thankful, could well be the one who was found living in Washington County, Virginia, and later in Knox County, Tennessee.

1. For at least fifteen years John lived next door to George Finley, proven son of John and Thankful. George and John were contemporaries.

2. John moved to Knox County, Tennessee, not far from the reported location of brothers Robert and James.

3. John of Knox County was born before 1754.

John Finley surveyed 87½ acres south of the French Broad River in Knox County, Tennessee, in 1807 and received a grant for that property in 1810. Also living nearby in Jefferson County south of the French Broad River, was William Finley, claimed by France to be John's son. While documented proof has not been found, time and proximity favor such a relationship.

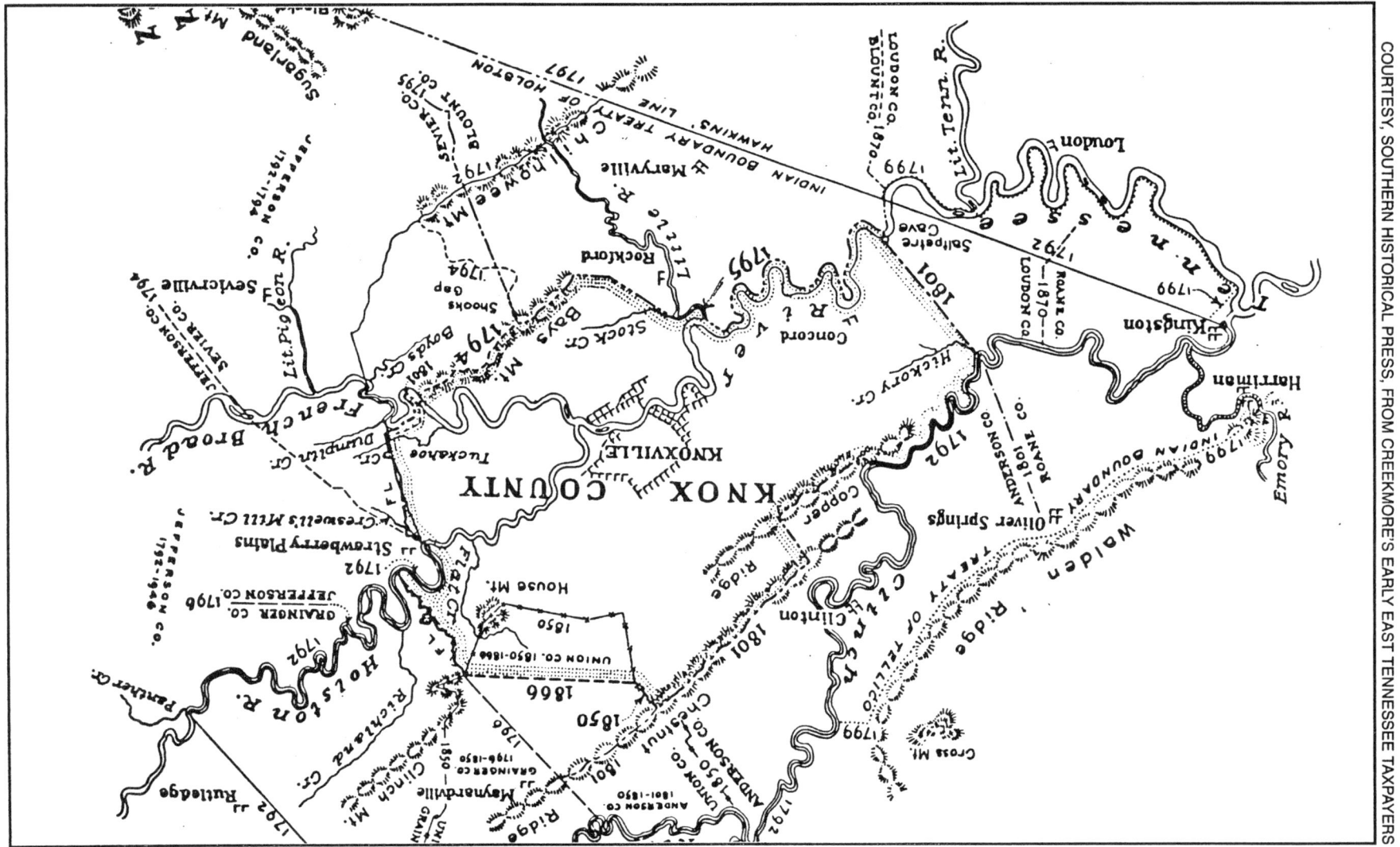

[handwritten will excerpt]

William Finley's will names deceased daughter, Mary Crockett and children John, William, and Polly.

The grave of William Finley, father-in-law of Davy Crockett, appears on the cover of "Stories in Stone: Jefferson County Cemeteries South of the French Broad River" transcribed by David Templin and Cherel Henderson.

4. John of Knox County assigned power-of-attorney to a David Finley and it was his brother David Finley, who was the executor for their father, John of Middle River. His brother David probably lived in or near Montgomery County, Kentucky, at this time, about 130 miles north of John. No other David Finley records were found in Knox County during this time period, indicating he was probably not a permanent resident of Knox County.

5. France reports that one of John's children, William, was the father of Davy Crockett's first wife, Mary (Polly) Finley. The relationship between William, daughter Mary, and Davy Crockett can be documented. Both John of Knox County and William were living in adjacent counties in a district described as south of the French Broad River.

This is certainly more support than could be found for the hypothesis that he ever lived in Lincoln County, South Carolina.

France believes the children of this John, son of the John who left the 1791 will in Augusta County, to be:[142]

34	i.	Mary[3] Finley, born 25 June 1763; married 11 January 1782, John Sevier; died in Sevier County, Tennessee.
35	ii.	William Finley, born 11 April 1765; mar-

PAGE 195

		ried 1783, Jean Kennedy; died in Jefferson County, Tennessee .
36	iii.	John Finley, born 17 February 1767 in North Carolina; married 13 November 1793, Margaret Kerr in Knox County; died in Tennessee.
37	iv.	Agnes Finley, born 20 October 1769; died unmarried in Gaston County, North Carolina, 20 October 1849.
38	v.	David Finley, born 22 May 1770; married 28 May 1791, Elizabeth Wilson in Staunton, Virginia.[143]
39	vi.	Alexander Finley, born 10 August 1772.
40	vii.	James Finley, born 10 March 1774.
41	viii.	Osbourne Finley, born 26 April 1776; died unmarried in 1799.
42	ix.	Infant daughter, born 1778; died 1778.
43	x.	Robert Miller Finley, born 18 September 1782 in Lincoln County, North Carolina; married 1808, Nancy Bryant, daughter of James Bryant; died 27 May 1869.

[Caution should be observed with this listing since there are clearly some errors, the most obvious being that David in this list is most likely John's brother].

7. Jean[2] Finley (John[1]) was the seventh child named in her father's will. Stout claims she was christened at Tinkling Spring in Augusta County, 16 February 1744.[144] However, Tinkling Spring records which exist for 1740-1749 do not list her. She married Joseph Trimble, son of John and Ann Trimble.[145] Joseph died prior to 29 October 1789.[146]

There were many Trimbles living in Augusta County during this general time period. A creditable job was done by Elam in sorting out some of them who were descendants of Walter and Rosannah Trimble. Joseph Trimble, who married Jean Finley, was not identified as a part of this line.[147] However, Elam believes Joseph's father, John, referred to as "North Mountain" John, was probably a brother of Walter.[148] The will of John Trimble, Sr., written 29 October 1789, named grandson, John Trimble, infant son of Joseph, deceased. William McPheeters was named an executor, along with John Trimble, probably son of John, Sr. and brother to the deceased Joseph Trimble. McPheeters was named, along with John Trimble and John Finley, a commissioner of Brown's Meeting House on 18 May 1769.[149] This, in turn, identifies the immediate family to which Joseph Trimble belongs. He had brothers and sisters: John, Margaret McClenachan, Mary Philson, Walter,[150] Robert, and Elizabeth Elliot and places them in the Middle River area near John and Thankful.

The only other document found for Joseph Trimble was the appointment of David Finley as guardian of John Trimble, orphan of Joseph. This was dated 15 December 1789.[151] It would appear that Jean (Finley) Trimble was widowed at a fairly young age.

The only known child of Joseph and Jean (Finley) Trimble was:

44	i.	John[3] Trimble.

9. David[2] Finley (John[1]) was probably the youngest child of

RELATED FINLEYS FOUND IN LEE COUNTY, IOWA

Recently, information from Lee County, Iowa, identifies a group of Finleys that most surely belong to the branch of Finleys originating with John and Thankful (Doak) Finley. However, their exact placement, as of this writing, is still clouded and unproved.

Documents in Lee County gives us fragments that allow us to make some educated guesses about the likelihood that the Finleys found there can be traced back to the Middle River Finleys. A Thankful Finley was born about 1794 in Tennessee. She had a son, David Finley, born 1824 in Tennessee, and she was the sister of Robert Finley. She moved with along with her brothers, John and Robert Finley, to Lee County, Iowa, about 1843.

The John Finley, found in Lee County, was born about 1800 in Tennessee; married Edy Saffel, 1 February 1825, Blount County, Tennessee; died Lee County, Iowa, prior to 23 June 1864.

Their children included:

i. Sarah Ann Finley, born about 1826; married Barker.
ii. Margaret Jane Finley, born about 1828; married Reuben Barker, 23 October 1845.
iii. Robert Carson Finley, born about 1830.
iv. Amy Eliza Finley, born 7 December 1831, Blount County, Tennessee; married David McCully, 3 May 1853 Lee County, Iowa; died 23 January 1918, Madison County, Iowa.
v. Nancy (or Lucy) Emaline Finley, born 28 March 1835, Blount County; married (1) Hugh McCullough, 17 August 1873; married (2) Solomon D. Johnson, 24 March 1875; died 2 January 1918.
vi. Samuel Saffel Finley, born 12 November 1838, Blount County; married Mary Jane Kyle Garrett, 7 October 1865, Burlington, Des Moines County, Iowa; died 13 October 1908, Louisa County, Iowa.
vii. John Henry Finley, born 9 December 1839, Blount County; married (1) Nancy Clark, 1 January 1865, Lee County, Iowa; married (2) Lucinda Randles, 21 January 1877, Marion County, Iowa; died while serving as City Marshal (location not identified), 5 October 1896.
viii. George Franklin Finley, born about 1843; married Harriet Hutson, 20 February 1865, Des Moines County, Iowa.
ix. Alexander Kanedy Finley, born about 1846; married Frances Davenport, 12 July 1865, Des Moines, Iowa.

At least two hypotheses suggest themselves. First, Robert Finley, born 1745, son of John and Thankful (Doak) Finley, settled in Blount County, Tennessee, when he was about fifty years old. He could have fathered the Lee County John Finley, born about 1800, as Robert did have a son John. Although we do not know the county of birth of the Lee County, Iowa, John Finley, we do know the state was Tennessee, and we do know that he was married in Blount County, Tennessee. If this hypothesis is true, John

Finley of Lee County would be third generation through John of Middle River by his son, Robert, i.e., John (Robert[2], John[1]).

Second, John and Thankful (Doak) Finley also had a son John, Robert's brother. The birthdate of John, son of John and Thankful, has not been verified. France believes this John's son John, was born 17 February 1767 in North Carolina, and married Margaret Kerr in Knox County, Tennessee on 13 November 1793. Knox County records do verify this marriage and date. Extensive research on John, son of John and Thankful, failed to find verification of his presence in North Carolina, but did find unmistakable evidence that he went to Knox County, Tennessee, and resided there from at least 1792 to 1819. It would not be unreasonable to believe that the John Finley born about 1800 in Tennesse who married Edy (Edith) Saffel in 1825 could be the son of John and Margaret (Kerr) Finley, and a great grandson of John and Thankful. If this hypothesis is true, John Finley of Lee County would be fourth generation through John of Middle River, by son John, and grandson John, i.e. John (John[3], John[2], John[1]). Frances believes this is the case. ❦

John and Thankful (Doak) Finley, born most likely between 1762 and 1765. He was married to Elizabeth Wilson, daughter of Joseph Wilson,[152] 10 March 1791 in Augusta County, by Reverend Archibald Scott.[153]

David was recommended and qualified as lieutenant in Captain Kirk's Company on 16 September 1783.[154] He is also shown in Captain Trimble's Company, but no date or rank is mentioned.[155] He appeared on the Augusta County tax rolls with his father, John, in 1786 and 1787.[156] From this we can make some assumptions as to David's approximate date of birth. To serve in the militia, a man had to be between the ages of sixteen and fifty.[157] A March 1781 order additionally required that those between sixteen and eighteen be identified separately.[158] It also seems unlikely that a man who qualified as lieutenant would be under twenty-one, since he had to take an oath upon accepting the office. If David was twenty-one in 1783, this would give us an estimated birth date of 1762. In 1786, when he first appeared on the tax rolls, the tithable age was twenty-one.[159] If he was just twenty-one in 1786, this would give us an estimated birth date of 1765. Therefore it seems highly likely that his date of birth was between 1762 and 1765, but probably at the lower end of this range.

On 15 December 1789, David was appointed guardian of his nephew John Trimble, orphan of Joseph Trimble.[160] On 17 January 1792 he was also appointed guardian for George Taylor, formerly bound to John Finley.[161] When David's father, John, wrote his will on 7 August 1791, David was named executor and received most of John's estate. Only small provisions were made for his brothers and sisters, his brother James excepted.[162] Apparently, John had a patent pending when he died, as David received a patent for 110 acres on 18 November 1791 and was referred to as "assignee of John Finley" at that time.[163] To settle the legacy of his brother James, David drew up a deed of trust to his brother-in-law John Shields, on 2 September 1793. The property was to be held until 2 September 1798 and could then be sold. This was to guarantee that James would receive his £120 plus interest.[164] Why David did not deal directly with James remains a mystery. However, David found a buyer for all of his father's estate on 1 October 1794 and sold 648 acres to John Johnston for £1,100.[165] Records for David in Augusta County, Virginia, then disappear.

David's connection to Montgomery County, Kentucky is based on circumstantial evidence, but seems reasonable. Descendants currently living in Santa Rosa, Sonoma County, California, have family records dating back to their David Finley, showing four children: John, Joseph Wilson, Thankful Sarah, and Ebenezer Finley. John was born 9 April 1792, about what might be expected for a 10 March 1791 marriage, and he was named for David's father. The second child, Joseph Wilson, was named for Elizabeth's father, while the third, Thankful Sarah, was named for David's mother.[166] The descendants also have correspondence which refers to a cousin, Sam Berry. There were Berrys living in the Middle River area and a James Berry was a witness when David made his final sale to John Johnston.

Tax records begin for a David Finley in Montgomery County, Kentucky, in 1797 and continue for 1799-1802 and 1804.[167] There is a David Finley on the 1810 census in the age range of twenty-six to forty-five. In his household are four males under ten, one male sixteen to twenty-six, two females under ten, and one female sixteen to twenty-six.[168] This would be consistent with a birth year of 1765 if David is at the upper limit of the age range in which he was count-

DAVID'S SALE OF HIS FATHER'S MIDDLE RIVER LANDS

An important document that ties together the relationships between the John Finley who lived on Middle River and his sons, David and James, is one showing the sale of 648 acres by David Finley to James Johnston in 1794. That total parcel consists of three smaller parcels containing 300, 238, and 110 acres. By description, the 300 acre parcel was patented to John Finley of Middle River in 1741. He acquired the 238 acres by patent in 1768. The 110 acre parcel was pending when John died in 1791 and was subsequently received by David as "assignee of John Finley." In addition, the 110 acre parcel is also mentioned in David's deed of trust to John Shields which protects the £120 legacy due his brother, James.

ed. However, the general constellation of the family, as we know it from later family records, is inconsistent. If this is the family of David and Elizabeth, it seems Elizabeth has disappeared. Son John, born in 1792 would have been eighteen years of age. He could not have a mother aged twenty-six or less. In the 1820 census, a David Finley is listed as over forty-five, with three males under ten, one male ten to sixteen, two females ten to sixteen, one female sixteen to twenty-six, and one female over forty-five.[169] Again this does not fit the pattern expected from later family records. There are at least three possible explanations for this. (1) Family records do not reflect all the children of David and Elizabeth; (2) some of the children do not belong to David and Elizabeth; (3) David and Elizabeth were living somewhere else and these are the records of some other David Finley—and there is evidence of another David Finley was in the area. They might well have been in Tennessee where brother Robert, and possibly John, was reported to be, and where census records do not exist for 1810 and 1820. By 1830, the David in Montgomery County had disappeared, but Ebenezer is shown, aged twenty to thirty,[170] with one male under five and one female twenty to thirty.[171] Other contemporary Finleys appear in these census years: Michael, Samuel, James, Joseph, William, Charles, John, and Polly, but speculation as to their possible connection to David would be just that. Unfortunately, many early Montgomery County records were burned during the Civil War and no record of David owning land has been found. A John and Michael Finley of Fleming County, Kentucky, sold a Negro boy to William Ramsay in Montgomery County on 20 September 1800.[172] And there were records for Finleys in Clark County (Montgomery County was formed from Clark County in 1797). Nothing further has been found for David for the period following 1794.

Known children of David and Elizabeth (Wilson) Finley include at least the following:

45	i.	John[3] Finley, born 9 April 1792, probably in Augusta County, Virginia.
46	ii.	Joseph Wilson Finley, born 27 February 1794.
47	iii.	Thankful Sarah (Sallie) Finley, born 7 July 1799.
+48	iv.	Ebenezer Finley, born 12 May 1802.

GENERATION THREE

48. Ebenezer[3] Finley (David[2], John[1]) was born 12 May 1802. Ebenezer died after 5 November 1889, probably in Missouri, having outlived at least four of his children.[173] He married (1) Narcissa Wilkerson about 1828, possibly in Montgomery County, Missouri. She was born 7 October 1810 in Kentucky and died 16 February 1848.[174] Ebenezer married (2) Mariah C. Moore in August 1848.[175] Mariah died 19 October 1852, probably in Morgan County, Missouri.[176] Another wife, (3) Elizabeth, appeared in land transactions in 1859.[177]

Ebenezer was first found in the Montgomery County, Missouri, census in 1830, age twenty to thirty. In his household were found a female in the same age range and one male under five.[178] There were two Wilkerson families living nearby, most probably kin of Narcissa.[179] By 1833 they had moved to Callaway County, Missouri, for there he witnessed the will of James Hulse, written 25 February 1833.[180] His wife, Narcissa, died early in 1848 and about six months later he married Mariah Moore. They were found in the 1850 census still in Callaway County, with seven Finley children and two who appear to be Mariah's,—by a previous marriage, John A., age four, and Martha, age ten.[181] Some time between 1848 and 1851, Ebenezer claimed two land entries of forty acres each in what is now Bates County, Missouri.[182]

In 1851 the family moved to Morgan County, Missouri, and then on to Bates County, Missouri, in 1853, Mariah having died in October of 1852. On 22 April 1854 Ebenezer bought an additional 200 acres adjacent to the land he had entered earlier from James F. and Elizabeth Hendricks.[183] In May and August 1859, he and his wife, Elizabeth, sold two twenty-five acre parcels to Alexander Williams and John H. Bowden, respectively.[184] This is the first mention of another wife and nothing further is known of her.

Known children of Ebenezer and Narcissa (Wilkerson) Finley include:[185]

49   i.   Jackson[4] Finley, born 12 November 1829, Montgomery County, Kentucky; died 20 October 1830, probably in Montgomery County.

50   ii.   Elizabeth Finley, born 14 July 1831, Callaway County, Missouri; married J.W. Montgomery, 29 August 1854 in Cass County, Missouri; died 1889, Italy, Ellis County, Texas.[186] Lived in Pulaski County, Arkansas, about twenty miles east of Little Rock in 1870. Wrote letters to brother, Harrison, from White County, Arkansas, between 10 May 1875 and 1 March 1880. On 29 November 1883, she wrote to him from Italy, Ellis County, Texas.

51   iii.   Joseph Wilson Finley, born 19 April 1833, Callaway County, Missouri; died 7/8 January 1863 while enrolled at Yale College, New Haven, Fairfield County, Connecticut. He is buried in the Yale Churchyard Cemetery. He wrote to his brother, Harrison, at Ione, Amador County, California, from Yale on 20 September 1862 asking for $300, saying he had been admitted to Yale. In it he said, "It will take me four Years to graduate here. Don't know whether I can stand the Yankees that long or not—they fleece a man on every turn." He died less than four months later. In November 1865, George F. Britton, a classmate, wrote to brother Harrison informing him that a monument had been erected over Joseph's grave—a brown stone indigenous to the climate, eleven feet high and engraved, "Joseph W. Finley, Of Weaverville California, A member of the Freshman Class, Yale College, Born April 19the 1833, Died January 7th 1863." Probate papers were found in Amador County, California, dated 24 October 1867, with H. or W. Finley, Esq., Administrator (probably Harrison, since expenses included three trips from Contra Costa County to

Jackson, and Harrison was living in Contra Costa County at that time). His estate amounted to $3,800.

52   iv.   William Wilkerson Finley, born 19 April 1835, Callaway County, Missouri. Fought in Civil War CSA, Company A, 1st Regiment, killed in action in November 1864 in the Battle of Franklin, Tennessee.

+53   v.   Harrison (Harry) Finley, born 26 December 1836, Callaway County, Missouri.

54   vi.   David Finley, born 4 July 1838, Callaway County, Missouri. Fought in Civil War, Company E, 8th Regiment CSA and killed in a skirmish 7 March 1865, in Carroll County, Arkansas.

55   vii.   Achilles (Chill) Finley, born 15 May 1843, Callaway County, Missouri; married Alice Wilkerson about 1876 in Fulton, Callaway County; died of Bright's Disease, 13 May 1916, Fulton, and is buried in the Hillcrest Cemetery there. Fought in the Civil War in Gates Regiment of Cockrell's Brigade. After the war he studied law at the University of Michigan and about 1870 taught school in Neosho, Newton County, Missouri, for a while. He later practiced law in Callaway County and was elected as State's Attorney in 1878. Correspondence to his brother, Harrison, included a letter dated 7 August 1868, from Carthage, Missouri, in which he gave birth dates of "father's family" and of his own siblings. He also says he will probably go to Ann Arbor the first of September. Another letter, written 23 July 1872 from Fulton, Missouri, told of his leaving Ann Arbor 10 August 1870. In the same letter he discusses the settlement of the estate of brother, Joseph Wilson. A final letter, dated 10 October 1904, with letterhead "A. Finley, Attorney at Law, Fulton, Missouri," tells of his marriage to Margaret, age 44, daughter of Thomas Wise.

56   viii.   Martha Louisa Finley, born 29 October 1845, Callaway County; married William (Buck) O'Neal.

GENERATION FOUR

53. Harrison (Harry)[4] Finley (Ebenezer[3], David[2], John[1]) was born 26 December 1836 in Callaway County, Missouri.[187] He died on 5 July 1917 in Santa Rosa, Sonoma County, California, and is buried in Stanley's Cemetery in Santa Rosa. He married Livonia Josephine Ray, born 9 June 1844 in Morgan County, Missouri, the daughter of Sanford and Matilda (Phillips) Ray. She died 14 December 1941 in Santa Rosa and is buried beside her husband in Stanley Cemetery. Harrison and Livonia were the third Finley family to settle in Sonoma County prior to 1900 and their story is told in chapter 3. They had ten children, all born in California:[188]

57   i.   Missouri E.[5] Finley, born 10 February

1863, Amador County, California; died 2 May 1863, Ione, Amador County, California, buried in Ione Cemetery.

58 ii. Mattie Zoe Finley, born 29 August 1864, Contra Costa County, California; married Claude D. Coates, 27 June 1902; died 15 December 1945 and is buried in Stanley Cemetery, Santa Rosa.

59 iii. Matilda Narcissus (Tillie) Finley, born 10 November 1866, Contra Costa County; married Henry Blank, 8 January 1908; died 2 August 1913 and is buried in Stanley Cemetery, Santa Rosa.

60 iv. Eliza Belle Finley, born 20 October 1868, Contra Costa County; married James Simcoe, 27 November 1917; died 29 August 1955 in Sonoma County.[189]

+61 v. Wilson Ebenezer Finley, born 3 February 1871, Contra Costa County.

62 vi. Mary Frances (Molly) Finley, born 23 January 1873, Contra Costa County; died 8 April 1893, Sonoma County and is buried in Stanley Cemetery.[190]

63 vii. Abigail Josephine (Abbie) Finley, born 31 January 1876, Contra Costa County; married Grant A. Laughlin, 25 April 1912; died 29 May 1977 in Sonoma County at the age of 101.[191] Grant died 4 September 1951 in Sonoma County.[192] Grant was the son of James Henry Laughlin whom migrated from Tennessee to the Mark West area in 1855. Grant was an attorney, having graduated from the Hastings School of Law in San Francisco in 1898, and practiced law several years before returning to Santa Rosa just prior to the 1906 earthquake. The Laughlin family home was built in 1876 and is on the National Register of Historic Places. It is located on what was Lone Redwood Road, now Airport Boulevard. Abbie and Grant lived there after the death of Grant's father. They had at least one daughter, Mary, who married Elmont Lane.

64 viii. Lucy Ray Finley, born 11 April 1879, Contra Costa County; married Archie L. Strout, 1 June 1911; died 6 February 1936 and is buried in Stanley Cemetery. Archie died 7 September 1970 in Sonoma County.[193]

65 ix. Livonia Louise (Lulu) Finley, born 21 July 1881, Contra Costa County; married S. Lesley (Lester) Cox, 21 January 1908; died 15 February 1971 in Napa County, California.[194]

66 x. Alicia V. Finley, born 26 September 1885, Contra Costa County; died 17 March 1889, Sonoma County and is buried in Stanley Cemetery.

GENERATION FIVE

61. Wilson Ebenezer[5] Finley (Harrison[4], Ebenezer[3], David[2], John[1]) was born 3 February 1871 in Contra Costa County, California, and 12 November 1952 died in Santa Rosa, Sonoma County, California. He married Alice Hudson, daughter of Cornelius and Lavina (Butler) Hudson, 28 November 1895 in Santa Rosa. Although Alice was a native of Calistoga, her father was from a pioneer Sonoma County family. She died in Santa Rosa 9 May 1970, at the age of 95 and is buried at the Chapel of the Chimes in Santa Rosa.[195]

Wilson spent his early years in Contra Costa County where he was born, moving to Sonoma County when he was seventeen years old. He completed his schooling at Santa Rosa High School and then worked full time helping his father operate the Finley ranch. When he and Alice were married they moved into a cottage on Mark West Creek where their first five children were born. Then in 1912, when Wilson's father bought additional property, they moved to an old farm house on Mark West Springs Road. They had two more children to complete the family. When Harrison Finley died, Wilson inherited fifty-two acres on Mark West Creek. His part of the ranch had about thirty-five acres in prunes and the rest in hay and pasture.[196]

The children of Wilson Ebenezer and Alice (Hudson) Finley, all born in Santa Rosa, Sonoma County, California, included:

67	i.	Lorena Frances[6] Finley, born 16 December 1896, Santa Rosa; married Anders Nielsen, 2 September 1919; died 26 November 1980 at age 83, Santa Rosa. The Nielsens were long-time owners of the Nielsen Christmas Tree farm located just off Chanate Road near the Community Hospital. In 1980 their children included: Donald A. Nielsen, Redwood City; Philip L. Nielsen, Cotati; Carol N. Underhill and Shirley A. Pelton, both of Santa Rosa.[197]
+68	ii.	Helen Alice Finley, born 16 January 1899, Santa Rosa.
69	iii.	Mervyn Harrison Finley, born 14 May 1901; married Hazel Elgin; died 8 June 1927 in Scotia, Humboldt County, California.
70	iv.	Wilson Cornelius Finley, born 6 December 1904; married Viola Brett 2 March 1929, San Rafael; died 11 February 1994, Santa Rosa.[198]
71	v.	Frederick Lee Finley, born 27 August 1907; married Mabel (May) Nidros; died 11 July 1946 in Sonoma, Sonoma County. He is buried at the Chapel of the Chimes.
72	vi.	Ruth Finley, born 24 November 1912, married (1) Harold Groom, (2) Lloyd Murphy; died 12 April 1990, Santa Rosa.
73	vii.	George Maurice Finley, born 12 March 1916, married Lillian Nelson 31 December 1940, Reno, Nevada; died 5 April 1992, Santa Rosa.

GENERATION SIX

68. Helen Alice[6] Finley (Wilson[5], Harrison[4], Ebenezer[3], David[2], John[1]) was born 16 January 1899 on her parents Mark

West Springs ranch just north of Santa Rosa. She died 17 July 1988 in Santa Rosa at the age of 89. She married James Hilliard Comstock, 20 July 1918 in San Diego, California. He was born 25 February 1891 in Evanston, Illinois, the sixth child of John Adams Comstock and Nellie (Hurd) Comstock. He died in 1967 in Santa Rosa.

It was Helen who, in 1970, wrote down her Rambling Reminiscences that contributed to the earlier feature chapter on her grandparents, the third Finley family to immigrate to Sonoma County prior to 1900. She also told of her experiences when it came time to attend Santa Rosa High School:

> In January 1913 I entered High School and Frances and I drove the 4 1/2 miles mornings and afternoon. The High School was on Humboldt Street and we stabled our horse "Lany" in Mr. Coon's barn which was across the street from the school. We paid $1 each month for that privilege. In those days the drive from our home to Santa Rosa was a pretty drive along tree lined dirt roads until about 1915 when concrete was laid on Old Redwood Hiway. That winter was dreadful. We drove thru deep mud to Coffey Lane, then to what is now Steel Lane and by much detouring finally arrived—rarely, but sometimes late.

After graduating from high school, she attended San Jose Normal School where she graduated in 1918. Shortly after, in San Diego, on 20 July 1918, she married Hilliard Comstock, who was at the time a captain in the Army. He left in August for overseas duty, to return a year later. He was already a practicing attorney in Santa Rosa before the war interrupted his young career. After his return, he continued in the practice of law and was appointed a judge of the Superior Court of Sonoma County

Helen Alice Finley's high school graduation picture, ca. 1916

in 1929, where he served until 1964.[199] The Comstocks were a prominent local family and contributed much to the welfare of the community.

Children of Helen (Finley) and Hilliard Comstock include:

74	i.	James Hilliard[7] Comstock.
75	ii.	Helen Margaret (Pudge) Comstock.
76	iii.	Marshall Hurd Comstock.
77	iv.	Harrison Finley Comstock.
78	v.	Martha Lee Comstock.

Five generations: Alice (Hudson) Finley; Helen Margaret (Pudge) (Comstock) Sloat holding daughter, Christine Ann; Lavina Ellen (Butler) Hudson; Helen (Finley) Comstock, 1948.

NOTES & REFERENCES:

INTRODUCTION

1. William Fletcher Boogher, comp., *Gleanings of Virginia History, An Historical and Genealogical Collection, Largely from Original Sources* (Baltimore: Genealogical Publishing Co., 1976), p. 113.
2. Carmen J. Finley, "John and Mary Finley of Montgomery (Wythe) County, Virginia," *The Virginia Genealogist*, 34 (Oct.-Dec., 1990), pp. 243-255; 35 (Jan.-Mar., 1991), pp. 18-33; 35 (Apr.-June, 1991), pp. 122-135; 35 (July-Sep., 1991), pp. 173-185; 35 (Oct.-Dec., 1991), pp. 251-262.
3. Carmen J. Finley, "John Finley of Montgomery/Wythe County, Virginia: Additional Children Identified," *The Virginia Genealogist*, 39 (Jan.-Mar., 1995) pp. 3-21; 39 (Apr.-June, 1995) pp. 94-103; 39 (July-Sept., pp. 202-212; 39 (Oct.-Dec., 1995) pp. 282-294.

CHAPTER ONE

1. Much of this chapter is based on the earlier work of Nettie (Head) McDonald and Clara (Keithly) Tarwater, great-granddaughter and granddaughter of John and Keziah. Nettie's published account of John and Keziah (Head) Finley, 1981, is available at the Sonoma County Library in Santa Rosa. Clara's articles on family history were published in the *Journal of the Sonoma County Historical Society*.
2. John and Keziah also had a son James William, who died at the age of two and a half in Bates County in 1850.
3. This part of the story that deals with Keziah's parents has not yet been confirmed. From Bible records it is known only that Keziah was born in 1828 in Tennessee and that her maiden name was Head. She is most certainly the granddaughter of Henry Head of Sumner County, but which of Henry's children is Keziah's parent has not been determined. However, Henry Head's son Pascal Head did arrive in Kentuckytown, Grayson County, Texas, in December of 1852. From research done on the Heads of Sumner County, it seems more likely that Keziah was the niece of Pascal Head. Hence family tradition, in this case, may be only partially true.
4. Dennis E. Harris, *1852 California State Census*, (Redwood Empire Social History Project), (Santa Rosa, Calif.: County of Sonoma, 1983), pp. 33-35.
5. Margaret Edith Trussell, *Settlement of the Bodega Bay Region*, Master's Thesis, University of California, 1960, p. 99. Potato crops in 1849 and 1850 had brought 20 and 10.7 cents per pound, but increased production dropped the price to a little over 5 cents in 1851 and 1852.
6. Harris, p. 97.
7. Honoria Tuomey, *History of Sonoma County, California*, vol. I (San Francisco: S.J. Clarke, 1926), p. 743 says, "English Hill is the name of the extensive and lofty elevation that may be roughly bounded as, by the lower lands on which stand Freestone, Valley Ford and Bloomfield and on its eastern base by Pleasant Valley. It was named 'the hill of the English' by the Spanish because some English-speaking people early made a settlement there on a ranch."
8. Tuomey, vol. II, p. 223.
9. Andrew Jackson was the grandfather of the author, and I have often wondered if the naming of his next older brother, Jefferson Davis, meant there was a division of sympathy between John and Keziah where the Civil War was concerned.
10. Sonoma Co., Calif., Deed Book 13:625-627.
11. Tish Levee, "The Mistress of Rancho Bodega," *Journal of the Sonoma County Historical Society*, 1983, no. 4, pp. 8.
12. Trussell, p. 41.
13. Tuomey, vol. I, p. 766.
14. It reached Bodega and Freestone in 1876 and Duncan's Mills in 1877.
15. Nettie McDonald, *John and Keziah (Head) Finley; Sonoma County, California* (Santa Rosa, Calif.: author, 1981), p. 5.
16. Sonoma Co., Calif., Mortgage Book 12:506.
17. Tuomey, vol. I, p. 750 says, "Irish Hill rises high above the north bank of Salmon Creek near its outlet at the Pacific. In 1857, two Irishmen, Andrew Fitzpatrick and William Fitzgerald, settled on ranches on this productive and extensive elevation, and soon the name of Irish Hill was evolved for the section."
18. Sonoma Co., Calif., Deed Book 268:355.
19. Harvey J. Hansen & Jeanne Thurlow Miller, *Wild Oats of Eden* (Santa Rosa: Hooper Printing, 1962), p. 109.
20. McDonald, p. 22.
21. Sonoma Co., Calif., Deed Book 39:302-303.
22. Sonoma Co., Calif., Probate File #357, #584.
23. Sonoma Co., Calif., Deed Book 42:257.
24. Sonoma Co., Calif., Deed Book 36:598.
25. John Schubert, "A Wild July in Guerneville," *Journal of the Sonoma County Historical Society*, 1990, no. 3, pp. 8-10.
26. Sonoma Co., Calif., Civil Court Case #345.
27. Sonoma Co., Calif., Liber R of Powers of Attorney, p. 309.

28. Clara Keithly Tarwater, "Family History," *Journal of the Sonoma County Historical Society*, 1983, no. 2, p. 11.
29. Great Register of Voters, Sonoma County, Calif., 1892, p. 45. Available at the Sonoma County Library, Santa Rosa, Calif.
30. Clara Tarwater, "The Corners, Smith's Ranch," *Journal of the Sonoma County Historical Society*, 1983, no. 2, p. 7.
31. Clara Keithly Tarwater, "Family History," p. 10.
32. McDonald, p. 8. This is an excerpt from a letter written by Mrs. James McCaughey to her son, Walter, on 4 September 1892.
33. Clara Tarwater, "The Corners, Smith's Ranch," p. 8.
34. Sonoma Co., Calif., Deed Book 188:201.
35. Sonoma Co., Calif., Deed Book 287:116.

CHAPTER TWO

1. Newton Gleaves Finley, *Memoirs of Travel* microfilm, #1206424, part 17, Family History Library, Church of Jesus Christ of Latter-day Saints, Salt Lake City. The Campbell family with whom they travelled were founders of what is now the town of Campbell, Calif. William Asa and Newton's mother was a Campbell, and a half-sister to Benjamin Campbell, who lead their wagon train. This account was written 30 December 1922 and submitted to the archives in Salt Lake City on 17 September 1981 by Dr. Alton Lovell Alderman of Athena, Oregon.
2. *Fourth Annual Catalogue of Officers and Students of the Pacific Methodist College, Vacaville, Calif., May 27th, 1864, to May 18th, 1865* (San Francisco: Towne and Bacon, 1865). Also, "From Backwoods Academy to Liberal Arts College..." *The Oregon Stater* (Corvallis, Oreg.: Oregon State University, February 1993), p. 1.
3. 1864 was the second graduating class in the history of Pacific Methodist College, the class of 1863 having but one graduate.
4. Oregon State University Archives has a thirty-six page scrapbook kept on William, plus some loose papers. A copy of the Pacific Methodist College Commencement, May 19th, 1864, is among the loose papers. There are also a number of his handwritten sermons, including his first sermon in December 1861, among the loose papers.
5. Rev. J.C. Simmons, D.D., *The History of Southern Methodism on the Pacific Coast* (Nashville: Southern Methodist Publishing House, 1886), p. 314. The history of his tenure in Oregon is preserved in the Oregon State University Archives: *Orange and Black*, 1938, pp. 7-12; and a series of articles written by Sarah (Latimer) Finley and published in the *Oregon State Monthly*, March, April, May, and June 1930. See also, "From Backwoods Academy to Liberal Arts College..." cited above.
6. Sarah Latimer was listed as a sophomore in 1864, the year William was graduated.
7. *Orange and Black*, 1938, pp. 9-10.
8. "From Backwoods Academy to Liberal Arts College..."
9. Wofford College was established by the Methodist Church in 1854 with the bequest of $100,000 by Benjamin Wofford, businessman and minister. At that time, the legacy was the largest gift made by an American Methodist for religious or educational purposes. Half of the original amount was lost after being invested in Confederate bonds during the Civil War. From Nolan B. Harmon, *The Encyclopedia of World Methodism* (Nashville: United Methodist Publishing House, c1974), p. 2586.
10. David Duncan Wallace, *History of Wofford College, 1854-1949* (Nashville: Vanderbilt University Press, 1951), p. 265.
11. Simmons, *History of Southern Methodism*, p. 314.
12. Twelve years later, on 1 June 1884, he was invited back to Corvallis to deliver the baccalaureate sermon. Local papers carried extensive reports of his visit. Oregon State University Archives, W.A. Finley Scrapbook, sheet 14.
13. *Orange and Black*, 1938, p. 12.
14. Oregon State University Archives, W.A. Finley Scrapbook, sheet 13.
15. Stephen E. Yale, Director of Archives, Commission on Archives and History, California-Nevada Conference, United Methodist Church, Berkeley, Calif. to author, 7 November 1994. Also D.M. Bishop, *Bishop's Stockton Directory for 1876-7 Containing a Business Directory, Street Guide Record of the City Government, its Institutions, etc.* (Stockton: B.C. Vandall, 1876), p. 95. Also George H. Tikham, *A History of Stockton from its Organization up to the Present Time* (San Francisco: Hinton & Co., 1880), p. 346.
16. *Sonoma Democrat* (Santa Rosa, Sonoma Co., Calif.), 5 Aug. 1876, p. 5; 21 Oct. 1876, p. 5.
17. Robert A. Thompson, *Historical and Descriptive Sketch of Sonoma County, California* (Philadelphia: L.H. Everts & Co., 1877), p. 78.
18. Gaye LeBaron, Dee Blackman, Joann Mitchell, Harvey Hanson, *Santa Rosa—A Nineteenth Century Town* (Santa Rosa, Historia, Ltd.: 1985), p. 78.
19. LeBaron, *Nineteenth Century Town*, p. 40.
20. Sonoma Co., Calif., Deed Book 65:355. Purchase date was 3 August 1878.
21. Oregon State University Archives, W.A. Finley Scrapbook, sheet 13, refers to Julia as an adopted

22. 1880 U.S. census, Santa Rosa, Sonoma Co., Calif., vol. 16 e.d. 124, sheet 43, line 39.

23. *Sonoma County Marriages: 1847-1902* (Santa Rosa, Calif.: Sonoma County Genealogical Society, 1990), p. 14.

24. Sonoma Co., Calif., Deed Book 90:566. Purchase date was 19 April 1884.

25. Ann M. Connor, *McDonald Avenue: A Century of Elegance* (Santa Rosa, Calif.: author, 1970), p. 94.

26. Sonoma Co., Calif., Deed Book 86:287; 90:564; 95:144; 1883 & 1884.

27. Connor, p. 94.

28. Sonoma Co., Calif., Deed Book 97:342; 112:393; 1884 & 1886.

29. The home at 1127 McDonald Avenue is currently occupied by Scott and Margaret Ogilvie Peterson, who graciously provided a copy of the picture included in this chapter.

30. He "wintered" in San Francisco.

31. Ernest L. Finley, *Santa Rosans I Have Known* (Santa Rosa, Calif.: Press Democrat, 1942), p. 76.

32. Santa Rosa in 1885 (Santa Rosa, Calif.: Elliott & Co. Lithograph, 1885). This map has a picture of the Santa Rosa Ladies' College.

33. Sonoma Co., Calif., Deed Book 110:576.

34. Ibid., p. 575.

35. Sonoma Co., Calif., Deed Book 114:222.

36. Sonoma Co., Calif., Deed Book 82:98.

37. LeBaron, *Nineteenth Century Town*, p. 69.

38. The Great Registers contain a listing of people eligible to vote in the State of California, beginning in 1866 when enacted by the State Legislature. They can generally be found in the County Office of the Recorder or in the State Archives. Those cited here were read at the Sonoma County Library in Santa Rosa.

39. Great Register, 1892, p. 45.

40. *University of Southern California Year Book*, 1889-90 (Los Angeles: Commercial Printing House, 1890), p. 10.

41. *Sonoma Democrat* (Santa Rosa, Sonoma Co., Calif.), 14 Sept. 1889, p. 1.

42. Ibid., 4 Jan. 1890, p. 3; 5 April 1890, p. 3.

43. *California State Gazetteer and Business Directory*, 1890, vol. II (San Francisco: R.L. Polk & Co., 1890), p. 987. Sarah's listing as "lady principal" leads one to speculate that it was probably Sarah who ran the school in her husband's absence.

44. J.P.H. Wentworth, Jr., *The Resources of California* (San Francisco: Wentworth, Feb. 1891), p. 4.

45. *Sonoma Democrat* (Santa Rosa, Sonoma Co., Calif.), 26 Sept. 1891, p. 3.

46. "Sunday School Workers," *Santa Rosa City Daily* (Santa Rosa, Sonoma Co., Calif.), 12 June 1891, p. 1.

47. Oregon State University Archives, W.A. Finley Scrapbook, loose items.

48. It seems reasonable to assume that he was in Southern California between 1891 and 1895, or at least not in Santa Rosa, since he was missing from the Great Registers of Sonoma County in 1892 and 1894. He did not reappear in the Great Register until 1900.

49. William A. Finley obituary, *The Press Democrat* (Santa Rosa, Sonoma Co., Calif.), 20 June 1912, p. 10.

50. *California Polk-Husted Directory Co.'s Santa Rosa City and Sonoma County Directory 1908* (Oakland Calif.: R.L. Polk, 1908), p. 71. Apparently he had ventured into the world of finance earlier as well. An item in the Sebastopol Times dated 28 August 1895 referred to him as a bondsman; reported in the *Sonoma Searcher* (Santa Rosa, Calif.: Sonoma County Genealogical Society, Mar. 1994), vol. 21, no. 3, p. 32.

51. Sonoma Co., Calif.: Deed Book 265:208; 23 Aug. 1906. Sarah also was gifted his home on Mendocino Avenue; Deed Book 265:209, 7 Nov. 1906. He also gifted property adjacent to 1127 McDonald Ave. to Asa A. Carter of San Bernardino County; Deed Book 265:207.

52. Sonoma Co., Calif., Death Certificates Book 3:142 and 12:369. Martha Ann Latimer died 7 December 1906 and Robert Atwell Latimer died 23 November 1910.

53. William A. Finley obituary, p. 10.

54. Sonoma Co., Calif., Deed Book 157:337.

55. Ibid., p. 496.

56. Sonoma Co., Calif., Deed Book 194:282. William's residence was given as Madera at this time.

57. Frank A. Brush, cashier of the Santa Rosa National Bank, was convicted of embezzlement of $382,392 in 1918. The bank went into receivership on 18 October 1918, about a year and a half after the final settlement of William Asa Finley's estate. From Ernest L. Finley, *History of Sonoma County* (Santa Rosa, Calif.: Press Democrat Publishing Co., 1937), p. 386.

58. Sonoma Co., Calif., Probate File #5569, 10-241, reel #157.

59. Records of the United Methodist Church, 2400 Ridge Road, Berkeley, California 94709, show Robert Atwell Latimer as an itinerant preacher from 1855 to 1870, serving the circuit areas of Stockton, Yolo, Montezuma, Chachville, Consumnes and Dry Creek, Yuba City, Gilroy, Santa Clara, Vacaville, Silverville, Chico, Bear River, San Jose, El Monte, and Los Angeles. Simmons (p. 173) says of him, "R.A. Latimer was an earnest, faithful man, a good and systematic preacher. His sermons were always short, but well arranged and interesting. He labored in the

Angeles Conference, where with ripening years he is waiting the call of his beloved Master to the rest of the faithful." And later (p. 376), "R.A. Latimer is our stand-by at Santa Ana. To him more than to any other man are we indebted for the neat and comfortable house in which our people worship there. His wise and brotherly counsels were of great service to me when on the district. In former years he was one of our most useful and laborious workmen, and wherever he went as preacher in charge signs of growth and improvement were sure to follow. He and his most excellent wife have a beautiful home at Santa Ana, and the neatness with which that house and premises are kept is a study and example to every visitor."
60. Sarah Finley obituary, *The Press Democrat* (Santa Rosa, Sonoma Co., Calif.), 16 Nov. 1937, p. 2. Also, *Fourth Annual Catalogue, Pacific Methodist College, 1865.*
61. *Fourth Annual Catalog, Pacific Methodist College, 1865.*
62. Oregon State University Archives, W.A. Finley Scrapbook, sheets 13, 15.
63. Lillian Burger Slater, *Rose Carnivals of Santa Rosa in Review: 1894-1932* (Santa Rosa, Calif.: Press Democrat, 1932), pp. 14, 18.
64. *Oregon State Monthly,* March 1930, p. 5.
65. Ibid., p. 8.
66. *Oregon State Monthly,* May 1930, pp. 9-10.
67. *Oregon State Monthly,* June 1930, p. 10.
68. Finley, *History of Sonoma County,* p. 257.
69. Great Register, 1912, Santa Rosa Precinct #1, line 99.
70. In 1922 her address was given as 605 College Avenue, where son, Ernest, was living.
71. Sonoma Co., Calif., Leases P:436.
72. Sonoma Co., Calif., Official Records, 138:11; 18 Feb. 1926.
73. California Death Index file #69050.
74. Sarah Finley obituary, *The Press Democrat* (Santa Rosa, Sonoma Co., Calif.), 16 Nov. 1937, p. 2.
75. "From Backwoods Academy to Liberal Arts College. . . "
76. "The Oregon Trail," *The Oregon Stater* (Corvallis, Oreg.: Oregon State University, Dec. 1992), p. 12.

CHAPTER THREE

1. *History of Contra Costa County, California,* originally published in 1882 by Slocum & Co., San Francisco (Oakland: Brooks-Sterling Co., 1974), pp. 557-558; Tuomey, *History of Sonoma County, California,* vol. II, p. 853.
2. Sonoma Co., Calif., Deed Book 116:321.
3. Sonoma Co., Calif., Deed Book 282:100.
4. J.P. Munro-Fraser, *History of Sonoma County, California* (San Francisco: Alley, Bowen & Co., 1880), p. 442.
5. *California State Gazetteer and Business Directory,* 1890, vol. II, p. 428.
6. Howard Smith, "Here's Story of Nine Pretty Girls," *The Press Democrat* (Santa Rosa, Sonoma Co., Calif.), 11 May 1949, p. 18.
7. LeBaron, *Nineteenth Century Town,* p. 60.
8. W.D. Reynolds & T.A. Proctor, comp. *Illustrated Atlas of Sonoma County, California* (Santa Rosa, Calif.: Reynolds & Proctor, 1898), p. 3 of section 2.
9. Helen (Finley) Comstock, *Rambling Reminiscences,* 1970. Notes in the possession of Christine (Sloat) Faux, 4611 Glencannon St., Santa Rosa, CA.
10. LeBaron, *Nineteenth Century Town,* p. 86.
11. Helen (Finley) Comstock, *Rambling Reminiscences.*
12. Wallace L. Ware, *The Unforgettables* (San Francisco: Hesperian Press, 1964), p. 70.
13. Helen (Finley) Comstock, *Rambling Reminiscences.*
14. Tuomey, vol. II, pp. 853-854.
15. Helen (Finley) Comstock, *Rambling Reminiscences.*
16. Harrison Finley probate records. Sonoma Co., Calif., Probate file #6530.
17. "Mrs. Livonia Finley, Pioneer County Resident, Dies at 97," *The Press Democrat* (Santa Rosa, Sonoma Co., Calif.), 16 Dec. 1941.
18. Sonoma Co., Calif., Deed Book 348:64.
19. Sonoma Co., Calif., Probate file #6530.
20. Sonoma Co., Calif., Deed Book 370:383.
21. Sonoma Co., Calif., Probate file #6530.
22. Sonoma Co., Calif., Deed Book 368:327-334.
23. "Mrs. Livonia Finley, Pioneer County Resident, Dies at 97." Also Finley, *History of Sonoma County,* p. 286.
24. Finley, *History of Sonoma County,* pp. 286-287.

CHAPTER FOUR

1. Joseph A. Waddell, *Annals of Augusta County, Virginia, from 1726 to 1871* (Bridgewater: Va.: C.J. Carrier Co., 1958), p. 63.
2. Wilson, *The Tinkling Spring: Headwater of Freedom, A Study of the Church and Her People 1732–1952* (Verona, Va.: McClure Press, 1974), p. 36.
3. Ibid., p. 42.
4. Elizabeth Venable Gaines, *Cub Creek Church and Congregation; 1738-1838* (Richmond, Va.: Presbyterian Committee of Publication, n.d.), p. 11.
5. Wilson, *Tinkling Spring,* p. 42.
6. Thomas A. Stallworth, Sr. *History of I: The Brooks Family; II: The Butler Family; III: The Caldwell*

Family; IV: Descendants of Margaret Rebecca (Caldwell) Stallworth (Chester, S.C.: privately printed 1992), p. 136.

7. Ibid., pp. 141-142.

8. Gaines, *Cub Creek Church*, p. 15.

9. Stallworth, p. 143.

10. Query, *Genealogy and History* (Washington, D.C.), 15 Dec. 1943, #8347. The unpublished data in the D.A.R. Library cannot be located there.

11. This section on the Reverend John Thomson is based on John Goodwin Herndon, *John Thomson, Presbyterian Constitutionalist Minister of the Word of God, Educational Leader and Church Builder* (privately printed, 1943), except as otherwise noted.

12. Only two known copies of the original exist. One is at the Historical Society of Pennsylvania in Philadelphia and the other is in the Library of Congress.

CHAPTER FIVE

1. Actually, two John Finleys settled in this part of Virginia about the same time, one on the Middle River of the Shenandoah and the other on the South River of the Shenandoah, about fifteen miles apart. Earlier researchers have intermingled the respective families of the two. The problem was compounded by the fact that there was considerable duplication of given names among their children. Between the late 1730s and 1800s, there were six John Finleys living in Augusta County. A sorting of some of these John Finleys has recently been published. See Carmen J. Finley, "The John Finleys of Augusta County, Virginia: Some Hypothesis," *The Genealogist*, in press.

2. Lyman Chalkley, *Chronicles of the Scotch–Irish Settlement in Virginia, Extracted from the Original Court Records of Augusta County* (Baltimore:

Genealogical Publishing Co., 1966), 2:375, 2:41.

3. Wilson, *The Tinkling Spring*, pp. 6–10.

4. Ibid., p. 62.

5. Ibid., p. 84.

6. Ibid., p. 3.

7. Ibid., pp. 88–90.

8. Ibid., p. 439.

9. Ibid., pp. 108, 113.

10. Ibid., p. 72.

11. Ibid., p. 474.

12. Augusta Co., Va., Deed Books 2:708–710, 2:711–714.

13. Wilson, *Tinkling Spring*, p. 431.

14. Ibid., p. 149.

15. Ibid., p. 158.

16. Ibid., p. 159.

17. Ibid., pp. 164–165.

18. Ibid., p. 166.

19. Augusta County, Va., Deed Book 11:808–809.

20. John G. Herndon, "Some of the Descendants of the Rev. John Thomson, (1690–1753)," *Virginia Magazine of History and Biography*, 51 (October 1943), pp. 394–404; reprinted in Genealogies of Virginia Families, 5 vols., (Baltimore: Genealogical Publishing Co., 1981), 5:454–464.

21. Prince Edward Co., Va., Deed Book 3:1–2.

22. Ibid., p. 21.

23. Montgomery Co., Va., Order Book 1:142.

24. Montgomery Co., Va., Deed Book A:283.

25. *Orange County, Indiana, Cemetery Records* (Paoli, Ind.: Lost River Chapter, D.A.R., 1943), 3 (Orleans, Finley Cemetery), p. 224.

26. Wythe Co., Va., Deed Book 1:95.

27. James Rood Robertson, *Petitions of the Early Inhabitants of Kentucky* (Louisville: John P. Morton & Co., 1914), p. 82.

28. Ibid., p. 121.

29. Madison Co., Ky., Tax Lists, Family History

Library microfilm #0008126.

30. Madison Co., Ky., Order Book B:356.

31. James F. Sutherland, comp., *Early Kentucky Householders, 1787–1811* (Baltimore: Genealogical Publishing Co., 1986), p. 62.

32. Lincoln Co., Va., Deed Book D:200.

33. Robert E. Glass, Special Collections, Grace Doherty Library, Centre College, Danville, Ky. to author, 15 December 1987.

34. 1810 U.S. census, population schedule, Lincoln Co., Ky., p. 116.

35. Bible record in possession of James D. Finley, 2320 Cheyenne Way, Modesto, CA 95356.

36. *Orange County, Indiana, Cemetery Records*, 3 (Orleans, Finley Cemetery), p. 224.

37. Garrard Co., Ky., Circuit Court, Box 2, Suit 39, Order Book 1:407. Also Anderson & Mounce, Order Book 10:224, Box 22, Bundle 86, Suit 633.

38. *Orange County, Indiana, Cemetery Records*, 3 (Orleans, Finley Cemetery), p. 224. Age at death given as 72 years, 5 days.

39. Kegley, *New River Tithables*, p. 27.

40. Montgomery Co., Va., Deed Books A:258, A:283.

41. H.V. McChesney, ed., "Certificate Book," *Kentucky State Historical Society Register*, 21 (Jan. 1923), p. 20. The spelling of the Dix (Dicks) River was not standardized until the late 19th century.

42. Virginia State Land Office, Richmond, Va., Grant I, 1783–1784, reel 50, pp. 322–324.

43. Mary B. Kegley, comp., *Militia of Montgomery County, Virginia, 1777–1790* (Wytheville, Va.: author, 1975), pp. 2, 39.

44. Mary B. Kegley, comp. *Tax List of Montgomery County, Virginia, 1782* (Wytheville, Va.: author, n.d.), p. 12.

45. Garrard Co., Ky., Circuit Court, Box 2, Suit 39, Book 1:407. Also Anderson & Mounce, Book

10:224, Box 22, Bundle 86, Suit 633.

46. Dale Van Every, *A Company of Heroes: The American Frontier, 1775–1783* (New York: William Morrow and Co., 1962), p. 296.

47. Carmen J. Finley, "Identifying the Revolutionary Soldier: James Downing of Lincoln County, Virginia (Kentucky)," *National Genealogical Society Quarterly*, 77 (Sept. 1989), pp. 169–185.

48. John Frederick Dorman, comp., "Mercer County Officers Before 1792," *Kentucky Genealogist*, 16 (Oct.–Dec., 1974), p. 135.

49. *Orange County, Indiana, Cemetery Records*, 3 (Orleans: Finley Cemetery), p. 224.

50. Eliza J. Turley to Pension Department, Washington, D.C., 30 January 1932, letter filed incorrectly under David Findley, W25577 in Revolutionary War Pension and Bounty–Land Application Files, microfilm M–804, roll 0975, National Archives. Eliza J. Turley, of Orleans, Ind., was a granddaughter of David by son, Cyrus.

51. Robertson, *Petitions of Early Inhabitants*, p. 68.

52. Ibid., p. 121.

53. "Lincoln Co., Ky., Order Books, 1781–1791," *Kentucky Genealogist*, 12 (Oct.–Dec., 1970), p. 138.

54. "Garrard County Wills," *Kentucky Genealogist*, 2 (Apr.–Jun., 1962), pp. 54–55.

55. Forest Calico, *History of Garrard County, Kentucky, and Its Churches* (New York: Hobson Book Press, 1947), p. 307.

56. Lincoln Co., Ky., Deed Book A:329.

57. Madison Co., Ky., Survey Book 1:326, warrant #3624, survey #506.

58. Ibid., p. 554.

59. Garrard Co., Ky., Deed Book C:367.

60. Records were found for David in Virginia, and in Lincoln, Mercer, Madison, and Garrard Counties, Kentucky. This reflects formation of new counties; David lived only in the Dicks River area of what is now Garrard County.

61. Garrard Co., Ky., Tax Records, Family History Library microfilms #007988 and #007989.

62. David Findley patents FC 170, 8 Oct. 1811, Credit Volume 14, p. 175; FC 189, 8 Oct. 1811, Credit Volume 15, p. 211; FC 190, 13 Aug. 1812, Credit Volume 15, p. 207; FC 263, 27 Dec. 1811, Credit Volume 15, Credit Volume 15, p. 406; FC 429, 3 Sept. 1813, Credit Volume 19, p. 268; FC 499, 15 March 1814, Credit Volume 20, p. 435; FC 551, 25 March 1814, Credit Volume 21, p. 17; FC 1851, 2 April 1818, Credit Volume 38, p. 419, U.S. Department of the Interior, Bureau of Land Management, Eastern States Office, Alexandria, Va.

63. Orange Co., Ind., Deed Book A:72–75.

64. Ibid., p. 70.

65. Orange Co., Ind., Tract Book #2, section 35, 4 December 1819.

66. Orange Co., Ind., Deed Book D:235.

67. Orange Co., Ind., Will Book 1:147.

68. *Orange County, Indiana, Cemetery Records*, 3 (Orleans, Finley Cemetery), p. 224.

69. Orange Co., Ind., Deed Book 13:205.

70. *Orange County, Indiana, Cemetery Records*, 3 (Orleans, Finley Cemetery), p. 224.

71. Orange Co., Ind., Deed Book 14:226–227.

72. Orange Co., Ind., Probate Order Book 4:111.

73. Garrard Co., Ky., Tax Lists, Family History Library microfilm #007988.

74. Ibid., microfilm #007988 and #007989.

75. 1820 U.S. census, population schedule, Lawrence County, Ind., p. 97.

76. "Burnt Tavern Cemetery at Bryantsville, Garrard County," *Kentucky Cemetery Records* (Frankfort?, Ky.: Kentucky Society, D.A.R. 1960), p. 171.

77. Estimated from age given on 1850 U.S. census, population schedule, Hopkins County, Tex., p. 22, dwelling #165, family #165; residence of Lewis Finley.

78. Bible record in possession of author.

79. Bible record in possession of Jeanne Branom, 1310 Aldridge Street, Commerce, Tex., 75428.

80. *Orange County, Indiana, Cemetery Records* (Trimble Cemetery), p. 245.

81. Family records in possession of Josephine Williams, 43570 Lake Hughes Road, Lake Hughes, CA 93532–1007.

82. Green Hill Cemetery at Orleans, Orange Co., Ind.; data read from tombstone marker described as "tall, substantial stone . . . letters very clear," by Pearl Wilson, records searcher, Route #3, Box 51, Paoli, Ind. 47454, November 1987. D.A.R. reading of this marker in error.

83. Information provided by Robert Morton, 2307 West 299th Place, Torrance, CA 90501, who has picture of tombstone marker; verified by author.

84. *Orange County, Indiana, Cemetery Records*, 3 (Orleans, Finley Cemetery), p. 224. Also *History of Orange County* (Paoli, Ind.: Stout's Print Shop, 1965), reprinted from *History of Lawrence, Orange & Washington Counties* (n.p., n. pub., 1884), p. 607.

85. Bible record in possession of James D. Finley, 2320 Cheyenne Way, Modesto, CA 95356.

86. Larry E. Pursley, comp., *7500 Marriages from Ninety–Six & Abbeville District, S.C., 1774–1890* (Easley, S.C.: Southern Historical Press, 1980), p. 65.

87. Ibid.

88. *A Register of Marriages Celebrated & Solemnized by Moses Waddel in South Carolina and Georgia*,

1795–1836 (S.C.?: Historical Markers Service of S.C., 1943), p. 6. Also Pursley, *7500 Marriages*, p. 65.

89. His will was probated 2 January 1832. Abbeville, S.C., Will Book 2:301.

90. Kegley, *New River Tithables*, p. 27.

91. Montgomery Co., Va., Record of Plotts B, 1782–83, p. 57.

92. Bible record in possession of James D. Finley. Andrew Swallow pension papers, file W61, National Archives and Records Service, Washington, D.C. Also in Thomas' will, Abbeville, S.C., Probate Box 34, Pack 732.

93. Andrew Swallow pension papers.

94. Abbeville, S.C., Will Book 2:301.

95. Abbeville, S.C., Probate Box 34, Pack 732.

96. Bible record in possession of James D. Finley.

97. Allen H. Stokes, Manuscripts Division, University of South Carolina, Columbia, S.C., to James D. Finley, 17 February 1977.

98. "Burnt Tavern Cemetery," p. 171.

99. Ibid.

100. Garrard Co., Ky., Marriage Records, Bond #198.

101. Calico, *History of Garrard County*, p. 80.

102. Annie Walker Burns, *Record of Wills in Garrard County, Kentucky, 1796–1851* (n.p., 1933), pp. 105–106.

103. Calico, *History of Garrard County*, pp. 40, 80.

104. J. Winston Coleman, Jr., *Historic Kentucky* (Lexington: Henry Clay Press, 1967), p. 31.

105. Burns, *Record of Wills in Garrard County*, pp. 105–106.

106. Calico, *History of Garrard County*, pp. 82–83.

107. *Kentucky Cemetery Records*, p. 171.

108. Stout, *Clan Finley*, p. 5.

109. Estimated from age given on 1850 U.S. census, population schedule, Hopkins County, Tex., p. 22, dwelling #165, family #165, residence of Lewis Finley.

110. Catherine named as wife in sale of property. Washington County, Ind., Deed Book, B:247.

111. Their son John was born in 1810 according to census records of 1850, 1860, and 1870, cited in full in text.

112. 1850 U.S. census, population schedule, Hunt Co., Tex., p. 416, dwelling #163, family #169; 1860 U.S. census, population schedule, Los Angeles Co., Calif., p. 537, dwelling #515, family #504; 1870 U.S. census, population schedule, Tulare Co., Calif., p. 276, dwelling #65, family #64.

113. Washington Co., Ind., Record of Land Entries, p. 13.

114. Washington Co. Ind.,Deed Book B:247.

115. 1830 U.S. census, population schedule, Wayne Co., Mo., pp. 38, 41.

116. 1840 U.S. census, population schedule, Van Buren Co., Mo., p. 138.

117. 1850 U.S. census, population schedule, Hopkins Co., Tex., p. 22, dwelling #165, family #165.

118. Cass Co., Mo., Deed Books C:389, F:10, F:127, F:148, F:448, F:456, G:127.

119. 1840 U.S. census, population schedule, Van Buren Co., Mo., p. 138.

120. 1850 U.S. census, population schedule, Hopkins Co., Tex., p. 22, dwelling #165, family #165; p. 20, dwelling #156, family #156.

121. Bible record in possession of author.

122. Macon Co., Ill., Probate Court, case #17, box 1, Family History Library microfilm #983,281.

123. Finley, "Identifying the Revolutionary Soldier," pp. 169–185.

124. Bible record in possession of author.

125. Ibid.

126. Macon Co., Ill., Marriages, p. 7.

127. "Muster Roll of Captain Charles Busey's Company of 5th Reg't Indiana Militia Infantry," 18 February to 19 March 1813, National Archives and Records Service, Washington, D.C.

128. Orange Co., Ind., Deed Book, A:72.

129. Ibid., p. 70.

130. Pearl S. Wilson, records searcher, Route #3, Box 51, Paoli, IN 47454 to author, 2 June 1984.

131. Macon Co., Ill., Marriages, p. 7.

132. Macon Co., Ill., Probate Court, case #17, box 1, Family History Library microfilm #983,281.

133. "Samuel Finley Land Grant," Illinois State Land Grants No. 2146 & No. 2410, 24 April 1820, Records of the Bureau of Land Management (Records Group 49), National Archives and Record Service, Washington, D.C.

134. Jean Parks Hauffe, *Abstracts of Macon County, Illinois, Probate Court Records, 1831–1847* (n.p.: n. pub., 1 October 1968), p. 4.

135. Macon Co., Ill., Probate Book A:76.

136. Ibid., Court Records, 1831–1848, 19 September 1836, 102–103, Family History Library microfilm #985,746.

137. Hauffe, *Abstracts of Macon County*, p. 16.

138. Macon Co., Ill., Probate File #11.

139. Ibid.

140. Macon Co., Ill., Marriages, p. 12.

141. Macon Co., Ill., Probate Book A:233.

142. Macon Co., Ill., Abstracts of Circuit Court Records, p. 26.

143. Hauffe, *Abstracts of Macon County*, p. 5.

144. Macon Co., Ill., Probate Court, case #17, box 1, Family History Library microfilm #983,281.

145. Bible record in possession of author.

146. International Genealogical Index (IGI),

Family History Library records for Mo.
147. Handwritten, undated letter obtained from 1, Family History Library microfilm #983,281.
145. Bible record in possession of author.
146. International Genealogical Index (IGI), Family History Library records for Mo.
147. Handwritten, undated letter obtained from Michelle Yahnian, 2607 E. Houston, Visalia, CA 93291, 10 June 1988.
148. Jackson Co., Mo., Marriage Book 1–2:153.
149. Cass Co., Mo., Circuit Court Book A:49.
150. Bates Co., Mo., Deed Book B:178.
151. 1850 U.S. census, population schedule, Bates Co., Mo., p. 265, dwelling #512, family #512; p. 271, dwelling #605, family #605.
152. Sonoma Co., Calif., Deed Books N:403, 7:452; 6:541, 8:426, 9:131.
153. Bible record in possession of Jeanne Branom.
154. Jesse was found living with son David in 1860 in Dunklin Co., Missouri, and had disappeared from this household in 1870. Complete documentation follows.
155. Washington Co., Ind., Marriage Records, vol. A:2. Rachel Findley was named in her father's will, 10 November 1822, Lulie Davis, *Abstracts of Wills of Washington County, Indiana, 1808–1902* (Salem, Ind., Christopher Harrison Chapter, D.A.R., 1971), p. 4.
156. Bible record in possession of Jeanne Branom.
157. Jesse and Rachel were found together in the 1850 census in Hunt County, Texas. Jesse was found, without Rachel, living in household of son David in Dunklin County, Missouri, in 1860.
158. "Muster Roll of Captain Charles Busey's Company of 5th Reg't Indiana Militia Infantry," 18 February to 19 March, 16 April to 15 May, 1813, National Archives and Records Service, Washington, D.C.
159. Bounty Land Warrant Application, National Archives and Records Service, Washington, D.C.
160. Orange Co., Ind., Deed Book A:72.
161. 1820 U.S. census, population schedule, Orange Co., Ind., p. 136.
162. 1830 U.S. census, population schedule, Wayne Co., Mo., pp. 38, 41.
163. 1850 U.S. census, population schedule, Hunt Co., Tex., 425, dwelling #232, family #243.
164. 1900 U.S. census, population schedule, Hopkins Co., Tex., e.d. 53, sheet 10, dwelling #184, family #189.
165. 1840 U.S. census, population schedule, Stoddard Co., Mo., p. 7.
166. Gifford White, *Mercer Colonists* (n.p.: n. pub., 1984), p. 21.
167. Hunt Co., Tex., Deed Book B–3:378, Surveyors Record, vol. A:468.
168. 1850 U.S. census, population schedule, Hunt Co., Tex., p. 425, dwelling #232, family #243; p. 429, dwelling #260, family #274; p. 429, dwelling #261, family #275.
169. Mrs. Jeff Wade, Jr., trans., *1860 Federal Census Dunklin County, Missouri*, also *1860 Mortality Schedules*, Microcopy No. M–653, Roll No. 618, National Archives (Bragg City, Mo.: author, 1975), p. 47.
170. Bible record in possession of Jeanne Branom.
171. Ibid.
172. Bible record in possession of Peggy Harding, 715 Emmons Street, Kilgore, Tex., 75662.
173. 1880 U.S. census, population schedule, Hopkins Co., Tex., p. 182, dwelling #218, family #218; 1900 U.S. census, population schedule, Hopkins Co., Tex., e.d. 53, sheet 10, dwelling #184, family #189.
174. White, *Mercer Colonists*, p. 21.
175. Hopkins Co., Tex., Marriage Records vol. 2:153.
176. *Orange County, Indiana, Cemetery Records*, 3 (Trimble Cemetery), p. 245.
177. Ibid.
178. Information provided by Carolyn Kraemer, 4875 N. 90th Street, Milwaukee, Wisc., 23 December 1982. The McKinneys were an old Augusta County, Va., family found both near Staunton and Middle River.
179. Ruth M. Slevin, comp., *Washington County, Indiana, Marriage Records, 1815–1847*, Books A–E, Part II – Index of Brides, 1970, 27, Book A:5. John Hay Center, 307 E. Market, Salem, Ind. 47167.
180. *Orange County, Indiana, Cemetery Records*, 3 (Trimble Cemetery), p. 245.
181. Orange Co., Ind., Deed Book A:75.
182. 1820 U.S. census, population schedule, Washington Co., Ind., p. 214.
183. June Voyles, *Guardianships, 1820–1859, Washington County, Indiana* (Salem, Ind.: Washington County Historical Society, 1989), pp. 24–25.
184. *Orange County, Indiana, Cemetery Records*, 3 (Trimble Cemetery), p. 245.
185. Pearl S. Wilson to author, 2 June 1984.
186. Washington Co., Ind., Probate Book 6:242.
187. Voyles, *Guardianships, 1820–1859, Washington County, Indiana*, p. 61.
188. Ibid., p. 65.
189. Ibid., p. 24. Vital data from Trimble Cemetery, p. 245, except as otherwise noted.
190. *Orange County, Indiana, Cemetery Records*, 3 (Trimble Cemetery), p. 245.
191. Tombstone marker read by local researcher, Pearl S. Wilson, November 1987.

192. Orange Co., Ind., Marriage Book C2:118.
193. *Orange County, Indiana, Cemetery Records,* 3 (Trimble Cemetery), p. 248.
194. Ibid.
195. Orange Co., Ind., Marriage Book C2:136.
196. There is a William A. Finley listed in the Cemetery Index, Orange County Library, Paoli, Indiana, born January 1831, died 2 June 1870.
197. Orange Co., Ind., Marriage Book C4:36.
198. Liberty Cemetery, p. 7.
199. Information on this family was provided by a great–great–granddaughter Josephine Williams, 43570 Lake Hushes Rd., Lake Hushes, CA 93532 from family Bible notes, except as otherwise noted.
200. According to a newspaper account, no date, no source, abstracted by Josephine Williams and titled, "Another Pioneer Gone," they were married in late 1815.
201. Orange Co., Ind., Deed Book A:73.
202. Voyles, *Guardianships, 1820–1859, Washington County, Indiana,* pp. 24–25.
203. Washington Co., Ind., Probate Book 6:242. Also Voyles, *Guardianships, 1820–1859, Washington County, Indiana,* p. 33.
204. Orange Co., Ind., Probate Order Book 4:111.
205. Unsigned, undated letter in possession of Josephine Williams. Letter includes reference to "Papa's (Joseph Jefferson Maxwell, Mary's son) Family record copied from Grandfather Maxwell's old Bible which Aunt has."
206. Orange Co., Ind., Marriage Record Index, 1816–1920.
207. Ibid.
208. Ibid.
209. Ibid.
210. Ibid.

211. Orange Co., Ind., Probate Book 7:388.
212. Green Hill Cemetery at Orleans, Orange Co., Ind; data read from tombstone by Pearl S. Wilson, Orange County researcher, November 1987. Stone marker described as "tall, substantial stone . . . letters very clear." D.A.R. transcription of his birth date from this marker is in error.
213. Orange Co., Ind., Marriage Record Index, 1816 to 1920.
214. *Orange County, Indiana, Cemetery Records,* 3 (Green Hill Cemetery), p. 158.
215. Orange Co., Ind., Deed Book A:74.
216. Voyles, *Guardianships, 1820–1859, Washington County, Indiana,* pp. 24–25.
217. Orange Co., Ind., Deed Book 13:205–206.
218. Orange Co., Ind., Order Probate Book 4:111.
219. Lawrence Co., Ind., Probate Box 42, file 30.
220. Birth and death dates for James, David, and Merrill in *Orange County Cemetery Records,* 3 (Green Hill Cemetery), p. 158. Data in *History of Orange County* (reprinted from *History of Lawrence, Orange, and Washington Counties [1884];* Paoli, Ind., 1965) are not in total agreement.
221. Date read from tombstone by local researcher, Pearl Wilson, November 1987.
222. Birth dates estimated from 1850 U.S. census, Orange Co., Ind., p. 414.
223. Orange Co., Ind., Marriages C5:422.
224. Ibid., p. 555.
225. Ibid., Marriages C3:148. *History of Orange County,* p. 607, gives 3 September 1847 as date of marriage.
226. Read from tombstone by local researcher, Pearl Wilson, November 1987. *History of Orange County,* p. 607, gives birth date as 2 September 1821.
227. *History of Orange County,* p. 607 except as oth-

erwise noted.
228. Ibid, p. 607.
229. Orange Co., Ind., Marriages C5:226.
230. *Orange County, Indiana, Cemetery Records,* (Green Hill Cemetery), p. 158, listed as Emma L.J. Finley. *History of Orange County,* p. 607 gives date of death as 27 February 1856.
231. Named in executor's report of her grandfather, Cyrus Finley, 14 December 1875 (Lawrence Co., Ind., Probate Box 42, file 30).
232. *History of Orange County,* p. 607 and Green Hill Cemetery records in conflict.
233. Ibid., p. 634.
234. Vital records taken from Green Hill Cemetery records except as otherwise noted, p. 158.
235. Orange Co., Ind., Marriages C5:573. *History of Orange County,* p. 634.
236. Orange Co., Ind., Marriages C3:384.
237. *History of Lawrence County, Indiana,* p. 258.
238. Information provided by Robert Morton, 2307 West 299th Place, Torrance, CA 90501, who has picture of tombstone marker; verified by author.
239. Garrard Co., Ky., General Index to Marriages, 1797–1958, Box 5, Bond 1092, Family History Library microfilm #0183255.
240. 1820 U.S. census, population schedule, Garrard Co., Ky., p. 109.
241. Orange Co., Ind., Deed Book D:235.
242. 1830 U.S. census, population schedule, Orange Co., Ind., p. 13.
243. Data provided by Robert Morton.
244. *Orange County, Indiana, Cemetery Records,* 3 (Orleans, Finley Cemetery), p. 224. Also some biographical material in *History of Orange County,* under son Samuel Finley, p. 607.
245. Ibid.
246. Orange Co., Ind., Marriage Record Index,

1816 to 1920.
247. *Orange County, Indiana,* Cemetery Records, 3 (Orleans, Finley Cemetery), p. 224.
248. *History of Orange County,* p. 638.
249. *Orange County, Indiana, Cemetery Records,* 3 (Trimble Cemetery), p.5
250. *Orange County, Indiana, Cemetery Records,* 3 (Trimble Cemetery), p. 224. Birth date given, but no date of death.
251. *History of Orange County,* p. 607.
252. Ibid., p. 639.
253. Andrew Swallow pension papers. Bible record in possession of Bonnie F. Sells, Livingston, Tenn. Also in will of Thomas Finley, Abbeville, S.C., Will Book 2:301.
254. Bible record in possession of Sally (Finley) Nance, Dunlap, Tenn.
255. Bible record in possession of James D. Finley.
256. Andrew Swallow pension papers.
257. Information provided by James D. Finley.
258. Overton Co., Tenn., Books 1:731; 1:180; C:241; R:82.
259. Letter addressed to Reubin (sic) Findley from Alexr. Hunter, Acting Executor of Thos Finley.
260. Bible record in possession of Sally (Finley) Nance.
261. Information provided by James D. Finley.
262. Ibid.
263. Vital dates come from a Bible record in the possession of James D. Finley.
264. Bible record in possession of Sally (Finley) Nance.
265. Ibid.
266. Letter from A. Hunter to Granville H. Finley, 4 March 1851, in possession of Sally (Finley) Nance.
267. Letter from A. Hunter to Granville H. Finley, 15 March 1851, in possession of Sally (Finley) Nance.
268. Diary kept by Mary Ann Hulsey, granddaughter of Reuben J. Finley, Jr. Copy in possession of Rex Hulsey, Walnut Creek, CA.
269. Bible record in possession of James D. Finley.
270. 1850 U.S. census, population schedule, Hunt Co.,Tex., p. 416, dwelling #163, family #169; 1860 U.S. census, population schedule, Los Angeles Co., Calif., p. 537, dwelling #515, family #504; 1870 U.S. census, population schedule, Tulare Co., Calif., p. 276, dwelling #65, family #64.
271. Bible record in possession of author. Also Ethel Work Balmer, *Garold's Great Grandfather and Great Grandmother*, written about 1916. Balmer was a granddaughter of John Findley through second wife, Sarah Masters.
272. Jackson Co., Mo., Marriage Book 1-2:153.
273. Tulare Co., Calif., Probate Court, Estate #118. Also Ethel Work Balmer, paper in possession of author.
274. Arba A. Frost, *Tulare County Killings*, vol. III (n.p.: n. pub., 1943), pp. 385A-1 through 392.
275. Macon Co., Ill., Probate Book A:76.
276. Hauffe, *Abstracts of Probate Records*, p. 14.
277. Macon Co., Ill., Abstracts of Circuit Court Records, pp. 21-24, 30.
278. Macon Co., Ill., Probate Box #1, case #17, Family History Library microfilm #983,281.
279. Ethel Work Balmer, granddaughter of John Findley by Sarah Masters, was born 16 June 1894, died 12 November 1978.
280. Mahala's brother John did have a set of twins.
281. 1840 U.S. census, population schedule, Van Buren Co., Mo., p. 129.
282. Macon Co., Ill., Marriages, p.13.
283. 1850 U.S. census, population schedule, Hunt Co., Tex., p. 416, dwelling #163, family #169.
284. William Thorndale & William Dollarhide, *Map Guide to the U.S. Federal Censuses, 1790-1920* (Baltimore: Genealogical Publishing Co., 1987), p. 34.
285. Eugene L. Menefee & Fred A. Dodge, *History of Tulare and Kings Counties, California* (Los Angeles: Historic Record Co., 1913), p. 840.
286. Hunt County, Tex., Surveyors Record, vol. A:468.
287. Menefee, *History of Tulare & Kings County*, p. 840.
288. 1860 U.S. census, population schedule, Los Angeles Co., Calif., p. 537, dwelling #515, family #504; p. 538, dwelling #523, family #512.
289. Ibid. Also 1870 U.S. census, population schedule, p. 538, dwelling #65, family #64.
290. 1860 U.S. census, population schedule, Los Angeles Co., Calif., p. 537, dwelling #515, family #504; p. 538, dwelling #523, family #512.
291. Ibid.
292. Tulare Co., Calif., Deed Book, F:494-495.
293. 1870 U.S. census, population schedule, Tulare Co., Calif., p. 276, dwelling #65, family #64.
294. Frost, *Tulare County Killings*, pp. 385A-1 through 392.
295. Ibid.
296. On 12 August 1871, the *Tulare Times* carried a similar item.
297. Three of the six included R.M. Work, J. Work, Wm. Work. John Findley's daughter Nancy Caroline had married Will Work in 1864.
298. Tulare Co., Calif., Coroner's Inquest No. 11.
299. Tom Woody's sister Ellen had married John's

son William, hence Woody was a brother to John's daughter-in-law.

300. Tulare Co., Calif., Probate Court, Estate #118.

301. Sonoma Co., Calif., Great Register, 1871, p. 23.

302. Sonoma Co., Calif., Deed Book 39:302-303 gives date of deed as 15 June 1872; however, papers in possession of the author indicate a mortgage was taken on 5 January 1872.

303. Tulare Co., Calif., Marriage Book A:328.

304. 1850 U.S. census, population schedule, Hunt Co., Tex., p. 416, dwelling #163, family #169.

305. Death certificate for Julia Ann Hart, local registered no. 10, Kern Co., Calif., County Recorder, Bakersfield, Calif. Certified copy in possession of author.

306. *Memorial and Biographical History of the Counties of Fresno, Tulare, and Kern, California* (Chicago: Lewis Publishing Co., n.d.), p. 727.

307. Julia Ann Hart death certificate.

308. *Memorial and Biographical History of the Counties of Fresno, Tulare and Kern, California*, p. 727.

309. 1850 U.S. census, population schedule, Hunt Co., Tex., p. 416, dwelling #163, family #169.

310. Death certificate for Nancy Caroline Work, local registered no. 94, Tulare Co., Calif., County Recorder, Visalia, Calif. Certified copy in possession of author.

311. *Tulare County, California, Marriage Records, Index, 1853-1892* (Visalia, Calif.: Sequoia Genealogical Society, P.O. Box 3473, n.d.), p. 53.

312. Nancy Caroline Work death certificate.

313. 1850 U.S. census, population schedule, Hunt Co., Tex., p. 416, dwelling #163, family #169.

314. Menefee and Dodge, *History of Tulare and Kings Counties*, p. 840.

315. Read from tombstone marker, Smith Mountain Cemetery, Dinuba, Tulare Co., Calif., by Michelle Yahnian, 2607 E. Huston, Visalia, CA 93291.

316. 1860 U.S. census, Los Angeles Co., Calif., p. 538 says she was born in California; however, it also says her half-brother David, who was 3 years younger, was born in Texas.

317. Birth information estimated from census records except for Catherine and Elizabeth. 1860 U.S. census, Los Angeles Co., Calif., p. 537; 1870, Tulare Co., Calif., p. 276.

318. Donna M. Hull, *And Then There Were Three Thousand* (Fresno: author, 1975), p. 236.

319. Ibid.

320. Ibid., p. 448.

321. Ibid., p. 149.

322. Ibid., p. 447.

323. Calculated from 1850 U.S. census, population schedule Hopkins Co., Tex., p. 22, dwelling #156, family #156.

324. 1840 U.S. census, population schedule, Van Buren Co., Mo., p. 138.

325. Cass County, Mo., Deed Books C:389, F:10, F:148.

326. 1850 U.S. census, population schedule, Hopkins Co., Tex., p. 20, dwelling #156, family #156.

327. Information supplied by Jeanne Branom.

328. 1860 U.S. census, population schedule, Hopkins Co., Tex., p. 602, dwelling #721, family #716.

329. Calculated from 1850 U.S. census, population schedule, Hopkins Co., Tex., p. 22, dwelling #165, family #165.

330. Information supplied by Jeanne Branom.

331. 1850 U.S. census, population schedule, Hopkins Co., Tex., p. 22, dwelling #165, family #165.

332. Lorraine Dodson Story, trans., *1860 Census of Hunt County, Texas* (Farmersville, Tex.: Search-N-Print, 1979), dwelling #56, family #50.

333. Bible record in possession of author.

334. Macon Co., Ill., Marriage Records, p. 10.

335. Macon Co., Ill., Abstracts of Circuit Court Records, p. 26.

336. Paul M. Hogan, Circuit Clerk of Macon County to author, 20 April 1981, claims estate file #43 for Alvin exists, but there are no file papers.

337. A marriage record is shown for Jacob Black, 12 November 1835, the same day Alvin Finley and Hannah Black were married.

338. Macon Co., Ill., Abstracts of Circuit Court Records, p. 32.

339. Bible record in possession of author.

340. John W. Smith, *History of Macon County, Illinois, from its Organization to 1876* (Springfield: Rokker's Printing House, 1876), p. 81.

341. Macon Co., Ill., Marriage Records, p. 7.

342. 1840 U.S. census, population schedule, Macon Co., Ill., p. 6.

343. Nancy Braden family Bible in possession of Susie Grohs, 1859 Archer Drive, Medford, OR 97501.

344. Nancy Braden family Bible.

345. 1860 U.S. census, population schedule, Analy Township, Sonoma Co., Calif., p. 491, dwelling #87, family #88; 1870 U.S. census, population schedule, Bodega, Sonoma Co., Calif., p. 259, dwelling #167, family #166.

346. This information provided by Glenva Conklin, 6205 Grant Avenue, Carmichael, CA 95608-3443, great grand-daughter of Nancy Finley

Braden.

347. Bible record in possession of author. His death certificate gives birth date as 6 June 1822, but photograph of tombstone is consistent with Bible record.

348. Bible record in possession of author.

349. Sonoma Co., Calif., Death Records Book 43:44. Also tombstone picture in possession of author.

350. John Finley death certificate, Sonoma Co., Calif., State Index, p. 503.

351. Photographs of tombstone markers in possession of author.

352. Bible record in possession of author.

353. Ibid.

354. *Portrait and Biographical Record of Arizona* (Chicago: Chapman Publishing Co., 1901), pp. 214-215.

355. Their oldest child, Martha, was born about 1850 according to 1860 U.S. census, population schedule, Bodega, Sonoma Co., Calif., p. 532, dwelling #382, family #382.

356. Tulare Co., Calif., Marriage Record Index, p. 16.

357. *The Sonoma Democrat* (Santa Rosa, Sonoma Co., Calif.), 29 July 1876.

358. Cass Co., Mo., Circuit Court Book A:49.

359. Bates Co., Mo., Deed Book B:178.

360. 1860 U.S. census, population schedule Bodega, Sonoma Co., Calif., p. 532, dwelling #382, family #382.

361. Bates Co., Mo., Deed Book B:178.

362. *Portrait and Biographical Record of Arizona*, pp. 214-215.

363. 1860 U.S. census, population schedule, Bodega, Sonoma Co., Calif., p. 532, dwelling #382, family #382; 1870 U.S. census, population schedule, Bodega, Sonoma Co., Calif., p. 254, dwelling #99, family #97.

364. *Sonoma County Journal* (Petaluma, Sonoma Co., Calif.), 27 Sept. 1861.

365. *Portrait and Biographical Record of Arizona* also claims he was a sheriff of Sonoma County, but no record has been found to substantiate this claim.

366. *The Sonoma Democrat* (Santa Rosa, Sonoma Co., Calif.), 29 July 1876.

367. *The Santa Rosa Times* (Santa Rosa, Sonoma Co., Calif.), July 1876.

368. *The Sonoma Democrat* (Santa Rosa, Sonoma Co., Calif.), 29 July 1876.

369. Ibid

370. Ibid.

371. *The Sonoma Democrat* (Santa Rosa, Sonoma Co., Calif.), 5 August, 12 August, 19 August 1876.

372. John Schubert, "A Wild July in Guerneville," *Journal of the Sonoma County Historical Society*, 1990, no. 3, pp. 8-10.

373. Pleasant Hill Cemetery has no record of the burial of either Samuel or Prudence.

374. *Petaluma Argus* (Petaluma, Sonoma Co., Calif.), 28 July 1876.

375. *Portrait and Biographical Record of Arizona*, pp. 214-215.

376. 1860 U.S. census, population schedule, Bodega, Sonoma Co., Calif., p. 532, dwelling #382, family #382.

377. 1870 U.S. census, population schedule, Bodega, Sonoma Co., Calif., p. 254, dwelling #99, family #97.

378. Tulare Co., Calif., Marriage Record Index, p. 16.

379. 1900 U.S. census, population schedule, Precinct #1, Pima Co., Ariz., e.d. 46, sheet 11, dwelling #196, family #204.

380. Birth dates are estimated from the 1860 and 1870 census, except as otherwise noted.

381. *Petaluma Argus* (Petaluma, Sonoma Co., Calif.), 28 July 1876.

382. *Portrait and Biographical Record of Arizona*, pp. 214-215. Most of the rest of James's information is also from this source except as otherwise noted.

383. 1900 U.S. census, population schedule, Precinct #1, Pima Co., Ariz., e.d. 46, sheet 11, dwelling #196, family #204.

384. Bible record in possession of author.

385. Their first child was born about 1855/56.

386. Tulare Co., Calif., Marriages Book A:328.

387. 1850 U.S. census, population schedule, Hunt Co., Tex., p. 416, dwelling #163, family #169.

388. Donna M. Hull, *And Then There Were Three Thousand*, p. 447.

389. 1860 U.S. census, population schedule, Los Angeles Co., Calif., p. 537, dwelling #515, family #504; p. 538, dwelling #523, family #512.

390. 1870 U.S. census, population schedule, Tulare Co., Calif., p. 276, dwelling #65, family #64.

391. Frost, *Tulare County Killings*; also *Visalia Weekly Delta* (Visalia, Tulare Co., Calif.), 10 August 1871; also *Tulare Times* (Visalia, Tulare Co., Calif.), 12 August 1871.

392. Sonoma Co., Calif., Deed Book 39:302-303. While the officially recorded deed is dated 15 June 1872, personal papers show a mortgage was taken on this property on 5 January 1872.

393. Sonoma Co., Calif., Probate File #584.

394. Ibid.

395. Tulare Co., Calif., Marriages Book A:328

396. Sonoma Co., Calif., Deed Book 42:257.

397. Sonoma Co., Calif., Probate File #584.

398. Donna M. Hull, *And Then There Were Three Thousand*, p. 236.

399. Akers Cemetery, also known as Kings River Cemetery & Centerville Cemetery, on Trimmer Spring Road, Fresno County, Calif. Listing provided by Donna M. Hull (now Agegberto), P.O. Box 1211, Frazier Park, CA 93225.

400. Bible record in possession of Jeanne Branom.

401. 1850 U.S. census, population schedule, Hunt Co., Tex., p. 425, dwelling #233, family #244.

402. Marion Day Mullins, comp., *Republic of Texas: Poll Lists for 1846* (Baltimore: Genealogical Publishing Co., 1974), p. 54.

403. Frances Terry Ingmire, comp., *Marriage Records of Hopkins County, Texas, 1846-1880* (St. Louis: author, 1979), p. 7.

404. Ibid.

405. Bible record in possession of Jeanne Branom.

406. Mullins, *Republic of Texas: Poll Lists for 1846*, p. 54.

407. Hopkins Co., Tex., Marriage Records, vol. 1:8.

408. White, *Mercer Colonists*, p. 20.

409. Hunt Co., Tex., 1850 U.S. census, p. 429, dwelling #260, family #274.

410. 1860 U.S. census, population schedule, Hopkins Co., Tex., p. 105/162, dwelling #755, family #747.

411. Bible record in possession of Jeanne Branom.

412. Mary F. Smith-Davis, *History of Dunklin County, Mo., 1845-1895*, II, 1896 Rpt. (St. Louis: Nixon-Jones Printing Co., Kennett, Mo.: Thrower Printing Co., 1962), pp. 191-193.

413. Ibid.

414. Ibid., p. 193.

415. Ibid., p. 191.

416. Downing & Wade, Jr., *1850 Dunklin County Census*, p. 3; Wade, *1860 Federal Census, Dunklin County*, p. 47.

417. Smith-Davis, *History of Dunklin County, Mo.*, p. 192.

418. Birth dates estimated from 1850 U.S. census records. Death dates estimated from Smith-Davis, *History of Dunklin County, Mo.*, p. 192.

419. Smith-Davis, *History of Dunklin County, Mo.*, pp. 191-193.

420. Bible record in possession of Jeanne Branom.

421. Lamar Co., Tex., Marriage Records, vol. 1:20.

422. Hopkins Co., Tex., Death Certificate, vol. 1:7.

423. Bible records in possession of Jeanne Branom.

424. Hopkins Co., Tex., Marriage Records, vol. 2:144.

425. Oakland Cemetery, Oakland Community, Hopkins Co., Tex.

426. Hopkins Co., Tex., Marriage Records vol. 2:258.

427. Emblem Cemetery, Emblem Community, Hopkins Co., Tex.

428. Hopkins Co., Tex., Marriage Records vol. 4:140.

429. Ibid., p. 102.

430. Ibid., p. 356.

431. Death Certificate, #31207, Texas Bureau of Vital Statistics.

432. Hopkins Co., Tex., Marriage Records, vol. 3:228.

433. Funeral Home Records, Antlers, Okla.

434. Hopkins Co., Tex., Marriage Records, vol. 6:171.

435. Confederate Cemetery, Austin, Travis Co., Tex.

436. Hopkins Co., Tex., Marriage Records, vol. 4:76.

437. Hopkins Co., Tex., Death Records, vol. 2-A:21.

438. Reeves Co., Tex., Marriage Records, vol. 1:1.

439. Hopkins Co., Tex., Death Records, vol. 2-A:454.

440. Hopkins Co., Tex., Marriage Records, vol. 9:517.

441. Hunt Co., Tex., Death Records, vol. 3:82.

442. Bible record in possession of Jeanne Branom.

443. Hunt Co., Tex., Marriage Records DA:404.

444. White, *Mercer Colonists*, p. 19.

445. 1850 U.S. census, population schedule, Hunt Co., Tex., p. 429, dwelling #261, family #275.

446. Hunt Co., Tex., Probate Records, vol. A:93.

447. Bible record in possession of Peggy Harding.

448. 1880 U.S. census, population schedule, Hopkins Co., Tex., p. 177b, dwelling #218, family #218; 1900 U.S. census, population schedule, Hopkins Co., Tex., e.d. 53, sheet 10b, dwelling #184, family #189.

449. White, *Mercer Colonists*, p. 21.

450. Confederate Pension Application, #25189, Texas State Archives, Austin, Tex.

451. Confederate Pension Application, #34761 (widow), Texas State Archives, Austin, Tex., statement appended, signed by M.A. Finley, dated 1 December 1917.

452. *Abstract of All Original Texas Land Titles Comprising Grants and Locations to August 31, 1941* (Austin: General Land Office, Bascom Giles Commissioner, n.d.), p. 461.

453. Confederate Pension Application, #25189, Texas State Archives, Austin, Tex.

454. Bible records in possession of Peggy Harding.

455. Death Certificate, #543, Texas Department of

455. (cont.) Health, Bureau of Vital Statistics gives date of birth as 12 February 1868.
456. Death Certificate #177, Texas Department of Health, Bureau of Vital Statistics gives date of birth as 15 August 1870.
457. Hopkins Co., Tex., Marriage Records, vol. 8:139.
458. Hopkins Co., Tex., Marriage Records, vol. 10:525.
459. Bible record in possession of Jeanne Branom.
460. Hopkins Co., Tex., Marriage Records, vol. 3:31.
461. Sonoma Co., Calif., Death Register Book 42:41.
462. White, *Mercer Colonists*, p. 21.
463. 1850 U.S. census, population schedule, Hunt Co., Tex., p. 425, dwelling #232, family #243.
464. Frances Terry Ingmire & Robert Lee Thompson, comp., *Johnny Rebs of Hunt County, Texas* (n.p.: comps., 1977), p. 121.
465. 1860 U.S. census, population schedule, Bodega Township, Sonoma Co., Calif., p. 536, dwelling #428, family #428.
466. Original in possession of Peggy Harding; copy in possession of author.
467. *Sonoma County Coroner's Inquests During the 1800s* (Santa Rosa, Calif.: Sonoma County Genealogical Society, 1989), p. 108.
468. Sonoma Co., Calif., Patents Book B:60.
469. Sonoma Co., Calif., Deed Book 59:329.
470. Sonoma Co., Calif., Deed Book 65:393-394.
471. 1880 U.S. census, population schedule, Redwood Township, Sonoma Co., Calif., p. 222, dwelling #139, family #76, dwelling #140, family #77, dwelling #141, family #78.
472. Sonoma Co., Calif., Deed Book 71:92.
473. Sonoma Co., Calif., Deed Book 170:493.
474. Great Register, Sonoma Co., Calif. began in 1867 and lists all registered voters in the county.
475. Great Register of 1898, Sonoma Co., Calif., p. 117.
476. From the 1870 and 1880 U.S. census of Sonoma Co., Calif. 1870 U.S. census, population schedule, Bodega Township, Sonoma Co., Calif., p. 257, dwelling #159, family #156. 1880 U.S. census, population schedule, Redwood Township, Sonoma Co., Calif., e.d. 130, sheet 18, dwelling #141, family #78. The 1870 and 1880 census records are not consistent in the reporting of birthplace for the children. 1870 gives birthplace of Mary and Sarah as California; 1880 shows all children born in Texas.
477. Orange Co., Ind., Cemetery Records (Trimble Cemetery), p. 5. A second transcription of Trimble Cemetery records is in conflict with this source in that it gives her date of death as 16 March 1868, p. 245; both give her age as 40y/2m/9d. If the age at death is correct, then the calculated date of birth as 20 January 1827 is more reasonable, considering her brother, Samuel, was born 10 July 1828.
478. *History of Orange County*, p. 634; also Orange Co., Ind., Marriages C3:170.
479. Orange Co., Ind., Probate Order Book 4:111.
480. Orange Co., Ind., Cemetery Records (Trimble Cemetery), p. 5.
481. *History of Orange County*, p. 634. 1860 U.S. census, Orange Co., Ind., p. 60.
482. *Orange Co., Ind., Cemetery Records*, 3 (Orleans: Finley Cemetery), p. 224. Birth date given, but no date of death.
483. *History of Orange County*, p. 607.
484. Identified in will of her grandmother, Rachel Elliott, probated 14 May 1868. Will Abstracts of Washington Co., Ind., p. 92. Washington Co., Ind., Will Book C:500-502, dated 8 April 1868.
485. *History of Orange County*, p. 607.
486. *Orange Co., Ind. Cemetery Records*, 3 (Orleans: Finley Cemetery), p. 224.
487. Identified in will of her grandmother.
488. Orange Co., Ind., Probate Order Book 4:111.
489. Orange Co., Ind., Deed Book 14:226-227.
490. Ibid., p. 227.
491. Orange Co., Ind., Deed Book 39:402-404.
492. *History of Orange County*, p. 607.
493. Ibid.
494. Orange Co., Ind., Marriage Records C6:173.
495. Orange Co., Ind., Marriage Records C7:532.
496. Orange Co., Ind., Marriage Records C8:94.
497. *History of Orange County*, p. 639.
498. Orange Co., Ind., Deed Book 14:227.
499. Orange Co., Ind., Marriage Records C3:512.
500. *History of Orange County*, p. 639.
501. Ibid.
502. Bible record in possession of Sally (Finley) Nance.
503. Ibid.
504. Abbeville, S.C., Probate Box 34, Pack 732.
505. Letter addressed to Dr. Thomas from Jane Findley, Abbeville, 20 December 1842. Original in possession of Sally (Finley) Nance.
506. Letter to Thomas M. Findley from A. Hunter, 29 November 1845. Original in possession of Sally (Finley) Nance.
507. Abbeville, S.C., Probate Box 34, Pack 732.
508. Bible record in possession of James D. Finley. Also letter from A. Hunter to Thomas M. Findley, 29 November 1845, in possession of Sally (Finley) Nance.
509. Letter from A. Hunter to Thomas M. Findley, 29

November 1848, in possession of Sally (Finley) Nance.

510. Letter from A. Hunter to Thomas M. Findley, 23 March 1846, in possession of Sally (Finley) Nance.

511. Abbeville, S.C. , Probate Box 34, Pack 732.

512. Ibid.

513. Ibid.

514. Bible record in possession of Sally (Finley) Nance.

515. The sections on the children of John and Keziah are taken from the earlier work of Nettie (Head) McDonald and published in 1981 by this author under the title *John and Keziah (Head) Finley*. Nettie (1906-1993) was the second cousin of this author, and although we lived for many years within 15 miles of each other, we did not meet until 1979. But in the fourteen years I knew Nettie, I learned much from her about the early Sonoma County Finleys. Nettie had a trunk full of original legal documents, including all the deeds showing John and Keziah's purchase of land in the Bodega Rancho. These documents are now in the possession of her grandson, Scott McDonald, 1890 17th N.E., Salem, Oregon 97303.

516. *Tulare County, California, Marriage Records, Index* (Visalia, Calif.: Sequoia Genealogical Society, n.d.), p. 16.

517. Michelle Yahnian to Carmen J. Finley, 18 October 1988. Michelle had visited the cemetery and copied the dates of birth and death. All information on the descendants of William J. Findley was supplied by Michelle Yahnian, 2607 E. Houston, Visalia, CA 93292.

518. Eugene L. Menefee, *History of Tulare and Kings Counties* (Los Angeles: Historic Record Co., 1913), p. 840.

519. Ethel (Work) Balmer.

520. Tulare Co., Calif., Death Certificate #105.

521. Bible record in possession of author, and Nettie McDonald manuscript.

522. Sonoma Co., Calif., Deed Book 34:519.

523. Nettie McDonald manuscript, p. 15.

524. Sonoma Co., Calif., Deed Book 287:116. This was comprised of two parcels; lot two , 106 acres and lot six, 150.46 acres.

525. Sonoma Co., Calif., Deed Book 363:446.

526. Sonoma Co., Calif., Official Records 445:31, 38.

527. "J.C. Finley Dies as Result of Fractured Skull," *The Press Democrat* (Santa Rosa, Sonoma Co., Calif.), 25 September 1920.

528. Bible record in possession of author, and Nettie McDonald manuscript.

529. Ibid.

530. Henry bought 408.78 acres from his parents on 2 April 1888 for $6,000. Sonoma Co., Calif., Deed Book 268:355.

531. Sonoma Co., Calif., Probate file #4981.

532. "English Hill is the name of the extensive and lofty elevation that may be roughly bounded as, by the lower lands on which stand Freestone, Valley Ford and Bloomfield and on its eastern base by Pleasant Valley." Tuomey, vol. 1, p. 743.

533. Bible record in possession of author, and Nettie McDonald manuscript.

534. Obituary, *The Press Democrat* (Santa Rosa, Sonoma Co., Calif.), 6 March 1953, p. 8, col. 2.

535. Sonoma Co., Calif., Deed Book 395:41.

536. Sonoma Co., Calif., Deed Book 396:429.

537. "Nancy Keithly, 98, Was County's Oldest Native," *The Press Democrat* (Santa Rosa, Sonoma Co., Calif.), 5 March 1953.

538. Howard Smith, "Who Is Oldest Native Resident? Women Vie for Sonoma Title," *The Press Democrat* (Santa Rosa, Sonoma Co., Calif.), 21 March 1948, sec. 2, p. 24.

539. Bible record in possession of author, and Nettie McDonald manuscript.

540. Ibid.

541. Sonoma Co., Calif., Deed Book 333:162

542. Sonoma Co., Calif., Deed Book 362:63

543. Sonoma Co., Calif., Deed Book 370:91

544. Sonoma Co., Calif., Deed Book 376:311

545. Sonoma Co., Calif., Deed Book 382:479

546. Sonoma Co., Calif., Official Records 242:90.

547. Sonoma Co., Calif., Official Records 299:147.

548. Bible record in possession of author, and Nettie McDonald manuscript.

549. Jefferson D. and Carrie Ann Finley, his wife, mortgaged their 109.3 parcel to R.J. Kee for $3,230 on 12 June 1914 (copy in possession of author). When Jeff sold his parcel of 103.48 acres to Henry on 29 March 1915, he was "unmarried."

550. Sonoma Co., Calif., Deed Book 288:383.

551. Sonoma Co., Calif., Deed Book 330:262. At this time, 29 March 1915, he was referred to as "unmarried."

552. Sonoma Co., Calif., Deed Book 333:162.

553. Carrie's handwritten birth dates of her children were found in the possession of her youngest daughter, Lillian Hodgson (Mrs. Carl), 1378 Funston Drive, Santa Rosa, 23 May 1991.

554. Sonoma Co., Calif., Marriage Index, Book 6:167.

555. Sonoma Co., Calif., Death Record Book 1972:2172.

556. Sonoma Co., Calif., Marriage Index, Book 6:76.

557. Ibid.

558. Sonoma Co., Calif., Marriage Index Book 6:76.

559. Sonoma Co., Calif., Death Record Book 1963:921.
560. Sonoma Co., Calif., Death Record Book 1926:154.
561. Bible record in possession of author, and Nettie McDonald manuscript.
562. *Portrait and Biographical Record of Arizona* (Chicago: Chapman Publishing Co., 1901), p. 214-215.
563. Orange Co., Calif., Deed Book 6:345.
564. Orange Co., Calif., Deed Books 54:59, 55:90-91, 55:142.
565. Sonoma Co., Calif., Deed Book 221:305.
566. Sonoma Co., Calif., Deed Book 282:248.
567. Sonoma Co., Calif., Death Records Book 40:1018.
568. "Accidentally Killed," *The Healdsburg Enterprise* (Healdsburg, Sonoma Co., Calif.), 20 December 1890, p. 6.
569. Bible record in possession of author, and Nettie McDonald manuscript.
570. Sonoma Co., Calif., Deed Book 213:323.
571. Madeline Miner to author, 10 January 1995.
572. 1870 U.S. census, population schedule Bodega, Sonoma Co., Calif., p. 258, dwelling #164, family #163.
573. Sonoma Co., Calif., Liber Z of Mortgages, p. 513, Liber 13 of Mortgages, p. 36, Liber 22 of Mortgages, p. 216, and papers in possession of author.
574. Sonoma Co., Calif., Liber B of Powers of Attorney, p. 309.
575. Birth dates estimated from 1880 U.S. census, population schedule, District #27, Madison Co., Mont., e.d. 27, sheet 4, dwelling #4, family #5.
576. *Portrait and Biographical Record of Arizona*, pp. 214-215. Most of the rest of James's information is also from this source except as otherwise noted.
577. 1900 U.S. census, population schedule, Tucson, Pima Co., Ariz., e.d. 47, sheet 7, 341 S. 3rd Avenue, dwelling #139, family #150.
578. Obituary provided by Department of Library Archives and Public Records, 3rd Floor Capitol, Phoenix, AZ, 85007. Also, *Arizona Historical Review,* January, 1931.
579. T.P. Cox, Personnel Division, Southern Pacific Transportation Company, One Market Plaza, San Francisco, CA 94105, to author 28 August 1980.
580. Michelle (Findley) Yahnian to author 27 May 1995.
581. Ibid.
582. From about 1911 to 1913.
583. Sonoma Co., Calif., Marriage Records 9:401.
584. Sonoma Co., Calif., Probate file #7024.
585. Sonoma Co., Calif., Marriage Records Y:2.
586. Obituary, *The Press Democrat* (Santa Rosa, Sonoma Co., Calif.), 9 May 1923.
587. California State Death Index, file #48-73449, #3735.
588. California State Death Index, file #48-42606, #322.
589. California State Death Index, file #14337, #83.
590. Sonoma Co., Calif., Deed Book 282:248.
591. Sonoma Co., Calif., Official Records 299:147.
592. Sonoma Co., Calif., Official Records 445:31, 38.
593. Certificate of Baptism, Church of the Assumption , P.O. Box 82, Tomales, CA 94971.
594. Interview with Edward Wilds, 3 April 1995, at his home outside Kelseyville, Lake County, California.
595. Certificate of graduation for Ocean View, dated 22 June 1923, verified during interview with Edward Wilds, 3 April 1995.
596. Alameda Co., Calif., Marriage Records Index for 1922, #255.
597. California State Death Index 1940-1949, registration #86, state file #34035 gives date of death as 18 June 1940, as does his obituary in the *Oakland Tribune* (Oakland, Alameda Co., Calif.), 19 June 1940. However, the Alameda County Death Records, microfilm #2610/86, 1940, p. 137 gives his date of death as 18 May 1940.
598. Certificate of Baptism, Church of the Assumption.
599. Interview with Edward Wilds, 3 April 1995, at his home outside Kelseyville, Lake County, California, and information provided by Horace Wilds by telephone, 1 February 1995. Both are nephews of Roy Finley.
600. Oakland City Directories.
601. Terril L. Shorb, *The Perry and Ardith Finley Story*, (Santa Rosa, Calif.: privately printed, 1991). Available through special collections at the Ruben Salazar Library, Sonoma State University, Rohnert Park, California.
602. Michelle (Findley) Yahnian to author, 27 May 1995.
603. Ibid.
604. "Symphony plays radio concert in tribute to KSRO," *The Press Democrat* (Santa Rosa, Sonoma Co., Calif.), 31 Dec. 1938, p. 2.
605. Jersey Neyman, Russian born and European educated noted mathematical statistician, was then director of the lab. This was during World War II and one of the more interesting projects on which I worked was the calculation of bomb damage done by allied planes over Germany.

606. With our selection as one of the state-wide computer centers, we outgrew our facilities and relocated in the old Santa Rosa Post Office, now the Sonoma County Museum.

607. Officially the Watson Laboratory at Columbia University, this facility was established in 1945 by Thomas J. Watson, Sr., then president of IBM to "serve as a world center for the treatment of problems in various fields of science whose solutions depends on the effective use of applied mathematics and mechanical calculations." Jean Ford Brennan, *The IBM Watson Laboratory at Columbia University: A History,* 1971, available through the IBM Archives, Somers, NY.

608. Carnegie Corporation and the Ford Foundation had sponsored the developmental phase of this project for the first six years, with the understanding that when it became functional, the Federal Government would continue to support it. For a brief history of the project's early phase as it relates to the development of testing materials, see Carmen J. Finley & Frances S. Berdie, *The National Assessment Approach to Exercise Development* (Denver, Co.: Education Commission of the States, 1970).

609. Ralph W. Tyler, well known for his work in curriculum and instruction, founder and Director of the Center for Advanced Study in the Behavioral Sciences at Stanford, was chairman of NAEP during its formative years. John W. Tukey, mathematical statistician at Princeton University, was chairman of NAEP's Technical Advisory Committee. Tyler and Tukey, together with other top professionals, designed and guided the developmental phase of NAEP.

610. The American Institutes for Research was founded by John C. Flanagan, veteran measurement researcher, who had designed the selection tests for the United States Air Force at Lackland Air Force Base in Texas during World War II.

611. Title I Education was, at that time, the largest single educational program funded by the Federal Government. Our service territory was Iowa, Kansas, Missouri, and Nebraska, and our budget, after the first year, was approximately one million dollars per year.

612. Organizations and journals for which I have held a variety of positions include the California Educational Research Association, California Journal of Educational Research, Journal of Educational Measurement, American Education Research Journal, National Council on Measurement in Education, Association of Measurement and Evaluation in Guidance, American Personnel and Guidance Association, American Psychological Association, the College Entrance Examination Board, and the Johns Hopkins University National Symposium on Educational Research.

CHAPTER SIX

1. Howard McKnight Wilson, *The Tinkling Spring, Headwater of Freedom, A Study of the Church and Her People, 1732-1952* (Fisherville, Va.: Tinkling Spring and Hermitage Presbyterian Churches, 1954), p. 474. According to Wilson, two James Finleys were born to the John Finley who also baptized Elizabeth, William, and

George (4 January 1748). If so, this James must have died in infancy.

2. The identification of this John Finley as the son of John, Sr., the Elder of Tinkling Spring, is based on a number of factors given in detail in the paper, "The John Finleys of Augusta County, Virginia: Some Hypotheses," cited above. Most notably, however, is the fact that he, as eldest son, had claim on the real property of his father when he died in 1782 in Montgomery County. John, Sr., had, however, given his remaining real property to younger sons David and Samuel in 1773 through Articles of Agreement (Montgomery Co., Va., Deed Book A:283). In order to make this earlier agreement a valid transaction, John, Jr., of Augusta County had to deed this same property back to David and Samuel on 12 June 1792 (Wythe Co., Va., Deed Book 1:84).

3. Augusta Co., Va., Will Book 10:172.

4. Named in will of father, 16 August 1789, Chalkley, *Chronicles of the Scotch-Irish Settlement,* 3:202.

5. Augusta Co., Va., Will Book 12:299.

6. Prince Edward Co., Va., Order Book 4:57.

7. Augusta Co., Va., Deed Book 19:414.

8. Augusta Co., Va., Personal Property Tax Records, Family History Library film #0029288.

9. Augusta Co., Va., Drawer 449, Gleaves vs Finley, March 1794.

10. Mary B. Kegley, comp. *Glimpses of Wythe County* (Central Virginia Newspapers, Inc., 1986), pp. 35-37. John Vogt & T. William Kethley, Jr., *Wythe County Marriages, 1790-1850* (Athens, Ga.: Iberian Publishing Co., 1985), p. 45.

11. Augusta Co., Va., Drawer 449, Gleaves vs. Finley, March 1794.

12. Ibid., Loose Papers (not recorded in any Deed,

13. Augusta Co., Va., Will Book 10:172.
14. Augusta Co., Va., Will Book 21:291; written 21? February 1836; proved 10? December 1836.
15. Montgomery Co., Va., Deed Book A:258, A:283.
16. Wythe Co., Va., Deed Book 1:82, 1:84.
17. Wilson, *Tinkling Spring*, p. 462.
18. Ibid.
19. Cecil McDonald, comp., *Some Virginia Marriages, 1700-1799*, vol. 17 (n.p., 1972), p. 13. Also Col. Thomas Hughart, *Record of Marriages Solemnized in the County of Augusta, from the 15th Day of March 1785* (D.A.R, 1970), p. 21.
20. Milford E. Barnes & Andrew Wallace Barner, Part II. *John and Margaret (Finley) Hutchison and Their Descendants* (Iowa City: author, 1965), p. 49.
21. Augusta Co., Va., Will Book 10:172.
22. Chalkley, 2:310. McDonald, *Some Virginia Marriages*, vol. 2, p. 6. Also Hughart, *Record of Marriages*, p. 22.
23. Wilson, *Tinkling Spring*, p. 474 gives the year as 1741. L.B. Hatke, *List of Baptisms by Rev. John Craig, Augusta County, Virginia, 1740-1749* (Staunton, Va.: author, n.d.), p. 2 gives the year as 1740/41. Since this predates the change from the Julian to the Gregorian calendar, 1740/41 is probably the more precise date.
24. Prince Edward Co., Va., Marriage Records, loose papers, 1754-1850, gives date bond was issued as 5 January 1764.
25. Wilson, *Tinkling Spring*, p. 426. Dorothy Day Gillespie, "Brief History of the Family of William Gillespie, Sr. (1734-1826)," *The Heritage*, 20th Anniversary, XV (Hot Springs, Ark., Historical Society, 1988), p. 36. Ms. Gillespie cites an importation order dated 24 July 1740 for the Gillespies stating they had come from Ireland (Orange Co., Va., Deed Book 4:122-124). Another descendant, Dan Welch, 6221 Armstrong, Kansas City, KS 66120 claims "family legend" says James was born in Scotland.
26. This was the location given when John Finley, Jr., stated his intention to obtain a deposition from James in 1794 when Matthew Gleaves brought suit against Finley. Augusta Co., Va., Drawer 449 cited earlier. A descendant has claimed that, "Recent research has revealed that this James Gilllespy was killed by Cherokee Indians in 1792 in Blount County, Tennessee." Dan Welch, to author 14 May 1993.
27. John G. Herndon, "Some of the Descendants of the Rev. John Thomson, 1690-1753)," *Virginia Magazine of History and Biography*, 51 (October 1943), 394-404; reprinted in *Genealogies of Virginia Families*, 5 vols. (Baltimore: Genealogical Publishing Company, 1981), 5:454-464.
28. According to Herndon cited above, Robert Baker had married Rev. John Thomson's daughter, Mary.
29. Augusta Co., Va., Will Book 4:263. The will was proved 20 October 1769.
30. Augusta Co., Va., Deed Book 19:414.
31. Augusta Co., Va., Deed Book 26:37.
32. Dorothy Day Gillespie, "Brief History", pp. 43-45. The location of the James Gillespys on Little River is confirmed by Matthew Gleaves vs. John Finley cited earlier.
33. Lillian Gillespie, 1821 Institute Drive, Longview, TX 75602, Dorothy Day Gillespie and Dan Welch cited above.
34. Descendants are not in agreement on the child as a part of the family.
35. Ibid.
36. Edith Little, *Blount County, Tennessee Marriages 1795 to 1910* (Evansville, Ind.: Whipporwill Publications, 1982), p. 103.
37. The reader will note similarities to William Joseph Finley (4-02-16) in Herald F. Stout, *The Clan Finley*, 2nd ed., 2 vol. in 1 (Dover, Ohio: Eagle Press, 1956), p. 62. However, Stout incorrectly identifies him as the son of John and Thankful (Doak) Finley who lived on Middle River. See Finley, "The John Finleys of Augusta County."
38. Wilson, *Tinkling Spring*, p. 474.
39. Wythe Co., Va., Will Book 1:202.
40. Mary Finley was named as daughter in the will of Dabney Pettus, 1 September 1788, as was son, Stephen, of Prince Edward County, Va. Charlotte Co., Va., Will Book 1:407a.
41. Their son, William was over 45 in 1820 census of Christian Co., Ky. 1820 federal census, population schedule, Christian Co., Ky., p. 43.
42. The date William and Mary, his wife, sold property in Prince Edward County to Joseph Fore; Prince Edward Co., Va., Deed Book 7:297.
43. On this date, his son, Dabney, brought suit against his father to recover slaves owned by Dabney's mother (William's former wife), at the time of their marriage. Wythe Co., Va., Deed Book 2:476-478.
44. Ila Earle Fowler, comp., *Kentucky Pioneers and Their Descendants* (Baltimore: Genealogical Publishing, 1978), p. 32.
45. Prince Edward Co., Va., Deed Book 3:1.
46. Ibid., p. 21.
47. 1820 federal census, population schedule, Christian Co., Ky., pp. 41, 43, 45. 1850 federal census, population schedule, Saline Co., Mo., p. 37,

dwelling #462, family #464.

48. Prince Edward Co., Va., Deed Book 5:63.

49. Prince Edward Co., Va., Order Book 5:301, 5:326.

50. Prince Edward Co., Va., Deed Book 5:184, Order Book 5:335.

51. Ibid., Order Book 5:440.

52. Herbert Clarence Bradshaw, *History of Prince Edward County, Virginia* (Richmond, VA: Dietz Press, 1955), p. 670.

53. Prince Edward Co., Va., Deed Book 6:439, 6:448.

54. Lewis Preston Summers, *Annals of Southwest Virginia, 1769-1800*, Volume in 2 Parts, Part 1 (Baltimore: Genealogical Publishing, 1970), p. 915.

55. Montgomery Co., Va., Survey Book D:220.

56. Montgomery Co., Va., Order Book 1:256.

57. Ibid., pp. 272, 288, Order Book 4:17.

58. Prince Edward Co., Va., Deed Book 7:297.

59. Lincoln Co., Va., Deed Book A:338.

60. Wythe Co., Va., Deed Book 1:82.

61. Ibid., p. 84.

62. Ibid., p. 95.

63. Ibid., p. 220.

64. Newton G. Finley, *Our Fore-Fathers*. Copied on 13 March 1870 from a letter written by "Uncle John P. Finley of Kentucky Dated January 25th 1854 to Uncle Asa W. Finley, Esq." Copy in possession of author.

65. Wythe Co., Va., Deed Book 2:476-478.

66. Wythe Co., Va., Will Book 1:202.

67. Birth dates, where given, are estimated from census records cited earlier, except as otherwise noted.

68. Family History Library Archive Record submitted by Richard Keith Finley, 9006 W. 75th

St., Merriam, Kansas (1959). Submitter cites family Bible record in possession of Mrs. Harry Smith, Nelson, Mo. as a source.

69. Vogt & Kethley, Jr., Wythe County Marriages, p. 20.

70. Ibid., p. 150.

71. Ibid., p. 150.

72. Wilson, *Tinkling Spring*, p. 474. This George is differentiated from the George Finley who was baptized 30 January 1743, son of John and Thankful (Doak) Finley in Carmen J. Finley, "The George Finleys of Augusta County, Va." *The American Genealogist*, v. 64, n. 4 (1989), pp. 216-225.

73. Hermione D. Embry, Genealogical Reference Librarian, Tennessee State Library & Archives to Mrs. Paul Hepple, 222 Douglas Avenue, Salinas, California, 21 February 1963. Copy in possession of author. Also *Wilson County, Tennessee Probate Records, 1814-1832*, Family History Library film #430841, p. 298.

74. Prince Edward Co., Va., Deed Book 3:487.

75. Shirley Dunn & Dorothy A. Griffith, comps., *Lincoln County Kentucky Marriages, 1780-1850, & Tombstone Inscriptions* (St. Louis: Genealogical Research & Production, 1977), p. 12.

76. Prince Edward Co., Va., Deed Book 3:487.

77. Ibid., pp. 1, 21.

78. Prince Edward Co., Va., Order Book 5:335. The deed itself, Deed Book 5:184, refers only to his "wife."

79. Montgomery County was officially created from Fincastle in 1776, but records were kept in the name of Montgomery County prior to this date.

80. Mary B. Kegley, comp., *New River Tithables, 1770-1773* (Wytheville, Va., privately printed,

1941), pp. 14, 29.

81. Ibid., p. 27.

82. Mary B. Kegley, comp. *Tax List of Montgomery County, Virginia, 1782* (Wytheville?, Va.: privately printed, 1974), p. 12. George's half brothers, David and Samuel, did appear on this list, but David had no tithes, slaves, horses, or cattle, one of several indications he had moved on by that date.

83. Michael L. Cook & Bettie A. Cummings Cook, *Fincastle & Kentucky County, Va.-Ky.: Records & History, Volume 1* (Evansville, Ind.: Cook Publications, n.d.), p. 272.

84. Reuben Gold Thwaites & Louise Phelps Kellogg, eds., *Documentary History of Dunmore's War, 1774* (Madison, Wisc.: Wisconsin Historical Society, 1905), p. 423.

85. Richard B. Harwell, ed., *The Committees of Westmoreland and Fincastle: Proceedings of the County Committees, 1774-1776* (Richmond: Virginia State Library Publications no. 1, 1956), pp. 103-104.

86. Madison Co., Ky., Deed Book D:63-64.

87. Finley, "The George Finleys of Augusta County."

88. This line has been researched by James M. Johnston, P.O. Box 4394, Carlsbad, CA 92008.

89. Dunn & Griffith, *Lincoln County Kentucky Marriages*, p. 12.

90. Lincoln Co., Ky., Deed Book C:331-333.

91. Garrard Co., Ky., Tax List, Family History Library film #007988.

92. Garrard Co., Ky., Deed Book A:718.

93. Mercer Co., Ky., Circuit Court Box F-9.

94. Mercer Co., Ky., Deed Book 7:229.

95. Hermione D. Embry to Mrs. Paul Hepple, 21 February 1963. Also Family History Library film

#430841, p. 298.

96. Wilson Co., Tenn., Probate Records, 1814-1832, Family History Library film # 430841, p. 314.

97. Mercer Co., Ky., Marriage Records, 30 May 1814, 22 September 1818, 4 October 1819.

98. Mercer Co., Ky., Circuit Court Box F-9.

99. Wilson Co., Tenn., Probate Records, Family History Library film #430841, p. 314.

100. This information from Stout and from descendant of Lucinda, Dorothy Chapman Van Slyke, S. 524 Scott Street, Spokane, WA 99202, except as otherwise noted. Mrs. Van Slyke has published extensive material on the Pennebaker family.

101. Foster G. Finley Bible Record, August 1847, copy in possession of author.

102. Information provided by Blanche Jernigan, Box 486, Pewee Valley, Ky., 40056.

103. Mercer Co., Ky., Marriage Records; mother, Mary Findley; bondsman, David Findley; witness, Ezekiel F. Gaines, give marriage bond date as 22 September 1818. Also Family History Library film #0191847.

104. Vital dates for Lucinda and William from Wm. Gaines Pennebaker Bible Record in possession of Dorothy Chapman Van Slyke. Van Slyke to author, 7 June 1993.

105. *Putnam County, Indiana Church Records,* Family History Library film #1455343, item 12, Deer Creek Baptist Church, p. 18.

106. Mercer Co., Ky., Marriage Records; mother, Mary Finley; bondsman, Ezekiel F. Gaines; witness, John Denny.

107. *Putnam County, Indiana Church Records,* Family History Library film #1455343, item 12, Deer Creek Baptist Church, p. 18.

108. Mercer Co., Ky., Marriage Records; bondsman, William Pennybaker.

109. Van Slyke to author, 7 June 1993.

110. Information on the Scott County Finleys was provided by Stella G. (Mrs. Henry Wilson) Finley, P.O. Box 612, Georgetown, Kentucky 40324, whose husband is a direct descendant of John Finley whose father, John, left 1807 will in Augusta County. She provided the following cemetery inscription handed down in her husband's family (name of cemetery not given): "Samuel Finley who departed this life Dec. 21, 1833 in the 64th year of his age. He was a believer in Christ, happy in life, patient in death. Beneath this silent Tomb His lifeless body lies. His soul in spotless innocence Has risen to the skies." To date, she has been unable to locate this cemetery.

111. Chalkley, 2:317. Samuel Finley and John Tate, surety. The father-daughter relationship is spelled out in two documents following the death of John Tate in December 1802. In Chalkley, 2:126, "Tate's heirs vs. Tate's executors . . . Answer 1804 by Jane Tate, widow and executrix of John Tate, Jr., and by Samuel Finley, who married Polly Tate, daughter of said John." In Chalkley, 2:212, "Finley vs. Tate . . . Bill by Samuel Finley and Mary, his wife, daughter of John Tate, who died December, 1802 testate." However, a Samuel Finley did leave a will in Augusta County dated 27 September 1841, proved 28 May 1849 (Augusta Co., Va., Will Book 29:287). This was a good fifteen years after the death of Samuel Steele Finley in Scott County. Neither Samuel had a wife named Mary at the time of their respective deaths. Stout claims the Samuel (4-14-12) who remained in Augusta County is the one who married Mary Tate, and that he was born in 1775 in Chester County, Pennsylvania, the son of Michael (3-14-1) and Mary (Waugh) Finley. He claims this family migrated to Rockbridge County some time after the birth of their last daughter, Elizabeth, in 1786 (Stout, *Clan Finley*, vol. 1, pp. 46, 47, 73, 74). This writer did not pursue the matter further.

112. Obituary of son, Samuel Thomson Finley states he was the son of Samuel and Martha Finley; *Marion County Democrat* (Palmyra, Mo., 27 February 1879). In addition, Samuel and Patsy Finley deed to Benjamin Bradford, property on the N. Elkhorn in 1817; Scott Co., Ky., Deed Book B:438.

113. Chalkley, 3:187.

114. Chalkley, 2:317.

115. Chalkley, 1:285.

116. Chalkley, 2:339.

117. Ibid., p. 344.

118. Chalkley, 3:222.

119. Augusta Co., Va., Will Book 19:242. This John Finley was the son of the William Finley who purchased a portion of the Robinson property from Samuel's grandfather, John Finley, an elder at Tinkling Spring. John, the elder, and William were most likely brothers. Readers wishing a more detailed discussion should see Finley, "The John Finleys of Augusta County."

120. Augusta Co., Va., Will Book 10:172.

121. There can be little doubt that Scott County is the location of Samuel and John, sons named in the 1807 will recorded in Augusta County. A copy of that same will was found recorded in Scott County October Court 1839, "Satisfactory proof was made this day in Open Court that the Original will of Record of John Finley Decd has been destroyed and a certified copy having been returned to Court and the Court having examined the same it is Ordered to be Recorded." Scott Co., Ky., Will Book G:70-71. One could surmise this may have been necessary to establish the legal claim of Samuel and/or John to the land inherited from their father.

122. Accelerated Indexing Systems, *Kentucky 1810 Census*, p. 188.

123. Scott Co., Ky., Deed Book pp. A2:279, 280. A fire had destroyed a portion of the documents, but fragmented pieces were copied from the original after the fire.

124. Scott Co., Ky., Order Book B:290.

125. Scott Co., Ky., Deed Book B:438.

126. 1820 federal census, population schedule, Scott Co., Ky., p. 124. 1 male under 10; 2 males 10-16; 1 male 45 and over; 1 female under 10, 1 female 10-16; 1 female 45 and over.

127. Scott Co., Ky., Order Book D:44-45.

128. According to the 1820 census, there were at least three additional older children.

129. *Marion County Democrat* (Palmyra, Mo., 27 February 1879).

130. Scott Co., Ky., Will Book F:42.

131. *Scott County Marriages: 1837-63*, Public Library Microfilm, reel #183225, Scott Co., Ky., #73. From notes handed down through family descendants, her tombstone inscription reads, "In memory of Martha Jane, wife of R.M. Hathaway, only daughter of Samuel Finley. Born Oct. 11th 1819, married April 7th 1840, died Feb. 3rd 1842." To date the cemetery has not been located.

132. Named in his father's will. Augusta Co., Va., Will Book 10:172.

133. On this date his inventory and appraisement was made. Scott Co., Ky., Will Book F:42-46.

134. From documents found in Scott Co., Ky., to be cited following.

135. Scott Co., Ky., Deed Book A:330.

136. Scott Co., Ky., Deed Book E:167.

137. 1820 federal census, population schedule, Scott Co., Ky., p. 112.

138. Scott Co., Ky., Will Book F:42-46.

139. Scott Co., Ky., Deed Book O:116.

140. Scott Co., Ky., Will Book F:396.

141. Purchased property of parents along with Benjamin Franklin Finley.

142. Tombstone inscription, Georgetown Cemetery, Georgetown, Scott Co., Ky.

143. *Scott County Marriages: 1837-63*, Public Library Microfilm, reel #183225, Scott Co., Ky., #73.

144. *Georgetown Times* (Georgetown, Scott Co., Ky., 22 February 1888), p. 3. Also tombstone inscription, Georgetown Cemetery, Georgetown, Ky.

145. Ibid.

146. Names of children supplied by Stella Finley.

147. *Georgetown News* (Georgetown, Scott Co., Ky., 18 December 1942), p. 1.

148. His will named brother Benjamin Franklin Finley. Accepted in May Court 1844, it said briefly, "I Joseph Walker Finley of the County of Scott State of Kentucky do make this my last will and testament in manner and form as follows. It is my will that should I die without issue that my Brother Benjamin Franklin Finley shall have my whole estate both real and personal that I am now possessed of or that I may hereafter acquire This 16th day of Oct 1843." Scott Co., Ky., Will Book H:361.

149. Assumed to be fourth heir; listed as receiving $14.20 along with Frank Finley, who received

$10 in settlement approved at October Court 1837. Scott Co., Ky., Will Book F:42-46.

150. *Scott County Marriages: 1837-63*, Public Library Microfilm, reel #183225, Scott Co., Ky., #73.

151. Christian County, Ky., Will Book C:556.

152. Wythe Co., Va., Will Book 2:180; will of John Barron of Gallatin, Sumner Co., Tenn., November 1815 lists Wm. Dabney Finley of Christian Co., Ky., as brother-in-law; Margaret Glevis (Gleaves), as sister-in-law. Christian Co., Ky., Deed Book F:300 gives William's wife's name as Nancy, 6 July 1816; hence we assume he married Nancy Barron. His sister Margaret married William Gleaves.

153. 1830 federal census, population schedule, Christian Co., Ky., p. 30. Eli, the eldest son, was in 20-30 age group; son William Adam was born in 1806.

154. Willard Rouse Jillson, *The Kentucky Land Grants*, 1 Volume in 2 Parts, Part 1 (Baltimore: Genealogical Publishing, 1971), pp. 311, 312.

155. 1810 & 1820 U.S. census, population schedule, Christian Co., Ky., p. (illegible section), p. 43.

156. Christian Co., Ky., Will Book C:556.

157. Christian Co., Ky., Deed Book P:374, 389, 391.

158. Cemetery card file, Marshall Public Library, 214 North Lafayette B, Marshall, MO 65340.

159. In 1844, Elizabeth and her husband deeded two acres to Cumberland Presbyterian Church at Salubrious Springs. At that time they were living in Saline County, Missouri. Christian Co., Ky., Deed Book 28:272-274.

160. Stout, *Clan Finley*, vol. 1, p. 108. Stout references are offered with caution, when no other source of supporting evidence has been found.

161. Christian Co., Ky., Marriage Book 8.

162. Age 32 in 1850 U.S. census, population schedule, Saline Co., Mo., p. 60, dwelling #765, family #768.
163. Stout, *Clan Finley*, vol. 2, p. 7. Stout references are offered with caution when no other supporting evidence has been found.
164. Ibid.
165. Referred to as one of two youngest sons in William's will.
166. Family History Library Archive Record submitted by Richard Keith Finley, 9006 W. 75th St., Merriam, Kansas (1959). He cites a family Bible record in possession of Mrs. Harry Smith, Nelson, Missouri.
167. Ibid.
168. Ibid.
169. Wythe Co., Va., Deed Book 2:476-478.
170. Jillson, *The Kentucky Land Grants*, p. 311.
171. Ibid., pp. 311, 312.
172. Christian Co., Ky., Deed Book P:105.
173. 1810 and 1820 U.S. census, population schedule, Christian Co., Ky., pp. 100, 45.
174. 1840 U.S. census, population schedule, Saline Co., Mo., p. 78.
175. 1830 U.S. census, population schedule, Boone Co., Mo., p. 98.
176. Saline Co., Mo., Will Records Book A:67-68.
177. Saline Co., Mo., Probate Record Book D:35.
178. Saline Co., Mo., Probate Record Book 1:390. Named were Eli, Philander, B.W., P.D., Thos. B. Finley and daughters' spouses Robt. Crocket, Rhoades Marshall, Hugh Crocket, Jas. Campbell, Jno. R. Hancock.
179. Saline Co., Mo., Probate Record Book D:35.
180. Ibid., p. 23.
181. Vital dates are those provided by a Family History Library Archive Record submitted by Richard Keith Finley, 9006 W. 75th St., Merriam, KS (1959), except as otherwise noted. Mr. Finley cites a family Bible record in the possession of Mrs. Harry Smith, Nelson, MO.
182. Saline Co., Mo., Probate Index 1:472, box 68, CE #692.
183. Ibid., p. 260, box 56.
184. Elizabeth Prather Ellsberry, comp., *Marriage Records of Saline County, Missouri, 1820-1850* (Chillicothe, Mo.: author, 1959), p. 13.
185. Ibid., p. 7.
186. Ibid., p. 16.
187. He was shown age 65 in the 1850 U.S. census, population schedule, Christian Co., Ky., p. 360; as 50-60 in the 1840 U.S. census, population schedule, Christian Co., Ky., p. 198.
188. Christian Co., Ky., Will Book R:376.
189. Christian Co., Ky., Marriages, Book 1:367.
190. Jillson, *The Kentucky Land Grants*, p. 311.
191. Ibid., p. 312.
192. Christian Co., Ky., Deed Books A:267; D:284, 391; F:132; G:441; I:52, 250; K:256, 260.
193. Christian Co., Ky., Will Book R:376.
194. Sue Lail, Corresponding Secretary, Christian County Genealogical Society, to Carmen J. Finley, 18 July 1990.
195. Sue Lail to Carmen J. Finley, 10 August 1990.
196. Christian Co., Ky., Will Book R:376.
197. Ibid., pp. 463-473.
198. Bettie, Afee, Soloman, Ned, George, Charlie, Hester, Urial.
199. Christian Co., Ky., Marriages, Book 8:241.
200. Campbell Museum, Campbell, Calif. Asa Wallace Finley, who reportedly wrote this statement, lived during the period 1822-1910.
201. Stout, vol. 2, p. 164.
202. 1820 U.S. census, population schedule, Christian Co., Ky., p. 41.
203. 1830 U.S. census, population schedule, Christian Co., Ky., p. 27.
204. 1840 U.S. census, population schedule, Christian Co., Ky., p. 198.
205. Christian Co., Ky., Marriages, Book 9:134.
206. Christian Co., Ky., Will Book L:482.
207. Christian Co., Ky., Marriages, Book 11:373.
208. Christian Co., Ky., Marriages, Book 8:241.
209. Estimated from 1850 U.S. census, population schedule, Saline Co., Mo., p. 37, dwelling #462, family #464.
210. Newton G. Finley, *Our Fore-Fathers*, copied on 13 March 1870 from a letter written by "Uncle John P. Finley of Kentucky Dated January 25th 1854," p. 1. Copy in possession of author.
211. Vogt & Kethley, Jr., p. 45.
212. From a family sketch written by Asa Wallace Finley, eldest son of Asa and Esther (Gleaves) Finley.
213. Ellsberry, *Marriage Records of Saline County*, p. 23.
214. Ibid., p. 8.
215. Jilleson, *The Kentucky Land Grants*, p. 312.
216. Christian Co., Ky., Deed Books A:390, I:298, K:562.
217. Newton Gleaves Finley was the son of James Washington Finley, second eldest son of Asa Finley.
218. 1840 U.S. census, population schedule, Saline Co., Mo., p. 78.
219. Saline Co., Mo., Will Record Book A:67-68.
220. Ellsberry, *Marriage Records of Saline County*, p. 23.
221. 1850 U.S. census, population schedule, Saline Co., Mo., p. 37, dwelling #462, family #464.
222. They are positively identified as Asa's

"younger children" in his will. Saline Co., Mo., Will Book A:253 (1-137, Box 65 & 66, CE #668).

223. Ibid.

224. Estimated from 1850 U.S. census, population schedule, Saline Co., Mo., p. 61, dwelling #775, family #778.

225. Ibid.

226. Newton Gleaves Finley, *Our Fore-Fathers*, p. 2.

227. Estimated from 1850 U.S. census, population schedule, Saline Co., Mo., p. 104, dwelling #509, family #511.

228. Family history notes written by Asa Wallace Finley, in possession of author, p. 1.

229. Estimated from 1850 U.S. census, population schedule, Cooper Co., Mo., p. 104, dwelling #498, family #498.

230. Ellsberry, *Marriage Records of Saline County, 1820-1850*, p. 15.

231. Ibid.

232. Estimated from 1850 U.S. census, population schedule, Saline Co., Mo., p. 37, dwelling #462, family #464.

233. Ibid.

234. Petitioned for her share of her father's estate with husband on this date. Saline Co., Mo., Index 1, p. 137, Boxes 65 & 66, CE #668.

235. Ibid. Petitioned for her share of her father's estate on this date and stated she was 21 on this date.

236. He was listed as age 1/12 in 1850 census.

237. Saline Co., Mo., Probate Book 1:559-560.

238. Foster G. Finley family Bible record. Copy in possession of author.

239. Ibid.

240. Records of the Veteran's Administration, Index to War of 1812 Pension Application Files,

film #0840462, WO36920 and WC 26127.

241. Lincoln Co., Ky., Deed Book F:113.

242. Ibid., Deed Book F:230. He bought this property for $80 and sold it for $560.

243. Records of the Veteran's Administration, Index to War of 1812 Pension Application files.

244. Ibid.

245. Ibid.

246. Mrs. Charles R. Emery, *Bible and Family Records* (G p.f.929.11 no. 3; G p.f. 929.11 no. 3 Supp.), Indiana State Library, 140 North Senate Avenue, Indianapolis, IN 46204. Also Oscar F. Curtis, *Cemeteries of Monroe County, Indiana* (Bloomington, Ind.: author, n.d.), p. 187. Available from the Indiana Room, Monroe County Public Library, 303 E. Kirkwood Ave., Bloomington, IN 47408.

247. Ibid.

248. Ibid. Some confirmation is found in that George Findley was listed in the Jackson County, Tennessee tax lists for 1804-1811. Christine Spivey Jones, Dero A. Darwin, Jr., & Charles Tomas, comps., "Jackson County Records, 1804-1811," *Upper Cumberland Genealogical Association.* v. 5, n. 2 (May 1980), p. 8.

249. Ibid.

250. Ibid.

251. Oscar F. Curtis, *Cemeteries of Monroe County, Indiana*, p. 187.

252. Martha Lou Houston, *1820 Census of Overton County, Tennessee* (Washington, D.C.: author, n.d.), p. 16. Available in the Overton County Library, Livingston, TN.

253. 1850 U.S. census, population schedule, Clear Creek Township, District 132, Monroe Co., Ind., p. 324, dwelling #403, family #403.

254. Monroe Co., Ind., Will Book 3:20-21.

255. The information on the children came from Clem Thompson, "A Remarkable Life: Aunt Polly Sharpe," *Free Press*, (Mt. Pleasant, Henry Co., Iowa), 21 July 1904 except as otherwise noted. Vital data are taken from Mrs. Charles Emery's *Bible and Family Records* cited above.

256. Emery gives date of death as 15 September 1851. However, descendant Blanche Jernigan claims this is in error since Bluford had six children after 1851. Should this be 1861?

257. Oscar F. Curtis, *Cemeteries of Monroe County, Indiana*, p. 187.

258. Newton Gleaves Finley, *Our Fore-Fathers*, p. 2.

259. Ibid.

260. Ellsberry, *Marriages of Calloway County*, p. 13 (listed as William W. Findley to Margaret J. Campbell).

261. Newton Gleaves Finley, *Our Fore-Fathers*, p. 2.

262. International Genealogical Index (IGI), Family History Library fiche, California, March 1988.

263. Newton Gleaves Finley, *Our Fore-Fathers*, p. 1.

264. 1840 federal census, population schedule, Saline Co., Mo., p. 95.

265. Ibid., pp. 96, 97.

266. 1850 federal census, population schedule, Saline Co., Mo., p..46, dwelling #570, family #572.

267. Ibid., pp. 45, 46, dwelling #'s 564, 565 and 575.

268. William Thornton and Veranda Rucker, with eight children; Ira Joseph and Ann Laurette (Campbell) Lovell, with eight children; Robert and Mary Ann Campbell, with four children. Ann Laurette (Campbell) Lovell was a sister of

Margaret Jane (Campbell) Finley. Benjamin Campbell, the leader of the wagon train, was a half brother of Margaret Jane. Campbell's wife was Mary Rucker.

269. Newton Gleaves Finley, *Memoirs of Travel*, Family History Library film #1206424, item 17.

270. Santa Clara Co., Calif., Old Probate Cases "A", Reel 20, March 1861-June 1868, case #348.

271. Birth dates from Newton Gleaves Finley, *Our Fore-Fathers*, p. 2. All children in the first family were born in Saline County, Mo.

272. *History of Oregon*, p. 384.

273. *The Polk County Itemizer* (Dallas, Polk Co., Oreg.), March 1925.

274. Birth dates of Thomas and Margaret were estimated from the 1860 census cited above. Birth dates for the remaining children were found in the Ancestry File, Family History Library.

275. Newton Gleaves Finley, *Our Fore-Fathers*, p. 2.

276. *Press Democrat's 1913 Directory of Santa Rosa, Petaluma and Sonoma County* (Santa Rosa, Sonoma County, Calif.: Press Democrat Publishing, 1913), p. 69.

277. 1850 federal census, population schedule, Horsehead Twp., Johnson Co., Ark., p. 140, dwelling #103, family #105.

278. Sarah E. Finley, "David and Jonathan," *Oregon State Monthly*, May 1930, p. 9. Available through the Oregon State University Archives, Corvallis, Oregon.

279. 1850 federal census, population schedule, Horsehead Twp., Johnson Co., Ark., p. 140, dwelling #103, family #105. Also *Orange and Black*, (Corvallis, Oreg.: Oregon State College), 1938, p. 12, available through the Oregon State College Archives, Corvallis, Oregon.

280. California Death Index File #68862.

281. Ernest L. Finley, *History of Sonoma County*, p. 376.

282. 1900 federal census, soundex, Sonoma Co., Calif., vol. 45, e.d. 174, sheet 14, line 71.

283. Newton Gleaves Finley, *Our Fore-Fathers*, p. 2.

284. Newton G. Finley death certificate, State of California, Department of Health Services, #33-035630.

285. A handwritten account made by Newton Gleaves Finley dated 5 October 1917 gives marriage date and states she died six years later. Cynthia (Finley) Elliott to author, 7 Jun 1993.

286. Rowena Finley death certificate, State of California, Department of Health Services, #26-061023.

287. Dr. Aldermann is no longer living, but his daughter, Mary Alice Ridgway, 511 N.W. Furnish, Pendleton, Oregon 97801, indicated in 1990 that a member of the family will be continuing the work on their branch of the family. Dr. Aldermann had in his file a beautifully preserved picture of William Asa Finley. Mary Alice Ridgway to Carmen J. Finley, 5 July 1990.

288. All sons are accounted for if we count both Jameses baptized at Tinkling Springs.

289. Unfortunately he does not name him. However, it is interesting to note that Stout identifies James and Elizabeth (Patterson) Finley of Cumberland County, Pennsylvania as the parents of John Finley of Middle River and they had 9 sons (France claims they had 7 sons). Stout further says James came to America in 1720 accompanied by two brothers, Samuel and John. An analysis of the naming pattern of John of Middle River and John of South River shows John of Middle River more closely resembles Samuel (whose wife was Jean Whyte) and John of South River more closely resembles James in their selection of names for their children.

290. 1860 federal census, population schedule, Santa Clara Co., Calif., p. 503, dwelling #503, family #299.

291. Handwritten account by Newton Gleaves Finley, dated 5 October 1917.

292. 1880 federal census, population schedule, soundex, Santa Clara Co., Calif., vol. 16, e.d. 124, sheet 43, line 39.

293. LeBaron, *Nineteenth Century Town*, p. 132.

294. *Great Register of Voters, Sonoma County, California*, 1892.

295. 1900 federal census, population schedule, soundex, Berkeley, Oakland Twp., Alameda Co., Calif., vol 4, e.d. 398, sheet 15, line 64.

296. Burial record, Chapel of Memories, Oakland, Calif.

297. According to family member, Cynthia (Finley) Elliott, Kate taught at least one year at Stewart's Point on the northern Sonoma County coast.

298. Dozier Finley death certificate, Alameda County Recorder. #6005-367.

299. Information provided by his daughter, Cynthia (Finley) Elliott.

300. *History of Oregon*, p. 384.

301. Newton Gleaves Finley, *Memoirs of Travel*.

302. 1860 federal census, population schedule, Santa Clara County, p. 503, dwelling #269, family #299.

303. *History of Oregon*, p. 384, 385.

304. Ibid., p. 385.

305. Oregon State University Archives.

306. Birth dates for Edna, Ada, and Percy taken from 1900 U.S. census soundex, 15th Pct., Monroe,

Benton Co., Oreg., vol. 1,e.d. 4, sheet 7, line 3.

307. 1880 U.S. census soundex, Monroe Pct., Benton Co., Oreg., vol. 1, e.d. 10, sheet 22, line 32.

308. Sonoma Co., Calif., Death Records reel 12:2428.

309. Sonoma Co., Calif., Marriage Book 3:255, license #5797.

310. Sonoma Co., Calif., Death Records reel 32:1470.

311. "E.L. Finley Guided the P.D. To Success, *The Press Democrat*" (Santa Rosa, Sonoma Co., Calif., Centennial Edition), October, 1956, p. 4.

312. Sonoma County Public Library Assessment Rolls located in basement; and Sonoma County Recorder's Office, Assessment Roll - Court House School District 1883-1890. It is interesting to note that other taxable items during these early years included furniture, a library, sewing machine, watch, a cow, and poultry.

313. Santa Rosa City Tax Assessor's Records; located in basement of Sonoma County Library. Sonoma Co., Calif., Assessment roll, Court House School District, 1883-1890, located in office of the County Recorder.

314. Ibid., loose papers.

315. LeBaron, *Nineteenth Century Town*, p. 146.

316. *California State Gazetteer and Business Directory, 1890*, vol II (San Francisco: R.L. Polk & Co., 1890), p. 987. Also *The Napa and Sonoma Counties Directory, 1889-90* (San Francisco: John F. Ulhorn, 1890), p. 402.

317. Sonoma Co., Calif., Marriage Book 3:255, license #5797.

318. Great Register of Sonoma County, 1914, Santa Rosa District #3, persons 114, 115; 1920, Santa Rosa District #4, persons 69, 70.

319. Sonoma Co., Calif., Official Records 46:88.

320. Gaye LeBaron & Joann Mitchell, *Santa Rosa: A Twentieth Century Town* (Santa Rosa, Calif.: Historia, Ltd., 1993), p. 109.

321. Sonoma Co., Calif., Official Records 88:388.

322. Sheri Graves Gayhart, "Finley—A man of vision left a legacy of idealism in action," *The Press Democrat* (Santa Rosa, Sonoma Co., Calif.), 3 Aug. 1975, p. 12D.

323. The Bridging the Golden Gate Association was formed by a group of businessmen who met on 13 January 1923. Ernest was secretary and primary leader.

324. Gayhart, *Finley—A man of vision*, p. 12D.

325. LeBaron, *A Twentieth Century Town*, p. 259.

326. Ibid., p. 110.

327. Gayhart, *Finley--A man of vision,* p. 12D.

328. "Ruth Finley Person: Accomplished musician and astute businesswoman," *The Press Democrat* (Santa Rosa, Sonoma Co., Calif.), 3 August 1975, p. 11D.

329. Gayhart, *Finley—A man of vision*, p. 12D.

330. LeBaron, *A Twentieth Century Town*, p. 273.

331. Gayhart, *Finley—A man of vision*, p. 12D.

332. Ibid., p. 12 D. LeBaron, *A Twentieth Century Town*, p. 206.

333. Sonoma Co., Calif., Death Certificate, reel 12:2428.

334. Ernest L. Finley, *Santa Rosans I Have Known* (Santa Rosa, Calif.: The Press Democrat, 1924).

335. "Mrs. Ernest L. Finley active humanitarian ," *The Press Democrat* (Santa Rosa, Sonoma Co., Calif.), 2 Aug. 1975, p. 12D.

336. "Mrs. Ernest L. Finley, P.D. Publisher, Dies," *The Press Democrat* (Santa Rosa, Sonoma Co., Calif.), 30 September 1973.

337. "Ernest L. Finley: Newspaper publisher honored," *The Press Democrat* (Santa Rosa,

Sonoma Co., Calif.), 4 December 1977, p. 15A.

338. "Gaye LeBaron's Notebook," *The Press Democrat* (Santa Rosa, Sonoma Co., Calif.), 23 Oct. 1994, p. A2.

339. Ibid.

340. *Mrs. Ernest L. Finley, active humanitarian,* p. 12D.

341. Sonoma Co., Calif., Marriage Record, reel 8:1815. Vital dates supplied by Evert B. Person.

342. The narrative that follows was taken primarily from two sources, except as otherwise noted. "Ruth Finley Person: Accomplished musician and astute businesswoman," *The Press Democrat* (Santa Rosa, Sonoma Co., Calif.), 3 August 1975, p. 11D. "Ruth Person, pianist, newspaper officer, dies," *The Press Democrat* (Santa Rosa, Sonoma Co., Calif.), 17 May 1985, p. 1.

343. The author was a member of the Santa Rosa Symphony Orchestra when Ruth performed as a soloist there, but did not know at the time there was a distant relationship.

344. "Ruth Finley Person: Accomplished musician" and "Evert B. Person Speaks: There have been many changes," *The Press Democrat* (Santa Rosa, Sonoma Co., Calif.), 3 August 1975, p. 12D.

345. *Gaye LeBaron's Notebook*, p. A2.

CHAPTER SEVEN

1. Virginia State Land Office, Patent #19, reel 17, p. 852.

2. Virginia State Land Office, Patent #20, vol. 1, 1741-1743.

3. Louis A. Burgess, *Virginia Soldiers of 1776*, vol. 2 (Richmond, Va.: Richmond Press, 1927), pp. 586, 733.

4. Augusta Co., Va., Deed Book 2:365-366.
5. Augusta Co., Va., Deed Book 18:92-93.
6. Augusta Co., Va., Deed Book 21:17 (lease), 21:19 (release).
7. Virginia State Land Office, Patent #37, reel 37, p. 281.
8. Others named were John Trimble, William McPeters, Jr., George Berry, and Hugh Young.
9. Augusta Co., Va., Deed Book 14:450.
10. Wilson, p. 485.
11. Augusta Co., Va., Will Book V:63.
12. Ibid., pp. 74-75.
13. J. R. Hildebrand, *The Beverley Patent, 1736, including original grantees, 1738-1815, in Orange & Augusta Counties, Va.,* folded map attached to back cover of Wilson's *Tinkling Spring.*
14. *Augusta Tithables, 1777-1778*, Family History Library film #0030312; *Personal Property, Augusta County, 1782-1790*, film #0029288.
15. The copy of the will made by the clerk incorrectly transcribed "James" as "Thomas." A comparison with the original, both of which are on file in the Augusta County Clerk's office, can easily see how this error was made. Confirmation that it is James, and not Thomas, is seen when David included the allowance for £120 plus interest to James in a deed of trust to John Shields 2 September 1793. Augusta Co., Va., Deed of Trust Book 1-A:122.
16. Augusta Co., Va., Deed Book 28:368.
17. Wilson, *Tinkling Spring*, p. 474.
18. Ibid.
19. Ibid.
20. Stout, p. 104, claims he was born 11 January 1742, but baptismal records at Tinkling Spring do not support this date.
21. Ibid., claims she was born 16 February 1744, but baptismal records at Tinkling Spring do not support this date.
22. Wilson, *Tinkling Spring*, p. 474.
23. Augusta Co., Va., Deed Book 18:92-93.
24. Augusta Co., Va., Deed Book 14:104-109.
25. Augusta Co., Va., Va., Deed Book 18:92-93.
26. Augusta Co., Va., Deed Book 21:17 and 21:19. These three transactions, from which George gained the most financial benefit, leads one to question the relationship between the Finleys and the Clendenens. Was George's wife, Jean/Jane, a Clendenen?
27. Augusta Co., Va., Survey Book 2:195.
28. Virginia State Library, Grants C, 1780-1781, reel 44, pp. 141-142.
29. Augusta Co., Va., Deed Book 27:268.
30. Lewis Preston Summers, *Annals of Southwest Virginia: 1769-1800*, 1 vol. in 2 parts, Part 2 (Baltimore: Genealogical Publishing Co., 1970), p. 952.
31. Summers, pp. 962, 974, 981, 1058, 1080, 1089, 1101, 1112, 1146, 1179.
32. Ibid., pp. 969, 1092, 1101, 1170.
33. Ibid., p. 952.
34. Ibid., p. 971.
35. Ibid., p. 1064.
36. Ibid., p. 1096.
37. Ibid., p. 1099.
38. Ibid., p. 1155.
39. Ibid., p. 1168.
40. Ibid., p. 1105.
41. Ibid., p. 1112.
42. Ibid., p. 30.
43. Ibid., p. 1390.
44. *The Virginia Magazine of History and Biography*, vol. VIII (Richmond: Virginia Historical Society, 1901), p. 196.
45. Ibid., p. 1032.
46. Sherwin McRae, ed., *Calendar of Virginia State Papers and Other Manuscripts, from August 11, 1792 to December 31, 1793, Preserved in the Capitol at Richmond* (Richmond: A.R. Micou, Superintendent of Public Printing, 1886), p. 102.
47. William P. Palmer, *Calendar of Virginia State Papers and Other Manuscripts, from January 1, 1785 to July 2, 1789, Preserved in the Capitol at Richmond*, vol. IV (Richmond: R.U. Derr, Superintendent of Public Printing, 1884), p. 5.
48. Ibid., p. 76.
49. Ibid., pp. 133-134.
50. Summers, p. 1216.
51. Virginia State Library, Grants 6, 1786, reel 72, pp. 451-453.
52. Virginia State Library, Grants 29, 1793, reel 95, pp. 179-180.
53. Washington Co., Va., Deed Book 1:140.
54. Ibid., pp. 407-409.
55. Washington Co., Va., Deed Book 2:201.
56. Ibid., p. 467.
57. Washington Co., Va., Deed Book 4:165.
58. Logan Co., Ky., Deed Book A1:165.
59. Summers, pp. 1262, 1263.
60. A transcript of this will, made by Edyth Rucker Whitley in 1930, was found in the Tennessee State Archives, Nashville Vertical Files. A notation stated the original will was in possession of M.L. Glenn of Sharon Grove, Kentucky in 1930. The Logan County Clerk's Office claims to have no copy of the will. The date that the will was proved was not included in the transcription.
61. Logan Co., Ky., Deed Book E:281.
62. Logan Co., Ky., Deed Books D:139, 140; E:298,

H:85, 183, 195.
63. Summers, p. 1262.
64. Ibid., p. 1263.
65. Wilson, *Tinkling Spring*, p. 474.
66. Alverta Brown Martin, *Finley Family History: Our Grandfathers* (Inglewood, Calif.: author, 1968), p. 5-6. While Martin does not say her ancestor, Robert, was the son of John and Thankful, she does say he came from Augusta County and she gives his birth date as about 1745. Wilson shows two Robert Finleys born that year. Robert, born into the same John Finley family as George (1743) and Margaret (1746), was christened 21 April 1745. Robert, son of William, was christened 23 June 1745. The latter Robert was still living in Augusta County in 21 December 1787, when his father wrote his will. Martin claims her ancestor Robert Finley had a daughter named Thankful.
67. Wythe Co., Va., Will Book 1:1.
68. Augusta Co., Va., Deed Book 14:104-106.
69. Augusta Co., Va., Will Book 7:404.
70. J. R. Hildebrand, cartographer, with information by F.B. Kegley, *A Settlement Map of Wythe County, Virginia*, available from the Roanoke Valley Historical Society, 1974. See Finley, *The John Finleys of Augusta County, Virginia: Some Hypotheses.*
71. Mary B. Kegley, *Militia of Montgomery County, Virginia* (Wytheville?, Va.: author, 1975), p. 53.
72. Montgomery Co., Va., Order Book 1778-1780, p. 338.
73. Montgomery Co., Va., Order Book 2, 1774-1782, p. 197, 299.
74. Montgomery Co., Va., Survey Book C:118.
75. Martin, *Findley Family History*, p. 6.

76. Trying to identify this John Finley would be pure speculation. Robert is said to have had a son, John; but with a 1777 marriage, even his eldest child would seem a bit young to be serving on jury duty. Could this John Finley be Robert's brother? Perhaps, but there was also a John Finley living near by in Knox County, who also meets several criteria for being Robert's brother. Could this John Finley be Robert's nephew? Perhaps. Brother John, is said to have had a son, John, born 17 February 1767 and who died in Tennessee. A John Finley was ordered to be a constable for Blount County in February 1798 (Blount County, Tennessee, Minutes of the County Court, vol. A-E, 1795-1818, Family History Library film #888,867). This would argue for a person mature enough to handle the job and one who is not in his waning years.
77. Blount Co., Tenn., Minutes of the County Court, vol. A-E, 1795-1818, Family History Library film #888,867, p. A-33.
78. The relocation of the Gillespys from South River to Blount County is discussed in more detail in Finley, *John Finley of Montgomery/Wythe County, Virginia: Additional Children Identified.*
79. Augusta Co., Va., Deed Book 14:450.
80. Augusta Co., Va., Will Book V:63.
81. Augusta Co., Va., Deed Book 28:268.
82. Augusta Co., Va., Will Book 7:404.
83. *Marriage Records of Augusta County, Virginia, 1785-1813* (Staunton, Va.: Col. Thomas Hughart Chapter D.A.R., 1970), p. 12.
84. Augusta Co., Va,. Will Book 7:431.
85. Augusta Co., Va., Deed Book 27:268.
86. Augusta Co., Va., Will Book 9:242.
87. Augusta Co., Va., Deed Book 1:77. See Finley, "The John Finleys of Augusta County, Virginia:

Some Hypotheses," for a fuller discussion.
88. On 21 March 1775, Robert Reed to son Alexander, tract on Middle River. Chalkley 3:542.
89. Blount Co., Tenn., Minutes of the County Court, p. A-251.
90. Blount Co., Tenn., Minutes of the County Court, p. B-259, 261.
91. Tennessee Land Grants Index, 1775-1905, 1911, Family History Library film #1002731, Book 1:349.
92. Blount Co., Tenn., Deed Book 2:53.
93. Ibid., p. 326.
94. She states all children except James never married. Birth dates and wives are claimed by Lee J. Bain.
95. Lee Co., Iowa, Will Book A:293-294.
96. Edith B. Little, *Blount County, Tennessee Marriages, 1795 to 1910* (Evansville, Ind.: Whippoorwill Publications, 1982), p. 90.
97. Duncan Hynes McIntosh, comp., *Shields Family Tree* (Richmond, Va.: author, 1965), taken from photograph by Dr. F.M. Shields, Sacramento, Calif. 1896. Family History Library film # 0874444, item 7.
98. Wilson, *Tinkling Spring*, p. 474.
99. McIntosh, *Shields Family Tree.*
100. Amhurst Co., Va., Deed Book I:405.
101. Augusta Co., Va., Deed of Transfer 1-A:122. The two parcels consisted of the 110 acre patent David received just after the death of his father, and another parcel described in this document as 76 acres, but which is actually the 176 acres which brother, George, had received from his parents, sold back to Robert Clendenen, who then sold it back to John Finley.
102. Augusta Co., Va., Deed Book 28:268.
103. Amhurst Co., Va., Deed Book I:405.

104. Amhurst Co., Va., Will Book 4:59-60.
105. Amhurst Co., Va., Deed Book K:323-324.
106. McIntosh's table includes a notation "also 1776."
107. Augusta Co., Va., Will Book 7:404.
108. See Finley, *The John Finleys of Augusta County: Some Hypotheses,* for a discussion of this problem.
109. Augusta Co., Va., Deed of Transfer 1-A:122.
110. Stout, p. 62.
111. Wythe Co., Va., Will Books 1:176, 1:220.
112. Stout, p. 62.
113. Carmen J. Finley, "Robert and James Finley of Augusta County, Virginia," *The American Genealogist,* 66 (Oct. 1991), 239-246.
114. Whitley Co., Ky., Will Book I:39, also Family History Library film #532,092.
115. Lynda Chalk Welch, 5535 Willow Lane, Dallas, Tex. 75230.
116. Stout, p. 104. Stout had copied this information from France.
117. Wilson, *Tinkling Spring,* p. 474.
118. France, p. 3 of section on Finleys of Virginia.
119. Miles S. Philbeck, Jr. & Grace Turner, *Lincoln County, North Carolina Will Abstracts: 1770-1910* (published by authors, 1986), entry #383.
120. R.B. Pruitt, *Abstracts of Deeds: Lincoln Co., NC, 1786-1793,* Books 3, 4, and 16 (published by author, 1988), p. 52.
121. Readers wishing a more in-depth discussion of the search for John Finley in the Carolinas should read Finley, *The John Finleys of Augusta County, Virginia: Some Hypotheses.*
122. Clarence E. Ratcliff, comp., *North Carolina Taxpayers: 1701-1786* (Baltimore: Genealogical Publishing, 1986), p. 69. Clarence E. Ratcliff, comp., vol. 2, *North Carolina Taxpayers: 1679-1790* (Baltimore: Genealogical Publishing, 1987), p. 66.
123. In 1779 Tryon County became a part of Lincoln County.
124. Brent Holcomb, abst., *Deed Abstracts of Tryon, Lincoln & Rutherford Counties, North Carolina: 1769-1786* (Easley, SC: Southern Historical Press, 1977), p. 40. This property had originally been granted to John and Thomas Beaty 24 September 1754?, conveyed by them to John Connelly, then to John Reed, adjacent to Thomas Beaty.
125. Finley, *The George Finleys.*
126. Summers, p. 957.
127. Ibid., p. 952.
128. Washington Co., Va., Minutes of the County Court, p. 957, 26 Feb. 1777. Also Lewis Preston Summers, *Annals of Southwest Virginia, 1769-1800* (Baltimore: Genealogical Publishing, 1970), pp. 957, 1390, 1419.
129. Washington Co., Va., Will Book 1:82.
130. Summers, p. 1064.
131. Virginia State Library, Grants 6, 1786, reel 72, pp. 451-453.
132. Summers, p. 1216. Surveys are shown for both John and George Finley, 400 acres on the North Fork of the Holston. John's survey is dated 1 September 1781 and George's is just dated 1781, with a settlement date of 1781. It is not known whether this is the same 400 acres of whether it represents two different 400 acre parcels.
133. Washington Co., Va., Deed Book 1:305. For a fuller discussion of John's records in Washington County see Finley, *The John Finleys of Augusta County.*
134. Readers wishing a detailed analysis should see Finley, *The John Finleys of Knox County, Tennessee.*
135. He paid no poll tax in 1804 through 1812, and persons 50+ were exempt from the tax.
136. *Tennessee Land Grants, 1810-1814,* vol. 3, grant #1790, Family History Library film #1012794.
137. Knox Co., Tenn., General Index to County Court Minutes, 5 July 1819, Book 10-2:70.
138. France, untitled manuscript, p. 3 of section on Finleys of Virginia.
139. John B. Shackford, ed., *David Crockett, The Man and The Legend* (Chapel Hill: University of North Carolina Press, 1986), p. 15. The author notes, "That instrument [marriage license] itself seems not to have survived, but the fact of its issuance and the date are recorded in the *Jefferson County Marriage and Bond Book, 1792-1940,* and reads: 'David Crockett to Polly Finley Aug 12 1806.'"
140. Jefferson Co., Tenn., Will Book 2:237-239.
141. David H. Templin & Cherel Bolin Henderson, trans., *Stories in Stone: Jefferson County Cemeteries, Volume I, South of the French Broad River and Dumplin Valley Sections* (Knoxville, Tenn.; author, 1986), cover page.
142. France, untitled manuscript, p. 4 of Finleys of Virginia section. Stout copied France's information and differs only slightly in dates.
143. This is incorrect. The David Finley who married Elizabeth Wilson in 1791 was the son of John and Thankful (Doak) Finley.
144. Stout, p. 104.
145. John Farley Trimble, *Trimble Families of America* (Parsons, W.Va.: McClain Printing, 1973), p. 212.
146. Chalkley, 3:191.

147. Lena Mae Elam, *Walter & Rosannah Trimble & Their Descendants* (Lynnwood, Wash.: Clint R. Jordan, 1987).

148. John Farley Trimble, *Trimble Families in America*, p. 212.

149. Augusta Co., Va., Deed Book 14:450.

150. This may signal a relationship to the immigrants Walter and Rosannah Trimble discussed by Elam.

151. Chalkley, 1:148.

152. Chalkley, 2:295.

153. *Marriage Records of Augusta County, Virginia, 1785-1813* (Staunton, Va.: Col. Thomas Hughart Chapter D.A.R., n.d.), p. 12.

154. Chalkley, 1:232.

155. John W. Gwathmey, *Historical Register of Virginians in the Revolution; Soldiers, Sailors, Marines, 1775-1783* (Richmond: Dietz Press, 1938), p. 272.

156. *Augusta Tithables, 1777-1778*, Family History Library film #0030312; *Personal Property, Augusta County, 1782-1790*, film #0029288. Also Augusta Co., Va., Personal Property Book B, p. 32? (82?), District of Joseph Bell, 1787.

157. William Waller Hening, *The Statutes at Large; Being a Collection of all the Laws of Virginia*, IX (Richmond: J. & G. Cochran, 1821), p. 27.

158. Hening's *Statutes*, X, p. 896, required the commanding officer of every county to transmit a census to the General Assembly of Virginia, "distinguishing all such as are under eighteen years of age."

159. Hening's *Statutes*, XI, p. 418, and XII, p. 431, established a poll tax of ten shillings for "every free male person above the age of twenty-one years who shall be a citizen of this commonwealth," in 1784 and repealed it in October 1787.

160. Chalkley, 1:260; 2:385.

161. Chalkley, 1:268.

162. Augusta Co., Va., Will Book 7:404-407.

163. Virginia State Land Office, Grants 24, 1791-92, reel 90, p. 385.

164. Augusta Co., Va., Deed of Trust 1-A:122.

165. Augusta Co., Va., Deed Book 28:268. This was comprised of three parcels of 300, 238, and 110 acres which corresponded to what John Finley had patented in 1741, 1768, and David had patented in 1791.

166. Christine S. Faux, 4611 Glencannon Street, Santa Rosa, Calif. 95405; Annabel Wesson, 5555 Montgomery Drive, K-2, Santa Rosa, Calif. 95409.

167. Montgomery Co., Ky., Tax Lists, Kentucky Department for Libraries and Archives.

168. 1810 federal census, population schedule, Montgomery Co., Ky., p. 367.

169. 1820 federal census, population schedule, Montgomery Co., Ky., p. 261

170. Ebenezer, born in 1802, would have been about 28 in 1830.

171. 1830 federal census, population schedule, Montgomery Co., Ky, p. 44.

172. Montgomery Co., Ky., Deed Book 2:512.

173. A series of letters written by Ebenezer to his son Harrison are still in the possession of family members Faux and Coffey. The latest letter from Ebenezer is dated 5 November '89 from Newtonia, Missouri.

174. Ebenezer Finley Bible Record, transcribed by Christine S. Faux, 16 January 1979, at the home of Ray Coffey in whose possession the Bible

was at the time.

175. Linda S. Barber Brooks, *Missouri Marriages to 1850* (published by the author, 1984), p. 141.

176. Ebenezer Finley Family Bible Record.

177. Bates Co., Mo., Deed Books E:570, F:40.

178. 1830 U.S. census, population schedule, Montgomery Co., Ky., p. 44.

179. Henry Wilkerson was found three lines down from Ebenezer. He was age forty to fifty with wife in same age range, along with four males and four females in the age ranges of under five to twenty, probably Narcissa's father. Hiram Wilkerson was found seven lines up from Ebenezer, age thirty to forty, with wife twenty to thirty and three children under ten, possibly Narcissa's older brother.

180. From Faux/Coffey notes; no reference given.

181. 1850 U.S. census, population schedule, 12th district, Callaway Co., Mo., p. 259, dwelling #916, family #916. On the next page was an Isaac Moore family, dwelling #924, family #924.

182. Missouri Original Land Entries, Clinton District, 1848-51, p. 160 lists 40 acres SESE Section 23, Twp. 41, Range 29; 40 acres NENE Section 23, Twp. 41, Range 29.

183. Bates Co., Mo., Deed Book C:140.

184. Bates Co., Mo., Deed Books E:570, F:40.

185. Vital data are from the Ebenezer Finley Family Bible. A rich resource for much of the other information included herein comes from a series of letters written by Ebenezer to his son Harrison, and by Elizabeth, Joseph Wilson, and Achilles to their brother, Harrison Finley. These letters date from 20 September 1862 to 10 September 1904.

186. Cass Co., Mo., Marriage Book B:58.

187. Ebenezer Finley Family Bible.

188. Information on the children was taken from

the family records of Christina (Sloat) Faux; Finley, *History of Sonoma County, California*, p. 286-287; Tuomey, *The History of Sonoma County, California*, p. 853-854; *Santa Rosa Rural Cemetery, 1852-1980* (Santa Rosa, Calif.: Sonoma County Genealogical Society, 1987) and "Mrs. Livonia Finley, Pioneer County Resident, Dies at 97" (obituary cited earlier), except as otherwise noted.

189. California Death Index, state file #55-71355, #178.
190. Sonoma Co., Calif., Death Records 40:37.
191. Sonoma Co., Calif., Death Records 36:1094.
192. Sonoma Co., Calif., Death Records 17:491.
193. Sonoma Co., Calif., Death Records 29:2253.
194. California Death Index, state file #6271, #95.
195. Sonoma Co., Calif., Death Records 29:1457.
196. Tuomey, vol. II, p. 853-854.
197. "Services are Saturday for Frances Nielsen," *The Press Democrat* (Santa Rosa, Sonoma Co., Calif.) 27 Nov. 1980.
198. Sonoma Co., Calif., Death Records 165:112.
199. Finley, *History of Sonoma County*, pp. 259-260.

INDEX

Abbot
  Bob, 99
Adams
  Robert, 148
  Sarah, 157
Agnew
  Robert Lee, 132
Akers
  William Alburtus, 83
Albini
  Malfalda Celeste, 125
Alderman
  Alton Lovell, Dr., 168
Alford
  Mary C., 98
Anderson
  James, Rev., 35, 37, 40
  Lucy B., 160
Applegate
  Anita, 125

Baker
  Robert, 144
  Samuel, 44
Baley
  Col., 77
Baller
  Adolph, 177
Balmer
  Ethel Work, 67, 79
Barker
  Reuben, 197

Barnett
  Thomas A., 86
Barnhart
  Irene, 172
Barrett
  Anna St. John, 27
Barron
  Joseph, 148
  Nancy, 154
Barsamian
  Ann, 133
Batten
  Dorothy (Freeze), 120
  Joe Michael, 120
  Wesley, 120
Bell
  John F., 163
Berrier
  Jacob, 142
Berry
  George, 182, 188
  James, 188, 199
  Sam, 199
Bessire
  Glen, 123
  Marion, 123
Best
  Elizabeth, 121
Beverley,
  William, 35, 46
Billingsly
  Dorothy, 100
Bishop
  Mary J., 96

Biswell
  Jana Michelle, 132
  Jason Tren, 132
  Steven, 132
Black
  Anthony, 182
  Hannah, 84
  Jacob, 67, 79, 84
  John, 182
  Rachel, 65
Blair
  John, 40
Blank
  Henry, 203
Blount
  Charles, 189
Bobst
  Ardith Bernice, 127, 129
  Jessie Maude, 127
  Richard Milton, 127
Boesch
  David Henry, 119
Bowden
  John H., 201
Boyd
  Elizabeth, 76
  James, 81
Braden
  Almyra J., 86
  Elizabeth P., 86
  George Marbern, 85
  Julia Ann, 86
  Nancy, 85
  Samuel, 85

PAGE 238

William James, 86
Bradford
   Benjamin, 153
Bradshaw
   Edward, 155
Branom
   Albert, 93
   David Merit, 93
   Eliza Jane, 93
   Elizabeth (Finley), 93
   Joseph Harvey, 93
   Julia Ann, 93
   Lucy Ardena, 93
   Malona Ellen, 93
   Mary (Polly) Ann, 93
   Merit, 92, 93
   Milton, 93
   Rachel Elizabeth, 93
   Tecumpseh C., 93
   Victorine, 93
   William J., 93
Breckenridge
   Alexander, 50, 52, 180, 185
   Ann (Doak), 185, 187
   George, 52, 180, 185, 187
   Sarah, 187
Brett
   Viola, 204
Brewster
   William F., 152
Brians
   Jackson, 87
   Prudence, 87
Britton
   George F., 201
Brooks
   Hannah (Sharrow), 77
   John Clark, 77

Miriam, 77, 96
Brown
   Catherine, 63
   Eugene Wakefield, 21
   John, 180, 182, 188
   Margaret, 180, 188
Bruce
   May Lena, 107
Brush
   Frank A., 25
   J.H., 25
Bryan
   Ellen, 153
   Samuel, 153
Bryant
   James, 196
   Nancy, 196
Burbank
   Luther, 169
Burns
   Ruth, 121
Burnside
   Hannah, 63
Busey
   Charles, Capt., 65, 69
Butler
   Susan Thereda, 93

Caldwell
   David, 37
   James, Rev., 38
   Jane (McGhie), 37
   John, 35, 37-39, 41, 42, 44, 52, 145
   Joseph, 37
   Margaret (Phillips), 37
   Martha, 39, 49
   Mary, 37, 39, 49, 52, 140, 179

Mary Jane (Parks), 37
Thomas, 37,
William, 37
Calhoun
   John Caldwell, 38, 39, 49
Campbell
   Arthur, 186
   James, 157, 179
   Margaret Jane, 166
   Sarah (McNary), 166
   William, 157, 166, 185
Cannon
   Adelaide, 76
   Julia, 21
Cantrell
   Bettie Finley, 154
Carder
   James, 98
Carmichael
   Alexander, 165
   Armstrong, 165
Carr
   Clay, 99
Carroll
   John B., 137
Carter
   Stephen, 190
Cauthorn
   Emma, 172
Chaffin
   Nancy A., 93
Chambers
   Emma, 83
Chilingerian
   Jonathan, 133
Chorzas
   Rosemary, 100

Christy
John, 49
Clark
Horace, 21
Jane, 60
John, 77
Nancy, 197
Clarke
Hester, 158
Clay
Henry, 62
Clendenen
Margaret, 180
Robert, 180, 185
Coates
Claude D., 32, 203
Cole
Josiah, 146
Colglazure
Jacob, 69
Rachel, 69, 95
Collier
Amanda C. (Boyd), 117
Cyrus B., 72
Moses, 58
Polly, 57, 58
Susan M., 117
Thomas, 117
Colter
Gen., 77
Comer
Marguerita Alice, 125
Comstock
Harrison Finley, 205
Helen (Finley), 205
Helen Alice (Finley), 30, 31
Helen Margaret (Pudge), 205
Hilliard, 205

James Hilliard, 205
John Adams, 205
Marshall Hurd, 205
Martha Lee, 205
Nellie (Hurd), 205
Conaster
Elizabeth, 78
Connelly
Thelma, 119
Cotton
Nan, 120
Council
Lee Ann, 134
Cowan
Eleanor, 145
Jane (Walker), 145
William, 145
Cox
S. Lesley (Lester), 203
Coyner
Michael, 144
Craig
Ina, 172
John, Rev., 45, 50, 140
Samuel, 182
Crockett
Davy, 193, 195
Hugh, 157
John, 193
Mary (Polly), 193, 195
Nancy, 157
Robert, 158
Samuel, 148
William, 193
Cross
Robert, 35
Crosswaith
Ida Finley, 154

Cruz
Richard, 99
Cunningham
Francis, 86
Robert, 49
Curtis
Tyler, 3

_____

Dalstrum
Lyn, 100
Daniel
Fannie, 98
Margaret L., 98
Daniels
Tullie, 100
Davenport
Frances, 197
Davies
Samuel, 40
Davis
Orinda, 92
Randall, 67
Robert, 180
Dawes
Bourbon, Mrs., 62
Day
Elizabeth, 76
Frank, 117
de Young
Charles, 177
M.H., 177
Dean
Carl, 99
Cleo D., 99
Forest, 99
Gilbert M.L., 99
Jack M., 99

James D., 117
John, 99
Levi, 99
Martha J., 117
Maude, 99
Deceare
    Basil Hudson, 120
Deck
    Ahi, 78
Dei
    John W., 109
DeMello
    Mary, 132
Denny
    Joseph, 152
Diffley
    Denise Jean, 120
    Florence (Doty), 120
    Joseph Lee, 120
Dillman
    Julia Ann, 165
Dixon
    Jonathan, 72
Doack
    David, 149
    Mary, 149
    Robert, 149
Doak
    Ann, 180
    David, 180, 187
    John, 187
    Robert, 187
    Samuel, 187
    Samuel Alexander, Col., 190
    Thankful, 180
    William, 187
Dorris
    Elias, 91

Downey
    Rachel, 73
Downing
    James, Capt., 43, 58, 65
    John, 58
    Martha (Patsy), 58, 65
    Nancy, 65
    William, 58
Dozier
    Cynthia (Carnes), 168
    Kate Rowena (Minnie), 168, 169
    Lewis Fort, 168
Drake
    Simon, 63
Dunks
    John, 76
Durso
    Edna (Sorensen), 108
Dutton
    Warren, 23

Edwards
    Brenda Lynn, 126
    Eliza J., 96
Elgin
    Hazel, 204
Elliot
    Andrew, 108
    Elizabeth, 196
Elliott
    Elizabeth, 96
    Ludwell, 96
Ely
    Mary, 105
Embree
    Clyde, 167
    Lillie, 167

    T.V., Dr., 167
    Van, 167
Emery
    Joseph, Rev., 167
Ennulate
    Yvonne, 133
Epperly
    Hiram, 87, 88, 116
Estes
    John W., 155

Fiedler
    Arthur, 177
Fielder
    John, 146
Findley
    Aaron B., 119
    Adeline Calla, 99
    Amy, 134
    Beverly, 132
    Blanch B., 117
    Byron F., 119, 132, 133
    Carolyn Jane, 132
    Carrie Lynn, 133
    Cathel, 100
    Catherine, 81
    Cecil M., 117
    Cyrus, 59
    Daniel, 120
    David, 64, 68, 81
    Dorothy, 132
    Earl Frances, 100
    Edmund, 59, 64
    Elizabeth, 82, 83, 90, 96
    Ellen, 98, 99
    Garold E., 117, 132
    Harvey, 59, 64, 81

Inez E., 117
Ira Sylvester, 100
Ivan, 99, 117, 119
Jeanne M., 134
Jefferson, 81
Jessie, 59
John, 6, 59, 63, 68, 80, 82, 83, 90, 91, 98, 147
John Moses, 99, 117
Judith Lou, 120
Kathleen Lea, 120
Kenneth Lee, 100
Lee Robert, 100
Lettecia, 84
Lewis, 64, 84
Mahala, 67, 68
Margarite, 100
Marian Ella, 120
Martha Alice, 90
Mary (DeMello), 132
Mary Elizabeth, 99
Mary Lou, 132
Melba, 100
Michelle R., 117, 133
Muriel Rose, 100
Myrtle L., 119
Nancy Jane (Daisy), 100
Natalie Lynette, 133
Oswald Allen, 100
Patrick Michael, 120
Reubin, 97
Richard I., 134
Robin Leigh, 133
Ruth Amanda, 119
S.J., 90
Samuel, 56, 59, 81, 82, 88
Sarah, 83
Sary, 187

Susan, 119
Thomas, 97
William, 89, 99, 142
William B., 133
William Cotton, 120
William Francis, 120
William J., 80, 98, 99
William Jackson, 99
Fin(d)ly
Elvira, 90
James (B.), 90
John, 81
John L., 90
Martha, 88
Nancy V., 90
Prudence, 88, 90
S.J., 88
Samuel W. , 90
Thomas, 90
Victoria, 90
Washington, 90
William, 81
Finley
Aaron, 92
Abigail Josephine (Abbie), i, 28, 29, 203
Achilles (Chill), 202
Ada V., 95, 172
Agnes, 196
Agness, 191
Albert Charles, 110
Alesia Vaneta, 101
Alexander, 191, 196
Alexander Kanedy, 197
Alfaretta, 14, 114, 123, 126
Alice (Hudson), 204
Alicia V., i, 28, 203
Almira, 165

Alvin, 65, 67, 68, 84, 103, 107, 108, 115
Alvin Wesley, 9, 14, 86, 114
Amanda, 159
Amanda M., 98
Amy Eliza, 197
Andrew Jackson, (Jack), 3, 9, 14, 86, 103, 111, 123
Anita L., 109
Ann, 61, 152, 165, 189
Ann Eliza, 167
Anna L., 172
Annette, 109
Ardith Bernice, 131
Arthur L., 172
Asa, 148, 154, 157, 160-163, 179
Asa W., 161
Asa Wallace, 159-161, 163
Benjamin Franklin, 154
Bessie, 108, 120
Betsey, 57, 58, 155
Betsy, 186
Bluford, 165
Brutus, 156, 166
Brutus William, 124, 157
Carmen Joyce, 131, 134
Carolyn Elaine, 177
Catharine Kitty Bruce, 152
Catherine, 64, 65, 79, 91, 165
Catherine M., 83
Cecile Vienna, 108
Charles, 200
Charles D., 164
Charles S., 96
Charles Wesley, 102
Clara, 117
Clara Eva, 117
Clark, 159, 160
Claude Thompson, 115

Cleveland Josiah, 101
Craig, 172
Cynthiana, 171
Cyrus, 58-60, 70, 71, 73, 77
Cyrus E., 75
Dabney, 148, 154-159, 161, 163, 179
Dabney B., 160
David, 39, 52, 56-61, 64, 65, 69, 70, 73,
    75-77, 79, 80, 83, 84, 92, 96, 139, 142,
    147, 149, 150, 165, 166, 182, 184, 185,
    188-190, 192, 193, 195-200, 202
David Edwin, 92
David M., 71, 92
David Merrit, 94
Dozier, 171
Earl Lester, 121
Ebenezer, 32, 199-201
Edith Mary, 121
Edmond, 69, 70, 94
Edmund, 60, 63-65, 69, 79, 83, 84, 91,
    139
Edna, 172
Edna Rowena, 171
Edward Leroy, 111, 114, 127
Eli, 155
Eli E., 157
Eliza, 92, 162
Eliza Ann, 70
Eliza Belle, i, 28, 33, 203
Eliza C., 92
Eliza J., 75
Eliza Jane, 75
Elizabeth, 49, 52, 57-60, 67, 68, 70, 71,
    76, 77, 79-81, 83, 91, 94, 140, 143,
    148, 154, 179, 188, 191, 199-201
Elizabeth (Betsey), 155
Elizabeth (McKinney), 70
Elizabeth (Mounts), 60, 61

Elizabeth (Wilson), 199
Elizabeth Ann, 70
Elizabeth Ellen, 70, 92, 93
Elizabeth F., 77, 96
Elizabeth Finetta, 3, 86, 105
Ellen, 92
Ellen R., 75
Elvira, 90
Emma, 95
Emma Ardena, 94
Emma J., 95
Ernest Latimer, i, ii, 19, 21, 23, 25, 27,
    30, 34, 168, 173-177, 179
Esau (Asa), 148
Esther, 161
Esther (Gleaves), 157, 162
Ethel Agnes, 111, 114, 126
Eva Cential, 101
Filander, 156
Florence Maurice, 115
Foster Gaines, 164
Frances, 32, 115, 205
Frances (Hancock), 164
Frances Elizabeth, 94
Frances Jane, 165
Francis Marion, 142
Fred Louis, 120
Frederick Lee, 204
Genevieve, 109
George, 43, 49, 69, 94, 140, 146, 149, 150,
    152, 164, 166, 179, 180, 182 184-188,
    190-193
George C., 159
George Franklin, 197
George Maurice, 204
George T., 88, 90
George W., 70, 93
Gilead E., 75

Grace Pearl, 100, 102
Granville Houston, 98
Granville Huston, 78, 97
Hannah, 84
Harold, 111, 114
Harrison, i, ii, 28-30, 32-35, 180, 201,
    202, 204
Harrison (Harry), 202
Harrison D., 117
Harrison Decatur, 118, 161, 163
Harvey, 58, 60, 65, 70, 71, 73, 83, 84
Helen, 161, 205
Helen Alice, 32, 204
Helen C., 161, 163
Henrietta, 161, 163
Henry, 3, 6, 9, 15, 103, 104, 107, 108,
    116, 121
Henry Harrison, 109
Henry Head, i, 2, 4, 9, 86, 102
Henry L., 75
Hester, 158
Hester (Clarke), 160
Hester M., 159, 160
Hugh Dozier, 171
Hugh McNary, 167, 172
Ida, 154
Irva Elizabeth, 120
Irving Hansen, 168
Isaac Newton, 78
Isaac Taylor, 164
Isabella, 191
Jackson, 201
James, 49, 52, 57, 67, 68, 73, 75, 79, 87,
    90, 91, 103, 117, 140, 149, 166, 182,
    185, 189-192, 196, 198, 200
James Benjamin, 167
James Buchanan, 87, 88, 90, 111, 116
James Christopher, 177

James Franklin, 101
James H., 154
James Harvey, 71
James Otis, 94
James Preston, 3, 9, 14, 86, 107, 126
James Washington, 161-163, 166, 167, 179
James William, 86
James, Capt., 148
Jane, 61, 94, 97, 165, 185, 189
Jane (Clark), 77, 78
Jane (King or Katherine), 78
Jane Ann, 39, 58, 60-62
Jane/Jean (Jinney), 143
Janet, 191
Jean, 182, 185, 186, 190, 193, 196
Jean/Jane, 185, 187
Jeff, 95, 107, 115, 129
Jefferson, 59, 60, 67, 68, 77, 79, 80, 83, 95
Jefferson Davis, 3, 9, 14, 86, 108
Jefferson L., 96
Jerome, 155
Jesse, 58, 60, 64, 65, 68, 69, 80, 91, 92, 95, 139
Jesse G., 164
Jo, 95
John, i, ii, 2-4, 6, 8, 9, 14-16, 28, 35, 37, 39, 41, 43-46, 49, 50, 52, 56, 57, 60, 65, 67, 68, 79-86, 91, 95, 100, 101, 103, 107, 111, 114, 121, 129, 139-142, 146, 147,149, 150, 153, 154, 159, 160, 168, 179, 180, 182, 184-189, 191-193, 195-198, 200
John B. , 164
John Henry, 197
John Jay, i, 2, 9, 14, 86, 102
John Lee, 88, 90

John Lewis, 61
John Moses, 117
John P., 155, 159, 163, 168
John Pettis, 148, 161, 167-169, 171, 172, 179
John Pettus, 148, 154, 156-160, 179
John S., 154
John T., 142, 153
John Victor, 120
Joseph Jefferson, 9, 69, 70, 94, 139
Joseph W., 168
Joseph Walker, 154
Joseph Wilson, 200-202
Josephine, 59, 77, 95, 96
Juanita Louise, 121
Judith, 145, 148, 149
Julia, 92
Julia Ann, 80, 83
Julia Ann (Dillman), 166
Katherine, 84
Kesia, 68
Keziah, i, 2-4, 6, 8, 9, 11, 14-16, 28, 34, 100, 101, 103, 111, 114, 121, 139, 191
Laura Ann, 94
Leon Grover, 111, 114, 123
Leora Martha, 108
Letitia, 64
Lettecia, 84
Lettie, 189
Lewis S., 65, 84
Lillian, 154
Lillian Eva, 110
Lily Maude, 101
Livonia, i, 28-30, 33, 34
Livonia Louise, i, 28, 32, 33, 203
Lorena Frances, 204
Louis Emanuel, 101, 120
Lucille Harriett (Hattie), 109

Lucinda E., 75
Lucinda W., 150, 152
Lucy, 33
Lucy Lavenia, 94
Lucy Ray, i, 28, 203
Lucy W., 98
Madeline Bernice, 115, 116
Mahala, 67, 68, 79, 80, 91
Manna, 92
Marenda, 3, 107
Marenda A., 86
Margaret, 69, 70, 92, 143, 148, 159, 179, 184, 189-191
Margaret (Peggy), 148
Margaret A., 64, 84, 157
Margaret E., 168
Margaret Emily, 71
Margaret Jane, 189, 197
Margaret Jane (Campbell), 166
Margaret Kerr, 198
Margaret S., 159, 160
Maria J., 154
Mariah, 165, 201
Marion, 69, 70
Marlena, 84
Marry, 191
Martha, 9, 65, 70, 75, 83, 87, 88, 116, 164
Martha (Downing), 65, 66
Martha E., 86
Martha Elvira, 101
Martha Jane, 153
Martha Louisa, 202
Mary, 49, 52, 56, 70, 83, 148, 150, 152, 156, 157, 187, 193, 195
Mary (Caldwell), 139
Mary (Gaines), 165
Mary (Lewis), 157

Mary (Pettus), 146
Mary (Polly), 60, 71, 93, 155, 195
Mary Alice, 101
Mary Ann, 84, 148, 149
Mary Ann (Polly), 78
Mary Dozier, 171
Mary E., 95, 157
Mary Elisabeth, 84
Mary Eliza, 164
Mary Elizabeth, 70
Mary Ellen, 94
Mary Frances, i, 28
Mary Frances (Molly), 33, 203
Mary Gaines, 165
Mary Jane, 70, 71, 101, 163
Mary Luella, 164
Matilda Narcissus (Tillie), i, 28, 203
Mattie, 154
Mattie Zoe, i, 28, 32, 33, 203
Melissa, 159
Merrill F., 75
Mervyn Harrison, 204
Michael, 200
Milton Ogden, 69, 92, 94, 159, 160
Miriam (Brooks), 96
Missouri E., 202
Moses, 92
Nancy, 5, 6, 8, 78, 84, 95, 97, 102, 155
Nancy (Barron), 155, 157
Nancy (McCulley, King), 77
Nancy Ada, 94
Nancy Ann, 79, 189
Nancy Caroline, 3, 83, 86, 103
Nancy Catherine (Rucker), 172
Nancy (or Lucy) Emaline, 197
Nancy J., 68, 85, 97
Nancy V., 90
Napoleon B., 164

Narcissa, 158
Narcissa (Wilkerson), 201
Nettie, 5, 6, 9,
Newton Gleaves, 16, 17, 23, 24, 161, 166, 168, 171
Obadiah G., 164
Obediah Gaines, 149, 150, 163
Oliver P.M., 96
Osbourne, 196
Patsy, 153
Percy E., 172
Percy Edward, 120
Perry Elmo, 111, 114, 123, 126, 127, 129, 131
Philander, 157, 166
Philena, 92
Phoebe Catherine, 172
Pois (Porus Dabney), 166
Polly, 77, 92, 155, 200
Porus Dabney, 157
Preston T., 96
Prudence, 2, 88, 90, 91
Rachel, 65, 69, 84, 91, 92, 186, 187
Rachel (Black), 67
Rachel (Colglazure), 80, 95
Rachel (Downey), 75
Rachel E., 75
Rebecca (McCoy), 167
Reed, 96
Reuben, 61, 78, 97
Reuben Edwin, 168
Reuben Jefferson, 60, 61, 77, 78
Reuben Oscar, 98
Rhoda, 77, 78, 148, 157, 161, 163
Robert, 45, 46, 182, 184, 187-192, 197, 198, 200
Robert Carson, 197
Robert Miller, 196

Robert Woolsey, 177
Rollin Pierce, 101
Ross, 172
Rufus, 164
Ruth, 151, 175, 179, 204
Ruth Woolsey, i, 176, 177
S.J., 111
S.W., 88
Sally, 143, 150, 157
Sally Dillard, 165
Sally Milton, 148, 149
Samuel, 2, 4, 6, 8, 9, 52, 56-60, 64, 65, 67-70, 77, 79, 82, 85, 90, 91, 95-97, 101, 111, 139, 142, 147, 152-154, 179, 191, 200
Samuel Edward, 102
Samuel Emanuel, i, 2, 14, 82, 86, 100, 121, 126
Samuel F., 83
Samuel J., 111
Samuel Joseph, 82, 87, 88, 90
Samuel Saffel, 197
Samuel Steele, 142, 152
Samuel Thomson, 153
Samuel Washington, 88, 90, 111
Sarah, i, 18, 21, 23-27, 34, 79, 80, 95, 141, 142, 161, 162, 188, 189
Sarah (Breckenridge), 188
Sarah (Sally), 142, 152
Sarah A., 164
Sarah Ann, 98, 197
Sarah Ann (Hodges), 163
Sarah E. Latimer, 17
Sarah Esther, 167
Sarah J., 95, 96
Sarah Jane, 159
Stephen Horne, 98
Susan, 96, 160

Thankful, 182, 184, 185, 187, 188, 190,
191, 193, 196
Thankful (Doak), 150, 180, 197, 198
Thankful Sarah, 199, 200
Thomas, 56, 57, 60, 61, 70, 77, 78, 84,
90, 97, 149, 190, 191
Thomas B., 157, 161, 163, 166, 168
Thomas Jefferson, 71
Thomas Milton, 78, 97
Thomson, 153
Travis, 191
Ulysses S.G., 96
Victoria, 90
Virginia, 157
Vivian Gertrude, 111, 114, 124
Vivian May, 121
Walker H., 155, 166
Washington, 87, 88, 90
William, 45, 46, 49, 52, 57, 69, 70, 80,
91, 92, 140, 142, 143, 145-149,
152-157, 164, 166-168, 179, 191, 193,
195, 200
William Adam, 155
William Alexander, 71
William Asa, i, ii, 16-19, 21, 23-28,
34, 35, 44, 140, 166, 168, 172, 179
William David, 9, 86, 114
William G., 154
William J., 83, 96
William L., 171
William Lovell, 172
William M., 164
William Orville, 78, 98
William Wilkerson, 202
William, Capt., 188
Willie C., 21, 168
Willie Calvin, 102
Wilson Cornelius, 204

Wilson Ebenezer, i, 28, 203, 204
Winfred Alberta, 109
Fisher
Amanda, 96
Clara J., 96
James, 96
John F., 96
Josephine, 59, 96
Laura, 96
Lydia, 96
Miriam E., 96
Fitzgerald
A.L., 19
Foe
Frances, 68, 80
Fore
Joseph, 146
Mary, 146
France
Albert Finley, 34
Franklin
Benjamin, 141
Frazer
Jane, 142
Joseph, 56
William, 56
Frazier
Jean, 143
William, 143, 152
Fregulia
Caroline (Sorensen), 108
Fresk
Erik, 119
Fridley
Fannie, 76
Fulton
Jane, 149
Thomas, 28, 149

Gaethle
Nancy, 125
Gager
George G., 85
Gaines
Mary, 149
Mary (Lewis), 163, 164
Polly (Mary), 150
William, 149, 150
William S., 163
Garden
Alexander, 180
Garloff
Bessie, 108
Henry R., 109
Walter W., 109
Mary Jane Kyle, 197
Garrett
Honour, 52
Jacob, 52
Gibert
Jean Louis, 60
Jeanne, 60, 61
Gillaspie
John, 188
Gillaspy
James, 143, 188
Jeannet, 143
Gillespy
Ann, 143
Campbell, 145
Elizabeth, 143, 144, 179
Ellen Jane, 145
James, 141, 142, 144, 145
James (Smoking Jimmy), 145
Jane, 144
Jennet, 143
John, 144

John Finley, 145
Mary, 144
Sarah, 145
William, 144
William Cowan, 145

Gillis
    Norman A., 93

Gleaves
    Elizabeth (Turk), 160
    Esther, 141, 160
    Matthew, 141
    William, 141, 148, 160

Glenn
    James, 186, 187
    Rachel, 187

Gomez
    Catharine Lorraine, 115

Gooch
    Gov., 35

Graff
    Alfaretta, 114
    Henry, 114

Graves
    Susan, 154

Greene
    Robert, 134
    Robert H., 152

Greenway
    John, 186

Gregg
    Samuel, 154

Grier
    William, 185

Griffith
    Sarah Francis, 93

Groom
    Harold, 204

Haire
    Alastair Lawrence, 133

Haley
    S., 76

Hall
    Lucy, 154

Hancock
    Frances (Fanny), 164
    John R., 157
    Martha (Patsy), 164
    William, 164

Hardcastle
    Bruce, 120
    Gregory Bruce, 120
    Susan Ellen, 120

Hardman
    William A., 96

Harley
    William, 186

Harlow
    Nathaniel, Jr., 190

Harness
    James, 132
    Marc Garold, 132

Harris
    John N., 84
    Mary T., 157

Hart
    Josiah, 83
    Julia Ann, 81
    Mary, 81
    Moses, 80, 83

Hartline
    Monte B., 119

Hathaway
    Robert M., 153

Hawkins
    Tamar, 76

Hawley
    Rufus, 173

Hay
    Peter, 186, 187

Head
    Albert Pike, 105, 107
    Clarence Elmore, 9, 14, 15, 102, 105, 107, 121, 129
    Elizabeth Finetta, 102, 107
    Frances Gertrude, 14, 114
    Keziah, 86
    Lulu Myrtle, 9, 15, 102, 105, 107, 121
    Margaret Janetta, 105, 114
    Nettie Mae, 107
    Robertson, 105, 114, 121
    Robertson Calvin (Rob), 9, 14, 15, 102-105, 107
    Ruth, 104

Hearst
    William Randolph, 177

Hebden
    Alice, 76

Helton
    Jesse, 150

Henderson
    Wm., 188

Hendren
    Ethel, 127
    Verner, 126, 127

Hendricks
    Elizabeth, 201
    James F., 201

Henry
    Patrick, 186

Hewett
    Josephus, 67

Hicks
    Mary Elizabeth, 168, 169

Higginbotham
  Elizabeth, 190
Hill
  Easter, 94
  Thomas, 185
Hilliard
  Elizabeth B., 174
  Henry P., 174
Hite
  Julia, 92
Hodges
  Phoebe, 92
  Sarah Ann, 160, 161
Hodgson
  Carl, 110
Hogan
  James, 153
Holman
  Hardy, 155
Holsey
  Thomas, 145
Hong
  Hom, 31
Hood
  W.S., 154
Horne
  Lutecia, 97
Horton
  John, 165
Houston
  Elizabeth (McCoskey), 144
  Elizabeth Gillespie, 145
  Esther (Hettie), 145
  Esther Jane, 144
  James, Maj., 144
  Lucinda C., 145
  Martha, 145
  Mary, 145

Melinda Gillespie, 145
Phoebe M., 145
Samuel, 144
Samuel Finley, 145
Sidney N., 145
Howarth
  Leonard, 175
Hudson
  Alice, 32, 204
  Cornelius, 32, 204
  Lavina (Butler), 204
Hughes
  Huie, 29
  LaVoy Eugene, 119
Hulse
  James, 200
Humphrey
  Frank, 83
Hunsaker
  George, 83
  Minnie, 83
  Nancy Ann, 83
Hunter
  Alexander, 77, 78, 97
  Joseph Hayes, 134
Hurd
  Nellie, 205
Hutchinson
  Franklin, 82, 91
  Thomas, 155
Hutchison
  John, 143
  Margaret, 143
  Robert, 143
Hutson
  Harriet, 197

Ingram
  James R., 93

———————————————

Jackson
  Andrew, Gen., 190
Jameson
  Asa, 162
  Janis, 162
Jeffress
  Coleman, 160
Jeter
  William O., 72
Johnson
  Adelaide, 165
  Amanda, 75
  Casey, 132
  Jesse, 163
  Kate, 94
  Mary Lewis, 163
  Sarah Ann, 163
  Solomon D., 197
Johnston
  John, 184, 199
Juell
  Dagney, 134

———————————————

Kalen
  Ira, 102
Kee
  Chong, 33
  Mary Elizabeth, 123
  R.T., 101, 107
Keithl(e)y
  Calvin, 8, 103-105
  Clara C., 8, 9, 11, 102, 104, 105, 121
  Nancy Caroline, 9, 15, 102-105

Keller
- Kim Roberta, 125

Kemper
- Martha, 63

Kennedy
- Jean, 196
- Pauline, 63

Kenner
- Mary Hampton, 190
- Matilda, 190

Kenney,
- Frank A., 172

Kerbo
- Arminda, 70
- Mary (Polly) Ann, 94

Kerr
- Margaret, 196, 198

Kersey
- Clarissa, 76

Kinder
- Catherine, 60, 61, 77

Kiner
- Clarice E., 99
- Denzelle, 100
- Elsie Kiner, 99
- Harold, 100
- Herman, 100
- John Fred, 99

King
- Nancy (McCully), 77

Kirk
- Capt., 198

Kirkpatrick
- Josiah, 115

Kneppler
- Florence (Matthews), 108

Kyle
- Thomas, 25

Lane
- Elmont, 203

Lashley
- Elizabeth, 91
- Seaborn N. (Zebe), 83

Latimer
- Malinda (Logan), 25, 168
- Martha, 24
- Robert Atwell, Rev., 23-25, 168
- Sarah, 17, 168

Latta
- Mary Bingham, 171

Laughlin
- Grant, 29, 33, 203
- James Henry, 203
- Mary, 203

Lawrence
- Ernest O., 135

Lechene
- Nohi, 76

Lee
- Carrie B., 76
- Eliza J., 75
- Gilead P., 75
- Iola, 99
- Merrill S., 76
- Sarah M., 76

Lehman
- Carolyn, 133

Lester
- James, 108

Letts
- Clara, 116

Lewis
- Aaron, Col., 155
- Elizabeth C., 71
- John, 45, 50
- Mary, 155
- Sarah Mary (South), 155

Liberman
- Alexander, 177

Lind
- Jenny, 62

Lindley
- Alfred, 72
- Martha Jane, 71

Linebaugh
- Robert, 108

Logan
- Harald, 177

Lorge
- Irving R., 136

Mackey
- Mary, 97

Mahan
- Ellen R., 75
- John W., 75
- Martha, 75
- Worth, 75

Mannheimer
- Frank, 177

Mantua
- Julius, 126, 127

Marles
- B.Q., Capt., 163

Marsh
- Lulu May, 107

Marshall
- Rhodes, 158

Martin
    Alverta Brown, 187
    Keziah, 191
Massey
    Marilyn Ruth, 119
    Marjorie Elaine, 119
    Walter Ernest, 119
Masters
    Caroline, 68
    Sarah, 67, 68, 79, 91
Matashuma
    H. (Martin), 31
Matthews
    George, 108
    William, 108
Maxey
    Mary, 78
Maxwell
    Almira, 71
    America Ann, 72
    Cyrus, 73
    Eliza Jane, 72
    George Washington, 73
    James, 71
    James David, 72
    John Tucker, 73
    Joseph W., 58, 70, 71
    Joseph Jefferson, 72
    Louiza, 72
    Martha Jane, 72
    Mary (Finley), 58, 71
    Mary Elizabeth, 72
    Polly, 59
    Sarah Brown(e), 73
McCaughey
    Howard, 4
    James, Mrs., 11, 102
    Walter, 102

McClenachan
    Margaret, 196
McClerry
    Sarah, 95
McCorkle
    Archibald, 163
    Eliza, 163
    Elizabeth, 163
    H.B., 163
    Mary Jane, 161
    William, 163
McCoy
    Rebecca Ivy, 166
    William, 76
McCready
    Caroline (Carrie) Anne, 108
    Jane (Boyd), 108
    Samuel, 108
McCullock
    Thomas, 185
McCullough
    Hugh, 197
    Thomas, 193
McCully
    David, 197
    Hugh, 67
    Rachel, 67
McDaniel
    Margaret, 92
McDonald
    J.B., 94
    Mark, 23
    Nettie, 4, 100, 102, 103
McFarland
    John, 52
McFarlin
    J.E., Dr., 93

McFarling
    Jessie Maude, 127
McGhie
    Jane, 37
McIntyre
    Linda, 126
McKarter
    Thankful, 182
McKean
    Mary, 41
McKinney
    David, 70
    Elizabeth, 70
    Margaret (Wallace), 70
McKinstry
    George D., 108
McKune
    Otis Edwin, 107
McNair
    David, 184, 185, 188
McNary
    Sarah, 166
McPheeters
    William, 182, 188, 196
McReynolds
    Isaac, 86
Mendes
    John, 100
Mikani
    Shizino (Judy), 99
Miller
    Hugh, Sr., 186
Minear
    Eliza Ann, 111
Miner
    David, 116
Misselbrook
    Bessie Elizabeth, 120

Catherine (Brown), 120
William, 120
Mitchel
    Francis, 61
    Thomas Finley, 61
Mitchell
    Nancy, 164
    Thomas Findley, 97
Mobley
    James, 185
Montgomery
    Elizabeth, 147
    James, Col., 189
    Ida Beatrice, 71
    J.W., 201
    John, 187
    Louise J., 71
    Rachel, 189
    Samuel, 146
    Theofilus, 71
    William, 70, 71
    William F., 71
Monyhan
    Mary (Nannie) J., 75
Mooney
    Margaret (Peggy), 142
Moore
    Mariah C., 200, 201
    Mary Rue, 93
    William Y., 159, 160
Mounce
    Elizabeth, 57
    Mary, 57
Mounts
    Elizabeth, 37, 39, 56
    Henry, 58
    John, 58
    Mary, 56
    Matthias, 56, 57
Murphy
    Lloyd, 204
Murray
    D.M., 108
Myers
    Mary, 63

Naish
    Joseph, 125
    Marie, 125
Neale
    Mattie Finley, 154
Nelson
    Lillian, 204
Newell
    Beulah, 93
Newlin
    Mahlon H., 72
    Mary Elizabeth, 71
Nichols
    Matilda (Mattie) F., 166
Nidros
    Mabel (May), 204
Nielsen
    Anders, 204
    Donald A., 204
    Philip L., 204
Nixon
    Richard M., Pres., 176
Nye
    George W., 149

Oakley
    Robert, 78
Odell
    Jane (Jinny), 93
    Simon, 93
Oliver
    Charles F., 116
    Eva, 116
    James, 116
    James F., 9, 88, 116
    John, 116
    Martha (Finley), 88, 116
    Mary E., 116
    Nellie, 116
    William, 116
Oman
    Alice (Finley), 88
    Arthur, 88, 91
Oppenheimer
    J. Robert, 135
Orr
    Hugh, 187
    Mary, 187
    Wesley Embert, 125
Osborne
    Felix G., 97
Otis
    Harrison Gray, Col., 177
Owens
    George, 8
O'Neal
    William (Buck), 202

Parker
    John, 86
Parks
    Mary Jane, 37
Pattee
    Carol Ann, 132

Debra Renee, 132
Jane Lucille, 132
William, 132
Patterson
Ray, 110
Patton
James, 50
Peacock
Mae, 101
Pedrazzi
Ethel, 101, 108, 114, 127
George, 101, 108, 114, 126, 127
Pelton
Shirley A., 204
Pennebaker
Catherine B., 152
Emeline, 152
George Finley, 152
John Hearst, 152
Lucinda, 152
Lucinda Prechus, 152
Mary Ann, 152
Samuel, 152
Samuel W., 152
Sarah Ellen, 152
William Gaines, 152
William Harrison, 152
Person
Evert B., 176-179
Ruth, 178
Ruth Finley, 176, 177
Perviance
Inez, 100
Peterson
Patricia, 125
Pettigrew
Sarah (McLane) Stedman, 60

Pettus
Dabney, 145
Elizabeth (Rodes), 145
John, 158
Mary, 145, 148, 156
Stephen, 146
William Overton, 158
Phillips
Andrew, 34
Margaret, 37
Matilda, 202
Philson
Mary, 196
Piazza
Alfred (Buck), 101, 127
Lorraine (Wilds), 101, 127
Pickens
John, 189
Letitia (Hannah), 189
Margaret, 189
Mary, 189
Pierce
Francis Edward, 101
Pippin
Tom U., 87, 88
Porter
Daniel, 79
Potter
Stella, 127
Preston
John, 50
Priest
Dean, 132
Purcell
Jeanne (Shaffer), 123

Ramsay
William, 200
Ramsey
Andrew, 152
Jess, 98
June, 125
Sally, 152
Randles
Lucinda, 197
Ray
Livonia Josephine, 28, 202
Matilda (Phillips), 34, 202
William (Sanford), 34, 202
Read
Alexander, 188
Reed
John, 191, 192
Martha, 191, 192
Reeves
George, 81
Reid
Alexander, 188
Thomas, 41
Renati
Mae (Sorensen), 108
Richardson
Alvira, 88
Beryl, 90
Charles F., 90
Riley
Thomas W., 71
William Alexander, 71
Roberts
Albert M., 98
Robinson
George, 49
Minnie, 100
William, 40

Rodrequiz
    Sarah, 132
Rogers
    Eldad, 23
Ross
    Chester Clyde, 94
Roth
    Harold, 126
Roy
    William B., 163
Rozell
    Wesley, 154
Rucker
    Nancy Catherine, 171
    Veranda, 171
    William Thornton, 171
Runyon
    Favel, 117

Saffel,
    Edith (Edy), 197, 198
Sankey
    Richard, Rev., 35, 42, 43, 50, 52, 144
    Sarah (Thomson), 144
Sayers
    William, 52
Schnabel
    Arthur, 177
Schoenfeld
    Charles B., 27
Schubert
    John, 88
Schwager
    Adrian, 133
Scott
    Archibald, Rev., 198
    George, Capt., 58

Sevier
    John, 195
Shadden
    Alexander, 188
Shadding
    Alexander, 188
Shaffer
    Clarence, 123
    Jeanne, 123
    Judy, 123
    Leonard, 123
Shannon
    James, 152
Sharp
    Edward, 185
Sharpe
    William P., 165
Shields
    Alexander, 189, 190
    David, 190
    Elizabeth, 190
    George, 190
    James, 190
    Jane, 190
    John, 189, 190, 198
    Margaret (Finley), 182, 189, 190
    Nathan, 189, 190
    Peggy, 189
    Rachel, 189
    Rebecca, 190
    Rebecka, 189
    Robert, 189, 190
    Thankful, 189
    William, 189, 190
Simcoe
    James, 33, 203
Simpson
    Elizabeth, 177

Sing
    Hop, 31
    Suey, 31
Singleton
    Robert, 58
Slaten
    Capt., 77
Slaves
    Abby, 148, 155
    Aia, 154
    Amy, 148, 156
    Betty, 189
    Boce, 162
    Caroline, 61
    Caty, 148, 155
    Charles, 148, 156
    Clark, 161
    Eli, 162
    Emily, 162
    Eve, 189
    Finda, 61
    Franklin, 61
    Green, 162
    Hagar, 148, 155
    Hanna, 148, 156
    Hannah, 182, 184
    Hanny, 61
    Hardin, 162
    Harry, 148
    Henry, 162
    Jack, 189
    Jinney, 61
    Jo, 155
    John, 189
    Joseph, 148, 156
    Jude, 61
    Lavery, 189
    Martin, 147

Milley, 154
Mourn, 148, 156
Nan, 147
Nancy, 162
Ned, 148
Nell, 189
Peggy, 61
Plim, 161, 166
Polly Ann, 162
Pompey, 189
Rachel, 148, 156
Reubin, 148
Robert, 61
Rose, 61
Sal, 148, 156
Sampson, 148
Sarah, 148, 156
Shadrick, 162
Spencer, 148, 156
Stephen, 155
Tom, 61
Wash, 162
Westley, 154
Willey, 61
William, 61

Sloan
Edward Sampson, 94

Small
Caroline (Sorensen) Fregulia, 108

Smith
Almira, 63
Anna Maria, 63
David Finley, 62, 63
Edmond, 58, 62
Edmund, 39
Edmund Finley, 62, 63
Elizabeth, 190
Elizabeth F., 63

Harold F., 62
Henry, 62
Henry E., 93
Jacob, 111
James, Rev., 58, 62
Jane Ann (Finley), 37, 59, 62
John, 62
Josephine Peachy, 63
Magdalene (Woods), 62
Manuela Torres, 3
Martha Jane, 72, 164
Mary, 62
Mary Jane, 63
Mary Virginia, 62
Merrill, 62, 63
Nathan L., 63
Oliver C., 160
Sally Ann, 63
Stephen, Capt., 3, 4
William, 62
Zebulon, 164

Sneed
Almira, 76
Benjamin, 76
David F., 76
Elizabeth (Finley), 59, 76
Harvey F., 76
Henry C., 76
Isabella H., 76
James B., 76
John A., 76
John Holman, 59, 76
Mary J., 76
Nathan, 76
Rufus, 76
Sarah (Johnson), 76
Sarah E., 76

Snyder
Henry, 67
Sorensen
Caroline, 108
Edna, 108
Mae, 108
Sam Hansen, 108
S(o)utherland
John, 95
Nancy, 94, 95
T.J., 95
Thomas, 95
Stanley
Julian B., 137
Mary Jane, 8, 100
Steele
James, 153
Martha, 152
Martha (Fulton), 140, 153
Samuel , 140, 153
Sarah, 140, 153
Stemple
Alfaretta Isadore, 111
Eliza Ann (Minear), 111
Henry Martin, 111
Stephens
Jehu, Capt. , 57
Stevens
J.G., Capt., 95
Stewart
Archibald, 49, 50
Edward M., 94
Martha A., 94
Mary Lillie, 94
Stockton
Dana Annette, 177
Strain
John H., 165

Street
    Doll, 100
Strout
    Archie L., 203
Stuart
    Archibald, 50
Stultz
    Wesley, 165
Sturgeon
    Wade, 127
Sullivan
    Monoah Hardin, 165
Sumner
    Charles, 99
Swallow
    Andrew, 61, 77
Swayne
    Wager, 177

Talbot
    Charles, 62
    John G., 63
    Presley, 62
Tarwater
    Arlene Frances, 121
    Clara, 10, 14
    Dolores, 121
    Francis Calvin, 121
    Helen, 121
    Marion Carroll, 121
    Martin, 121
    Martin Raymond, 121
    Orville Glenn, 121
    Vernon Keith, 121
Tate
    John, 152
    Mary, 152

Taylor
    Altamire G., 164
    George, 198
    Isaac, 164
    Julia, 76
    Margaret, 164
Tegarden
    Andrew, 77
    Annie (Todd), 77
    Basil, 77
    Elizabeth, 75
    George W., 96
    John, 75
    Lucinda (Irvine), 75
    Miriam, 96
Thomas
    John, 179, 184
Thompson
    Arthur, 58
    Margaret Janetta, 105
Thomson
    Esther, 39
    Hannah, 41
    John, Rev., 35, 37, 39-45, 49, 50, 52, 140, 149
    Lewis, 154
    Mary, 49
    Sarah, 52, 144
Thorndike
    Edward L., 136
    Robert L., 136
Thorp
    Thomas J., 163
Townsend
    James H., 108
Trimble
    Ann, 196
    Capt., 198
    Jean (Finley), 182, 196
    John, 182, 188, 196, 198
    Joseph, 185, 196, 198
    Robert, 196
    Rosannah, 196
    Walter, 196
Trombetta
    Judy (Shaffer), 183
Trombley
    George, 134
Tucker
    John W., 72
Turley
    Benjamin F., 75
    Eliza, 75

Underhill
    Carol N., 204
Unisck
    Sonny, 100

Vahldick
    Teresa Marie, 126
Vanoni
    Antonia Renee, 134
    Brenda Jeanne, 134
    Joseph Attilio, 134
    Joseph E., 134
    Maria Kathleen, 134
Violetti
    Dick, 131

Wade
    Leticia, 84

Walker
    Elizabeth (Finley), 97
    Helen M., 136
    Henrietta Lora, 78
    Mary, 97
    William, 78
    William H., 97
    William R., 97
Wallace
    Caleb, 40
    Mary L., 155
Wallin
    Mae, 121
Ward
    Sarah M.E., 93
Ware
    Hester C., 159
    James D., 159
    Jane, 162
Warren
    Earl, Gov., 135
Washington
    George, 50
    John, 187
Wasson
    Bettie A., 163
Watson
    Patrick, 186
    Thomas, 185
Wear
    Eliza, 161
    Elizabeth, 163
    Ellen, 163
    Finley, 163
    Francis, 163
    George, 163
    Louisa, 163
    Margaret, 163

    Mary, 160, 163
    Susan, 163
    Wallace, 163
    William, 163
    William B., 161-163
Weaver
    Belle Kennemer, 93
Weisner
    Roland, 99
Welch
    Mattie, 93
West
    William Marcus, 28
White
    John, 186
    Joseph, 186
    Moses, 186
Wilds
    Celesta Jane (Young), 124
    Edna Thelma, 125
    Edward Jackson, 125, 127
    George Edward, 124
    Horace E., 125
    Jesse S., 124, 125
    Lorraine, 101, 127
    Vivian, 125
    William S., 125
Wilkerson
    Alice, 202
    Narcissa, 200
Wilkes
    Maria, 87, 90
Williams
    Alexander, 201
    Dorothy Marie, 132, 133
    Hannah Catherine (Harrison), 124
    Jacquie Marie, 124, 125
    James Weston, 124, 125

    John Weston, 124
    Nettie Sarah (Eaton), 132
    Rube, 187
    Vivian, 124, 125
    William E., 132
Wilson
    Elizabeth, 188, 196, 198
    F., 50
    Fletcher, 76
    Gordon, 100
    James, 184
    John, 186
    Joseph, 188, 198, 199
    Robert, 188
Winkler
    Oliver, 104
Wirht
    Vearldeen Agnes, 100
Wise
    Margaret, 202
    Thomas, 202
Wiseman
    John, Rev., 152
Wold
    Arne J., 125
    Curtis Lynn, 126
    Rick Layne, 126
    Roy Lee, 125
    Roy Peter, 125
    Terry Dean, 125
    Timothy Allen, 125
Womer
    Frank B., 137
Wood
    Edward, 146
    Stephen, 146
    Thomas, 146

Woody
- Ellen, 91
- Ellen Louisa, 98
- Thomas, 81, 91, 98

Woolsey
- Frank, 173, 174
- Ruth, 173, 174
- Sarah (Caldwell), 173, 174

Work
- Nancy, 81
- Will, 83
- William, Mrs., 82

Wright
- Joseph, 88
- Sarah Marilda, 75

Yahnian
- Dodd, 133
- Dodd Steven, 133
- Janet Lynn, 133
- Marc A., 133
- Michelle (Findley), 117, 132

Yew
- Fong, 33

Young
- Celesta Jane, 124
- Hugh, 182
- James, 185
- Nancy, 85
- William Wesley, 93
- Wm., 188

ERRATA SHEET FOR PAGES 169–171

Note of Correction provided by William Earl Finley: William Earl Finley has provided a correction and supporting Documentation regarding his Grandfather Dozier Finley. His name was Dozier Finley not Hugh Dozier Finley. This is evident as well in the letter entitled, "Our Fore Fathers" written by Newton Gleaves Finley, the father of Dozier Finley, wherein Newton Gleaves Finley records in his own handwriting his sons first name as being Dozier. Also, all Finley's in the Finley family genealogy written down by Newton Gleaves Finley in this same letter and appear at the end of the letter are listed by their first names only. Of further note, Cynthiana Finley Elliott, daughter of Dozier Finley, who provided this information originally spells her name first name Cynthiana not Cynthia. William Earl Finley is the youngest son of William Latta Finley who was Dozier Finley and Mary Bingham Latta Finley's eldest son.

Other Heritage Books by the Sonoma County Genealogical Society, Inc.:

CD: *Sonoma County [California] Records, Volume 1*

Early School Attendance Records of Sonoma County, California, Beginning 1858

Early School Attendance Records of Sonoma County, California, Volume II: 1874-1932

Index and Abstracts of Wills, Sonoma County, California: 1850-1900

Index to Naturalization Records in Sonoma County, California, Volume 1: 1841-1906

Naturalization Records in Sonoma County, California, Volume II: 1906-1930

Index to The Sonoma Searcher*: Volume 16, No. 1 to Volume 28, No. 3*
(Including Index to The Sonoma Searcher*: Volume 1, No. 1 to Volume 15, No. 4, SCGS, August 1993)*

Index to Vital Data in Local Newspapers of Sonoma County, California, Volume 1: 1855-1875

Index to Vital Data in Local Newspapers of Sonoma County, California, Volume 2: 1876-1880

Index to Vital Data in Local Newspapers of Sonoma County, California, Volume 3: 1881-1885

Index to Vital Data in Local Newspapers of Sonoma County, California, Volume 4: 1886-1890

Index to Vital Data in Local Newspapers of Sonoma County, California, Volume 5: 1891-1899

Index to Vital Data in Local Newspapers of Sonoma County, California, Volume 6: 1900-1903

Index to Vital Data in Local Newspapers of Sonoma County, California, Volume 7: 1904-1906

Indigent Records in Sonoma County, California 1878 to 1926, Volume 1: The Indigents

Indigent Records in Sonoma County, California 1878 to 1926, Volume 2: Taxpayers Who Certified Indigent Need

Militia Lists of Sonoma County, California, 1846 to 1900

Santa Rosa Rural Cemetery, 1853-1997

Sonoma County, California Cemetery Records, 1846-1921, Third Edition

Sonoma County, California Death Records, 1873-1905, Second Edition

Sonoma County California Reconstructed 1890 Census

The 1930 School Census of Sonoma County, California